For Celia

About the Author

As well as writing two very popular and well-reviewed historical thrillers, *The Night He Left* and *Fields of Blue Flax*, Sue Lawrence is one of the UK's leading cookery writers, with eighteen published cookbooks. Having trained as a journalist in Dundee, she won BBC's MasterChef in 1991 and became a food writer, regularly contributing to *Scotland on Sunday*, the *Sunday Times* and many leading magazines. Born in Dundee and raised in Edinburgh, she now lives near Newhaven in North Edinburgh. She has won two Guild of Food Writers Awards and a Glenfiddich Food and Drink Award.

Piers Morgan

Misadventures of a

Big Mouth Brit

EBURY
PRESS

Piers Morgan has asserted his right to be identified as the author of this Work
in accordance with the Copyright, Designs and Patents Act 1988

The Random House Group Limited Reg. No. 954009

Addresses for companies within the Random House Group can be found at
www.randomhouse.co.uk

A CIP catalogue record for this book is available from the British Library

The Random House Group Limited supports The Forest Stewardship
Council (FSC), the leading international forest certification organisation.
All our titles that are printed on Greenpeace approved FSC certified paper
carry the FSC logo. Our paper procurement policy can be found at
www.rbooks.co.uk/environment

Printed in the UK by CPI Cox & Wyman, Reading, RG1 8EX

ISBN 9780091913946

To buy books by your favourite authors and register for offers visit
www.rbooks.co.uk

ACKNOWLEDGEMENTS

I'd like to thank the usual suspects for another sterling collaborative effort on this, my third volume of diaries.

Eugenie Furniss from William Morris, my ruthlessly brilliant literary agent provocateur .

Jake Lingwood from Ebury, my equally ruthless and brilliant – and often utterly exasperating (but only because he's usually right) – editor.

Jake's diligent, committed and highly professional team at Ebury, including Ken Barlow, Sarah Bennie, Hannah Robinson, Katie Johnson, Hannah Telfer and Mel Yarker. And everyone in the sales team.

My two TV agent provocateurs – in Britain, Peter Powell, from James Grant Management; and in America, John 'The Ferret' Ferriter, also from William Morris. Both are great agents, great friends, and great shoulders to cry, rage, laugh and whoop on.

My various other editors – Dylan Jones at *GQ*, Peter Wright and Gerard Greaves at the *Mail on Sunday*, and Paul Dacre at the *Daily Mail* – for the astoundingly free rein they afford me to prod, goad, intrude on, embarrass and generally abuse the rich and famous.

Simon Cowell, for taking me to America to live the Hollywood dream, and to re-think my view of the world's No. 1 superpower in the process.

My beloved co-judges – Sharon Osbourne, Amanda Holden and The Hoff – for all the laughs. And the occasional, usually well-deserved, whack.

Tracey Chapman, so much more than a PA, who does whatever I ask her, whenever I ask her, with no fuss, no complaint, and nothing less than first-class professionalism.

And my large and splendid family; led of course by my three magnificently entertaining sons Spencer, Stanley and Bertie, my parents, my grandmother, my brothers and sister, and all my nieces, nephews and goddaughters (They said they'd never speak to me again if they didn't get a namecheck – so here goes: Gabby, Phoebe, Georgina, Finlay, Milly, Lucy, Rosie, Katie and Alice), who all contribute so much to my diary, put up with my constant foreign absences, and carry the burden of being related to such a 'popular' public figure with such remarkable good humour.

I tried to warn everyone ... the *Mirror* front page just before
George W. Bush was elected President in 2000.

prologue

I vividly remember the first time I went to America.

It was 1984, I was a 21-year-old showbusiness hack on the *Sun*, and I'd been sent to New York to interview Sylvester Stallone.

From the moment I arrived, and made my way to my hotel in Manhattan, I felt a surge of exhilaration at the sheer power, size and energy of the place.

Everything, and everyone, seemed bigger, faster, brasher.

The streets were huge, the cars even larger. And vast skyscrapers reached to the skies all over the city as a constant reminder that I was now in the heart of the world's undisputed superpower.

New York in the eighties radiated cash, success and excitement.

And I hated it!

All the Americans I met on that week-long trip seemed cocky, humourless, very intense and very aggressive.

Their attitude towards Britain seemed totally dismissive, as indeed was their attitude to anywhere outside of America.

For the next few years, I made numerous further trips to New York, Miami and Los Angeles, and my opinion didn't change much.

America, it always seemed to me, was just a big, loud, brash kinda place full of big, loud, brash kinda people. And while I came to enjoy going, a few days was usually quite enough. For both of us.

They didn't get my jokes, finding my typically British brand of sarcasm, irony, cheerful cynicism, and downright abuse, both weird and obnoxious. They also, despite their claims to 'love the Brits', actually, it seemed to me, found us rather pompous, prickly and vaguely irrelevant. I, in turn, thought they were fairly ghastly, too. A bunch of swaggering, self-interested isolationists.

But then, in the nineties, I toured the centre of America, covering a tour by the pop group, New Kids on The Block. I flew to places like Kentucky, Dallas and Alabama. And I realised there was a whole different America out there, full of very different people with very different attitudes. They seemed gentler, slower, friendlier and less in your face. I met some lovely people, though they also seemed a little bit mad – obsessed with guns, abortion, religion and hunting.

On this trip, I realised, too, just how massive the United States is; a great sprawling landmass that takes over six hours to cross in a plane, with 300 million people inhabiting it.

I came home feeling definitely warmer towards America, a view later enhanced by the Clinton years. I thought Bill Clinton was a fantastically charismatic president, a great speaker and a man who preferred peace to war. He presided over an America that commanded respect and admiration the world over.

But then came sleaze, scandal, terror and George Bush.

By the time Dubya came to be president in 2000, I was editor of the *Daily Mirror*, and immediately viewed him as the absolute personification of redneck idiocy, and everything I had originally disliked about America.

Ironic really given that he came from the part of the country that I had liked the most.

Bush was loud, sneering, dumb-sounding, gun-toting and arrogant; he'd only been out of the United States twice, and didn't, memorably, know the prime minister of Pakistan's name. Texan-born, a lover of Stetsons and stirrups, a leading figure in the oil community, and prone to outbreaks of cruelty and bad behaviour, Bush could have been JR Ewing's evil little half-brother.

When it looked like he was heading into the White House, someone at the *Mirror* had the bright idea of checking his execution record as governor of Texas. It turned out that in just five years he had personally ordered the killing of 150 people, more than any governor in American state history. One of his last was to be a man with a mental age of six. (The final tally was 152.) Thanks to America's freedom of information bills, we were able to track down all the personal details of each of the people he executed, and ran their stories under a front-page headline saying simply: 'LETHAL.' And inside, I personally wrote the following leading article: 'Tonight a man with a mental age of six called John Paul Penry will be executed by lethal injection in Texas. His death is a sinister milestone – he is the 150th person killed by personal order of state Governor George W. Bush. Bush has sanctioned 38 executions in this election year alone, breaking all American records. The *Mirror* would never defend the appalling crimes of the men and women listed here. But a civilised society must never take a life for a life. Bush makes no apology for his hideous track record. He believes he's doing society a favour by murdering murderers. And disturbingly, he has mass support from Americans, driven by their out-of-control gun culture and bloodlust for retribution. If Bush wins the increasingly farcical race to be president, he will take charge of the largest military power in history. Do we really want a man like him making snap decisions on whether to drop bombs or go to war? Do we really like the idea of his finger on the big trigger? No, we don't. There are many sound reasons why Bush should not be president. But surely there is no more compelling reason than the 150 men and women he has executed with impunity. He is a thoroughly dangerous, unpleasant piece of work who shouldn't be let anywhere near the White House.'

Bush was tested almost immediately with the 9/11 outrage, and reacted exactly as we had feared – like a roughneck cowboy intent on bloody revenge at all costs.

For the next eight years, Bush slowly turned America into the most hated country on earth.

And by doing so, he brought this once super-confident nation to its knees.

In 2006, I went to work in America on a show called *America's Got Talent* for Simon Cowell.

And what I found was a place consumed by fear, vulnerability, ravaged by war, natural disaster and an economy teetering on the brink of collapse.

Something extraordinary had to happen.

And it did.

In the shape of an extraordinary young man called Barack Obama, who burst through the barriers of racism and stupidity to almost single-handedly turn the political and social landscape of the United States right on what I, and many others, believed was its bigoted, small-minded, insular head.

All with a mantra of hope and change.

And it wasn't just America that transformed as Obama worked his magic. I did, too. Travelling across this vast, extraordinary country, immersing myself in the culture of the place and meeting many more of the people who live there, I came to realise that my own views about America had also been bigoted, small-minded and insular.

This, then, is a tale of two journeys: how America went through a stunning new revolution. And how I, to my utter amazement, fell in love with her in the process.

'Now, Gordon, far be it for me to interfere,
but what I'd do if I was running the country is...'

1

'My parents gave me an African name, Barack, or blessed, believing that in a tolerant America your name is no barrier to success. That is the true genius of America, a faith in the simple dreams of its people, the insistence on small miracles. That we can say what we think, write what we think, without hearing a sudden knock on the door. That we can have an idea and start our own business without paying a bribe or hearing a sudden knock on the door. That we can participate in the political process without fear of retribution, and that our votes will be counted.' BARACK OBAMA

MONDAY, 23 OCTOBER 2006

Barack Obama, the dynamic young black American senator, has said he will 'consider' running for president in 2008 – sending the American media into a maelstrom of excitement.

Obama is 45, fresh-faced, articulate, purposeful, charismatic and engaging to the mass populace in a JFK kind of way, with huge crowds turning up at his recent book-signings.

When asked if he was 'ready to be president', Obama smiled and replied: 'I'm not sure anybody is ready to be president before they're president.'

By coincidence, I've been reading Obama's new book, *The Audacity of Hope: Thoughts on Reclaiming the American Dream*.

He is clearly an intelligent and thoughtful man. Prone, perhaps, to a slightly 'preachy' tone but full of sensible, if not particularly radical, thought processes: Iraq was a bad idea, America must end its reliance on oil, fairer taxation and health care plans for the less well off, etc.

Most significantly, he argues very coherently about the 'need for change'. And that, right now in America, is going to be a powerful message.

Bogged down in two seemingly interminable wars, and hated by most of the rest of the world, the world's greatest superpower is lacking in confidence, vulnerable and angry.

There is something very likeable about Obama, too. The natural warmth of his big smile, the knowledge that he comes from a diverse background, has a close and loving family and is markedly reluctant to abuse his rivals or deploy the clichéd political rhetoric that has grown so stale on the global stage.

I concur with one Amazon reviewer's verdict of the book: 'Readers will come away thinking of Barack more of a neighbour than a politician.'

The one fairly massive barrier he faces, of course, is how to convince a still deeply conservative country – particularly those vast swathes of gun-toting, abortion-banning, gay-hating and, dare I say it, ever-so-slightly-racist Middle and Southern Americans who elected the imbecilic Bush twice – to vote for an anti-war black guy, whose middle name is Hussein.

I just can't see it happening. And even if it did, there would have to be, as someone suggested on TV tonight, a high probability of him getting shot by one of those mad, dumb, white supremacists you find with alarming prevalence lurking in places like Alabama.

WEDNESDAY, 25 OCTOBER 2006

NBC has 'picked up' my option for a second series of *America's Got Talent*, which means I'll be spending another three or four months in the States next year.

Obviously, I'm thrilled that the show's a success. But I can't pretend that my first thought isn't to instantly wonder how many Arsenal matches, Newick cricket games and great parties I will miss back in Britain again. This summer, my American schedule seems to coincide with just about every major sporting or social event of the year. More importantly, how many of the boys' school events will I miss, too? I used to make sure I got to practically every one of them when I was a newspaper editor, however busy my day was. But getting to Clapham from Canary Wharf was a little easier than getting there from Beverly Hills. The boys are very good about it, and they don't seem to mind too much. But I mind.

There will be a lot of lonely nights amid all the frivolity, too. Working in Los Angeles is great for the CV and the suntan; but like many Brits who work in the entertainment industry there, I know that more often than not, I'll find myself sitting in my hotel room alone at night, watching mindless TV, eating another bowl of spaghetti Bolognese, drinking some God-awful Californian Merlot and waiting until midnight for someone in Britain to wake up so I can have a conversation that doesn't end with, 'Have a nice day now, Mr Morgan.'

I also know I'm going to severely miss the following, in no particular order: Heinz baked beans, Ambrosia creamed rice, Branston pickle, PG Tips, proper milk, genuine (not faxed) English newspapers, Sainsbury's pork pies, Harvey's real ale, small roads, small cars, country fields, a chicken tikka masala from the Newick Village Tandoori, and yes, even the rain. In fact, especially the rain. When you've woken up every day for six weeks to clear blue skies and 90-degree heat, you start to yearn for a cold, drizzly day. It's strange, but true.

Having said all this, there will almost certainly come a moment when I am snaking up Sunset Boulevard in a convertible Aston Martin, shades on and Aerosmith blaring, heading towards my trailer in the fabulously glamorous studio where *America's Got Talent* is filmed, and Hollywood life won't seem quite so intolerable!

TUESDAY, 7 NOVEMBER 2006

Kicking around the flat tonight, I found myself flicking through various American news channels.

They're as fascinating as they can be alarming.

Rupert Murdoch's Fox News, for example, is already aiming its powerful turrets squarely at Barack Obama, in a way that would be unthinkable on British television.

Americans like extreme TV, whether it's the crazy acts on *America's Got Talent*, or loudmouth political pundits like Fox's Bill O'Reilly ranting about 'pinko liberals' on prime time. There's no room for a middle ground; you rarely hear anyone pop up on American TV talking about anything remotely serious where their opening line is: 'I'm kinda sitting on the fence with this one.'

No, in the States they do their TV news and politics hard core, particularly in the run-up to a presidential election.

And the Fox network, led by O'Reilly, is already painting a picture of Obama as the potential devil incarnate. He's 'too young', 'too inexperienced' and, although obviously they don't actually say this, the possible implication to someone not very bright is also that he's too 'non-white'. The Fox news machine is ferociously right wing, almost comically partial and brashly unashamed about it. But there's at least an honesty to their coverage which is lacking on, say, the BBC, where the left-wing bias is real, but exercised in a much more surreptitious manner. You know where you stand with Fox, even if you disagree with everything they stand for. And I wish there was someone like O'Reilly on British television – a smart, aggressive, highly opinionated political commentator, right in your face every weeknight about issues that really matter. He, and other high-profile American pundits like the left-wing Bill Maher, make the politics there interesting, combative and entertaining.

THURSDAY, 9 NOVEMBER 2006

Lunch at Langan's with three of my oldest Sussex village mates, Miles, Sloan and Malcolm. I bought my first house with them in Morden, South London, just before the property crash in the late eighties. We lost £4,000 each after three miserable years, during which we got burgled so many times that in the end we left the door open with a sign saying 'Note to thieves, don't bother – it's all gone'. It made us all realise that the much-fabled mantra handed down by our parents – 'You'll always make money from bricks and mortar' – was bullshit. Property prices can go down as well as up, something that those getting over-excited by the current ridiculously inflated market should seriously consider. My own mantra, post the Morden Road debacle, is this: if house prices seem too good to be true, then they are.

The Times says today that many people have doubled their money in just four years on their properties, which is an unsustainable rate of growth. The bubble, surely, can't be far from bursting.

As we ordered our food, a thick-set bearded man in his early seventies approached the table.

'Hello, Piers,' he said in a strong South London accent.

'Hello,' I replied.

'I'm Charlie,' he said.

'Hi Charlie,' I replied, again.

Pause.

'Charlie Richardson.'

I looked again at this smiling, benign-looking, vaguely familiar gentleman, and the penny suddenly dropped like a two-ton 'sleep with the fishes' lead weight in my stomach.

Charlie had been leader of the infamous Richardson Gang, sworn enemies of the Kray Twins in London in the sixties.

They were also known as The Torture Gang, as a result of their varied techniques of whippings, cigarette burnings, nailing limbs to the floor, bath electrocutions and ripping toes off with bolt cutters. And, my personal favourite, the removal of teeth via pliers without anaesthetic, at which gang member 'Mad' Frankie – aka 'The Dentist' – Fraser was especially skilled.

Charlie – described in his heyday as 'the most dangerous man in Britain' – could not have been more charming as we exchanged small talk, but still exuded an undeniable air of controlled menace and was treated with impressive respect by other diners.

Cabinet ministers, editors, football managers, and just about anyone else who holds high office, lose all their power the moment they lose their job.

But if you were once the 'most dangerous man in Britain' then that status never leaves you. And it's strongly advisable to know what these people look like.

Dad once helped run a fashionable London nightclub called Churchills in the sixties, and barred entry one evening to a rough-looking gentleman.

The man concerned stared at Dad like he wanted to kill him. Which, as it turned out, he might well have done.

'What the hell are you doing, Glynne?' chastised a colleague. 'That's Ronnie Kray!'

Dad swivelled round, barely catching a breath, and said: 'Mr Kray, what a terrible misunderstanding, please allow me to escort you to your usual table.'

I remembered this nifty quick-thinking when Charlie walked off to the bar.

'Does anyone ever have a go at your husband to make a name for himself?' I asked his wife.

'God, no!' she shrieked with derisive laughter. 'You wouldn't want to upset my Charlie.'

As she joined her husband I summoned the maître d'.

'Please ask Mr and Mrs Richardson what they would like to drink and put it on my bill.'

The maître d' nodded.

'Very wise, Mr Morgan. Very wise.'

SATURDAY, 11 NOVEMBER 2006

There are some invitations that scream 'Yes, Yes, YES!' like Meg Ryan in *When Harry Met Sally*.

And the words 'Gordon Ramsay invites you to his fortieth birthday party' are definitely in that category. Particularly when the venue tonight was the Banqueting House of the great Whitehall palace.

Rather like the wedding reception of Gordon's great rival Marco Pierre White, you can assume certain things before you even get there: delicious food, sumptuous wine, and Michael Winner sitting on the best table.

But there were some surprises, like the half-naked woman waiting for us in reception, painted green, sitting in foliage and lovingly feeding grapes to a half-naked man.

'This is going to be fucking great!' bellowed our host on arrival, like a hyperactive boxer dog.

And he was right.

The meal, ah, the meal... I'm going to be specific here, because when one of the world's best chefs wines and dines you at a party, you don't want to forget it.

Starter: evaporate-in-the-mouth lobster thermidor, washed down with 2003 Chassagne-Montrachet 1er Cru Morgeot.

Main course: whacking great big Aberdeen Angus rib-eye steaks with home-made chunky chips, Béarnaise sauce and Caesar salad – complemented by 2001 Château Haut-Gravet, St Emilion Grand Cru.

Dessert: blackberry and apple macadamia crumble with custard – and 1996 Castelnau de Suduiraut Sauternes pudding wine.

It was all a bit like Gordon, simply presented but laced with excitement, energy and flamboyance.

Over dinner, I got into a splendidly heated argument over who was the most beautiful famous woman in the world.

'Scarlett Johansson,' I suggested. 'She's the only one who doesn't look like she's been sculpted by a surgeon.'

'Liz Hurley,' countered Elton's boyfriend David Furnish.

'Oh God, no,' I rejoined. 'Mutton dressed as posh mule.'

'No, no,' insisted Furnish. 'I've seen her without make-up first thing in the morning, and she's amazingly beautiful even then.'

The entertainment was equally entertaining: Rory Bremner, the stars of the musical *Cabaret*, and pub landlord Al Murray on the anchor leg.

As midnight arrived, the dance floor ripped into life and I bustled for space with Penny Smith from GMTV (slinky mover), Radio 1 DJ Chris Moyles (not so slinky mover), David Furnish, Kirsty Young, my bête noire Jeremy Clarkson ('We've got to stop meeting like this,' he said, and meant it) and, of course, the great Winner – though I'm not sure he was dancing, just wobbling gently on his way to the loo.

But most of the 350 guests weren't famous at all. They either worked for Gordon, were related to Gordon or just mates with Gordon. And they were all having the time of their lives. Such a refreshing change from the normal, and ghastly, 'all my mates are celebrities, aren't I clever?' party guest list you see every week in *OK!* magazine.

There were bowls of sweets everywhere – jelly babies, liquorice allsorts, sherbet bangers, wine gums. And a cocktail bar serving up strawberry mojos, tiramisu Martinis and pomegranate caipiroskas.

I felt so utterly consumed with pleasure by the end that I asked the DJ to play a song for me.

'Say this is from Piers to Jeremy,' I said to him as he cued up Elton John's disco classic, 'Are You Ready For Love?'

Unfortunately, he misheard me, and said 'David' not 'Jeremy', which raised several eyebrows. Not least from Mr Furnish.

At 1 a.m., the Birthday Boy joined the dance floor like a hurricane joining the South Coast. It was time to leave.

'Had a good time?' shrieked Gordon as he launched into a frenzied Full Monty ten-step.

'It was fucking great!' I replied, in the only language he'd truly appreciate.

SUNDAY, 12 NOVEMBER 2006

A terrible day in Iraq – seven British troops killed and wounded in an attack on their patrol boat, and another 100 civilians dead or injured after six separate bombs in Baghdad.

All, with appalling irony, on Remembrance Sunday.

Tony Blair once told me that sending British servicemen into action was the most difficult thing he had to do as prime minister.

'It keeps me awake at night,' he said, pursing his lips in that 'Diana was the People's Princess' way we all know so well.

It's tempting to believe him, and assume that's why he's looking so tired all the time.

But I suspect the real reason for his drooping eyelids is all those late-night calls he must be getting from Dubya in Washington asking: 'Tone, buddy, get me outta this mess.'

Even the American public is slowly starting to doubt the legitimacy of the war in Iraq. Which for a country that prides itself on its military, and its unbending patriotism, is remarkable. But then they are starting to see genuine parallels with Vietnam – an increasing number of bodybags coming home, with no end to the carnage in sight, and no apparent concept from the administration of when or how victory might be achieved. Americans like things to be resolutely black and white, and wars are no exception – 'The Japs attack Pearl Harbor? Then we nuke 'em, game over.'

What they hate is complexity, ambiguity or, God forbid, possible failure.

So when Bin Laden took down the World Trade Center, they wanted, no needed, Bin Laden to be killed. And he hasn't been.

Similarly with Iraq. They bought into the concept that Saddam Hussein's a bad guy, so they must therefore invade Iraq, take out the monster and instill 'freedom'. Hence the national jubilation when Bush declared the war was won in March 2003.

Yet they turn on their TV set today and see that the war they thought was won is clearly still raging, and they feel confused and betrayed, because they think Bush misled them.

Americans are a trusting people, and they trusted their president.

MONDAY, 13 NOVEMBER 2006

Not a week passes without me being invited on to some ever more ridiculous reality TV show.

I never thought I'd receive a dumber request than *Celebrity Shark Bait*, where famous people were taken by ITV to the middle of a South African ocean, lowered into the water in steel cages and filmed shrieking in terror as sharks attacked them. But today I was approached by an independent production company and asked if I would like to fake my own death, and witness how the news is then received.

'Obviously this needs to be hush-hush,' read the letter, 'and certain people would need to know...'

Yes, I guess my parents, and my kids for that matter, ought to have an advance nod of my departure from the world. Just out of courtesy.

I think I can spare them the production costs.

Unfortunately, I fear I know exactly how news of my death will be received. Which is why I intend staying alive for as long as humanly possible.

TUESDAY, 14 NOVEMBER 2006

Breakfast with Gordon Brown at the Treasury at 9 a.m. Well, in the chancellor's true prudent style, a cup of tea anyway. We used to meet regularly when I was *Mirror* editor, and it's rather touching to be invited back now I'm comparatively useless to him. And I'm curious, too: has he still got the fire in his belly to run the country?

I was supposed to be there for 40 minutes, but finally emerged blinking into the sunshine at 11.23 a.m. after a quite fascinating one-to-one morning with the man who is expected to take over as prime minister next summer.

There's a real anti-Brown bandwagon stirring at the moment. 'He's too old, too serious, too dour,' is all I ever hear.

Well, I beg to differ. I'm done with pop-star politics. All that cheesy grin, insincere, 'I'm a straight kinda guy' guff that so typifies Blairism – and Cameronism, for that matter. I'm ready for an older, more mature and sober prime minister. Someone who wears a tie, possesses a fierce intellect, can run something as complex as the economy with superb efficiency, and bores me comfortingly rigid when he speaks on TV.

Brown started our meeting, in a typically spartan annexe to his office, looking tired and distracted. He'd probably been up since 6 a.m. getting his head around some horribly difficult budgetary issue. (Blair once told me, when they were still speaking, 'Gordon is the cleverest person I know in politics. He has a brilliant mind, much more brilliant than mine.')

But after a while Brown relaxed, and when he relaxes he is charming, funny, passionate and inspiring. Four things you would never guess from his *Thunderbirds*-style public persona.

We discussed everything from Iraq, the Olympics and President Bush to child poverty, education and *The X Factor*. (He is not happy with the inexplicably unstoppable progress of the MacDonald brothers, a Scottish singing duo who have stayed in the competition despite murdering every track they sing, and being repeatedly insulted by Simon Cowell. 'They're giving Scotland a bad name,' Brown moaned.) And yes, even our great mutual friend, Cherie. Whenever I mention her name, Gordon's whole body tenses like someone's just inserted an electric charge into his abdomen.

I liked what I heard, and the way he said it. Brown understands Britain and its values. He knows what the problems are, and has original ideas for how to solve them. And underneath that dour Presbyterian exterior burns real fire.

But until Blair finally buggers off (and what, pray God, can he possibly still be waiting for?), Brown is left prowling around like a caged lion waiting to be released from captivity.

Listening to him vent his absurdly knowledgeable cerebral mass, I suddenly realised the way he should respond when the battle commences for real with David Cameron next year.

'Have you seen the film *The American President*?' I asked.

'Yes,' Brown replied.

'Then you will remember what President Andrew Shepherd [Michael Douglas] says when he storms the White House press conference to defend his girlfriend [Annette Bening] from his smarmy lightweight political opponent Bob Rumson [Richard Dreyfuss]?'

'Erm, not entirely. What did he say?'

'He made a virtue out of being serious. A serious man doing a serious job for his country. And the public loved him for it.'

Brown nodded, and smiled.

'Well, politics is a serious business.'

So I wouldn't be surprised if, come next summer, we saw our new prime minister charging into a Downing Street press conference, grabbing the microphone, declaring, 'We've got serious problems, and we need serious men to solve them. If you want to talk about character and British values, Dave, then fine. Just tell me where and when, and I'll show up. This is a time for serious men, Dave, and your 15 minutes are up. My name is Gordon Brown, and I AM the prime minister.'

I asked him who he thought would be the next US president.

'Hillary Clinton's got a great chance if she runs,' he said.

Gordon goes back a long way with the Clintons, so a Hillary win would suit him perfectly.

THURSDAY, 16 NOVEMBER 2006

Flew to Rome for the day, to speak to a bunch of financial types at their annual conference.

Public speaking is a nightmare if you have to follow someone like Bill Clinton, but a little easier if, like today, one takes the stage after an hour-long presentation delivered in a monotone by a jut-jawed, humourless American banker and titled: 'Hedge Funds: Where Are We Going?' (The answer, judging by the faces on the audience, was: 'into a coma, fast'.)

During the Q and A session, someone asked me about Gordon Brown – the mention of whose mere name triggered a low-level booing.

'Well,' I replied, 'I know this isn't a popular view right now, but what's so wrong with making the cleverest, most serious man in the government prime minister? Running the country is a pretty serious job, haven't we had enough of pop stars doing it?'

To my astonishment, the audience promptly erupted into rousing cheers. I think I might be on to something.

An hour later, I got back to Rome airport to be met by a wall of paparazzi.

'Surely they're not all for me?' I pondered to myself, ruffling my hair into a suitably cool pap-friendly bouffant.

They weren't. They were there for Tom Cruise's wedding guests.

'Get outta the damn bloody way!' shrieked one Italian photographer as Jim Carrey arrived, completing my humiliation by barging me to one side, and on to a luggage carousel.

FRIDAY, 17 NOVEMBER 2006

Matthew Freud and I have finally thrown the towel in on *Press Gazette*, the trade magazine for journalists that we bought 18 months ago. We've done everything we can to make it work – upping the pagination, improving the paper quality, hiring a raft of new columnists and writers, moving the staff back up to London from Croydon and landing them huge scoops like an interview with Rupert Murdoch.

There's no doubt that we've made the magazine a better read than it's been for years.

But our reward has been for most of the industry to announce they are going to boycott the magazine's annual British Press Awards, despite this year's event being, by common consent, a huge success.

Without the awards, the magazine is an unsustainable loss-maker.

And the only reason they all want to boycott it is because they just resent the idea of me and Matthew owning their trade magazine. Which is just pathetic, childish and unbelievably frustrating. But also, sadly, a fact.

So we've bailed out, at a cost to me personally of £250,000, and Matthew well over £1 million.

I'm sure this decision will bring plenty of chortles and back-slaps around Fleet Street. But let's see how smug they're all feeling when the magazine slips back to an unreadable load of old guff with no investment.

SATURDAY, 18 NOVEMBER 2006

Had a big family lunch down in Sussex, and we all got stuck into a delightful roast chicken.

Jeremy, now a lieutenant colonel in the Royal Welsh regiment, was scathing about what the Americans are doing in Iraq.

'They're just a bunch of John Waynes,' he said, with disgust, 'only without the heart or the intelligence. Most of the American military is fervently Republican, and blindly loyal to Bush. The more gung-ho his rhetoric has got, the worse they have behaved. They've been like the Romans – they don't do meetings and they kill everything that gets in their way. They're arrogant, antagonistic, isolationist, deeply entrenched in their ideology, naïve and like something out of the nineteenth century. Essentially, America is a very inward-looking nation that doesn't understand the rest of the world, but still thinks it has the right to stomp around imposing its idea of democracy on countries that don't want it. Iraq has been a disaster, and probably an illegal disaster. But you'll never hear an American soldier say that. They just march around like they own the place, trigger-happy and bullish, and rather than see this as a chance to genuinely instil freedom and democracy in Iraq, they just see it as a war against an enemy that must be won at all costs. And that is an incredibly dangerous attitude, especially when you consider how many senior members of the American military are Christian fundamentalists who look upon the campaigns in Iraq and Afghanistan in the same way the medieval crusaders viewed their campaign in the Holy Land.'

Coming from someone who supported the war, and has served in Iraq twice with the Royal Welsh Regiment, this is an incredibly damning and dispiriting verdict.

Later in the afternoon, when we were having tea, I casually asked if I could 'have a cookie'.

There was a sudden, deafening, grotesque silence in the room.

'A *what*?' scoffed Jeremy, incredulous.

'A...biscuit please.'

It's so easy to lapse into Americanisms when you've spent some proper time there. But it's actually a necessity. I have to be very precise with my words in the States, or nobody understands what I'm on about.

If you want to really, really confuse an American, then go into a super-market and ask an assistant something like this: 'Hi, old chap, I wonder if you could furnish me with a plaster, a tin of mince, four nappies, a rubber, some chips, and a jar of strawberry jam, please?'

To translate this request into something even remotely intelligible, you'd need to say: 'Hello, sir, I need a Band-Aid, a can of chopped beef, four diapers, an eraser, some fries and a carton of jelly, please.'

A lift is always an 'elevator', a row is an 'argument', a pram a 'baby carriage', the loo is the 'rest room', petrol is 'gas', a motorway is a 'freeway', the post is 'the mail', nought is 'nothing', trousers are 'pants', full stop is 'period', to hire is to 'rent', football is 'soccer', the bin is a 'trash can', lorries are 'trucks', waistcoats are 'vests', arse is 'ass', and if you want a biscuit you won't get one unless you ask for a cookie.

I spent the first series, sorry 'season', of *America's Got Talent*, mystifying Americans with my phraseology.

Words like 'blimey', 'bloody', 'cheeky', 'cobblers', or 'codswallop' just left them all shaking their heads.

I told an illusionist he was 'dodgy' and he just stared at me, none the wiser.

I called a hoop act the 'dog's bollocks', and she looked deeply offended.

I said to one singer, 'I've haven't heard that kind of singing in donkey's years,' and he just stood there, utterly nonplussed.

And the dancer who left me 'gobsmacked' was herself…well, 'gob-smacked' by my response.

Jeremy eventually handed me a 'biscuit', but only after I asked for it in the correct manner.

Having said all that, with more American TV coming up, I should possibly lay off the biscuits/cookies anyway. Double chins are only allowed on screen over there if you're starring in one of those fat-busting shows like *The Biggest Loser*.

SUNDAY, 19 NOVEMBER 2006

Take That, minus Robbie Williams, are back in the charts after more than ten years. I was the band's official biographer, and still have a copy of the first book we did together – a No. 1 bestseller – signed by the band. Gary, Mark, Howard and Jason all wrote heartfelt, generous words of gratitude. Robbie, bitter about my royalties, just scrawled: 'To Piers, fuck you and fuck all your money.'

The little charmer is now, ironically, worth £100 million. But he's also a lonely, self-obsessed, recovering alcoholic. And his new record has tanked and thousands of unsold copies are, genuinely, being used to make pavement slabs in China.

It's nice to see the good guys have the last laugh.

MONDAY, 20 NOVEMBER 2006

'Come and do a Comic Relief challenge,' pleaded Emma Freud on the phone this morning. She and her filmmaker husband Richard Curtis, who created the annual event, could sell Big Macs to Posh Spice.

'What is it?' I asked, instantly suspicious.

'It's a one-off celebrity episode of *The Apprentice*,' she replied.

'Ah, I get it, you want me to get fired again, only this time on national television...'

'No no no no no, absolutely *not*,' insisted Emma, perhaps protesting a little too much. 'We just want you to have fun and raise a lot of cash for charity. It's going to be a boys' team versus a girls' team, and Sir Alan Sugar will decide who gets fired.'

Despite my firm belief that they *do* want me as their sacrificial firing lamb, it sounds like fun, and I think I'll do it.

TUESDAY, 21 NOVEMBER 2006

Jude Law's a strange little cove, isn't he? (And I mean little, he's tiny).

Barely a week seems to go by without him whining about the press invading his privacy, and that of his children who, he says, are constantly harassed by paparazzi.

So I was surprised to see him with his kids at the glitzy re-opening of the Somerset House ice-skating rink tonight. (Celia's been trying to get me to learn this ridiculous pursuit for a month now, and it's not going well, to put it mildly.)

I mean, why, if you feel so strongly about it, would you voluntarily expose your young children to dozens of photographers, even if there was a charitable aspect to the night?

I found myself sitting next to Jude as we changed our skates. Him taking his off, me putting mine on.

'All right?' he said, nodding at me in that rather condescending way big stars do when they spot lesser 'celebrities'.

'All right?' I replied, defiantly adopting exactly the same attitude. We both work in Hollywood, after all. 'How was the ice?'

Jude flashed those come-to-bed-nanny blue eyes intently at me, deep paranoid suspicion etched all over his face.

It was like I'd just asked him to run naked over Waterloo Bridge hand in hand with Ann Widdecombe.

Several seconds passed, the temperature plummeting a few hundred degrees as he digested the vulgarity of my question.

Then he threw back his head, flicked an imaginary hair from his perfectly groomed eyebrow, smirked broadly, and said, slowly and deliberately: 'Cold.'

Jude then chuckled to himself, and turned away.

My audience was over.

WEDNESDAY, 22 NOVEMBER 2006

One of the joys of being a football fan is that you can usually take out all your fury at losing a match on one man: the referee.

He is the epicentre of hatred and revulsion, whatever he does. And most referees, like traffic wardens and BBC motoring presenters, absolutely love being despised. You can see it in their horribly smug grins as 60,000 people chant 'Who's the wanker in the black?'

But there's still something innately dissatisfying about not being able to physically harangue a ref. I don't mean give him a proper beating, but a mild slap round his jowly chops or flick of his self-important ear would ease so much simmering tension created by his incompetence.

For instance, I should have left the new Emirates Stadium last night feeling jubilant at Arsenal's brilliant 3–1 Champions League dismantling of Hamburg. But instead, I was fuming with rage at Thierry Henry's absurdly unfair booking, which means he misses the crunch match away to Porto next week.

The Danish referee, Claus Bo Larsen, offered no explanation for the miscreant yellow card.

And I retired to Fredericks restaurant in Islington for a fuming post-match inquest, ruminating noisily on Mr Larsen's myopic disability.

A waiter heard me in full spleen-venting wrath, leant down and whispered: 'You might like to know that the referee you're talking about is eating dinner over there...'

I looked up and saw Larsen chuckling at a nearby table, felt the blood curdle inside me, and I got up and went over to him.

'Sorry to trouble you,' I said, interrupting him in full chortle, 'but why did you book Henry?'

Larsen smiled, irritatingly. 'I apologise if it upset you...'

'It upsets me because thanks to you he now misses the Porto game.'

'Oh really? I didn't know that,' he smiled again, even more irritatingly.

'Yes, well you know now.'

'Yes, I do. Would it make you feel better if I changed my match report and exonerated Henry?'

This, of course, completely threw me.

'Er, yes, it would actually.'

'OK, no problem. Consider it done.'

'Thank you.'

I went back to my table and sat down, feeling dissipated.

He didn't mean it, obviously.

THURSDAY, 23 NOVEMBER 2006

Three of my favourite women were back in the news today: Kate Moss played a 'total slag' in a live *Little Britain* show for Comic Relief tonight, looking as rough as a badger's derrière, and snarling in that adorable Sarf Croydon twang: 'I'll give you a gob job for a bag of quavers.' (Trust me, this was no act…)

Lady Heather Mills McCartney then popped up on American TV doing her hilarious 'I'd rather be deaf, dumb, blind, limbless and vegetative than marry an *icon* again' act. (Perhaps if she'd viewed her husband as a 'human being' it might have helped?)

And finally, Cherie Blair told a bunch of students that journalism is 'not a noble cause' and we hacks have 'no ethics'. Says the woman who used notorious conman Peter Foster to help buy a couple of flats in Bristol for her son.

All three are fast becoming National Treasures, of the sunken, soiled, barnacled variety.

At 2 a.m., I sat down in the flat to watch the first ball being bowled in the new Ashes series in Australia – with Roger Alton and Rob McGibbon.

There's been a huge pressure building on the England team in recent weeks, as it's become clear that our heroes have spent most of the time since we won the Ashes last summer celebrating, while the Aussies have been training like madmen in hellhole bootcamps.

So we were all praying we'd get off to a good start.

Fast bowler Steve Harmison ran in, and bowled his first ball straight to second slip, one of the biggest wides I've seen in my life.

'Right, well that's it, then,' said Roger, grimly. 'We're completely fucked.'

FRIDAY, 24 NOVEMBER 2006

Alastair Campbell rang at 8 a.m. (old habits die hard for workaholic ex-spindoctors).

'You doing this *Celebrity Apprentice* thing?' he asked.

'Yes, thinking about it,' I replied. 'You?'

'I will if you will,' he chuckled. 'At least that way I won't be the most unpopular person on it.'

It was very weird to be talking to him about doing a reality TV show together, even if this is for charity. Three years ago we were both in positions of huge influence – me editing the *Mirror*, and him running Blair's spin machine – and falling out over the Iraq War.

Now we're reduced to debating the finer points of who might end up getting fired by Sir Alan Sugar for the delectation of the public.

I think we both share a sense of slight embarrassment at even contemplating it.

It was the first time we'd talked in two years, and towards the end of the conversation, he said something that left me bemused all day. 'You know, Tony always said about you, "Piers is someone we should never underestimate, or overestimate."'

I still can't work out if I should feel flattered or insulted.

Later, Sir Alan Sugar called to politely try and persuade me to do his *Apprentice* show.

'Morgan, just fucking do it, you useless little bastard. It's for charity.'

Well, since he put it so kindly…

SATURDAY, 25 NOVEMBER 2006

The Newick Cricket Club annual dinner/dance ended tonight at 2 a.m., with me lying on the floor of the coach going home being repeatedly punched and kicked by eight junior players.

I think it's fair to say my village has concluded that I've grown a little big for my showbiz boots.

SUNDAY, 26 NOVEMBER 2006

Stanley has recently been diagnosed with a very mild form of dyslexia. And has wasted no time in turning this to his advantage.

'Can you clean your room, please?' I asked him today.

'Sorry, Dad, but my dyslexia is playing up again.'

MONDAY, 27 NOVEMBER 2006

Tonight, I attended the annual PEN literary quiz.

For some reason I seem to particularly irritate literary types, and my heart sank when I arrived and was promptly asked to run the auction.

'But I'll get booed,' I said.

'No, you won't,' came the response.

I walked onstage at 9 p.m., and got roundly booed.

Right, I thought, time for a bit of politically incorrect fun with these ungrateful, right-on, liberal wretches.

'OK, the first item is a U2 album, signed by the band. And Bono and the boys have specifically requested that not a penny go to Africa from this one.'

To my surprise, and dismay, the audience started cheering.

'The next item is a philosophical dinner with Alain de Botton,' I announced. 'And there is a runner-up prize of TWO philosophical dinners with Alain de Botton.'

More dispiriting cheers and laughter.

It was time to be really disgraceful.

'And finally, a very special prize,' I said, as I was handed a cardboard box by hostess Mariella Frostrup, 'that's been donated by Nigella Lawson.' I stared at the box mournfully. 'In fact, I can reveal that it *is* Nigella Lawson. God rest her soul. Now, who will start me at 50 pounds?'

I stood back to receive the inevitable torrent of sickened catcalls. But instead, I got a virtual standing ovation.

And in that moment I realised that the reason the literary world dislikes me is because I'm nowhere near as vile as they are.

Later in the evening, I got into conversation with an American writer, who I'd never heard of and who grew more repellently bombastic with each drink.

I've noticed that when Americans get drunk, which most of them rarely do, they morph into hideously boorish cowboy caricatures.

It's like they mentally transport themselves to a horse on a prairie back in the days when cowboys saw off the 'injuns', with big Stetsons, bigger buckles, even bigger spurs, and the largest gun imaginable.

When the subject of Iraq cropped up, and I dared to criticise America's policy, he could barely disguise his disgust.

'You Brits would have lost the Second World War without us,' slurred my 'friend'. A vacuous taunt that always seems to creep out of an American mouth at closing time.

I find their relentless boasting extraordinarily tiresome, mainly because it is so devoid of charm. Americans just don't do self-deprecation. In fact, they don't even understand the concept of it. To them, self-criticism is a shocking sign of weakness. So they go the opposite way, talking themselves up at every opportunity.

'I've written several best-sellers,' he announced at one stage. A declaration that back in the States would have earned him instant respect, and sincere comments like, 'That's so awesome! Congratulations!'

'Really?' I replied, 'On what – modesty?'

He stared at me, first bemusement, and then fury in his sodden eyes.

'I think that's a very disrespectful thing to say,' he eventually said, haughtily.

'I think you need to wind your neck in,' I replied.

TUESDAY, 28 NOVEMBER 2006

I was invited to dinner at No. 11 Downing Street tonight with Gordon Brown and Simon Cowell. The former's almost certainly going to be running the country very soon; the latter already thinks he is.

I accepted with almost distasteful haste, and it didn't disappoint.

Before the meal, we were given a guided tour of No. 10. 'Tony's away,' explained Gordon.

'Never mind him,' I said. 'Where's his missus?'

'I believe Cherie is also away,' he grinned. 'So we're safe.'

We entered the cabinet room.

'Simon, I'd like to discuss a very urgent matter of state with you,' boomed Gordon, as we stood by the famous decision-making table.

The other guests – including Richard Curtis and Hammasa Kohistani, the dazzlingly beautiful, first-ever Muslim Miss England – went silent.

What was it to be? Iraq? The pension crisis? How to cure the NHS?

The Chancellor mustered up his most serious face.

'Those MacDonald brothers on *X Factor* are bloody terrible!' he declared. 'Something must be done about them…'

Cowell burst out laughing.

'Tell me about it, Gordon. I've tried everything to get rid of them but they keep getting voted back.'

'Sounds not entirely dissimilar to what's been happening in Downing Street,' I suggested.

'Piers,' said Gordon, sternly. 'If you can't behave you will have to leave.'

'Right, sorry,' I replied, as I tried in vain to open the side door into what I knew was Tony Blair's private office.

'Stop it!' commanded Gordon. And this time, I think he almost meant it.

I sat next to Sarah Brown over dinner.

'How are your boys?' I asked.

'They're great,' she replied, with a glow of maternal pride and joy that was lovely to see after all the hell she and Gordon suffered when their baby daughter Jennifer died.

It was a fun, slightly surreal evening, culminating in Simon giving Gordon his views on various world issues. He talks about politics in much the same way as he talks about everything else – with firm opinion, and an absolute belief that he's right.

'If you want to stop knife crimes, then give people who get caught carrying knives ten years in jail,' he declared as the dessert arrived, causing Gordon to choke slightly on his trifle.

WEDNESDAY, 29 NOVEMBER 2006

I was watching Arsenal lose embarrassingly at Fulham tonight, when I received a text from Sarah Brown.

'The newspapers are running a story on our boy Fraser's health tomorrow. Please don't worry – he's doing really well and we have no real concerns right now. Both John and Fraser are growing up fast and very lively!'

I rang Sarah, and discovered that Fraser has cystic fibrosis.

They must be worried sick, but never even hinted at any problems yesterday.

'We've been through worse than this,' she said. 'And when you experience certain things it puts other problems into perspective. We don't see it as a new heartache, as some of the headlines are suggesting tonight, we see it as a challenge to overcome.'

It seems utterly cruel and heartless that they are having to endure this so soon after losing their baby daughter Jennifer. I feel so sorry for them.

THURSDAY 30 NOVEMBER 2006

A letter arrived from PEN's director, Jonathan Heawood. 'Thank you again for turning our auction into a major fundraising event. Thanks to your bullying charm we managed to raise an extra £2500 in under 25 minutes. I was sorry to hear, though, that you set out to fuck off all the liberal wankers in the room, as I don't think many of the liberal wankers were particularly fucked off. You must try harder!'

Celia dragged me out ice-skating again today, and I strained my groin doing a particularly ungainly pirouette, thus turning this into one of the most self-defeating exercises any woman has ever asked their boyfriend to perform.

FRIDAY, 1 DECEMBER 2006

Despite all my TV work, I like to keep my hand in as a journalist, so this morning I interviewed *Guardian* editor Alan Rusbridger for *GQ* magazine, and in the space of 90 minutes he managed to dig himself into a hole the size of the Grand Canyon.

He admitted sending his kids to private school while he believes Labour politicians should send theirs to comprehensives, he drives gas-guzzling cars while espousing the supposed joys of the Gee-Whizz style green vehicles and he earned £520,000 last year, including a £170,000 bonus, while, of course, hammering greedy fat-cat public figures every chance he gets in his paper.

Not quite the stuff his sandal-wearing liberal staff may expect from The Boss...

By the end, I was enjoying myself so much I started lobbing in any questions I could think of guaranteed to make him squirm a bit.

'If you were offered photos of *Daily Mail* editor Paul Dacre snorting coke with hookers, would you publish the story?'

'If he admitted it, then that would be fairly irresistible, yes.'

'And if it was just the hookers, and not the coke?'

'I don't think I'd...'

'If it was a hooker he had picked up off the street. In other words, illegally?'

'Erm…well, that wouldn't be so good.'

'And if Paul Dacre got a picture of you snorting coke with a couple of hookers, would you get sacked?'

'I don't know, you'd have to ask my bosses, the Scott Trust.'

'Would you resign?'

'If I was caught snorting cocaine with a couple of hookers?'

'Yes.'

'Erm…I would probably have to consider my position, yes…'

Rusbridger seemed to be fairly amused by it all, judging by an email he sent me tonight saying: 'Big Boy, enjoyed our bit of jousting…'

Though he then went into a lengthy 'off the record' briefing outlining exactly why he is entitled to his whacking great big bonus.

I think a little panic might be setting in.

TUESDAY, 5 DECEMBER 2006

Simon Cowell has asked me to be a judge on *Britain's Got Talent*, the home-grown version of the American show. Cowell will be on the panel too, but there's been no decision yet on who the third judge will be. It will be fascinating to see what it's like starring in a big prime TV show in this country. I'm sure it will be very different to anything I've done before in terms of media attention and public recognition, both in a good and bad way.

'I see this as my chance to rehabilitate you with the British public,' Cowell said this afternoon.

'Oh, why do I need rehabilitating?'

'Because, and I realise this may come as a shock to your ego, you're not exactly Mr Popular in this country, Piers.'

WEDNESDAY, 6 DECEMBER 2006

Caroline Graham, one of my oldest journalistic friends, is back from America for Christmas. We worked together on *The Sun* 20 years ago, and she's been living in LA as the *Mail on Sunday*'s US correspondent for the last 14 years. When I first came over last summer, she was brilliant in showing me the ropes, introducing me to people and explaining the weirdness of the place.

We had dinner tonight with Celia and James, a DVD distributor friend of

Caroline's who also works in LA, and the conversation turned to the dating scene in California.

James smiled, ruefully.

'It's a nightmare. Californian women can't just go on a date, they see each encounter as a potentially life-or-death relationship dealbreaker. You've seen *Friends* and *Sex and the City*, right? Well, it's like that, only worse. They're neurotic, health-obsessed, teetotal and aggressive.'

God, this had got my attention!

'Carry on...'

'Well, they spend an extraordinary amount of their free time on their bodies, for starters. They have regular manicures and pedicures, teeth-whitening sessions, facials, Brazilian waxes, hair extensions and highlights. They go to the gym four times a week, have massages afterwards, and then see their life coaches. Most of them have pale skin because they are terrified of skin cancer, and have had some form of plastic surgery – a breast enlargement, collagen lip implant, stomach tuck, bingo-wing-removal operation, or lashings of Botox. So their faces are taut, wrinkle-less.'

Caroline laughed.

'That's all true, but you have to remember the biggest difference between American and British women is that American women feel entitled to certain things. A Brit might get her hair done once a week, and have the odd trip to a spa. Out here, basic maintenance takes a village of people.

'A weekly mani-pedi and blow-out is considered essential. I have the girl who does my nails and the two who do my hair – one is a colour specialist, the other cuts it. Then there is my beautician who waxes my eyebrows, upper lip and bikini line. There's another girl who dyes my eyelashes a rather fetching shade known as boudoir black. I get a monthly facial and also go to the derma-tologist at least three times a year to get my red veins zapped with a laser. And I've had new veneers put in and had a breast reduction operation – my surgeon said: "You're the only girl in this town who wants to make them smaller."

'At home I have three Mexicans who come twice a week to do my garden for 200 bucks a month, along with a maid once a week to clean. My Man Friday, Gus, does all the things a husband would, fixes plugs, hangs things, does basic plumbing, fixes the stove, etc.

'Then there is the personal trainer and the Russian acupuncturist.

24

'My cat has a staff of two, the cat sitter who looks after him while I'm away and the mobile pet groomer who comes once a month to trim his nails and wash/condition/de-furball/stick the flea stuff on.'

I burst out laughing. 'Are you serious?'

'Trust me, Piers, I am considered low maintenance. In LA you are simply not allowed to age. It is forbidden. I don't know where all the old ladies go but you never see any on the street. What frequently does happen is you are driving along and see some amazing vision in white spray-on jeans, with a mane of beautiful blonde hair, wiggling along outside Neiman Marcus (or Needless Mark-up as it's known). You pass her and then glance back to see a face that looks like a baboon's bottom – a slightly odd pink from too much laser resurfacing to remove the wrinkles, botoxed to within an inch of her life and with fake lips that look like she's gone ten rounds with Lennox Lewis. There are a lot of those women of indeterminate age in Los Angeles. I know. I am rapidly becoming one of them.

'Everyone has fake acrylic nails and the current fad is for hair extensions like Britney and Lindsay. An Aussie bloke I know says his bed after a good night's shagging looks like road kill.'

I turned back to James.

'What are LA women like to take on a date?'

'Hard, hard work. If you actually get them to dinner, then they will spend half an hour studying the menu before ordering a salad, and glass of sparkling water or green tea. Alcohol is "impure", and none of them smoke because it "ages".

'Then they start bombarding you with material questions – where do you live, how big is your house, what car do you drive, how much do you earn, what's your bonus, where did you go to college, what do your parents do, what religion are you, do you eat red meat, are you or have you ever been an alcoholic, have you ever taken drugs, do you believe in the reincarnation, what's your favourite colour…and that's before you get to the main course.'

'Are they any positives?'

'Yes. Once you eventually get them into the sack, they're surprisingly good. Must be all that pent-up energy.'

Caroline laughed, then said: 'If you think the women are bad, you should try dating an American man out here. My God!'

'Go on...' I urged.

'They haven't a clue, honestly. They dress terribly – they're like big kids when it comes to clothes. You'll see 40-year-old men with beer bellies walking around in shorts, sneakers and baseball caps. Even the billionaires dress like bums. A friend of mine works for a big designer store on Rodeo Drive, and says some of the richest guys in Hollywood – like Spielberg – come in wearing jeans and tattered Nike trainers, and just ask her to dress them. These guys make multi-million dollar deals every day, but ask them to decide between black or blue trousers, and they fall to pieces.

'And they're obsessed by money. I went out on a date with a banker last summer and he sat across the table from me at Il Sole and told me the cost of everything in his life – his house, his Maserati, his watch, his last holiday, his bloody bichon frise dog. My eyes were glazing over by the time the starter arrived. I endured another hour of small talk and was totally bored by the time I got back into his Maserati, at which point he looked at me and said, "My place or yours?" I got out and called a cab.

'They all date numerous women at the same time, and work out who is the best catch as they go. They can be very unreliable, too. I dated one guy called Ramon, who was half-Texan, half-Mexican, and was funny but so pug ugly I was sure he'd never cheat on me! The guy looked like Marlon Brando: the later years. He was very wealthy and fairly thick but had a kind nature and adored me. He suited my lifestyle. I was always jetting around, he travelled frequently for business (with an entourage that included a personal attorney) and we'd meet up in New York or Miami or spend weekends at his beach house in La Jolla. This all went swimmingly for a year until my phone went one day and the woman on the other end told me she was Ramon's wife, had found my number on his cellphone bill and did I know I was one of a stable of mistresses that included a model in New York, a secretary in Texas and a woman who looked after his business interests in Mexico? Oh, and by the way, he was the father of triplets.'

We all fell about laughing.

'LA is the worst place in America for a woman to date,' sighed Caroline. 'They are all either married, or gay. Or married and gay. It's a nightmare.'

We ordered another bottle of wine.

'But at least I can get pissed here!' she laughed. 'God, if we drank this much in LA they would frogmarch you out of the restaurant and straight to Alcoholics Anonymous.'

THURSDAY, 7 DECEMBER 2006

Slightly bizarre evening.

I was having a drink tonight with Paul Dacre at the Berkeley Hotel in Knightsbridge, when the Duchess of York suddenly bounded over from a dimly lit recess.

'How *are* you!' she shrieked in that wonderfully over-the-top jolly-hockey-sticks voice. To my surprise, it turned out that they'd never met. And it was a bit like Hannibal Lecter coming face to face with Agent Starling in *Silence of the Lambs* – you know they both probably want to do each other immeasurable harm, but there was a strange, mutually respectful, if slightly awkward, courtesy to the encounter.

When Dacre left, she beckoned me over to her table, where she was planning her chaotic diary with a few staff.

'How's your love life?' I asked.

'Bloody terrible!' she shouted, raising a few eyebrows at other tables. 'Honestly, why is it so difficult to find a decent man these days?'

'We're all taken,' I replied, prompting a huge guffaw, and the splendidly sneering retort: 'I'm not *that* desperate, Piers!'

Fergie, it has to be said, looks great – slimmer than I've seen her for a long while, and radiating good health.

'How are the royals treating you?' I asked.

'Oh, well, the top ones treat me very well, they always have. Her Majesty is so kind to me. And so are Charles and Camilla. In fact, Camilla always makes sure that my girls are OK at functions if I'm not there, which is very sweet of her.'

'So you're back in the fold then, are you?'

She shook her head. 'Not exactly, no. I was introduced to Lady Helen Windsor in Drones Club the other night, and she just looked me up and down and then turned away from me without saying a word. That was quite hurtful.'

It's not just hurtful, it is shockingly rude. It's sad the way many of the lesser royals still behave towards Fergie. At least she's had the balls to get back on her feet and earn a proper living. Unlike 'The Lady Helen' – as she calls herself these days – who doesn't seem to do very much at all.

We ordered more wine, and she told me a hilarious story involving Sharon Osbourne and her daughter Kelly last week.

'We all had dinner in Le Caprice,' she said, 'and after a few drinks we thought it would be quite fun to go down to the ladies' and pretend to be loo attendants.'

'You did *what*?'

Fergie exploded with giggles.

'I know, it's very naughty, isn't it. But, God, it was funny. We were down there for half an hour, and Sharon insisted we do it properly – handing people their towels, opening cubicle doors for them. Most of them knew who we were, and just smiled or looked really bemused. But one lady didn't recognise us at all, and got very irritated when Sharon started asking her where she got her dress from. She just thought we were being rude! It was hilarious!'

We swapped notes about Americans.

'I'm still not sure I really like them very much,' I said. 'And I think the feeling's mutual.'

Fergie shook her head vigorously.

'No, no. Americans are wonderful people. They accept you for what you are, not what you've been or where you come from. I've been able to rebuild my life out there, in a way that Britain just wouldn't let me do because of all my baggage. My advice is just to be yourself out there.'

SUNDAY, 10 DECEMBER 2006

Just got back from a lovely weekend in Paris for Celia's birthday. On Friday night, we were having dinner in a lovely little restaurant in the Latin Quarter when I observed, with some dismay, that I never get recognised in France.

'That's because the French have taste,' she explained.

At which point, a young Parisienne woman approached our table and asked excitedly in broken English: 'Hello, is it possible for me to have a photo?'

I smirked at Celia, felt my chest imperceptibly puff with pride, and stood up to pose for the picture, putting my arm around the woman's shoulder.

She looked embarrassed, pointed at her camera and then to herself, and said: 'No, no, it is perhaps possible for *you* to take *my* photo? Is OK?'

As I went crimson with mortified embarrassment, and took the photo, Celia giggled uncontrollably. An extra birthday present had just arrived.

MONDAY, 11 DECEMBER 2006
Had lunch at the Ivy with Alastair Campbell today.

'How do you think we should play this *Celebrity Apprentice* thing?' he asked.

'I think we should tear into each other, rip into the other luvvies and then make sure one of us gets fired. Because that's exactly what Sir Alan and the public will want…'

'I bet I get fired,' he said.

'Hmmm, I wouldn't be so sure if I were you,' I replied. 'Sugar's waited years to do this to me…'

We compared notes on public speaking, which we both do a lot of at the moment.

'The biggest laughs I get are when I tell humiliating stories about you,' I said.

'Ditto,' he replied.

WEDNESDAY, 13 DECEMBER 2006
Comic Relief: The Apprentice seemed such a good idea two weeks ago.

Now, having agreed to do it, I'm suddenly not so sure. Spoke to the boys this morning before I set off, and Spencer summed up their collective thought process: 'Dad, please don't get fired again. It would be sooooooo embarrassing.'

I arrived at the West London location to find out who my fellow apprentices are.

The boys' team consists of me, Alastair Campbell, Rupert Everett, Ross Kemp and Danny Baker. The girls' team is Trinny Woodall, Karren Brady, Jo Brand, Maureen Lipman – and Cheryl Cole, wife of the great traitor himself, Ashley Cole, or 'Cashley', as we Arsenal fans call him after his money-grabbing defection to Chelsea.

Cheryl and I exchanged some early verbal swords as we all sat waiting to be briefed, and then her mobile rang. It was Cashley.

'Here, give me that,' I commanded.

She inexplicably handed me her phone.

'Hi Cashley, it's Piers Morgan, how are you, mate?'

'I'm good, thanks mate, how are…'

'Yes, well, let's cut the crap, shall we, "mate"? We need to raise a lot of money and I've just thought of a very good way to do it. If you don't send my team a cheque for £1 million within an hour then I am going to kidnap your wife at the hotel later and do unspeakable things to her.'

There was a long pause.

'Is this a wind-up?' he eventually squeaked.

'No "mate", it's not. So I'd give the bank a call if I were you. Sharpish.'

I handed the phone back to Cheryl, who was giggling so loudly I thought she was going to explode.

I instantly warmed to her. A pop star with a sense of humour, quite extraordinary.

Richard Curtis arrived and explained what our challenge was going to be.

'You are setting up a fairground in Central London that will have eight rides on it. Each team will get four rides to run as a business, and we expect you to invite 100 wealthy and famous guests to come and spend small fortunes on them. Oh, and you've got 48 hours to do it. The winning team will be the one that raises the most money. And one of the losing team will get fired by Sir Alan.'

Ah, yes, Sir Alan. We were led through to the infamous *Apprentice* boardroom to meet the monster, and he swiftly proceeded to humiliate, degrade and generally abuse all of us one by one. I found it hilarious, but others were less enthralled as the vicious barbs were exhaled from his toxic mouth.

'Mr Everett, you're one of those poncey actors, right? Can't say I've ever seen any of your films, so you can't be very good…'

Poor Rupert looked slightly shell-shocked. I suspect nobody had ever talked to him like this before.

We returned to the hotel where we would spend the next three days, and appointed Campbell as our leader on the basis that he always claimed to run the country anyway.

But we had a problem.

By now, Mr Everett was holding his head in his hands and repeatedly muttering 'I can't do this'.

'Rupert,' I said, 'can you start phoning your showbiz mates and get them to give us some cash?'

'Like who?' he whimpered.

'Like Julia Roberts perhaps? Can you get her to offer a kiss to the highest bidder?'

He looked utterly horrified.

'I don't think she'd do that. I could do it maybe?'

'No offence, Rupert, but I think we'd have more success with Julia. Now what about Madonna, it's about time she stopped stealing kids from Africa and actually helped the ones still out there. Can you call her?'

'You can't…erm…you can't just call Madonna, you have to write to her…'

We all burst out laughing, but he was deadly serious.

'Oh God, I can't…I just can't do this…OK, look, can I buy myself out? What if I paid 10,000 pounds of my own money, could I go home then?'

I looked at the others, who were as disgusted as I was by this pitiful display.

'No. It's 100K or you're staying.'

He stared into space, his eyes glazed with horror. Campbell and I exchanged wry smiles, both thinking the same thing: 'What a complete and utter berk.'

THURSDAY, 14 DECEMBER 2006

Woke at 6 a.m. for a team meeting. Everett, predictably, didn't show. He went home last night, and ran away when a car came to pick him up this morning. It was all too much for the poor lamb.

'I didn't know it was all going to be on camera,' he apparently wailed to the producers. Which was rather strange given that we were making an episode of a world-famous reality TV show. And even stranger that this should bother him given that he is a professional bloody actor!

Down to four, we had our work cut out – and began hitting the phones to anyone rich or famous we could think of. Philip Green, Richard Branson, Goldman Sachs, Michael Winner, Jeffrey Archer – anyone and everyone with cash.

It was a long, hard, fractious day. Enlivened only when an Italian chef from Cecconi's restaurant arrived in our suite by mistake, having been recruited by the girls.

We kept him hostage until Trinny Woodall burst in and began kickboxing me and Campbell around the room, demanding we release the startled chef. She was like a crazed, mad-eyed, shrieking banshee: quite terrifying.

I escaped tonight to Matthew Freud and Liz Murdoch's annual Christmas party, where I knew there would be very loaded people to tap up for donations.

Everyone was there, from Mick Jagger and Sting to Claudia Schiffer and Lady Helen Windsor.

I didn't get much money, but I did have a long chat with David Cameron on the stairs. He's a charming and intelligent man. There's nothing offensive about him at all. But there's nothing that impressive about him either. There are thousands of perfectly affable Old Etonians like him out there, and most of them wouldn't know how to run a whelk stall, let alone a country.

Cameron was half furious and half admiring of the way that the sensational breaking news this afternoon – Tony Blair's questioning by police over the cash-for-honours scandal – had 'coincidentally' taken place at the same time former Met Police chief John Stevens' report into Diana's death was being released.

'How does he fucking get away with it?' said Cameron.

'Because he always fucking gets away with it,' I replied. 'That's why they call him Teflon Tony.'

FRIDAY, 15 DECEMBER 2006

Showtime. The sheer logistics of organising this challenge have been mentally and physically exhausting, but by 5 p.m. we got there. And I have to say, I've loved every second of it. Long hours, adrenaline rushes, constant need for quick wit and creative thought, badgering the rich and famous for help...it's been the nearest thing to editing a newspaper I've experienced in two and a half years.

Celebrities streamed into the makeshift fairground. Most of them straight into various ambushes.

The girls had the bright idea of getting Take That to run their dodgems, so we retaliated by promptly kidnapping Mark Owen and sticking him on top of our Ferris Wheel until they paid a hefty ransom for his release.

I had a quiet chat with Gary Barlow after Mark was freed.

'Fantastic to see you back at number one, mate,' I said.

'Cheers, mate, we can't quite believe it either,' he replied.

Long pause.

'Tragedy about Robbie's new single tanking in the charts, isn't it?' I said.

'Awful, terrible, I'm so sorry for him...' replied Gary, with the biggest, smuggest smirk you've ever seen in your life.

Buoyed by the success of our Mark Owen mission, we then tried doing the same with Ashley Cole as he and John Terry rode in a dodgem car. But were prevented by a still-screaming Trinny flinging herself on the two footballers. 'My back, my back!' yelped Terry, a most pleasing sound to any Arsenal fan's ears.

Highlight of the night, though – apart from Tracey Emin arriving with specially painted pink breast coconuts for our shy – was definitely our medieval stocks.

Anne Robinson stunned me by agreeing to be doused by John Terry, and so did Marks & Spencers boss Sir Stuart Rose, who let a very enthusiastic Peter Stringfellow do the same to him.

Simon Cowell point blank refused (I suspect he was worried his hair might run...) and Sir Alan Sugar just ran off, sneering 'NO FUCKING CHANCE!' when I suggested it.

As the evening got increasingly silly, I personally paid £2500 to drench Cashley with a full bucket of freezing cold sponges, crying the immortal words, 'On behalf of every Gooner in Britain, you treacherous bastard!'

And then Cheryl paid for, and performed, the same act on me – as Spencer, Stanley and Bertie watched in hysterics.

It must be strange for them to see their father make such a complete public arse of himself. But then I guess they're getting used to it.

As the evening drew to a close, I gathered our team together and made a suggestion: 'Let's call Rupert.'

'Oh, YES!' they cried in unison.

We were all wet, cold, and exhausted. The perfect state to have a little chat with the gutless thespian coward.

His mobile went into voicemail, so on a count of three we all shouted at the top of our voices: 'Rupert, you WANKER!'

SATURDAY, 16 DECEMBER 2006

Back to the boardroom for the 'verdict'.

After a brief preamble, Sir Alan cut to the chase. The girls had raised £774,000 (apparently Trinny wangled £150,000 out of one rich Russian woman at the Freud party, while I was busy spitting blood about Blair with Cameron). Our depleted boys' team had raised £286,000, of which I had personally brought in more than three-quarters of the cash.

But this was only ever going to end in one of two ways.

Campbell and I looked at each other.

'It's going to be you,' I snarled.

'I'm not so sure now,' he smirked.

Sugar was loving every minute of the suspense, urging me and Campbell to abuse each other for 20 minutes or so before finally calling a halt to proceedings.

He then summed up both our numerous inadequacies before announcing: 'Mr Piers Morgan...you are FIRED!'

Campbell turned slowly, with a revolting leer on his face. '*Again*?'

But since this was pre-recorded, I wasn't going to let Sugar have his moment of fun without a fight.

'Bollocks. I've been fired by better people than you,' I retorted.

Cue mass convulsions of nervous laughter from the film crew.

Sir Alan wasn't laughing.

'Very funny Morgan, let's do it again.'

'Mr Piers Morgan, you're FIRED!'

'Tell someone who gives a fuck,' I responded this time, to more laughter.

Sugar was ready to smack me, I could tell.

Eventually I let him have his moment, and we were released back into the community.

It's been a mad, intense three days. And given the fact that they've got 200 hours of tape for a one-hour show, they can either make me look very, very stupid, or the smartest tool in the history of tools.

I won't be rushing to put money on the latter.

I called the boys as I was being driven home.

'How did you do, Dad?' asked Stanley.

'Not great, mate.'

'You weren't fired again, were you?' he sighed.

'I'm afraid I was, yes.'

There was a pause, then I heard Stanley shout: 'HEY GUYS – GUESS WHAT, DAD GOT FIRED AGAIN!'

Spencer came to the phone.

'You have to keep it a secret until the show gets aired,' I told him.

'Dad, why would I even think of telling anyone…?'

Tonight, it was revealed that John Terry pulled out of today's Chelsea match complaining of 'an aggravated back injury'.

So at least some good has come out of it all.

The *Britain's Got Talent* stars all vie for who can pull off the cheesiest showbiz grin.

'I was pretty cynical about the American mentality before I worked there, but now I preach it. They have such a positive outlook, I find it very infectious. If you buy yourself a new Ferrari there for $400,000, nobody abuses you or tries to scratch it. They are more likely to say how much they like the car, and to congratulate you on working hard enough to get it.' SIMON COWELL

SUNDAY, 17 DECEMBER 2006

It's hard to know how Simon Cowell could be more insufferable, given his sickening new £20 million ITV deal.

But I picked up the papers this morning and read that he has been voted the seventh most famous person in the world by British schoolchildren – after God, President Bush, Madonna, Jesus, Father Christmas and the Queen.

When I phoned him to break this horrific news, there was a long pause before he cackled, then said, slowly and deliberately: 'I...LOVE...IT!'

Cowell's dazzling Hollywood gnashers are clearly going to be in permanent smug 'gleam' for the next few weeks, which is why I've booked a last-minute flight out of the country to avoid him.

'Have a great Christmas,' he said. 'Where are you spending New Year?'

'Well away from you,' I replied. 'In Barbados.'

Another pause, another cackle.

'Fantastic! So am I...'

MONDAY, 18 DECEMBER 2006

GQ have declared Gordon Brown 'Britain's Most Powerful Man' and asked me to interview him to celebrate this accolade.

I haven't interviewed Brown for about ten years, and given that we have since become pretty good friends, this was going to be a weird experience. But also, I hoped, a very enlightening one. This is, after all, the man who most people assume will be prime minister before too long.

We sat, again, in the small poky ante-room off his Treasury office, completely in keeping with his resolute, and totally genuine, disinterest in flash trappings.

He poured me a coffee, and I flicked on the tape-recorder.

'Good luck...' I joked.

'Just behave yourself,' he chuckled.

'So, Gordon, how does it feel to be the most powerful man in Britain?'

'I have never thought of this job in terms of power. I think of it in terms of how much I can influence things.'

'But the mere fact that you are now the longest-serving chancellor for 200 years suggests you are one of the most powerful men in Britain, does it not?'

'Actually the only chancellor who served longer than me is Nicholas Vansittart, who lasted 12 years, and that's because he abolished income tax.'

Gordon's knowledge of political history borders on the autistic.

'So can we expect any announcements of a similar nature?'

'I wouldn't hold your breath, Piers...'

'You once said that all power corrupts, and no power corrupts...'

'I actually said that all power corrupts and lack of power corrupts absolutely. And I was talking about the Conservatives.' He laughed loudly.

Gordon poured me another cup of coffee, and chuckled again. He's an adept interviewee, and thus very difficult to trip up, or squeeze much revelation from.

We then got on to economics. 'Do economic statistics turn you on, then? Do you get a buzz out of them?'

'I'm not obsessed by the minutiae of obscure financial statistics if that's what you're getting at...'

'No, but when you ceded independence to the Bank of England, was that better than sex?'

Gordon rocked back in his chair like he'd been smacked in the face.

'Erm...(rolls his eyes, puffs his cheeks)...I don't think I'm going to answer that. But it was important.'

'And exciting?'

'Erm...' He reaches desperately for his coffee.

'Come on, it must have been a hell of a thrill?'

'It was important, Piers. Let's leave it there.'

'If you were describing your personality to someone, how would you describe yourself?'

'I think I'm quite determined.'

'Obstinate?'

'No, determined.'

'Don't the two go hand in hand?'

'No, because I would like people to think that I listen before making a decision. I hear all the arguments and then decide what to do. You have to listen.'

'What other characteristics do you think you have?'

'I liked Churchill's line about people being resolved to be irresolute or adamant for drift. I like to make my mind up about things and then actually do it.'

'Are you a passionate man?'

'Yes, I think so. About the things I believe in, whether it's supporting your football team or helping someone who you believe has something to offer.'

'Are you romantic?'

'Yes.'

'In what way?'

'By believing in the best in people. That's what romanticism is about. Wanting people to make the best of themselves. Though you may have other definitions of romance on your mind...'

'I was really wondering if you were romantic to your wife, Gordon!'

'Yes (laughs). I think so (loud chuckle).'

'In what way?'

'Well, we get on very well, we do lots of things together. And we've been through a lot together. We respect each other and we like going places together.'

'Are you a chocolate and flowers man?'

'Er...' (Looks embarrassed, starts to blush.)

I can see he finds this kind of questioning excruciating, whereas Blair used to love it.

'Candelit restaurant type of guy?'

'Er…(now visibly cringing)…I'm not going to get into all that, Piers. You go to the Ivy restaurant, don't you?'

'I took your wife for lunch there actually…you never go there, though, do you?'

'It's very difficult when you have young children to go out, even with the help of other people.'

'How important has Sarah been to you?'

'She's been great, just great. And having children together has just been the greatest thing of all.'

'When did you actually meet her?'

'Er…in the 1990s…'

'Do you remember the moment?'

'Well, we met on a number of occasions. She was working on stuff, and came to see me, and we met through other friends… But, look, that's a story to be told some other time.'

'Why some other time? This would seem a perfect moment to spill the beans.'

(Laughs.) 'Nooooo. I think we'll just keep that for later. I think that the thing people are really interested in about me is the job I can do for them, and whether I do it well or badly. And I don't think people are as interested in my personal life as you are, Piers!'

'Of course they are. And I think you should talk about it, because the Gordon Brown I know is very different to the man people see on telly. Why do you insist on being so serious and dull on TV when you're nothing like that away from the cameras?'

'I think that most of the times I appear on TV, I am appearing as the chancellor and talking about things that are very important to people. I give news about the economy or a budget statement. And so the scope for great humour isn't really there. (Bursts out laughing.) I can't just start cracking jokes about taxation, can I? I prefer to walk into a room, tell people I have listened to the arguments, and then say: "OK, this is what I believe, and this is what I think is right." And then you are tested by democracy as to whether your decision making is right or wrong.'

'Are you frustrated in always being the bridesmaid, never being the bride?'

(Laughs.) 'No.'

'Come on, you must be.'

'I think…erm…(sighs)…I have done things that had to be done. So I can't say it is a limited job in that sense, it is very important.'

'What's the truth about your relationship with Tony Blair?'

I know the truth, which is that they've been at loggerheads for several years now. But there was no way Gordon would admit that in an interview.

'He's a good friend of mine and we have worked together for 23 years…' he replied, deadpan. I laughed out loud, but Gordon ignored me. '…we shared an office, worked on similar projects, and still work together on projects now.'

'Fancy telling me what things irritate you about Tony?'

'No. But what I can say is that people will look at our record. We are the longest-serving prime minister and chancellor team.'

'Are you a political Lennon and McCartney then?'

'Er…which one's McCartney?'

'You tell me.'

'Well, it was Bono who first used that analogy and he didn't actually say who he thought was Lennon and who was McCartney.'

'Well, presumably you're Lennon, aren't you?'

'(Chuckles) Bono didn't say, and I don't know.'

'Lennon was always the edgy one with real depth, McCartney was just the pretty boy pop star, wasn't he?'

'They were both very good entertainers.'

'Two geniuses together?'

'They were, yes, so you can't compare them to mere politicians like me and Tony.'

'Do you like the idea of being two genius entertainers, though?'

'No, I don't think that really suits.'

It was time for some fun.

'Do you think you're in touch with the real world?'

'I…erm…yes, I like to think so.'

'OK, then, how much is a pint of milk?'

Gordon froze.

'I can tell you….er…generally…erm…the price of milk and bread and so on. The price of milk hasn't gone up much at all in recent years.'

'Go on then, how much is a pint?'

'About 30…(gives sudden desperate look to his aide)…yes, about 30p.'

'Loaf of bread?'

'About 65p.'

'Do you ever buy these things?'

'Yes, I go to supermarkets in Scotland.'

'Do you haggle over prices?'

'I might have done 20 years ago. (Laughs.) I used to sell football programmes with my brother at Raith Rovers, so I have been a salesman.'

'You have been through some pretty harrowing things as a parent, Gordon. Culminating in the recent news that Fraser has cystic fibrosis. How difficult has it been for you, given the particularly demanding nature of your job, to deal with these things?'

'We have lived through all the tests from the day Fraser was born, and didn't expect or want it to become public. But it has, so we have had to speak about it. But I am very optimistic about cures, and the opportunities that sport and fitness give to someone with this condition. We are both very optimistic.'

'You and Sarah have shown extraordinary courage, given what else you had to go through.'

'I think most parents in our position just get on with it, because you know your child is depending on you. And it is really important to remember that it's not important what you feel, it's making sure that your child has the best chance that really matters.'

'Sarah said to me that after what happened to your daughter Jennifer, nothing could ever be that bad again. And that made it easier to deal with the news about Fraser.'

'Yes. I think there is nothing that can ever rival the loss of a child. Nothing ever.'

Gordon stopped talking at this point, dropped his head and looked tearful. I'd never seen him show such emotion, and was slightly taken aback by it.

'I'm sorry, Gordon, are you OK?'

He looked up at me, his face blackened with grief. 'Yes, sorry, where were we?'

Part of me wanted to change the subject, but that would have been unprofessional. I was conducting an interview, not having a private chat with him.

'In terms of what you said about character earlier, how did what happened change you as a man?'

'I think every event that you face shapes you. All of us are shaped and reshaped by events, and how you deal with them. I think people know that I spent a huge amount of time in hospital when I was a teenager after getting a rugby injury that cost me an eye.'

'How bad was it?'

'I was 16, and playing rugby, and I got whacked in the eye in the scrum and knew something had happened but I carried on playing anyway because I was concussed. It turned out to be a retinal detachment and the only way they could deal with it was for me to lie flat for weeks on end in total darkness.'

'God, sounds absolutely horrific. What were you thinking about as you lay there?'

(Laughs.) 'I was thinking about all sorts of things! I could listen to music and hospital radio, and talk to the nurses. But otherwise I just had to lie there.'

'Did you ever fear you might go completely blind?'

'At one point I did, yes.'

'How did that feel?'

'I just had to stay determined and positive. I think I am a very fortunate person. I've had to meet challenges, from losing my sight in one eye at 16 and nearly losing the other to more recent events. I was lucky, though, because some new technology came in that saved my other eye. And that shows you what the National Health Service can do when it is at its best. It saved my sight with new laser treatment; it was a young surgeon who was carrying out his first operation with these new techniques and I was very fortunate to find him, or rather for him to find me.'

'Finally, have you sent your neighbours at No. 10 a Christmas card yet?'

'Yes, of course.'

'To both of them?'

'Yes, of course.' (Smiles.)

'And have you had one back yet?'

'Yes, I'm pretty sure I have…but this interview is coming out in February isn't it?' (Roars with laughter.)

I left the Treasury feeling, as always when I see Gordon Brown, impressed by his energy, intellect and sense of purpose.

His public image is something he's brought on himself, and bears little reflection on the man I know in private. If he does become prime minister, it will be fascinating to see if he can show us the real Gordon, or whether this straitjacket he's stuck himself in remains rigidly in place.

TUESDAY, 19 DECEMBER 2006

'Fancy lunch at the Ivy?' asked Celia this morning.

There was something about her tone that made me suspicious.

'What's the catch?'

'I will be dressed as Ugly Betty.'

'I see. Why?'

'Because the *Telegraph* want me to spend the day as her to see what it's like.'

Two hours later, I entered the Ivy and went to wait for her at the table.

'Betty' arrived minutes later, and I was shocked. She looked *identical* to the TV character: the long dark hair, glasses, hideous skirt, orange puffy vest and psychedelic patterned blouse. And then she smiled, and I saw a set of horrific fake braced teeth looming out at me.

'Celia, you look disgusting.'

'Thank you,' she said, delightedly.

I overheard a woman at the next able ask her companion: 'Is that Nana Mouskouri?'

We ordered our food, and I spied Neil Reading, a PR man and old mate of ours, sitting two tables away. I summonsed him over, and introduced him to 'Betty'. He never twigged for a second, just looked slightly appalled that I was dining with such an ugly woman.

Then Alan Yentob passed by, and I stopped him, too.

'This is Betty,' I said.

He shook her hand, and said hello. Again, not a flicker of recognition.

When the time came to leave, I guided 'Betty' through the restaurant, and could see numerous diners nudging each other, all thinking: 'Poor old Morgan, is that the best he can do?'

WEDNESDAY, 20 DECEMBER 2006

My phone rang.

'Piers, it's Gordon. Now, this thing about the price of a pint of milk...'

'Yes, Gordon...'

'I don't want to look a fool here...'

'No, Gordon.'

'It's just that someone in my office says it is nearer to 45p than 30p.'

I laughed.

'Gordon, I haven't the foggiest how much it costs.'

'So you asked me the question without knowing the answer?'

'I'm afraid so, yes. Bloody journalists, eh...but for what it's worth, I reckon it is nearer 30p than 45p, definitely. I'll have a quick check, though, and let you know.'

I hung up and clicked on the Sainsbury's, Tesco's and Asda websites.

The price of a full-cream, non-organic pint is 32p.

I rang him back.

'You're in the clear. It's "about 30p" – just as you said.'

I could almost hear the sigh of relief willowing down from No. 11. Prime ministers, or even prime ministers in waiting, can survive many things – prison break-outs, natural disasters, philandering ministers, even illegal wars.

But I doubt they could survive getting the price of a pint of milk wrong by 50 per cent.

THURSDAY, 21 DECEMBER 2006

A Christmas email arrived today from Sir Alan Sugar:

Dear Piers,

I wanted to send some sort of holiday greeting to my friends, family and clients but it is so difficult in today's world to know exactly what to say without offending someone. So I met with lawyers yesterday, and on their advice I wish to say the following:

Please accept with no obligation, implied or implicit, my best wishes for an environmentally conscious, socially responsible, low stress, non-addictive, gender neutral celebration of the solstice holiday, practised with the most enjoyable traditions of religious persuasion or secular practices of your choice with respect for the religious/secular persuasions and/or traditions of others, or their choice not to practise religious or secular traditions at all.

I also wish you a fiscally successful, personally fulfilling and medically uncomplicated recognition of the onset of the generally accepted calendar year 2007, but not without due respect for the calendars of choice of other cultures whose contributions to society have helped make our country great (not to imply that Britain is necessarily greater than any other country) and without regard to the race, creed, colour, age, physical ability, religious faith or sexual preference of the wishee.

By accepting this greeting, you are accepting these terms:

This greeting is subject to clarification or withdrawal. It is freely transferable with no alteration to the original greeting. It implies no promise by the wisher to actually implement any of the wishes for her/him or others and is void where prohibited by law, and is revocable at the sole discretion of the wisher. This wish is warranted to perform as expected within the usual application of good tidings for a period of one year or until the issuance of a subsequent holiday greeting, whichever comes first, and warranty is limited to replacement of this wish or issuance of a new wish at the sole discretion of the wisher.

Sir Alan Sugar

FRIDAY, 22 DECEMBER 2006

I interviewed Naomi Campbell today, and after 40 minutes or so, she suddenly pulled out a notebook and shouted, 'MY TURN!'

'What are you doing?' I said, with a jolt.

'I am now going to interview you, Piers.'

'Oh no you're not…'

'Oh yes I am.'

I sat back and laughed.

'Oh sod it, go on then…'

'So, Piers, how does it feel now you're a TV star in America to have people snooping around your private life?'

'I like it, it's funny. I got exposed over a whole page of the *National Enquirer* recently, and I thought I was hilarious.'

'And was it true or false?'

'Most of it was true. But it wouldn't have bothered me either way. It was funny.'

'Was it right of you to run Paul Burrell's story in the *Mirror*? How did you know it was accurate?'

'I believed every word he wrote.'

'So why did he have to leave the country and go and live in America then?'

'Because the media who didn't get his story destroyed him.'

'Now then, let's talk about your partner Celia Walden. I have to ask, had she been drinking when she met you? Ha ha ha ha ha ha ha ha ha!'

'Ho ho. Yes, she had. And she is drinking a lot more heavily now, I can tell you, as the full horror sets in.'

'Were you guilty of insider dealing?'

'No. I was cleared. But journalists don't want to hear that. They would rather I was guilty.'

'Did you lose any journalist friends over it?'

'No, but I had to laugh at the way some journalists took the high moral ground given what I know about them. But then journalists have always been the most hypocritical people on God's earth.'

'Oh wow! What is your stance on racism?'

'I think I did a hell of a lot to promote positive race stories in the *Mirror*.'

'Yes, but what about your front page "Achtung Surrender"!'

'Ah well, that wasn't racism, that was taking the piss out of the Germans.'

'But they have had the piss taken out of them enough in their lives.'

'Sorry, no they haven't.'

'You are a famous Arsenal fan. What did you think of Ashley Cole going to Chelsea?'

'I think he's a treacherous little swine who should be hung, drawn and quartered then burned at the stake in Trafalgar Square.'

'I hear you threw a bucket of water over him for Comic Relief?'

'I did. And loved every second of it.'

'And what did you do to my friend Rupert Everett in the same Comic Relief thing?'

'He is a big girl's blouse.'

'He's not, he is a wonderful person and a great British acting export.'

'Absolute bollocks. He's a lily-livered little limpet who buggered off after five hours of our *Apprentice* challenge crying that he couldn't do it. It was Comic Relief, raising money for Africans, you of all people should agree with me on this one.'

Naomi squealed with laughter.

'Should you have checked those Iraqi photos a bit more before you published them?'

'No, because the abuse was going on and since been proven to have been going on in various court cases.'

'Now, what do you do to cleanse yourself of all the negativity in your life as a result of being a journalist?'

'I accept that journalists are very cynical, particularly about celebrities. And often with good reason. We tend to view people like you as soap opera characters, not real human beings. And perhaps we need to think of you as a human being sometimes. When I look back on that court battle we had over privacy, I think my overriding thought is that going after you for your drug-addiction treatment was not how I would wish to be remembered as a journalist.'

'Do you have any skeletons in your closet that you would rather not come out?'

'Yes, millions. Where do you want to start?'

'Do you drink, or take drugs?'

'Whooaah there, tiger. I'm not having you invading my privacy, I'm sorry, Naomi.'

'EXACTLY! Thank you!'

The whole thing was an exhausting, but fascinating experience, and enjoyable too. Naomi may be a piece of work, but she's an entertaining piece of work – I'll give her that.

MONDAY, 25 DECEMBER 2006

Spent Christmas Day without the boys for the first time, and really missed them. Marion and I separated six years ago, and have finally started formal divorce proceedings. But I'm sure they will be quick and amicable, we've stayed good friends.

WEDNESDAY, 27 DECEMBER 2006

I've managed to go 41 years without ever losing a bag at an airport. But the moment I disclosed this fact to Celia as we arrived in Barbados today…her bag obviously failed to arrive.

For a woman, losing every favourite dress, bikini, item of underwear and shoe on day one of a holiday is just about the worst thing that can happen to you. And Celia took it well.

'This is going to RUIN my holiday,' she pronounced, firmly, as we sat staring at a virtually empty carousel.

Our hopes were temporarily raised when we suddenly spotted another very similar bag, and realised that Celia's must have been taken by genuine mistake. Unfortunately, further investigation revealed it belonged to a local Bajan called Arthur Taylor, who had paid cash for his ticket, and left no address.

And since Arthur's bag contained just some unwashed socks and a large jar of Marmite, our hopes crashed again. Why would he come back for that if he now had thousands of pounds' worth of designer clothes?

We trudged to our hotel, Celia's jet-black mood darkening faster than the sky.

Then, at 9 p.m., my mobile rang. It was a man from Virgin Atlantic.

'Mr Morgan, your bag has been returned.'

I was flabbergasted.

'God, really? How? Why?'

'Oh, you're going to like this. Mr Taylor really wanted his Marmite back.'

FRIDAY, 29 DECEMBER 2006

I had my feet massaged on the beach today by a six-foot-six Rastafarian called 'The Doctor'.

'I've done all the big stars,' he boasted, unfathomably oblivious to my own celebrity status.

'Who has the best celebrity feet then?' I asked.

'Alan Shearer. Very smooth.'

'And the worst?'

'Hugh Grant. Short and fat.'

SATURDAY, 30 DECEMBER 2006

Saddam Hussein was hanged today. And I won't lose any sleep over the loss of this mad old tyrant. It always bemuses me that people think if you opposed the war then you must love Saddam.

The truth is that while he was a deeply unpleasant piece of work, he posed little or no threat to anyone by the time we invaded, and the safer and more sensible thing to do would have been to keep him clinging on to power as long as possible, and let the Iraqi people work out for themselves how they wanted their future to look once he'd died naturally.

But Saddam still killed and tortured millions of his people, and I'm glad he's gone.

SUNDAY, 31 DECEMBER 2006

Simon Cowell invited us to join his table at the Sandy Lane Hotel New Year's Eve party tonight.

'It's fancy dress,' he assured me this afternoon. 'Aliens and seafood.'

I have learned the hard way not to believe everything Mr Cowell tells me, so I double-checked with the Sandy Lane reception.

'No, no, it's formal black tie,' came the predictable reply.

'It's not,' Cowell insisted when I confronted him. 'It's aliens and seafood.'

'Great,' I replied. 'In that case, I'm going to come naked, wearing a giant aqualung, and say I'm with Simon Cowell.'

'I will alert security,' he said.

I bottled it, of course, and turned up in a shirt and trousers – only to be met by what looked like Dolly Parton's birthday party.

The whole beachside area of the hotel had been turned into a country and western extravaganza. The staff were decked out as cowboys and Indians, there were giant 'Wanted' posters everywhere, a huge marquee festooned with cowboy-style paraphernalia, and right in the middle of it all was Cowell, wearing jeans and the biggest grin of his life (and you can imagine how big that must have been), tucking into a huge plate of lobster.

'I told you,' he said. 'Aliens and seafood.'

I sat next to Cowell's mother Julie, a wonderful lady in her eighties, who was recently run over by a car and hurt quite badly, but who didn't seem remotely concerned.

'It would take a lot more than broken hips and knees to stop me coming out here,' she said.

Down the table was Sir Philip Green. And his wife Tina, sporting the biggest diamond necklace I have ever seen.

'It's 52 carat,' she said.

'God, was that a Christmas present from Philip?'

'No, he bought me a fabulous ring from Graaf, but wouldn't let me wear it tonight.'

'Why ever not?

'Because he said it would be too flashy.'

The buffet was equally extravagant. There must have been 50 tables groaning with giant slabs of fresh lobster, crab, caviar, sushi, every form of roast meat, more varieties of salad than I knew existed, and puddings to commit mass murder for.

'Not a bad spread, is it?' chuckled Philip, spearing what looked like a small shark on to his plate.

We all gorged ourselves stupid for the next two hours, washing down the food with chilled Cristal champagne and decanters of fabulous red wine.

One surprise absentee was Michael Winner, who had been struck down with a mystery illness and was confined to his bed upstairs.

'Trust me,' said Simon. 'For Michael to miss this meal it must be life threatening.'

At midnight, everyone congregated on the dance floor for the countdown to New Year. If you had kidnapped all the highrollers I spotted at that moment, you could eliminate the national debt of most African countries.

Then a huge and magnificent fireworks display erupted from a large boat offshore.

As it did, I shook hands with one of the richest people there, Irish magnate Dermot Desmond who co-owns the hotel.

'The secret to life is being kind,' he said, without prompting, 'just be kind, show goodwill to people, and you'll have a good life.'

I turned back to Philip. 'This is a quite amazing party, isn't it?'

He chuckled. 'Do you want to see what a *really* amazing party looks like?'

Then he and Tina led me and Celia back to their nearby suite (the best, obviously), and stuck on the DVD of Green's fiftieth fabled birthday bash in Greece. When I tell you that it lasted three days, and that the entertainment for the 220 toga-clad guests – ferried there by private plane – included Earth Wind and Fire, George Benson and Rod Stewart, then you get the general idea.

'When are you 55?' I asked.

'Very soon,' he replied.

'Having another party?'

'Of course.'

'How's the guest list coming along?'

'Nearly finished.'

'Is there any chance...'

'Piers, don't be vulgar.'

At 2.30 a.m., I cracked open one last bottle of champagne with Cowell.

'How are you enjoying America?' he asked.

'I think "work in progress" is the phrase I'd use. I find all their chest-beating a bit over-bearing to be honest.'

Simon burst out laughing.

'That's pretty rich coming from you! You know, I was pretty cynical about the American mentality before I worked there, but now I preach it. They have such a positive outlook, I find it very infectious. If you buy yourself a new Ferrari there for $400,000, nobody abuses you or tries to scratch it. They are more likely to say how much they like the car, and to congratulate you on working hard enough to get it.'

'But I find their humour so one-paced.'

'It can be, but they find our humour pretty weird, too. They hear us taking the piss out of each other, and they're genuinely horrified that two people who are supposed to be friends could abuse each other like that. And they've got a point!'

'What do you think of the presidential election race?'

'I keep out of it, and my firm advice to you is to do the same. They take their politics bloody seriously in America, and you're either one side or the other. So why alienate half the population with a silly quote?'

I got back to my hotel to find a text message from brother Rupert back in London.

'Really sorry I couldn't make the New Year's Eve party, I'm a little hung over from last night. Best wishes, Saddam Hussein.'

TUESDAY, 2 JANUARY 2007

I'm not saying I get an unfair press in Britain, but the Ephraim Hardcastle gossip column in today's *Daily Mail* carries a New Year quiz that includes the following question:

'Former Tory MP George Walden was anxious, I reported, about his comely daughter Celia's friendship with this man: a) The Yorkshire Ripper; b) Saddam Hussein; c) Piers Morgan.'

WEDNESDAY, 3 JANUARY 2007

My Caribbean ordeal continued tonight with a lavish dinner on the beach back at the Sandy Lane Hotel, laid on by Philip Green and his wife Tina.

As the fine wine flowed, and private chefs prepared a gourmet feast (aided by Tina, who tossed up an extremely good salad), the guests – including Simon, his girlfriend Terri Seymour, and Rebekah Wade – began to debate great matters of state.

Not for us the complexities of the Middle East or Saddam's public hanging, though. No, the burning question, as proposed by Cowell, was this: who is the biggest prima donna in the world of showbusiness?

His criteria were straightforward: 'These have to be people who we have all heard are nightmares, whether our sources are cabbies, make-up artists, stylists, producers, or our own personal experience.'

It was a spirited, heated and intense discussion. After all, there are so many names to choose from.

But eventually we agreed on the top 10 celebrity divas.

In reverse order, they were:

10. P Diddy – 'Oh, a complete nightmare,' said one diner. 'Everyone who works with him says it. The jumped-up little plonker genuinely thinks he is the biggest star in the world.'

9. Liz Hurley – 'Pretends to be so high and mighty, but apart from wearing a dress with safety pins at her boyfriend's premiere 12 years ago, what the hell has she ever done?' was one guest's withering observation. 'Ego writing cheques the body can no longer cash,' said another. (Yes, I am a massive *Top Gun* fan.)

8. Naomi Campbell – 'Ooohhhhh, sheer emotional, psychological and physical hell on magnificent legs was one comment. I tried to defend Naomi, but I was shouted down. 'Piers, stop being so pathetic just because she fluttered her eyelashes at you.' Harsh but fair.

7. Madonna – 'She has to be in there, can you even begin to imagine what she must be like to live with?' chuckled one of the male guests. 'The ultimate pain in the backside,' said another who once had to interview her.

6. Annie Lennox – came out of left field, this one. But the accuser was adamant. 'She was quite breathtakingly grand and offensive to me. I was shocked. But then other big stars told me she's always like that.'

5. Katie Holmes – another surprising choice, perhaps. But one female member of the group (who was stroking Cowell's neck at the time)

insisted: 'Oh my God, she was the rudest woman I have ever met. Quite appalling.' And then the words nobody thought they would ever hear: 'I feel sorry for Tom Cruise.'

4. Mariah Carey – everyone simply nodded when her name came up. 'Actually has a red carpet and scented candles waiting for her when she arrives at hotels in the middle of the night,' said someone, almost admiringly.

3. Hugh Grant – all the media-related guests were unanimous on this one. 'If I have to hear that spoiled, upper-class brat whining one more time about fame, I'm going to take an axe and sever him at his pampered little neck,' was one of the more generous reflections.

2. Bobby Brown – 'Literally unbearable. The worst of the worst. A man who treats everyone around him like a personal slave. Truly awful man.' And that was about the best that anyone had to say about him. 'He has only one thing going for him,' said another contributor. 'He's not his wife.'

1. His wife – Whitney Houston: a comfortable winner. Everyone had some form of terrible first-hand experience of this creature. 'Think Cruella de Ville without the charm,' was one verdict. Take your pick from other descriptions: 'Rude, arrogant, treats people like dirt, unreliable, difficult, stroppy little madam.'

THURSDAY, 4 JANUARY 2007

Celia and I had just strolled back along the beach from a nice, relaxing lunch today when another guest at my hotel, the Sandpiper, rushed up and said: 'Mr Morgan, I just thought I should warn you that there's some bloke buried up to his chest in sand over there taking photographs of you.'

I laughed. This was a wind-up, obviously.

But he wasn't joking. I looked to where he was pointing and saw the unmistakable features of a paparazzi lurking 50 yards away.

Oh, the irony. After 12 years of buying 'pap' photos of celebrities along these very beaches for newspapers I edited, I was now a victim.

Even worse, it was someone I recognised – an operative from the Big Pictures agency, run by that crazy, Mohican-haired Australian, Darryn 'Dazza' Lyons.

'How did you know I was here?' the photographer asked when I walked over to him.

'Mate, you're fully clothed, you're buried in sand, and you've got a three-foot camera lens in your hands. It wasn't difficult. What did you get?'

'Oh, you and the bird, walking along the beach.'

'You'll never sell it…'

'Already have, mate.'

'Who to?'

'Can't say, sorry.'

Quite extraordinary how fast they work these days. He had taken the pictures, sent them digitally to his London office, and they had been sold somewhere in the world (America, probably) – all within about four minutes.

It's also quite bizarre how invasive it feels. Even for a tabloid poacher turned gamekeeper like me. Because the truth is that I had never spotted him at all. My torso is now 'currency' in the paparazzi game, for the first time. And that's slightly unnerving, to put it mildly.

To make matters worse, the Ephraim Hardcastle column has had another pop this morning, describing me as 'portly'. I spent the rest of the day walking around in a T-shirt, with my stomach tucked in, and tightening my arm muscles in a desperate effort to look more Daniel Craig than Demis Roussos.

My only consolation is that Cowell's been all over the papers this week too, for his so-called man-boobs or 'moobs' as the *Mail* have dubbed them.

FRIDAY, 5 JANUARY 2007

Cowell bought us a farewell dinner at the Lone Star restaurant.

'I don't think we can have anyone called "portly" starring in *Britain's Got Talent*,' he taunted, laughing so hard I thought he might delight the world and self-combust, 'you'd better do something about it, fast.'

'Very funny, Mr Moobs,' I retorted. 'At least I haven't got breasts bigger than Pamela Anderson.'

Terri was sporting some lovely diamond earrings that Cowell had bought her for Christmas. 'The only problem is that compared to the enormous ring Philip Green bought Tina, they look tiny,' he moaned.

'I'm sure Terri's got used to tiny things by now, Simon,' I replied.

WEDNESDAY, 10 JANUARY 2007

President Bush has announced a dramatic change in strategy in Iraq – ordering an extra 20,000 troops into the region.

'Failure in Iraq would be a disaster for the United States,' he said, stating the bleeding obvious. Americans hate losing at tiddlywinks, never mind a war.

Announcement of what they are calling the 'Surge' has gone down badly – with most experts thinking that sending more troops out there is like chasing gambling losses in a casino, it's only ever going to end in more tears.

I don't really know what to think.

Something big has to happen in Iraq to quell the mayhem, that much is undeniable.

If more troops can bring some stability now, then I would reluctantly go along with it. The argument about whether the war was right or not is history now. All that matters is that Iraq comes back from the abyss.

THURSDAY, 11 JANUARY 2007

Michael Winner DID have a life-threatening illness that caused him to miss New Year's Eve. In fact, the poor man nearly lost his leg in an appalling allergic reaction to some food he'd eaten.

And he's not the only one to come back from Barbados feeling rough.

Cowell, Celia and I have all been wiped out by some horrible debilitating virus that has no real symptoms other than making you feel absolutely bloody knackered all the time.

My doctor says he's had over 1,000 people go down with it in the last month, all after trips to the Caribbean. It lasts six weeks, and there's no effective treatment.

My recovery plans weren't helped by picking up a copy of *OK!* magazine and reading details of a 'speciality Brussels sprout recipe' that Cherie Blair has donated to a new book.

And talking of things that make me gag, it's heart-warming to see 'Lady' McCartney in the papers on the ski slopes, doing her Franz Klammer impression.

It seems only last month that she was claiming in her divorce papers to be so appallingly disabled that she couldn't drag herself up the stairs of an evening.

The wonders of modern medicine never cease to amaze me.

FRIDAY, 12 JANUARY 2007

David Beckham has quit Real Madrid, and announced he is joining LA Galaxy in Hollywood in a deal said to be worth £128 million.

His joy is, I suspect, dwarfed by the unmitigated ecstasy Victoria will be feeling at moving to her spiritual home. I can see her now, prancing down Rodeo Drive in her Gucci hotpants and stilettos, paparazzi going crazy, Tom Cruise's wife on her arm.

It's going to be most amusing seeing how they go down out there. Despite his claims to the contrary, they must be going for the lifestyle and show-business career opportunities rather than the football.

The 'soccer' scene is almost non-existent in LA, as it is in most parts of America. They love their own football, the one with pads and helmets, and their baseball, ice hockey and basketball.

And that doesn't leave much room for our version, which is weird given that soccer is played in virtually every other country in the world. And even weirder when you consider that America, with its 300 million inhabitants, would almost certainly dominate the sport if they could be bothered to take it seriously.

The reason they don't like it is because a lot of soccer matches end in boring 0–0 draws, a concept that American sports fans find baffling and pointless.

'You mean, nobody scores anything?' The Hoff exclaimed to me last summer, when we talked about soccer on the set of *America's Got Talent*.

'Nope.'

'Man, that's so whacked out!'

SUNDAY, 14 JANUARY 2007

I rang Caroline Graham in Los Angeles to wish her a belated Happy New Year.

Caroline's one of the most positive people I know.

But today she sounded unusually down.

'You OK?' I asked.

'Not really, no.'

'Why?'

'I've been diagnosed with rectal cancer. And there is only a 50/50 chance of me surviving it.'

I'm absolutely stunned. Caroline is just 40.

It's always impossible to say something either original or even vaguely helpful in situations like this. But my mind flew back to when Marion was a nurse at a busy London hospital.

'Marion told me that the attitude of seriously ill patients often determined whether they lived or died,' I said. 'The power of positive thought is massive, Caroline.'

She laughed. 'That's funny. Andy Coulson just sent me an email saying "If the cancer knew who it had taken on, it would be very scared indeed…"'

'Where are you going to have your treatment?'

'Oh God, here definitely. The one thing Americans do brilliantly is this kind of thing. They attack it like their military would attack something – very, very aggressively.'

I put the phone down, reeling from the news, and checked out rectal cancer survival rates on the Internet. In Europe, it's just 42 per cent, but in America it's 59 per cent. So Caroline's got a 17 per cent better chance of living just by staying right where she is.

TUESDAY, 16 JANUARY 2007

Barack Obama has officially entered the race for the White House. What a moment this is for America.

The Obama bandwagon has been growing steadily in the last two months since he first hinted he might run, but I honestly never expected him to actually go through with it. I really don't think the United States is prepared to vote for a black man at its ballot box yet. But the fact Obama's going for it means he thinks they might be, and that in itself is a stunning revelation.

I watched his speech today, announcing the decision, and he was, again, superbly eloquent and articulate. Such a refreshing change from the gurning, slow-witted, intellectually moribund Bush.

WEDNESDAY, 17 JANUARY 2007

I watched a re-run of Oprah Winfrey's TV show this afternoon, an addictive guilty pleasure that I like to succumb to occasionally.

It is impossible to exaggerate how powerful Oprah is in America. She is their unofficial queen, a woman who transcends almost every aspect of the average American's life.

She hosts the most popular talk show in the history of world television, attracting 30 million viewers a week, has a book club that is the most influential literary force in the country, is an Oscar-nominated actress, publishes two of the most successful magazines in America and runs a website that gets 100 million page views a day.

Her life story would sustain a guest appearance on her own show for months. Born in Mississippi in 1954, her parents – a barmaid and a coal miner – separated almost immediately afterwards, and she was sent to live with her grandparents in abject poverty, where things were so bad that Oprah often wore dresses made from potato sacks. At the age of six, she moved back to live with her mother in Milwaukee, where she was subsequently repeatedly raped and sexually molested by a cousin, uncle and family friend from the age of nine, battled drug and alcohol problems and, at 14, gave birth to a baby son who died in infancy. Her mother, having lost patience with her apparently uncontrollable daughter, sent her to live with her father in Nashville, Tennessee, and it was then that her life changed for ever.

Her dad, now a barber, enforced a mix of strict discipline and devoted love that rescued Oprah from her despair, and drove her to get a university scholarship.

'I knew there was a way out,' she said later, 'I knew there was another kind of life because I had read about it.'

The rest is the stuff of American folklore. Oprah landed a radio job while still in high school, began anchoring local evening news at 19, and quickly landed a little-watched talk show in Chicago that she took to the top of the ratings.

And displaying dazzling business acumen, Oprah promptly launched her own production company and syndicated her show across America.

The reason it was, and is, so successful is that she helped pioneer the genre of tearful, confessional conversation.

She urged guests to show their feelings, to talk about their most private affairs in a way that had never been seen before. Oprah's shows would tackle sexual abuse, divorce, infidelity, eating disorders, domestic violence and self-help. Lots and lots of self-help. And the searingly powerful twist to all this was that Oprah had been through the lot of it herself.

Even now, her marital problems, fluctuating weight, eating disorders and occasional bouts of depression fill the tabloids every week.

But she has been a force for massive social change, too, giving formerly taboo American TV issues like homosexuality and AIDS unprecedented airtime, and shaming bigoted Americans about their prejudice.

In one memorable show, she focused on a man with HIV who had been shunned by his local conservative town in West Virginia, to the extent that the local mayor had even drained a swimming pool that the man had used.

'I hear this is a God-fearing town,' said Oprah. 'Where's all the Christian love and understanding?'

Time magazine said about her: 'Few people would have bet on Oprah Winfrey's rise to host of the most popular talk show on TV. In a field dominated by white males, she is a black female of ample bulk. What she lacks in journalistic robustness, she makes up in plainspoken curiosity, humour and above all, empathy. Guests with a sad story are apt to raise a tear in Oprah's eye. They, in turn, often find themselves revealing things they could not imagine telling anyone else, much less a national TV audience. It is not so much a talk show, as a group therapy session.'

Or, as TV critic Howard Rosenberg put it rather more succinctly: 'Oprah's a big, brassy, aggressive, hyper, laughable, lovable, soulful, tender, low-down, earthy, ad hungry, full-course meal.'

These characteristics have turned Oprah into the planet's richest black woman, according to *Forbes* magazine, with an estimated fortune of over $1 billion. She is said to have earned over $250 million last year alone. CNN recently anointed her as 'the most powerful woman in the world'. And in a recent poll, she was named the 'Greatest Woman in American History'.

And this makes her, right now, probably the most important endorsement that any presidential candidate could possibly wish for.

Oprah, who is close friends with the Clintons, has never publicly endorsed any politician.

But is she going to ignore the emergence of the first African-American man to seriously challenge for the White House?

I don't think so.

If Obama gets Oprah, it's no exaggeration to say he'd be halfway to the presidency.

THURSDAY, 18 JANUARY 2007

Bumped into Sarah Brown, escorting Al Gore to an event at the Guildhall honouring 'Great Britons'.

She was still reeling from Gordon's white legs being exposed to a horrified nation on Andrew Marr's show last Sunday.

'He will never wear short socks on TV again,' she said, shuddering at the memory.

It was interesting to watch Gore speak. Since he was robbed of the presidency in 2000, he has built a brilliant reputation for himself promoting his environmental movie *An Inconvenient Truth*. He spoke about global warming tonight with passion and real knowledge. I would love to see him run for the White House again.

FRIDAY, 19 JANUARY 2007

Breakfast in Chelsea with Kevin Pietersen, back home nursing a broken rib after being the only England player to emerge with his reputation enhanced from the Ashes debacle (we lost 5–0 to Australia, and Harmison's bowling never improved from that first ball).

He wasn't happy. 'I lost one competitive cricket match in the first 18 years of my life. And one rugby match. I don't like losing.'

I may be biased, because he's a mate, but we could do with someone like KP leading the team, although he's too young obviously. He's aggressive, positive, the best player we've got and, strangely for a man born in South Africa, he seems to have more English patriotism in his fibre than most of his England-born teammates.

SATURDAY, 20 JANUARY 2007

Hillary Clinton has now confirmed that she is running for president too, saying: 'I'm in, and I'm in to win.' No woman has ever been nominated by a major party for president. But then Hillary is no ordinary woman.

And with the awesome power of the Clinton brand behind her, pundits are already saying she is the Democrat front-runner.

It's very early days in this race, but already it promises to be a thrilling, and historic, one. A black or female president would have been unthinkable to Americans even ten years ago. But since 9/11, times have changed in America, and changed fast.

I've been boning up on the way their presidential election system works, and although it can seem quite hideously long and complicated to outsiders, Americans pride themselves on what they see as the most truly democratic process in the world.

Essentially, it's a simple two-party race. Since 1872, America has only ever voted for a Republican or Democrat president. Although many smaller parties do field candidates.

The first formal stage is called the 'primaries'. A series of small mini-elections around the country.

The primaries always start in the January preceding the election (so, in a year's time from now), with numerous candidates from the same party competing with each other for the nomination. Anybody can turn up and vote, just as they would in a full election. But more importantly, these primaries also select the official 'delegates', a few thousand men and women who will make the final nominee selection at the party's national convention in the summer of 2008.

To complicate things even further, some states, such as Iowa and Maine, use a 'caucus' system rather than a primary, to choose their delegate.

Whereas in primaries, where people simply vote at a ballot box for the delegate they support, caucuses select their delegates through a more tortuous route involving a number of different stages, and community meetings, the rules of which vary from state to state.

Once the caucuses, and primaries, are over, the race moves to the conventions.

These are huge, glitzy affairs where the remaining candidates (many will have dropped out by now) await to see how many delegates have voted for them.

The candidate with the most delegates wins.

Stage three is the presidential campaign, where the chosen nominee goes head to head with his opponent from the rival party. This usually lasts around four months, and includes three live presidential TV debates in front of the whole country.

Finally, there is election day itself, which is always held on the first Tuesday after the first Monday in November, four years after the previous election.

Here, it all gets messy again.

Americans are all invited to the polling booths to cast their vote.

After the votes are counted in each state, the process moves to what is called the 'electoral college'. Each state has a different number of electoral college members, reflecting its representation in Congress, the American version of Parliament. Whichever candidate wins most votes in each state, wins all of that state's electoral college members.

Once a candidate gets a majority of those members from across the states, the election is effectively over.

Somehow, this all seems to work!

But between now and next January, when the first caucuses and primaries start, the candidates will be doing everything in their power to drum up support, and, crucially, money. Because winning a presidential race requires at least a billion dollars.

Or, as I heard one pundit put it today on the NBC news: 'The guy who can buy the most votes wins!'

SUNDAY, 21 JANUARY 2007

When I first used to go and watch Arsenal, back in the early seventies, it was a fairly grim affair.

I'd stand for hours on the decaying, stinking, concrete terraces of the North Bank. Lunch was usually a plastic glass full of urine lobbed from some kind soul 20 rows back, and most of the match would be spent being slammed over barriers by the swaying drunken crowd or dodging flying darts and missiles hurled by visiting fans.

How times have changed…

Today, I was invited to sample the delights of the Diamond Club, an unbelievably lavish £25,000-a-year members' area inside the new Emirates Stadium.

Lunch was overseen by the superchef, Raymond Blanc. It included crudités with artichoke and black Périgord truffle, Gressingham duck confit, the best roast beef I've ever tasted, and caramelised fig tart with spiced wine syrup. All washed down with Château Mouton Rothschild 1995 at £420 a bottle.

Oh, how I yearned for the inedible old rubbery burgers I used to endure at Highbury.

The match itself was sensational, Arsenal coming from 1–0 down to win 2–1 with a last-minute Thierry Henry goal.

And equally entertaining was the unexpected presence of my new best friend, Naomi Campbell, on her first-ever visit to an English football match.

'Piers, my darling!' she squealed, showering me in kisses to astonishment from other guests. 'What a lovely surprise.'

She then joined my table, with Celia and Raymond, where she was candid, gossipy, flirtatious and – I have to admit – a lot of fun.

When it was suggested that she should have married Eddie Murphy and they could thus have saved everyone else a lot of pain, she laughed: 'I was warned off Eddie.'

Pause.

'And he was warned off me...'

She also eats like no other model I've ever seen, wolfing down a full roast lunch, giant hotdog, two mini burgers, various bread rolls, a large chocolate mousse and biscuits. All while conducting five different simultaneous phone conversations on various mobile phones.

As the wine flowed, I took one of them off her, and called Dad at home in Newick.

'I've got a young lady who'd like a word with you...' I said.

She rose to the challenge magnificently.

'Hi, Glynne, it's Naomi,' she purred seductively, before flirting with him for a few minutes.

I can imagine Dad down the Royal Oak tomorrow night, boasting, Pete and Dud style, 'I had that Naomi Campbell on the phone yesterday, trying it on with me,' and all his mates thinking, 'Poor old Glynne, he's lost his marbles.'

'You're not as mad as everyone thinks, are you?' I said to her, as I presented her with a 'NAOMI 14' Arsenal shirt I had specially made during the second half.

'No,' she giggled. 'But I like the fact everyone thinks I am, because it means I can get away with murder.'

MONDAY, 22 JANUARY 2007

An extraordinary night.

I was in a bar in Victoria with Celia and Ellie, one of her old Cambridge friends, when a drunken man staggered over, and offered to buy us all champagne. Or rather, he offered to buy the ladies champagne, not seeing me stuck round the back of a small pillar.

They politely declined, so he took a deep theatrical bow, thanked us for our time, and staggered off again to a table 15 feet away. He seemed a perfectly harmless, if rather sozzled, old duffer.

Half an hour later, an American woman, sitting near to him, suddenly leaped to her feet and began screaming.

'What the fuck did you say? How *dare* you? Nobody ever speaks to me like that!'

The whole bar fell silent.

The old drunk looked baffled.

'I'm so sorry, I think you misunderstood…'

'No, I fucking didn't, you sonofabitch. I heard you. And it was *disgusting*! You should be jailed!'

She then demanded to see the manager.

'That man should be arrested!' she shrieked. 'No man should ever be allowed to say that!'

By now, we were all gripped by the unfolding drama, and fascinated to discover what on earth the old drunk – now being evicted – had said.

The American woman sat down, tears of anguish pouring down her face.

By her accent, I'd say she was from New York.

'What did he say?' I asked.

'He came over,' she wept, 'and asked if we wanted champagne… and…(now almost wailing)…and when we said "no", he turned to my friend and said, "You're going to have to beat her into having a drink." Can you *believe* that? I feel so violated!'

We all looked at each other in astonishment.

'That's it?' said Celia, incredulous.

'What do you mean, "that's it"?'

'He was obviously joking,' said Celia.

'*Joking*? There's nothing funny about domestic violence!'

And then she ran off to the loo, still sobbing uncontrollably.

TUESDAY, 23 JANUARY 2007

America has appointed a new commanding officer in Iraq, General David Petraeus. And his first speech shows encouraging signs of a change in the usual war-mongering US rhetoric.

'In the end, Iraqis will decide the outcome of this struggle,' he said, 'our task is to help them gain the time they need to save their country. To do that many of us will live and fight together.'

The key thing here seems to be inclusion. The old, bombastic 'we'll kill everyone who gets in our way' attitude seems to be gone, replaced by a 'let's work together to make this a better place' stance.

'Our priority is achieving the security of the population, in partnership with the Iraqi Security Forces,' Petraeus added.

No more of that 'we're gonna beat these evil ragheads' nonsense. I like the sound of this guy. He seems like a total breath of fresh air.

THURSDAY, 25 JANUARY 2007

I watched *The Bodyguard* movie again last night, featuring Whitney Houston, Kevin Costner and our very own Gary Kemp as the slippery amoral PR man. That bloody Bryan Adams song drives me bonkers, but it's a great no-brainer film for a drizzly Wednesday night, with heavy emphasis on the no-brain. And it ends properly. (I like films which end the right way; if I had my way, then Ingrid Bergman would never get on that plane in *Casablanca*, Celia Johnson *would* get on the train in *Brief Encounter*, and Ali McGraw would definitely pull through in *Love Story*).

Tonight, by strange coincidence, I felt a hand grab me as I passed a table at the hot new St Alban restaurant in Regent Street. It was Gary Kemp.

'Gary, I've got to ask, who was the biggest piece of work in the making of *The Bodyguard* – Whitney or Kevin?' I expected him to say Whitney, obviously.

But to my surprise he replied: 'Oh, Whitney was great, I really enjoyed working with her, and she was very nice to me. But Costner was…well, he wasn't quite so great.'

'What do you mean?'

'I mean that most big stars help out up-and-coming actors by staying in position for when you are doing your lines, even if they are not going to be seen on camera. But Costner just used to disappear the moment his lines were finished, and leave you with a stand-in. It was beneath him.'

FRIDAY, 26 JANUARY 2007

Brandy, my co-judge on *America's Got Talent*, has been involved in a fatal car accident. Her car ran into the back of a Toyota on the 405 Freeway in Los

Angeles, and the driver of the other car was killed. Brandy wasn't drunk or on drugs, and it all seems to have been just a terrible accident. But the family of the dead woman have now launched a $50-million lawsuit against her, and her future on the show must be in serious doubt. I feel so sorry for her, she's such a sweet girl.

This whole 'compensation culture' syndrome is such nonsense.

America has become almost paralysed by lawsuits.

The very fear of being sued is enough to stop many people leading normal lives.

As Lord Levene, a vociferous British opponent of this legal absurdity, said recently: 'Is "better safe than sorry" the spirit that built America? I don't think it was on Christopher Columbus's mind somehow, do you? The Pilgrims would probably need to have insurance against passengers becoming seasick or against food poisoning from rotten vegetables. If you sold a saddle to a pioneer who wanted to travel west, you'd need him to promise he wouldn't sue for becoming saddle-sore. If you exhorted another to "go west", you'd want to protect yourself against being sued for making false claims.'

American lawsuits have increased 50-fold in the last 50 years, one in three Americans has now been sued, and the total legal costs work out at over $1,000 per citizen per year.

It's virtually impossible to over-exaggerate the stupidity of some of these suits.

A man called Robert Glasser, for example, sued San Diego city and its Jack Murphy Stadium for $5.4 million after he arrived at a Billy Joel/Elton John concert, and discovered the loos were unisex.

His lawsuit claimed he was unable to urinate for four hours as a result of the embarrassment caused by 'finding women in the rest room'.

Glasser lost.

But a burglar in Detroit who broke into a house to steal things, and cut himself on a knife while doing so, sued the home owners, and WON.

And there are no depths litigants won't stoop to. One woman had a collision with a snowboarder, who died. She sued the snowboarder's widow for the 'psychological injuries' caused by watching him die. A family sued Disney for 'emotional stress' suffered when an employee wearing a Mickey Mouse outfit took his head off for some fresh air – 'shattering' their fantasy.

A student in Illinois was doing a 'moonie' out of his fourth-floor campus room when he fell out. He successfully sued the college for 'not warning of the dangers of living on the fourth floor'.

Even a surfer sued another surfer in Malibu for 'taking his wave'. The case was only dismissed because the court felt unable to 'put a price on the pain and suffering' endured by watching someone ride the wave that was 'intended for you'.

'Britain is falling into the same abyss,' warned Levene, 'the traditional village fete, with cucumber sandwiches, bouncy castles and donkeys is now being threatened as liabilities for all aspects of health and safety rise. This compensation culture on both sides of the Atlantic has got to be reversed.'

TUESDAY, 30 JANUARY 2007

Channel 4 threw a party for their 'talent' tonight, and as I went to get a drink from the bar I was stopped by Phil Spencer from *Location, Location, Location*.

'Hi, Mr Cameron,' he said. 'I'm Phil Spencer.'

I laughed.

'Very funny.'

He looked embarrassed.

'Oh God, sorry, are you not David Cameron?'

'No, I'm Piers Morgan.'

'Oh dear…'

THURSDAY, 1 FEBRUARY 2007

Stanley had a solo part in his school play today, playing a genie who pops out of a giant pot and sings in an American accent.

He's been practising for weeks, and taking it terribly seriously. He's got natural theatrical flair and is great with impressions, but you never know how nerves will get to young people when the curtain goes back and they see the audience waiting.

So I sat halfway back, praying he'd get through it OK.

I needn't have worried. From the moment his little head popped out of the pot, and he started singing in perfect pitch with his outrageously over-the-top vaudeville voice, he had everyone in the palm of his hand.

And I could tell he loved every single second.

FRIDAY, 2 FEBRUARY 2007

'We are pleased to tell you that you've been selected by the *Cosmopolitan* Magazine 2007 Nomination Committee to join the Centrefolds VIP Hall of Fame,' read a letter in this morning's post.

'Centrefolds is a nude shoot. However, you will have a closed set, a male photographer if requested, and nothing untoward will be seen in the final shot. The desired effect is cheeky or classy, never smutty. Your modesty will remain intact!'

I'm sorely tempted to do it, obviously. Especially as it is for the Everyman Male Cancer Campaign. But I just can't expose the other naked Cosmo celebrities to inevitable comparative humiliation, it wouldn't be fair.

SATURDAY, 3 FEBRUARY 2007

Celia and I have fled back to Paris again to escape the madness of London. Only for a series of incredibly irritating things to conspire to ruin our idyllic plans.

A terrifyingly annoying young English woman wearing a turquoise jumper (always a bad sign), and clutching the *Guardian* (ditto), spent the entire two hour and forty minute train journey to the Gare de Lyon noisily munching crisps, bawling inanities into her mobile phone, then watching the Ray Winstone movie *Henry VIII* on her laptop with her gormless boyfriend, but unfortunately *without* earplugs – even having the brass neck to ramp up the volume for all the battle scenes.

On arrival, I then suffered an allergic reaction to antibiotics I've been pointlessly taking for this wretchedly persistent Barbados virus, and couldn't eat or drink anything for two days.

Finally, I sought solace in a bar showing the Arsenal/Middlesbrough game, only for things to deteriorate even further. The digital TV picture kept freezing, the sound didn't work properly, and just after Arsenal had a player sent off and conceded a penalty goal, a short fat ugly posh twit wearing fake pink plastic breasts and an England rugby shirt came up to me and the following conversation ensued:

'Billy, isn't it?'

'Er, no.'

'No, it is, you're Billy.'

'I'm not Billy, mate, I'm just trying to watch the game.'

'No, you're definitely Billy.'

His mouth was dribbling with lager.

'I'm not…'

'Yes you are…you're BILLY NO-MATES.'

TUESDAY, 6 FEBRUARY 2007

Gordon Brown called this morning, inviting me to pop round to his Downing Street flat tonight for a quiet drink.

Security seemed tighter than ever, though impressively courteous.

'Would you like to step into the shadows, sir?' said the armed policeman as a colleague searched my car.

'Erm, why?' I replied, nervously.

'Oh, to avoid any embarrassment with the passing public as I frisk you,' he said.

'But I *want* people to see me coming in here,' I protested, to no avail.

'Champagne or wine?' Gordon asked, as we plonked ourselves down in the kitchen to discuss urgent matters of state.

I had the wine, he had the champagne.

After half an hour, an aide rushed in with a message.

Gordon read the note, looked surprised and picked up the phone.

'Ah, yes, hello No. 10 switchboard, it's Gordon here, please put him through to the kitchen.'

A few moments passed, then I heard the words: 'Hi Tony…'

Gordon ushered me (with a hurried hand and a smirk) into the next-door sitting room – where I found his two young sons watching TV. Young Fraser looked, I was delighted to see, a picture of health. And the way John quickly assembled a large toy abacus in front of me suggests the future of our economy is in safe hands too.

I was summoned back to the kitchen 15 minutes later.

'Has he quit?' I asked, more in hope than expectation.

'No,' replied Gordon. 'He just wanted a chat.'

'Does he normally call you at night for a chat?'

'No, hardly ever.'

'And was it important?'

'No, not really.'

'Bit strange?'

'Very!'

We spent the next hour talking about what I thought Labour should be doing to stop the rot.

'Get Britain's kids off the streets,' I said. 'We've got the worst youth obesity, youth crime, youth binge-drinking and youth drug abuse in Europe. There's no respect, the gangs are increasing, knives and guns are everywhere, and I think I know how to deal with it.'

'How?'

'Sport. You lot have been as bad as the Tories in selling off playing fields, and not letting kids play sport enough at school.

'As a result they're bored out of their brains, and have nowhere to let off steam. It's no wonder they're all behaving so badly.

'Bring back compulsory sport for all schoolchildren every day. Parents will love you for it, and the kids will too.'

Gordon scribbled this all down furiously – he's a frenetic note-taker.

'And while you're at it, unleash the country's young talent, too.'

'What do you mean?'

'I mean you should use the impetus created by all these talent shows on TV, and extend it to find our next brilliant young scientists, poets, philosophers, engineers, writers, actors. It's positive, aspirational and good for votes.

'We've got the Olympics here in six years – you should use that to get Britain fit again, and to show off our talent.'

'You should come and work for me,' he laughed, as I concluded my impassioned rant.

'You can't afford me, Gordon,' I replied. 'And anyway I've got more skeletons than Mandelson's dog.'

WEDNESDAY, 7 FEBRUARY 2007

I've joined Facebook, the new 'social networking' website that started in American universities and has swept like wildfire around the world, hoovering up millions of people in the process.

The premise is simple. You create a profile, detailing who you are, what you like and dislike, and then start collecting contacts by formally inviting them to be your official 'friend'. Others can then check out your profile and see exactly how many 'friends' you have, and who they are.

I put 'friends' in inverted commas, because of course there is no way of anyone else knowing if any of them are actually 'friends' at all.

Facebook was created by a young geek called Mark Zuckerberg at Harvard University, who got the idea from the paper facebooks depicting members of American campuses that get given to every incoming student as a way of getting to know everyone quickly.

All those social-networking concepts seem to start in the States, and I'm not surprised. Because Americans like to be liked, and have a strong sense of community, and this is a perfect way of showing how popular they are.

It will be interesting to see who contacts me. And probably quite worrying, too.

THURSDAY, 8 FEBRUARY 2007
Lunch with Labour's rising star David Miliband, at Quirinale restaurant in Westminster, currently the favourite haunt of politicians.

'Nobody is going to catch me being unsupportive of Tony as our current leader, or Gordon as our next leader,' he insisted.

I agreed that this was particularly important in the current febrile climate.

'I'm doing *Question Time* tonight,' the environment secretary added, as the main course arrived.

'Well, in that case be extra careful!' I warned.

I tuned in to watch the show, and with five minutes left, Miliband had played a blinder – confident, assured and authoritative.

Then he was asked whether Blair is hanging on too long to power, and answered thus: 'I promise you that if I come back on this show in six months' time, people will be saying "wouldn't it be great to have that Blair back because we can't stand that Gordon Brown?"'

What?

I grabbed my Sky Plus remote and rewound quickly.

Yep, he had said what I thought he said. He'd dropped the baton on the last leg of the relay.

Sure enough, within an hour the TV news shows were all running with 'Miliband says we won't be able to stand Brown as leader.'

FRIDAY, 9 FEBRUARY 2007
Spoke to Caroline, who has started chemotherapy and radiotherapy.

'It's been unbelievably full on,' she said. 'It's like they've invaded my body. I've had CT scans, PT scans, MRI scans, X-rays, and endless probes, enemas and other tests. Within 24 hours of my oncologist or radiologist demanding something, they do it. Thank God I've got insurance, or I'd never be able to afford it. I'm spending $20,000 a week. Even the anti-nausea pills cost $40 each.'

This confirmed that America has both the best and worst health care in the world.

Their system outspends any other nation's, both in spending per head, and as a percentage of its GDP.

The World Health Organisation ranked the US first in terms of responsiveness, and as a leader in medical innovation.

But, and it's a massive but, health care is not universal in America, relies heavily on private funding and is the most expensive in the world. Nearly 50 million Americans have no health care insurance at all, and that means they get virtually ignored by the system.

'Every day I realise I am one of the lucky ones,' said Caroline. 'I get whizzed through the emergency room at UCLA or Cedars Sinai and see the sea of Hispanic faces staring back at me. Whoever wins the next election will have to deal with the economy and war, but they will also have to fix the health care system to make it fairer than it is now.'

She's being treated at the Tower Hematology Oncology unit.

'It's affectionately known as Beverly Hills chemo,' she laughed, 'they serve caffè lattes in the lobby and bring round trays of cookies and fresh fruit while you're having all this poison pumped into your arms.'

SUNDAY, 11 FEBRUARY 2007

Up to Birmingham to start filming the *Britain's Got Talent* audition shows.

The third judge was going to be Cheryl Cole, but on Friday she pulled out at the last minute.

Last night, Cowell texted me the name of her replacement: Amanda Holden.

Uh-oh.

The *Mirror*, under my editorship, exposed Amanda's affair with Neil Morrissey while she was still married to Les Dennis. Hardly the best way to endear myself to my co-panellist.

We met for the first time in the hotel bar tonight, and she was cordial, but understandably guarded.

Mind you, she's now engaged to a dashing young music producer and they've got a beautiful baby daughter. And her career has gone from strength to strength, with her currently starring in the smash hit drama series, *Wild At Heart*.

So, as I pointed out to her, 'You should really be thanking me, Amanda.'

She paused for thought. 'You're right,' she replied, her voice drowning in sarcasm. 'Thank you *so* much, Piers.'

But after a few more drinks, we were getting along fine. She seems a fun, lively little number. Perfect, as she put it, to play the 'rose between two thorns' on the show.

Cowell arrived in the bar at 10 p.m., furious. 'I'm checking out.'

'But you've just got here,' I said.

'Yes, I know. But you can't open any windows in the room, and I've got to have air.'

And with that he was gone.

MONDAY, 12 FEBRUARY 2007

The *Britain's Got Talent* hosts are Ant and Dec, two guys I hugely respect but barely know. And I was curious: are they as close in real life as they are on TV? So many of these double acts can't stand the sight of each other away from the cameras.

Fortunately my make-up artist today was in rather a good position to tell me – she's Ant's wife, Lisa.

'Oh my God,' she groaned. 'It's worse in real life. They're totally inseparable. Dec lives round the corner from us, and whenever we're at home Ant just puts this sheepish grin on his face and asks: "Can my mate come round for tea?" Then Dec will turn up, and they'll start mucking around or watching the football until I eventually have to send them to the pub to get them out of my hair.'

'Sounds like there are three of you in this marriage,' I said.

She giggled: 'That's *exactly* what it's like!'

Cowell arrived at 11.40 a.m., beaming from ear to ear.

'I think we're going to have some fun today,' he declared.

Minutes later (to my astonishment, Cowell's make-up preparation isn't the three-hour vanity trip I feared it would be – just a quick powder, and hair trim beforehand), we met the contestants backstage.

'Now, I don't want you to feel nervous,' Cowell told them all, 'but get this wrong, and it could be the end of your career...and life, probably.'

We walked out to a thousand-strong audience in the theatre.

Me to apathy and jeers.

Amanda to rapturous applause.

And finally Cowell, to the kind of hysterical screaming that made the Beatles pack in live gigs.

His fame is now at a preposterous level. The mainly female crowd went bonkers, chanting 'Simon, Simon' and chucking everything from sweets to knickers at him. He, of course, loved every second.

'It wasn't always like this,' he admitted during a fag break (he smokes 40 cigarettes a day). 'I remember early on in America being stopped on a red carpet by a TV crew and the interviewer was in mid-question when she suddenly screamed, "Oh my God, BRITNEY, BRITNEY!" and just ran off. Mortifying.'

It was fascinating to observe Cowell in his natural lair. He's never conducted auditions in front of a live baying audience, nor had use of a loud buzzer to express his disapproval.

Both new tools delighted him.

During one terrible act this afternoon, Cowell hovered his hand over his buzzer like a Roman emperor, as the febrile crowd chanted, 'PRESS IT, PRESS IT, PRESS IT!'

Minutes later, a crudely made-up transvestite tottered on stage in high heels, pulling a small box containing a singing dwarf.

Cowell leant over and whispered: 'Did you ever think it would come to this, Piers?'

Later, a lovely old chap called Ted stumbled on, deaf as a post, and started tap-dancing.

Cowell called over. 'Piers, buzz him. Quickly.'

So I did.

Only for Cowell to promptly feign horror, urge Ted to finish his dance and milk the applause of the crowd as he told him: 'That was brilliant, Ted, I can't believe Piers was so cruel...'

I stared at Cowell, open-mouthed: 'You slippery, devious toad.'

He just cackled, delighted at his stitch-up.

A few minutes later, I saw a chance for revenge when he sneered: 'Piers, with the greatest of respect, what do you know about singing?'

I turned slowly: 'Ah yes, says the man who gave the world Zig and Zag.'

Cowell sat bolt upright.

'I've sold 150 million records,' he retorted testily.

'Oooohh, get him,' I replied, as the audience revelled in his obvious irritation.

It was a rare victory for me, though. Competing with Cowell on a judging panel is like wrestling with an enraged gorilla – it's only going to end one way.

I got back to the hotel feeling absolutely exhausted. People think this judging lark is easy, but eight hours of watching horrific auditions in front of a live audience would test anyone.

TUESDAY, 13 FEBRUARY 2007

Another day, another collection of socially dysfunctional misfits convinced they are the next Whitney Houston or David Blaine.

Hopeless magicians, terrible jugglers, shocking singers and creepy weirdos who left us all feeling distinctly uncomfortable.

Amid the carnage was the odd genuinely great talent. But I suspect the real stars will be the hilariously awful trainwreck acts.

The warm-up man, Ian Royce, summed it up perfectly: 'We should rename this show, *Britain's Got Special Needs.*'

Royce, a London policeman, torments Cowell all day about his teeth, trousers, ego, smoking habit and height – chanting 'Hi Ho' every time he walked out.

In the bar tonight, I finally got asked for my autograph (I normally get shoved out of the way in the stampede for the others'). Or rather, Simon's huge, bald bodyguard Tony brought over a woman to meet me.

'I was hoping it would be Simon or Ant and Dec, but you'll do,' she said, thrusting a piece of card into my hand.

I looked down at what seemed like some form of medical pamphlet, and eyed Tony suspiciously – but he was laughing too much to speak.

She, however, was deadly serious.

'Can you write, "I support Chlamydia screening," please. Thank you.'

FRIDAY, 23 FEBRUARY 2007

Spent the morning interviewing Abi Titmuss for a new BBC1 series I'm making called *You Can't Fire Me, I'm Famous*.

And despite every sinew of my flesh willing me to dislike her, I enjoyed her company.

She was feisty, flirty, fiery and fun.

'Fancy lunch?' she said afterwards, fluttering her eyelashes.

'I can't, I'm afraid. I've going to spend the afternoon getting some of Britain's most revered BBC news stars blind drunk.'

I walked down to the Ivy, where I met up with Jeremy Bowen, Sophie Raworth and Emily Maitlis.

The last time I 'lunched' with Bowen and Raworth, we were kicked out of the very same restaurant at 8 p.m. for making too much noise with Adam Faith and Emma Noble. Today was just as surreal (at one stage Victor Meldrew came over and paid his respects), just as hilarious (a competition to discover who had performed the most demeaning corporate gig was won by Jeremy, who'd once spoken to a group of waste disposal experts, though Emily thought her BBC *News 24* pal Ben Brown had gone one better by addressing the nation's leading undertakers…) and just as hard on the liver (seven bottles before we hit the hard stuff).

I finally stumbled into the street at 7.30 p.m., to be met by a lone paparazzi.

'Mr Cameron! Mr Cameron!' he shouted, and began snapping me furiously.

This Cameron thing is getting ridiculous.

A text from Ms Raworth arrived at 9.30 p.m. 'You're losing your touch Morgan, JB and me are still here…'

Being out-drunk by the sweet, innocent, presenter of the *One O'Clock News*. Oh the shame…

SUNDAY, 25 FEBRUARY 2007

Having finally recovered from the world's most depressing virus, I woke up in Newick today with horrific food poisoning from a Chinese take-away.

Stanley surveyed the unedifying scene as he visited my bedroom, and observed: 'Dad, I think you need to go into rehab.'

WEDNESDAY, 28 FEBRUARY 2007

John McCain has said he's going to run for president, joining a Republican candidate list that now includes Rudy Giuliani, Mitt Romney and Mike Huckabee.

As with the Democrats, this promises to be a hugely entertaining battle. McCain is a 70-year-old self-styled 'maverick', and Vietnam veteran war hero. Giuliani was the New York mayor who won huge plaudits for his leadership after 9/11. And Romney and Huckabee are two classic Republican presidential candidates – white, middle-class and very, very conservative.

None of them, of course, is either black or female.

THURSDAY, 8 MARCH 2007

Question Time in Newcastle. I've done it at least a dozen times now, but it is always the one TV programme that gets the nerves jangling more than others, because the panellists genuinely have no idea what questions are going to come up.

And bitter experience has confirmed to me that if the host David Dimbleby suspects you are a little 'under-researched' on a particular topic then he will flash that mischievous smirk of his and say: 'Right, let's start with…Piers Morgan.'

Tonight's show was a lively, amusing affair. I got randomly attacked over share-dealing by a heckler, accused of 'going to fancy restaurants where cocaine is served' by co-panellist and PR man Colin Byrne and given the chance to defend two old mates currently mired in controversy – Mohamed Al Fayed and Lord Levy.

Both were very nice to me after I was sacked from the *Mirror*, proving that there really is no greater way to judge someone's character than loyalty when the chips are down.

I don't believe Mohamed's wilder conspiracy theories (though come to think of it, Prince Philip has never actually denied being a Nazi, has he?) but I absolutely defend his right to find out what happened to his son Dodi in the same legal way any of us would be entitled to.

As for Levy, his only real crime appears to be raising all the money for Tony Blair to get elected – which admittedly is fairly heinous given what our Tony then did with the power that came his way, but not a hanging offence.

At 2 a.m., I was smoking cigars, drinking Jack Daniel's, and gambling in a hotel bar with David Dimbleby and Tory shadow minister Alan Duncan.

Well, when I say gambling, I bet Duncan that Gordon Brown will beat David Cameron at the next General Election.

'Put your money where your mouth is,' he challenged me.

'A thousand pounds?' I suggested.

'Erm…how about one hundred?' whimpered Duncan.

Dimbleby was indignant. 'That's not a bet, Alan. Come on, dig deeper, man.'

'Oh God, OK. One hundred pounds and a fine bottle of wine.'

I accepted. But then my idea of a fine bottle of wine is a Château d'Yquem 1787, currently trading at around £55,000.

FRIDAY, 9 MARCH 2007

My mobile rang on the train back from Newcastle and a mad voice started screaming at me.

'IT WAS ME!' he shrieked. 'I did it ALL! I decided who got all the fucking honours, and I just told fucking Tony who to give 'em to! It was all down to ME!'

I was bemused. Who was this crazed lunatic?

'Did you hear me?' he continued. 'I run the fucking country and I decided who gets what!'

I could see people around me raising eyebrows at the sheer volume of noise emanating from my phone, so decided to interrupt whoever it was with a curt 'Excuse me, but who the hell is this?'

There was a pause, then another high-pitched explosion.

'It's ME, the man who runs the fucking world.'

I laughed. Perhaps it was Tony Blair, and he'd finally gone bonkers.

Or even worse, Rory Bremner, targeting me as his next phone prank victim.

'Come on, who is it?'

Another pause, then a normal, more familiar voice:

'It's Levy.'

'Michael?'

'Yes. Just my little joke there…I am ringing to thank you for supporting me on *Question Time* last night. Gilda [his wife] and I really appreciated it.'

'No problem,' I replied. 'I think the whole thing's ridiculous. How are you coping?'

'It's been tough, very tough. Especially for the family. But what doesn't break you makes you stronger, as they say.'

'Where's it all going to end?' I asked.

'I've no idea, mate, honestly no idea. The police seem determined to keep hammering away, and we will just have to wait and see. But I know I did nothing wrong. And I believe that will be shown in the end.'

'Are you being hung out to dry by Downing Street?'

'I don't think so…I don't know…I'm not allowed to talk to anyone there for obvious reasons.'

'Including Tony?'

'Nobody. It's been hard.'

SATURDAY, 10 MARCH 2007

Spoke to Caroline in LA, who sounded utterly miserable.

'They sent me to this therapist who specialises in cancer,' she said, 'and was supposed to help me face up to issues like death. But I left her after three sessions because I told her I really wasn't in the right frame of mind to face up to death quite now, thanks all the same. It was a classically American thing to do. They think of the worst-case scenario, and try and "deal" with it. Whereas a Brit prefers not to think of the worst-case scenario at all.'

MONDAY, 12 MARCH 2007

The Democrats have cancelled plans to take part in a Fox News presidential race debate in Nevada, after Roger Ailes, the head of the network, cracked this joke during a speech: 'It's true that Barack Obama is on the move. I don't know if it's true that President Bush called Musharraf and said, "Why can't we catch this guy?"'

This cheap dig at Obama's name sounding like Osama bin Laden's has, of course, merely served to confirm all the suggestions that Fox is biased against the Democrats, and Obama in particular.

Fox's indignant defence is not helped by the fact that Ailes served as a campaign adviser to previous Republican presidential candidates including George Bush Senior and Ronald Reagan.

Larry King recently said: 'Fox News is an extension of the Republican Party, with some exceptions.'

And even their own Bill O'Reilly has admitted: 'Fox does tilt to the right.'

The question is: does this kind of bias in the media matter that much? And I'm not sure it really does, so long as other voices can still be heard loud and clear on the airwaves and shouting off the newsstands.

In Britain, the *Daily Mail* tilts so far to the right that even Genghis Khan would be a bit embarrassed to be caught reading it some days. But it doesn't seem to have much effect at the polling booths. Despite 85 per cent of the paper's stories on Tony Blair being negative in his first term of office, more *Mail* readers voted for Labour when he was re-elected in 2001 than voted for him in 1997. And the *Mirror* is just as biased against the Tories, so it balances out.

What we've seen in American media generally is the increasing emergence of 'infotainment', using news as a ratings-driving entertainment vehicle.

Whether it's hurricanes, wars, political sex scandals, or celebrity murders, the whole focus is linked to commercial gain.

The American TV system is a very simple, uncomplicated beast. They don't have the whole public service broadcasting or BBC licence fee issues to worry about.

All that matters is ratings, because if you get those then the advertisers will follow.

Profit is thus inextricably attached to viewing figures, and how you get those viewers is irrelevant. The market mechanism rewards volume, not quality, of viewers.

And that's led to news networks like Fox treating news as hard-hitting, provocative entertainment that will titillate the masses in the manner of a mass-market tabloid paper.

Critics of infotainment in the States say it has led to all news being treated in a straight black-or-white manner – little guys versus big guys, good versus evil, appearance versus reality, efficiency versus inefficiency, and unique and bizarre events versus ordinary events. Everything gets simplified to this unrealistic either-or template, and that creates totally unrealistic but highly commercial news bulletins.

I have to say, though, it makes them a damn sight more interesting to watch, which is why Fox is killing everyone in the ratings.

WEDNESDAY, 14 MARCH 2007

Amazing, isn't it? We can't afford to give our nurses and doctors a proper pay rise, but we can find £20 billion to renew our Trident nuclear weapons programme.

I would normally have been totally opposed to this.

But the horrible irony is that Blair's appalling foreign policy has made it almost imperative that we renew Trident, because the prospect of us being attacked by someone with WMD is about 100 times higher now than it was in 1997.

THURSDAY, 15 MARCH 2007

Spent two hours at the dentist this morning having some old fillings replaced, emerging into the sunlight with my entire lower mouth still grotesquely numbed.

I felt, and spoke, like a drunken version of Marlon Brando in *The Godfather*.

It's at moments like this that you just hope and pray you don't meet anyone you know. So, predictably, I bumped straight into GMTV's Fiona Phillips taking her son for a check-up.

'Hello!' she said.

'Gnnnntrnng,' I gurned.

She looked momentarily alarmed.

'Are you all right?'

'Yeth,' I replied. 'Fnnnnine phanknnns.'

Fiona started giggling.

'This is great, you've finally been silenced *and* you look ridiculous.'

We parted, and my phone rang outside the surgery.

It was Cowell again, calling from the private jet that had ferried him from LA to Cardiff for the second round of *Britain's Got Talent* auditions starting tomorrow.

'Hello, darling, how are you?'

'I'm fnnnnine phanknns,' I phlegmed.

'Morgan, are you drunk again?'

'No. I'th been to the thdentisth.'

Cowell roared with laughter.

'I knew it. You've had veneers haven't you? I want my £100.' (He recently bet me £100 that I would succumb to plastic surgery within the next five years.)

I tried to argue, but the words just wouldn't come out.

Arrived at the Cardiff hotel to find Ant and Dec in the bar watching Newcastle's UEFA Cup game. I'm always suspicious about celebrity football fans – they've usually supported about eight teams, and think Didier Drogba is a form of exotic plant.

But these Geordie boys are the real-deal fans. I could tell by the demented way they stared at the TV screen, the genuinely agonised yelps that erupted every time Newcastle missed a sitter, and the blind fury that erupted when the other team scored twice.

Fearing that things might turn rather nasty as Newcastle slid to defeat, I retired to my room to watch *Comic Relief: The Apprentice* on BBC1.

There is something rather uncomfortable about watching yourself on TV, alone. Particularly when you've filmed 200 hours of reality television and have no idea what they are actually going to use.

To be honest, they edited me pretty fairly, though the row with Trinny Woodall was slanted to portray Campbell and me as vicious brutes, when the truth is that she was the one smacking us around.

Judging by the messages I was getting throughout the show, everyone was thoroughly enjoying every toe-curling second. And that's before they get to me being fired tomorrow night.

But I consoled myself with the knowledge that however badly I emerged from the wreckage, I could not possibly look more ridiculous than Heather Mills.

Today 'Lady' Heather revealed video footage of herself with a load of greedy pigs and insisted: 'I am not a publicity-seeker.'

A claim she made on dozens of TV and radio interviews throughout the day.

Heather will cement her non-publicity seeking by appearing on a TV show called *Dancing With The Stars* in America, watched by over 20 million viewers. Her miraculous recovery from being barely able to walk continuing apace.

FRIDAY, 16 MARCH 2007
Woke up to the sound of yelping from the room next door (the walls are ridiculously thin in this hotel).

It was, unmistakably, Amanda Holden.

Now there are men out there who would pay a lot of money to hear Amanda yelping at 9 a.m. But I was concerned. She seemed to be in a lot of pain, and not of the pleasurable kind.

We met in the green room later.

'Were you OK earlier?'

She laughed.

'I knew you were in the next room, and I knew you'd be wondering what the hell was going on…'

'Well?'

'Well, if you must know, I burned myself ironing.'

Cowell arrived.

'Amanda, I don't mean to be rude [always a sign that he is about to be shockingly rude] but can you please make sure you're always fully made up when I see you. Something dies inside me when I see you without your make-up on.'

Amanda, of course, looks absolutely lovely with or without make-up.

'Simon, are you always this charming?' she retorted.

'I just have this thing about women and make-up,' he replied. 'I remember going away with this girl for the weekend once, and as soon as we got to the hotel she went to the bathroom and reappeared *au naturelle*, without any make-up. It was the biggest turn-off I've ever experienced.'

'What did you do?' Amanda and I asked in appalled unison.

'I told her to go back into the bathroom and put it all back on, obviously.'

My *Apprentice* firing was aired tonight, to what looked like scenes of national jubilation on the Comic Relief live set.

Within seconds, my mobile started buzzing off the bed.

'Well, here we are again,' wrote James Nesbitt. 'Travesty barely does it justice indeed. An outrage. Don't let the bastards grind you down.'

Cowell was less sympathetic. 'Hee hee. Great.'

Alastair Campbell was more positive. 'Reckon your agent should plant a story that TV companies are queuing up to sign us up as a new double act and we are playing hard to get,' he suggested, showing all the honest, non-spinning qualities we've come to know and love in the man.

'Yes,' I concurred. 'It could be *The Two Ronnies* meet the Krays.'

'With Sir Alan as Mad Frankie Fraser,' he added.

SATURDAY, 17 MARCH 2007

Everywhere I go, people are shouting 'You're fired!' at me in the street with great big satisfied grins on their faces.

It took two years for the public to stop doing that after I left the *Mirror*. And now this…Christ!

SUNDAY, 18 MARCH 2007

Enjoyed a ferociously long lunch at Andrew Neil's house today.

Halfway through, I launched into a loud denunciation of the current Muscovite invasion of Britain.

'Every Russian woman in London right now is basically a hooker,' I declared.

There was a chilly silence around the table. I turned to Ozwald Boateng, the dashing designer sitting to my right, for support.

'Don't you think so, Ozwald?'

He stared at me, shaking his head in a half smile of pity.

At which point Andrew Neil intervened.

'Piers, allow me to introduce you to Ozwald's wife Gyunel…' I turned to a beautiful, immaculately attired lady at the other end of the table, '… she's Russian.'

Got home, drunk and shamed, to find that, coincidentally, Freddie Flintoff has been sacked as England vice-captain after he fell off a pedalo and nearly drowned while drunkenly attempting to sail out to a yacht at 4 a.m. during the cricket world cup in St Lucia.

Everyone's getting terribly worked up about it, but I don't remember the same critics caring when Freddie caned it after we won the Ashes.

Like Ian Botham before him, he's a big man who enjoys the occasional big drink, but who never puts less than 110 per cent into playing for his country.

All seems a pathetic over-reaction to me.

MONDAY, 19 MARCH 2007

I interviewed Thierry Henry today. Well, when I say interviewed, it was more a one-man obsessed fan convention.

'Thierry,' I began, 'forgive me if I seem a little nervous but this is a rather emotional moment for me…when I do these interviews I don't normally enter a room and find a man in front of me who has such a profound effect on the way I feel or the way I live my life.'

'OK, OK...' he giggled, 'I understand.'

'I only really have one question for you that matters.'

'Tell me?'

'Promise me you'll stay at Arsenal.'

'Oh, that is for sure. For *sure*.'

'You promise?'

'Yeah, yeah. Definitely. I did think about leaving last season, I have made no secret of that. If Barcelona come in, then you're going to listen. But the love I have for Arsenal, the relationship I have with the fans, and obviously with Arsène Wenger, meant I couldn't leave. People still keep wondering if I am going to go or not. But there is no way I could leave now. I have grown to know what it means to wear the Arsenal shirt, and it is the most important thing of all. For me, the club, the fans. So let me say it to you once more: I am not leaving.'

When we finished, I asked him to sign three shirts for the boys, which he did with great care.

Then he stood up, with a large grin on his face, and said: 'I have a little surprise for you now, Piers.'

And then handed me one of the very rare genuine premiership shirts only Arsenal players get to see or wear.

He took a pen, and wrote: 'To Piers, a true Gooner, from Thierry Henry, a Gooner for Life.'

I nearly cried.

MONDAY, 26 MARCH 2007

Few things make me so angry that I want to physically break something. Arsenal going out of every competition last week was one such recent example. As was the news that Snoop Dogg's British tour has been cancelled because the government wouldn't let him in. (I mean, what the hell am I now supposed to do next weekend?)

But the sacking of newsreader Moira Stuart from Andrew Marr's Sunday *AM* show on BBC1 has left me wanting to single-handedly demolish whole cities with my television. There is not a make-up artist, producer, presenter, tea-boy or doorman at the BBC who has a bad word to say about her.

Moira also defies all the usual rules of age. She is apparently 55, but doesn't look a day older than she did 25 years ago when she first started appearing on our screens.

Yet apparently she is now 'too old' for the job. What a load of balls.

The woman is, as many are now saying in the wake of her disgraceful sacking, a national treasure, not to mention a magnificent black role model. And in the States, she would be reading the news until she was 80 if she wanted to. The Americans don't get everything right in their broadcasting (allowing me to star in a No. 1 show was a lamentable lapse in judgement, for example) but they are spot on in their theory that increased age and experience brings increased trustability in a newsreader.

WEDNESDAY, 28 MARCH 2007
Jeremy Clarkson has been photographed on a Barbados beach sporting the biggest pot belly seen since Vanessa Feltz was last pregnant.

Take some advice from a mate, Jezza: get out of those cars and on to a treadmill before they have to rename your show *Spare Tyres*.

FRIDAY, 30 MARCH 2007
My new book *Don't You Know Who I Am??* has been serialised this week in the *Daily Mail* and appears to have upset almost everyone. Elton's apparently 'not happy', Sharon Osbourne's 'flaming mad', Janet Street-Porter's 'spitting feathers' and Rod 'The Toad' Liddle is 'calling Nicaraguan hitmen' (allegedly).

All of which I can probably cope with, however painful it may be.

But my favourite fit of pique award goes to Jack Straw. I recounted how I met Straw on *Question Time* last year, and during a surprisingly indiscreet conversation backstage in the green room, he responded to my suggestion that John Reid might stand against Gordon Brown for the leadership of the Labour Party by saying: 'I hope so, yes.'

There was no doubt what he said, I was standing right next to him. As was Ken Clarke and at least four other people.

At the time, of course, Straw was not in Brown's camp and was still firmly sucking up to Blair every chance he got.

But earlier this week it was revealed that he now might actually be running Brown's leadership campaign. Which is why my revelation, and the timing of it in particular, has caused him acute embarrassment. Because it confirmed what most people think of Straw – that, as his name suggests, he moves (politically) wherever the wind is blowing strongest.

Today, a curious letter appeared in the *Mail* from a Mr Mark Davies, who bills himself as 'Advisor to the Leader of the Commons'.

It read: 'I was with Jack Straw the whole of the time he was in the company of Piers Morgan and others while waiting to appear on *Question Time* last September. At no stage did he use the words attributed to him by Mr Morgan and nor would he have done.'

Hmmm. Sounds like Straw and his lickspittle are calling me a liar.

In which case, they should obviously sue me for libel.

SATURDAY, 31 MARCH 2007

I'm on holiday with the boys and Rupert in Antigua, watching some of the cricket world cup.

Today, we came across actor Patrick Stewart on the beach at our hotel, reading *Macbeth* and talking in an extremely loud grandiose manner to his son in the water about the finer complexities of their family tree. It was true thespian behaviour, designed to create the impression of a very serious, very important member of the theatrical community.

This charming vignette was slightly marred, however, by the late arrival of Spencer, who gleefully pointed to him with the immortal words: 'Hey, Dad, look, it's the bald bloke off *Star Trek*.'

It's been great spending some proper time with the boys.

They put up with all my endless travelling with remarkably good humour, but it must grate with them that I am often out of the country when they have something important on.

It's another sacrifice that you make to the strange altar of fame, and there are many nights, when I'm stuck in some godforsaken foreign hotel, that I seriously question whether it's really all worth it.

Keeping in touch with the boys is miles easier than it used to be thanks to things like iChat, email and texting. And I speak to them all every day. But nothing can beat that intimacy of physical contact.

Part of me is looking forward to going to America this month, for work. Another part of me, the paternal part, is dreading it.

SUNDAY, 1 APRIL 2007
The first fund-raising totals for the American presidential candidates have been revealed, always a major indicator of who the favourites are going to be. Americans, after all, don't like to back a loser.

Romney is in the lead for the Republicans, with $21 million raised since January. Giuliani is second, with $15 million, and McCain third with $12.5 million. As for the Democrats, Hillary Clinton is way ahead with $36 million, Obama second with $25 million. And the rest, nowhere.

As a result of all this, Hillary is now the clear favourite to be the next president, because she is the one raising the most cash. And in America, it's the colour of your money that really counts in election races.

MONDAY, 2 APRIL 2007
Oh dear, slightly scary news today. One of the celebrities least amused by the new book was Sharon Osbourne, who was apparently very upset that I'd repeated rather insulting remarks she made in a *GQ* interview with me about Madonna ('cunt'), Bryan Ferry ('tosser'), Mick Jagger ('twat') and just about every other star in the world.

Today I learned that Brandy Norwood has resigned from *America's Got Talent* to focus on defending herself legally over the fatal car crash she was involved in earlier this year. And Sharon is going to replace her! Which means we're going to be sitting next to each other for days on end for the next three months.

Normally the producers of these shows urge us to spice things up a bit if we're all getting too chummy – it makes for better viewing.

Somehow I don't think Sharon's going to need any encouragement.

TUESDAY, 3 APRIL 2007
For 20 years I have reviled, scorned and scoffed at celebrities who appear in magazines like *Hello!*

Today, I myself appeared over six gloriously cheesy pages of the latest issue to promote the book, complete with smug gurning photos that would have done that bronzed movie icon George Hamilton proud.

I don't know what on earth they do with the pictures over there, but the sheer scale of Gorgonzola dripping from my beaming visage made me feel quite nauseous. So God knows what everyone else is going to think.

Celia rang after seeing it, and did nothing to ease my concerns. 'Did they spray-paint your head with brown lacquer or something?'

THURSDAY, 5 APRIL 2007

I don't really 'do' chat shows. When your standing in public life nestles somewhere between Saddam Hussein and Neil and Christine Hamilton, then it is best to try and avoid exposing yourself to situations with obvious maximum ridicule potential.

But if there's a new book to flog, all bets are off.

So, this afternoon, I trudged down to ITV's studios for the new *Dame Edna Experience*, weary both from jetlag (I flew in from Antigua this morning) and a mounting sense of abject fear. I mean, why on earth would I subject myself to the most notoriously sharp and offensive chat-show host of them all?

The answer, of course, is greed and arrogance. I want to sell loads of books, and I quite fancy being the one who finally got the better of the Dame in front of millions of viewers...

Most chat-show stars meet their guests before the show for a quick hello and perhaps a drink.

Not Edna.

Most chat-show stars get their researchers to give you a full detailed briefing on what might be coming your way.

Not Edna.

Most chat-show stars show even the vaguest modicum of concern for the wellbeing of their victims.

Not Edna.

I sat in the green room with a few of the production team as the show started. You always hope that you're following a humourless, smug clinker like John Redwood or Paul Daniels, so the audience will automatically find you funnier, cleverer and more entertaining.

The first guests were *Little Britain* – David Walliams and Matt Lucas. Dame Edna duly treated them like comedy gods, and the laughter in the studio was prolonged and awestruck.

I nibbled on my Twiglets feeling apprehension mounting.

After 45 minutes, I was summoned to the waiting area behind the studio.

'You OK?' asked a nice polite young production assistant.

'Not really…' I mumbled back, as the roars of amusement echoed around us. 'How long am I on for?'

She smiled a long, gleeful smile.

'For as long as Dame Edna thinks she needs with you…'.

Gulp.

Little Britain came to the end of their stint, and received the biggest ovation since Elvis first played in Vegas.

Then I heard that hideously familiar Australian twang saying: 'And my next guest is an incredibly unpopular person…Mr Piers Morgan.'

Cue boos, jeers and the odd excited handclap at the salivating prospect of my impending suicide mission.

I marched on determined to fight fire with fear. But it was like an arthritic sea urchin coming face to face with a Great White Shark.

'People either love you…or DETEST you, don't they, Piers?'

The emphasis on the second descriptive word indicated where Edna thought most views lay.

'These guys like me…' I said, pathetically, as I turned to Walliams and Lucas. They'd always been fairly friendly whenever I'd met them anyway.

Both stared straight ahead, unsmiling, raising eyebrows to the ceiling.

I was on my own, and it was becoming a desperately lonely place.

'Well, I love you,' Edna lied, 'and I'd like you to wear this tie to prove it.'

I was handed a bright pale blue tie with the words 'Edna loves me' on it.

It only served to make me look even more absurd than I already felt.

For the next 20 minutes I sat on the corner of the sofa, ludicrous tie gripped around my sweating neck, as I was treated to the full range of the *Dame Edna Experience*. It was possibly the most uncomfortable 'experience' I have endured since a 75-year-old Japanese crone jumped up on my back during a supposedly 'recuperative massage' in downtown Tokyo.

Edna verbally degraded me. There is no other word for it. And the audience revelled in my misery from start to finish.

When the massacre ended, Blondie star Debbie Harry came onto the sofa. She used to be my pin-up when I was a teenager, and still looks amazing for nearly 60.

'How do you still look so good?' I asked ungallantly during a commercial break.

'I have a very good plastic surgeon,' she laughed back, with commendable honesty. 'Actually, several very good plastic surgeons.'

As the show drew to a close, a producer came up and asked me and *Little Britain* to join in the finale by dancing along as Blondie sang with Dame Edna.

'Who with?' I asked.

'Erm, with Valmai please.'

Ah yes, Edna's fat, ugly, kleptomaniac daughter.

So I did, and yes it was as appallingly cringe-making as it sounds.

Edna shook my hands afterwards. 'That was fun, wasn't it, darling?'

No, it wasn't, darling. It was torture.

SATURDAY, 7 APRIL 2007

I picked up the papers and saw a headline screaming back at me saying, 'ANT AND DEC SIGN £40 MILLION ITV DEAL.'

If ever there is a story guaranteed to utterly enrage Simon Cowell, this is it. He, after all, recently became the 'highest-paid TV star in Britain' himself with a mere £20 million deal. And the Geordie boys, who share the same agent as Cowell and me – former Radio 1 DJ Peter Powell – are currently presenting our show.

I raced to the London theatre where we are finishing the auditions, to savour the atmosphere.

'Good morning, Simon.'

'No, it isn't,' he snarled, hurling the papers into a nearby bin.

'I'm sure these figures are exaggerated,' I said, stifling a giggle.

'That story made me feel physically sick while eating my porridge,' he replied.

Ant and Dec then appeared, with the biggest grins seen since Cherie Blair heard I'd been sacked from the *Mirror*.

'Hi Simon...'

Silence. Then he looked them both straight in the eye. 'There are two of you, right?'

'Er, yes,' they replied.

'So that's only £20 million each, isn't it? We're level.'

Lisa had an understandably big smile on her face as she applied my make-up.

'How are you going to spend all that cash?' I asked.

'Oh God, don't, it's embarrassing,' she blushed. 'Mind you, I've had my eye on this pair of Ugg boots for a while now…'

TUESDAY, 10 APRIL 2007

Barry Humphries left a voice message on my mobile this morning. 'The show's looking great, Piers. It's really…funny, and I think you and your loved ones are going to really…enjoy it.'

The pauses suggested a certain insincerity to the statement, although my 'loved ones' will definitely enjoy it if it's as bad as I think it is.

The call was final confirmation, if any was needed, that I must have died a slow, horrible death in the editing suite. I feel like the inmates must do on Death Row at San Quentin prison when the governor pops his head round the door of your cell to say: 'The electric chair is looking fabulous…'

SATURDAY, 14 APRIL 2007

Dame Edna aired tonight. And yes, it was just as ghastly as I'd feared. I can always tell when an interview is really bad because Mum says, as she did tonight: 'Well, your suit looked lovely, darling.'

MONDAY, 16 APRIL 2007

It's very hard to take anyone seriously when their full name is Alexander Boris de Pfeffel Johnson.

Particularly when the gentleman concerned has done his level best for 42 years to prevent anyone even thinking of taking him seriously.

I like Boris, though. He's incredibly bright, instinctively funny and great at a party. But do I want him running the country? That's a rather less appealing prospect, to be honest.

We met for an interview in his chaotic office next to Big Ben.

'Now, no funny business, Morgan,' he cajoled, slapping me hard on the back (Boris is built like a Sherman tank).

'Right Boris, let's start with…'

I pulled out a large notepad laden with juicy titbits to hurl at him.

'Whoooooahhhh. Hang on a second, let me see those questions…'

He made a mad snatch for my pad, but I skilfully avoided him with a deft snatch of my own.

'No Boris, it doesn't work like that I'm afraid…'

'It does in my interviews…' (Makes a second desperate lunge for my notepad.)

'Not in mine it doesn't, mate.'

'You stitcher-upper.'

'Boris, I couldn't help noticing in today's papers that you appear to have earned £545,000 this year outside of your parliamentary salary. Accurate?'

'I've no idea but it sounds pathetic.'

'What do you mean "no idea"? You've declared it, haven't you?'

'Yuh, but you only declare the ballpark figures within various frameworks, so it could be a lot less.'

'Or a lot more, presumably?'

'Not more, no, not really. That is the top estimate. I can't believe it's that much, it doesn't feel it's that much. Anyway, what's really pathetic is how far behind William Hague I am. What am I doing? I'm earning chicken feed compared to him, I've got to pull my socks up. Even old Winny [Ann Widdecombe] is chasing my tail.'

'You're stinking rich, aren't you?'

'No, I'm not, you keep coming back to this script of yours in your wooden way.'

'It's not a script, Boris, the criticism of this money thing would be, and let me stress that I don't share this view…'

'In which case why bother to bloody make it? Come on, have the courage of your convictions, man.'

'OK, I will. Are you a politician, or just a greedy, grasping little mercenary bastard?'

'You mean there's a contradiction in terms there?' (Laughs.)

'I'm just curious why you bother being a politician at all when you can rake in all this cash doing other things.'

'I believe wholly in what I am doing. But I have also got to put bread on the table, I've got a lot of mouths to feed.'

'Yes, indeed you have. And that's just the ones we know about…'

(Silent smirk.) 'I'm not going to respond to…go on.'

'Do you think you're a celebrity?'

'I think Disraeli was once asked why people went to the House of

Commons, and he said "we do it for fame". And I think it was Achilles who said…you're a classics scholar, right?'

'Not massively, no. I did Latin and Greek at school though. Can you do the Greek alphabet?'

'Er…yes, of course I can. So Achilles said…'

'Go on then, do it now.'

'I'm trying to tell you about Achilles. Oh God, all right then…alpha, beta, gamma, delta…' (He completes it quickly and successfully.)

'OK, a few pronunciation issues but that was basically right.'

(Explodes indignantly.) 'There were no pronunciation issues!'

'Back to Achilles, please.'

'Right, well, he was asked…well, the thing is that fame or the desire to be known is not in itself necessarily disreputable. Achilles said he was doing it all for the glory of song and immortality.'

'Is that your game then?'

(Chuckles.) 'Yes, to be immortal!'

'Do you think you've become immortal yet?'

'It was Vespasian who said on his death bed…'

'It's no good trying to impress me with all these classical names, Boris, it leaves me cold.'

Boris looks at me with a look of appalled condescension.

'Anyway, back to this fame thing, there's no problem desiring it provided you do some good with it as well. It is possible to have a pretty good life and career being a leech and a parasite in the media world, gadding about from TV studio to TV studio, writing inconsequential pieces and having a good time. But in the end feeling a great sense of personal dissatisfaction. Even you, Piers, must have moments when you feel a need to put something back…'

'I don't feel that great calling, to be honest. I'm quite happy judging dancing cows in America with The Hoff.'

'Well, OK, that is a wonderful thing to do, I agree.'

'It's more fun than politics, most of which is bloody boring.'

'It is boring…but in my thirties I began to feel totally hacked off with just being a journalist and I wanted to do something more meaningful.'

'Do you think you could be prime minister one day?'

'I think it's highly unlikely.'

'That's bollocks. Inside you, you do think you can be, don't you? Why bother with it all otherwise?'

'Well, look…we're all in a…I think…listen, David Cameron is going to be an absolutely fantastic prime minister.'

'I don't mean now, I mean one day. Is there any reason why you shouldn't be?'

'What, biological? Intellectual? Moral? Aesthetic?'

'No, I mean do you think that this country would ever elect a buffoon as prime minister?'

'Have I over-buffooned it? Hmmmm.'

'Do you think you can be a prime minister and a buffoon? That's my point really.'

'I think it's very difficult to be both, I agree.' (Chuckles.) 'Mind you, there have been quite a few prime ministers who've done a pretty good job of it, come to think of it!'

'Do you want to be taken seriously?'

'The awful truth is that people already take me seriously. I judge that by the amount of rage I seem to inspire with my casual remarks.'

'You see, I don't really buy into this buffoon thing. I think you play it all up to make money and charm the public, when underneath it all lurks a calculating, ambitious and very serious brain.'

'That's very kind of you but you must consider the possibility that underneath it all there really may lurk a genuine buffoon.'

Boris diverts to the TV screen, where Gordon Brown is arguing with George Osborne about pensions. 'Balls, balls, balls!' he shrieks. 'You've ripped everyone off!' Pause. 'They're history these guys. Look at them.' He then grabs my list of questions…

'"Fatso?" What the hell does this mean?'

'You campaigned in the *Telegraph* to be allowed to use that word if you wanted. A curious thing to get worked up about.'

'"Checking your hair in the *Question Time* camera?"'

'You did, I saw you. You looked at the camera and adjusted your hair.'

'It's possible…'

'The same hair that you like to claim never gets brushed. Another con. The unruly mop is carefully crafted.'

'Dear oh dear, all right.'

His aide entered the room at this point to ask if the *GQ* photographer could set up.

'It's going very badly,' Boris informs him. 'But we're nearly finished...'

I laugh. 'Oh no, we're not. We've only just begun. How much will your image have to change as your political career develops? I mean, going back to my earlier point, you cannot go on playing the buffoon if you ever actually seriously aspire to be leader of this country.'

'Very true. And that may be why I am finally prohibited from getting very much higher. Because it may be that the psychological effort needed to haul myself round into a more serious, gaffe-free zone proves too difficult.'

'I repeat, you do want to be prime minister one day, don't you?'

'Well, of course. In an ideal world. Listen, man, we've done politics, celebrity, the media, we're done aren't we?'

'No mate, I need to fill six pages with this at least.'

'Jesus Christ! I haven't got six pages in me. I'm a defunct volcano.'

'Do you think you're a sex symbol?' (Boris stares at me, silent and aghast.) 'Why are you shying away from such obvious questions? You're Boris Johnson, for God's sake, not the Pope.'

'I have no idea if I'm a sex symbol.'

'You must get loads of female fan mail, though?'

'Yes, but mainly asking me to help them with their drains...'

'Are you not familiar with that euphemism, Boris?'

(Chuckles.) 'Noooooo. Andrew, help me here (turns desperately to his young work-experience aide), what shall I say?'

Andrew replies: 'Say that if you get into power then you will be much more of a sex symbol.'

To which Boris roars: 'That's right, brilliant answer.'

'Do you think power is more of an aphrodisiac than celebrity?'

'Oh God, stop it, Piers.' (Rolls his eyes.) 'I'm starting to feel a bit beaten up here.'

'Oh, don't be ridiculous. This is hardly the Spanish inquisition, is it?'

'No, but your readers don't want to know about my private life.'

'Of course they do. Are you good in bed?'

'What? I have...I've no idea...no...'

'No?'

'Is there some other subject we can talk about?'

'You got fired over a sex scandal. You can hardly blame me for asking you about sex.'

'The memory is a bit sketchy...'

'I bet it is. But look, you're a celebrity politician who got sacked over sexual misbehaviour. I'm perfectly justified to quiz you like this.'

'OK, OK, fire away then.'

'What was it like to be fired for something a lot of people think should be private?'

'It was politics.'

'Should politicians in the modern age be judged on personal morality issues?'

'If they're kleptomaniacs, yes.'

'And if they're sex maniacs?'

'Erm...I don't think so, no.'

'If you were prime minister, would you ever fire anyone for a legal sexually related matter?'

'I don't see why I should, no.'

'What did you think of Cameron standing his ground over the drugs issue and refuse to say whether he had ever taken them?'

'Yes, I thought he was right. I'm not a great drug man myself.'

'You once alluded to the fact that you tried cocaine but sneezed on it.'

'Yes. I tried it at university, and I remember it vividly. And it achieved no pharmacological, psycho-tropic or any other effect on me whatsoever.'

'Some of it did creep into your big hooter then, despite the sneeze?'

'It must have done, yes, but it didn't do much for me, I can tell you.'

'Have you ever tried any other drugs? Any dope?'

'Cannabis, you mean? Yes, I have. There was a period before university when I had quite a few spliffs. But funnily enough, not much at university.'

'Did it do much for you?'

'Ummmm. Yeah, it was jolly nice. But apparently it is very different these days. Much stronger. I've become very illiberal about it. I don't want my kids to take drugs.'

'Without dwelling on your personal failings in this area, would you say you are better behaved sexually now?'

'That's a trap question. You're asking me to concede that I have behaved badly in the past, which I'm not prepared to do.'

'The evidence to the contrary is fairly overwhelming.'

'I lead a life of blameless domesticity and always have done.'

'That's a lie. Do you honestly feel you shouldn't have to answer these kind of questions?'

'I do a bit, yeah.'

'As a journalist, would you ask them of a politician who'd resigned over a sex scandal?'

'I think after a while I'd think it was impolite. I admire your heroic persistence but I'd have thrown in the towel a lot earlier.'

'I'm made of tougher stuff. Are you a man's man, or a woman's man?'

'I don't know…' (Shuffles uncomfortably.)

'You look like a rabbit in headlights.'

'Look, I love women who run things.'

'Which famous women do you admire?'

'Scarlett thingummy…'

'Johansson?'

'Yah. God, this is such a useless interview, isn't it? I'm so sorry, Piers. Do what you can to resuscitate this corpse.'

His aide returns to say it's time to wrap things up.

'Piers has got nothing out of me. Not a word. It's been blood from a stone.'

'I don't think I'd be quite so confident if I were you.'

'You're not allowed to editorialise anything. Make out that "Johnson sat there, keeping schtum but with the sweat pouring off his brow as he was bombarded with yet more personal questions – morphing into a politician as I watched."'

'No, no. As I said, you're a politician who got sacked over a sex scandal but doesn't want to talk about sex. Fair enough. But you can't blame me for trying to ask you about it, or take umbrage as you have done.'

'I didn't take umbrage.' (Turns to junior work-experience aide Andrew.) 'I didn't, did I?'

Andrew: 'Well, maybe there was a little hesitation occasionally.'

'Have you had to change as a person, though, since becoming a politician?'

Junior aide Andrew interrupts: 'I think he's learned to talk more slowly, giving himself more time to think.'

'Well...' (long sigh) '...we all have things for which we reproach ourselves.'

'How much reproaching do you do?'

'A lot.'

'You must be in almost permanent reproach mode...'

(Laughs loudly.) 'It's a non-stop orgy of reproach.'

'Do you fancy Cherie Blair?'

'Well...erm...I like her. I suppose I...I suppose I do a tiny bit.'

'Could you ever imagine having sex with her?'

'I could, yeah... no, don't put that in! God!' (Roars with laughter.)

'What do you think of George Bush?'

'I've met him. And he got in a frightful rage about the watch I was wearing because it had a picture of Che Guevara on it. He said, "We don't like folks who wear things like that, we shoot them." It was interesting. But I thought he was a charming fellow, much smarter than people think. I tell you what, though, Clinton is incredibly smart. I would even consider voting for Hillary if it meant getting Bill back. Because I think he gave the world a much better image of what America is and stands for than, I'm sad to say, the current White House does. The world was better run under him as president, there was a greater sense of optimism, the potential for harmony between different countries and religious groups. And we didn't have this terrible thing that Bush has brought in of this "you're with us or against us" mentality. That view has hugely antagonised a lot of people. I'd love to see Bill back to restore things. He represented America better, and that is so important. I love America.'

'Last question: you can be prime minister but you have to give up sex. Would you take the deal?'

'No.' (Roars with laughter.)

At the end of the interview, Boris squealed with joy. 'You got NOTHING, Morgan, not a line.'

'Well, let's wait and see, shall we?' I laughed back.

He slapped me hard on the back again.

'Just watch it.'

TUESDAY, 17 APRIL 2007

There's been a horrific shooting at an American university in Virginia, leaving 32 people dead and dozens more injured.

The perpetrator was a young student called Seung-Hui Cho, who apparently suffered from psychiatric problems.

And after it emerged that Cho, an individual formally recorded as being 'mentally unsound', was able to buy various handguns without any detection from the authorities, it's already sparked a massive renewed debate about gun laws in America.

Americans love their guns, and buy more than half the firearms manufactured worldwide each year.

The FBI estimates that there are over 200 million privately owned guns in the country, and if you add those owned by the military, law enforcement agencies and museums, there are 12 weapons for every man, woman and child in the United States.

And you see them pervading every part of contemporary American popular culture – TV, movies, music, books, magazines and video games.

Most Americans believe in their 'right to bear arms', as laid down by the American constitution. And they believe in this right as passionately as we Brits believe in our right to attend a pub.

WEDNESDAY, 18 APRIL 2007
Simon Cowell is in trouble after appearing to disrespect a contestant on *American Idol* paying tribute to the victims of the Virginia university shootings.

He was caught rolling his eyes and raising his eyebrows while the young singer spoke, and some nerdy geek immediately posted it on the Internet as 'Cowell's shocking snub to Virginia'.

The eye-roll has already attracted a million hits on YouTube in less than 24 hours, turning his alleged treason into a national talking point.

I watched it on GMTV with Celia this morning, and could tell immediately that he hadn't been listening, and just thought the kid, Chris Richardson, was making another of those ridiculous 'I can prove you wrong, Simon' speeches they are prone to make whenever he criticises them.

But the film evidence – unless, like me, you know him well, and have worked with him – is damning.

THURSDAY, 19 APRIL 2007
Simon's issued a fulsome apology.

'I may not be the nicest person in the world,' he said, 'but I would never disrespect those victims or their families. I didn't hear what Chris was saying.'

Within an hour of his mea culpa, the scandal was over as fast as it began. He had come out, explained what happened, America understood and everyone went back to work.

It was a fascinating example of how powerful the Internet is, and how fast you need to act to protect yourself from it.

Simon rang tonight, still reeling from the shock of the whole thing.

'It was terrifying! I didn't even know what I was supposed to have done, and suddenly the whole of America is going bonkers.'

I myself fly back to America tomorrow to start filming the second series of *America's Got Talent*, and can't wait.

Who wouldn't enjoy the prospect of four weeks in sun-kissed Hollywood?

But it's always tough saying goodbye to the boys, even if they react, as they did this afternoon, with stunning stoicism.

'Have a nice time, Dad,' said Bertie, 'can you get me some pants from Abercrombie and Fitch?'

'Pants?'

'Yes, they've got really cool ones.'

'Bertie, you're seven years old, you shouldn't be worrying about designer pants.'

'But I like them,' he said, firmly, 'and they're really cheap in America. They're like ten dollars or something.'

He was right; clothes are cheap in America. Bloody cheap. In fact, with the dollar rate hovering around two dollars to one pound, everything seems like it's half price out there.

I packed my suitcases, and had another chat with Simon.

'This is a really important time,' he said. 'A lot of shows start well in America, and then disappear without trace. I don't want that happening with *Talent*. So give it everything you've got in the next few weeks to build on the success of the first series. We've got to get the ratings up.'

Ah, yes, the ratings.

The absolute, non-negotiable, barometer of success in American entertainment.

I thought British television was pretty tough until I experienced the sheer, unrelenting pressure of the American networks.

Shows live, or die, by their ratings. All that counts is your score on the Nielsen fast ratings service, which publishes last night's figures every day on the Internet at 8 a.m.

TV critics are nowhere near as important or influential in America, because they don't have national newspapers in the way that we do in Britain.

The place is so huge that it would be impossible to distribute them properly, or produce a paper relevant to every state. So each city has its own big daily paper, usually more than one.

And as a result, very few papers are read outside of their specific area – the exceptions being the *New York Times*, *Washington Post*, *Wall Street Journal* and *USA Today*.

So while a critic reaches just a couple of million readers if he's lucky, almost every paper publishes the national TV ratings, so everyone knows exactly how every show is doing. And this piles on the tension.

If *America's Got Talent* does well in this second series, then I can look forward to at least another two or three years in Hollywood. If its ratings plummet, then I can look forward to the next plane home.

Sometimes I hate my job. Nancy Dell'Olio and Victoria Beckham
compete with each other for my affections at a party.

'America...just a nation of used car salesmen with all the money we need to buy guns and no qualms about killing anybody else in the world who tries to make us uncomfortable.' HUNTER S. THOMPSON

FRIDAY, 20 APRIL 2007

I arrived at the British Airways check-in to be told that my standard-sized carry-on bag was now 'too big' for new safety regulation. By one inch.

As I vented my spleen about how absurd this new law was, I heard an even angrier voice next to me doing the same.

It was government minister Ed Balls, the Economic Secretary to the Treasury. 'But this is ridiculous, I'm going to Berlin and I need my stuff to work on the plane,' he insisted, to no avail.

Eventually a special services manager arrived to deal with us.

'Whose stupid idea is this new rule?' I demanded. 'British Airways?'

'No, sir,' he said.

'The airport authorities?'

'No, sir.'

'Well, who the hell do I blame then?'

'It is a new law brought in by the British government, sir.'

I turned slowly to Mr Balls, who at least had the good grace to blush.

'You mean *him*,' I said.

The special services manager smiled, and nodded.

Arrived in Los Angeles and went straight to dinner at the excruciatingly trendy Mr Chow's in Beverly Hills, with senior producers on *America's Got Talent* and the show's two new stars, Sharon Osbourne and Jerry Springer, who is taking over from the host Regis Philbin.

Obviously, I wasn't exactly looking forward to seeing Sharon. It all went fine for the first hour, until I made the fatal mistake of asking Sharon if she had forgiven me yet.

'No. Don't you ever call me unprofessional again, you pen-pushing little TWAT!!!' she snarled. 'You've been fired from every job you've ever had, and you're so desperate to be famous it's pathetic!'

I regret to say that I reacted to this charming (if undeniably accurate) tribute in an equally unedifying manner by saying: 'Save it for someone who gives a flying fuck, Sharon.'

'Shut up, you middle-class fucking pillock,' she snarled back.

By this time, the table had fallen into the kind of silence reserved for when your barmy uncle suddenly announces he is in love with your mother over the Christmas lunch table.

I started laughing, which just sent her even more off the dial. 'You're Simon Cowell without the talent or fucking class, darling.'

'Whatever. You won't manipulate me like you manipulate everyone else in your life, Sharon. I'm not a pushover like you're used to, I'm afraid.'

Sharon suddenly stood up and marched over to where I was sitting, her own chair crashing over in the process. And then started prodding my face like she was testing a steak to see if it was cooked enough. 'You're a fucking lucky sonofabitch who is only here because you crawled up Simon's arse.'

'Get your hands off me,' I spat back.

You know things are getting out of hand when even Jerry Springer starts to look uncomfortable. But he eventually took charge of the situation, as you'd expect given the practice he has on his show, and led a still raging Sharon out of the room as other guests spluttered into their glasses. 'I'm not finished with you!' she shrieked, as she disappeared from view.

I sat back, looked at the rest of the stunned guests and took a long, slow, sip of wine.

'Well, that went well,' said Georgie Hurford-Jones, one of the producers, prompting everyone else to collapse with laughter. Or should I say, nervous laughter. I left soon afterwards, went back to my hotel room, took a sleeping pill and conked out, still reeling from the encounter.

SUNDAY, 22 APRIL 2007

I woke up with a heavy head and very vague memories of someone ringing me in the middle of the night.

I got to the studio.

'I'm glad we had that chat last night,' Sharon said.

'What chat?' I said, bemused.

'Don't you remember? I rang you when I got home. Ozzy told me I was being silly.'

I laughed.

'I'll have to take your word for it. Let's forget it anyway, we've got it off our chests now.'

By the time we got to the actual filming, we were laughing and joking as if nothing had happened. And I could see the American executives all shaking their heads, and thinking to themselves: 'These Brits are even crazier than we thought...'

One thing's for sure, working with Sharon's going to be very entertaining.

TUESDAY, 24 APRIL 2007

The great thing about LA is that you literally do meet a celebrity every day.

I was by the hotel pool this morning when a familiar British face gave me a cheery, 'Hello, there.'

It was the actor Tom Conti, who is filming a pilot comedy show for Fox.

We'd never met but there's a strange camaraderie between all Brits in Hollywood, and within minutes he'd invited me to dinner with him and his actress wife Kara.

It was a hilarious night at their favourite local Italian restaurant, culminating in a loud and sustained debate about God. I'm a believer, they're not.

I honestly never thought I'd be drinking Barolo with Tom Conti while simultaneously shouting: 'Yes, but what happened *before* the Big Bang, eh?'

WEDNESDAY, 25 APRIL 2007

The Queen has been revealed as a secret Arsenal fan, Heather Mills was booted off that American TV dance show she has been so shamelessly flashing her false leg on, Hugh Grant was arrested for throwing baked beans at a photographer and my book went to No. 1 in the charts.

What a stupendously good day to be alive.

THURSDAY, 26 APRIL 2007

Sharon stormed off set twice during filming today, calling me 'horrific' and 'disgusting'.

She's opinionated, fiery and unpredictable. And, it has to be said, fantastic television!

FRIDAY, 27 APRIL 2007

The first Democrat presidential debate took place last night, and the general view is that Hillary did the best, showing up Obama for his lack of experience. I think this will be an absolutely key factor in who wins the nomination. Never mind the fact that Obama is black in a country where racism is still widespread, he's also very young by presidential standards, and has had very limited exposure to the front line of politics. Hillary, by contrast, lived in the White House for eight years while her popular husband ran the country.

On the flip side, Obama opposed the Iraq War, while Hillary supported it. And there is a rising tide of anger about Iraq that could tilt the foreign policy debate back Obama's way. He also sounded intelligent, thoughtful and sensible last night, three words you wouldn't use about the current president.

There was a big NBC press day today, where you basically spend five hours as a performing monkey for endless US media crews.

Most of the fun was to be had walking up behind the interviewers as they grilled Cowell or The Hoff and saying something like, 'Hey, Simon, have you told them about the penis enlargement?'

But the most bizarre moment came when I met Howie Mandel, a big TV star over here who hosts the American version of *Deal or No Deal*.

When I tried to shake his hand, he offered me his clenched fist instead, saying: 'I do those.'

I was a bit confused.

'Sorry, what are those?'

'Knuckle shakes. I don't do the shaking hands thing any more – I've got OCD and it used to kill the rest of the day.'

He wasn't joking.

And nobody else seemed remotely perturbed by this lunacy.

'He's got a point, there are a lot of germs out there,' one of the NBC crew said, matter-of-factly.

Californians are health obsessed. I'd go as far as to state that hypochondria is almost a state disease.

Never make the mistake of saying you've got a cold here, or you'll still be talking about it two hours later. I'm thinking that next time, I'll use the correct medical term 'acute viral nasopharyngitis' instead, as I'm sure it will send them racing for their gas masks and saline drips.

SATURDAY, 28 APRIL 2007

After a soothing Vietnamese mani-pedi (I didn't even know what that phrase meant a year ago, let alone permit myself to have a manicure and pedicure – which must mean I am slowly but surely disappearing up my LA backside), I dined with Celia at the Ivy – which is no relation to the London restaurant, but just as starry.

Sitting next to us was a rather plump young woman opposite a bearded, perma-tanned, grey-haired TV producer.

The following conversation took place:

'So, look, you've got the role.'

'Oh my *GOD*!'

'And I don't think you'll even have to audition.'

'Oh my God!'

'And you're going to be brilliant, and the show's going to be brilliant.'

'Oh my God!'

An hour later, he paid the bill and said: 'So, back to my place then?'

The woman squealed with excitement.

'Oh my God! Yes!'

This really happened. I heard it with my own ears.

The Hollywood casting couch is alive and throbbing.

SUNDAY, 29 APRIL 2007

Ordering a simple thing like breakfast can be such an ordeal in America. You can't just ring room service and ask for 'cereal, toast, eggs, juice and coffee please', because the list of supplementary questions will be so long and tedious that you'll be re-ordering for lunch by the end of it.

You need to know the right terminology, and be highly specific.

So I've developed a firm, but time-effective, manner of ordering now, which went like this today:

'Good morning, Mr Morgan, this is in-room dining, how may I help?'

'Good morning, I'd like a large pot of decaffeinated Colombian dry-roasted coffee, with 2 per cent cold milk on the side [that's 2 per cent fat, or semi-skimmed as we would call it]. Two cartons [never say packet, they don't know what that means] of Special K, with 2 per cent cold milk on the side. Then three boiled eggs, cooked for three minutes and 22 seconds [they won't bat an eyelid at this ludicrously precise schedule, it's perfectly normal in the States to be that anal], with wheat bread toasted for two minutes.

'And fresh grapefruit juice, no ice, or lemon, in a tall glass.'

They then read this all back to you, and once you have clarified the order, they say: 'Thank you for placing your order with in-room dining, Mr Morgan. It will be with you by 8.34 a.m.' The Beverly Wilshire guarantees to serve you every meal within 30 minutes, which is why they always give you a time exactly half an hour after you place the order.

At 8.34 a.m., a charming old Mexican man will arrive with the order, and spend a few minutes reading out absolutely everything on his tray.

And finally, exhausted by the sheer scale of the mental demands required for what should be one of the simplest procedures in the world, you eat.

Americans love all this. Food is almost as important to them as the weather. They adore hideously complicated menus that run for 30 pages, full of infinitesimally small variations.

MONDAY, 30 APRIL 2007

Corporal Donald Payne, Britain's first convicted war criminal, was today kicked out of the Army and jailed for a year for the inhuman treatment of Iraqi civilians in Basra in 2003.

He was in the Queen's Lancashire Regiment, the same lot the *Mirror* accused of abusing innocent Iraqis during the 'fake photo' scandal that cost me my job.

TUESDAY, 1 MAY 2007

It's often said about Americans that they don't understand irony or sarcasm, but I'd say that is only half true. It depends on the situation. I had a hilarious moment on a plane recently where, after several requests to have a faulty reading light fixed, I finally lost patience and said to the steward: 'Is there any danger of any light around here?' He reacted like I'd just told him I was hijacking the jet. 'Danger? *Danger?* There's a dangerous light around here?'

I tried to explain what I meant, but it was pointless. The steward then spent the next 20 minutes dealing with the 'dangerous light' emergency.

But there is another half of America that loves, and totally 'gets', heavily ironic TV shows like *Seinfeld*, *Frasier*, *The Simpsons* and *The Office*.

Eddie Izzard, who draws heavily on irony in his act, has played to sell-out crowds everywhere from New York to Detroit.

And when Ricky Gervais accepted two Golden Globe awards with the words 'Two bookends, excellent!' the audience laughed, quite naturally.

If Americans expect to find irony, most of them will recognise it and laugh.

It's when you slip it unexpectedly into normal conversation that it can cause confusion.

If a restaurant waiter asks me how my food is, I might reply: 'Terrible, thanks.' Purely for the puzzled look this provokes on their faces.

Conversely, we Brits often seek evidence of irony or sarcasm in American language where it doesn't exist. If you tell an American you have a cold, and they reply, 'Oh no, I feel so bad for you,' then they're not taking the piss, as we'd assume. They actually mean it.

It's a minefield, though, and probably the safest thing when in America is to add the words 'Only joking' after every ironic or sarcastic outburst.

Take this afternoon, for example, when a group of old grannies hobbled on to the AGT stage with Zimmerframes and announced they were going to do a 'Zimmer-rap'.

I stopped them in their decrepit tracks, and asked: 'Excuse me, but I have to ask, are you the Dallas branch of the David Hasselhoff fan club?'

They looked totally bemused.

'No, sir, we're not.'

I turned to David, who shook his head vehemently. 'No, man, I don't know these ladies.'

And all around me, I could see the confused audience just muttering to each other.

The only person who laughed was Sharon. But then she was the only other Brit in the room.

Tonight, I dined at the Beverly Wilshire's new restaurant Cut, currently the buzz of the town. In the last week alone, it has played host to Jennifer Aniston, Eva Longoria, Kevin Costner and Al Pacino.

But today, I couldn't see anyone famous at all.

'Admit it,' I asked Dana, the sommelier, 'I am the biggest star in here.'

She grimaced. 'Yes, Mr Morgan. Tonight, unfortunately, I think you just might be.'

Five minutes later Dana was back with a gleeful smirk.

'See that guy sitting in the corner with his jacket pulled up over his ears?'

'Yes.'

'Mel Gibson. Enjoy your meal.'

WEDNESDAY, 2 MAY 2007

The Hoff, who has been on splendidly entertaining form for the last week, was in a weird mood today. He seemed edgy, distracted, and at one stage turned his judging seat round and sat with his head in his hands for at least two minutes looking like a broken man.

Normally I tease him mercilessly during filming until he eventually snaps, calling me a 'tabloid wanker' – his favourite phrase. But today he seemed too tense to toy with.

'You OK, David?' I asked during a tea break.

'Yeah, yeah, man, it's fine,' he replied.

But I could tell he wasn't.

'What's going on?' I probed.

'It's just some domestic shit,' he said, shaking his head sadly.

An hour later I discovered what it was. A video of him, very, very drunk, has been leaked to the media. It had apparently been recorded by one of his children three weeks ago in Las Vegas, where he is starring in the Mel Brooks musical *The Producers*.

The firm suspicion is that his estranged wife Pamela is behind the leak, the latest salvo from their horribly bitter divorce.

No wonder he's so depressed. Poor bloke.

Had dinner at Ago restaurant tonight, a delightful Italian place owned by Robert De Niro.

The guests were me, Simon Cowell, Jerry Springer and Dermot O'Leary – the new *X Factor* host.

It's Cowell's favourite eaterie because they let him smoke outside, which in LA these days is a sin akin to publicly injecting oneself with heroin.

Obviously, the first topic of conversation was The Hoff video.

There are plenty of cowardly TV executives in Hollywood who would instantly drop a star over an embarrassing 'scandal' like this.

But Cowell, who produces *America's Got Talent*, was resolute.

'David's going to get my full support. Privately and publicly. We've all been drunk. We just haven't had our family video tape it, thank God.'

We all agreed, and promptly ordered another bottle of red wine with amaretto chasers.

THURSDAY, 3 MAY 2007

Saw The Hoff outside his dressing room first thing in the morning, surrounded by agents and lawyers. The video is apparently being shown on national TV tonight.

I patted him on the shoulder. 'Mate, what's happened to you is disgusting and we're all right behind you.'

'Thanks man, I appreciate that.'

When filming started, he walked out to find half the audience wearing 'Don't Hassel The Hoff' T-shirts.

They gave him a rousing cheer.

Sharon and I joined in the applause. He may be a legend in his own mirror, but The Hoff has a big heart and we both feel for him.

'What's it like waiting for something like this to be aired?' I asked, as we waited for an act to start.

'Oh man, you know what? It's like a gigantic gong is sitting over my head and some guy is waiting to whack it as hard as he can.'

Sharon and I both burst out laughing, and so did he.

'Jesus, it's so *exhausting*!' he added. 'I wouldn't mind so much but it's my own kids who took the video!

'I told them to film me if I fell off the wagon again because I wanted to know how bad I was when I got like that. But I never wanted it put on TV obviously...'

We got back to judging a reverend who hurled knives, tomahawks and machetes at his beautiful assistant with unnatural enthusiasm for a man of the cloth.

'I'd like to do that to my ex-wife,' The Hoff observed. 'And miss...'

As the hours ticked by, he grew tense again.

'What time are you premiere-ing tonight?' I asked.

'God, I don't know, man. Soon, I guess.'

'How bad is it?'

'It's awful. They've all got it – the whole world's going to see The Hoff lying on the floor so drunk he can't even eat a burger.'

We returned to our dressing rooms, the audition stage of the show finally over after two weeks.

I packed my things, and knocked on his door.

'Good luck, mate, just try and keep your calm and don't hit back – stay dignified.'

'Thanks for the advice. You should know, I guess, being a tabloid wanker.'

Then The Hoff started to well up with tears.

There are millions of benefits to being a celebrity, and he has milked them all.

But in a moment like this, I wouldn't swap places with David Hasselhoff for all the money, freebies and upgrades in the world.

Underneath all the superstar bluster, he's a nice guy struggling to make his weird, chaotic, dysfunctionally iconic life work.

'You don't deserve this,' I said. And I meant it.

I got back to my hotel room and turned on the TV to find 'breaking Hasselhoff news' erupting everywhere.

The video was awful: The Hoff reduced to a pathetic shambling wreck, lying half-naked on the floor, mumbling incoherently, food flying out of his mouth.

'Why do you do this?' his daughter asks him in the middle of it.

'Because I'm lonely,' he said.

I'm sure millions of people will laugh at The Hoff when they see the video. But I didn't. One thing's for sure, though – he'll survive. He always does. And there is no better place to fall off your perch than America, because they have a far more pronounced sense of sympathy towards erring celebrities here than in Britain.

Most Americans won't revel in The Hoff's misfortune, they will feel sorry for him. It's one of their more endearing qualities.

SUNDAY, 6 MAY 2007

I'm back in the UK, and Michael Parkinson and I had a little spat on his Radio 2 show today about what constitutes talent.

'Are you seriously trying to tell me that David Hasselhoff has entertained

more people than Frank Sinatra?' he asked, before playing 'I Get A Kick Out
Of You' to prove his point.

'Yes,' I answered, when the song finished. 'You've obviously never seen
the video to his single "Jump In My Car", have you?'

MONDAY, 7 MAY 2007

I've taken on a new agent in Hollywood, John Ferriter from the William
Morris agency.

He's like the one in *Entourage* – smart, funny, ballsy, and resigned to the
fact that most of his clients are less intelligent than him, and therefore prone
to frustrating acts of gross stupidity.

But I have one great advantage over his other clients.

'I read your book this weekend,' he said today. 'There is no greater moti-
vation for an agent than to know that if you screw up, your client will write
about it…'

It's vitally important to have a good agent in Los Angeles. Without
one, as he pointed out to me, 'you're swimming uphill in a river full
of piranhas'.

In Britain, I will often talk directly to TV executives about future
projects. But in LA, that would be deemed rank stupidity and commercial
suicide.

'Your job,' said Ferriter, 'is to look pretty, smile a lot and do your work
well. My job is to screw the bastards into the ground.'

WEDNESDAY, 9 MAY 2007

A familiar unshaven, tousled, swarthy, scowling head slithered past me at the
Conrad Hotel in Chelsea this morning.

It was José Mourinho, manager of a 100 billion rouble Chelsea team
that has lost out on both the Premiership and Champions League in the last
fortnight.

I jumped out of my seat.

'José, how do you do, I'm Piers Morgan.'

He stared ahead with the most vacant, dismissive, 'I'm not listening'
blankness I've been afforded since meeting Prince Philip at Prince Charles's
fiftieth birthday party.

''Allo,' he grunted.

'I just wanted to congratulate you,' I said, shaking his hand.

He looked bemused.

'On what?'

I smiled. 'On the last two weeks. I'm an Arsenal season ticket holder, and it's been the only thing that's made us laugh all season.'

He looked repulsed, shook his head and marched off.

THURSDAY, 10 MAY 2007

If you've ever wondered what it's like to make a complete chump of yourself in front of all your heroes, I'm now in a position to know.

Tonight was the twenty-first birthday party of a charity celebrity cricket team called the Bunburys, run by a great guy called David 'The Loon' English. Everywhere I looked in the Great Room of the Grosvenor Hotel was another cricketing legend – Botham, Gower, Lamb, Gooch, Gatting.

From rugby, world champions Martin Johnson and Matt Dawson. From football, my all-time Arsenal favourite Ian Wright. From music, Eric Clapton, Bill Wyman and Bee Gee Robin Gibb.

My role was simple – do a quick live chat with as many stars as I could find.

But the organisers told me not to mention Barry Gibb's name when I interviewed Robin Gibb, because they have recently fallen out.

So, as I walked towards Robin, I kept saying to myself, 'Don't mention Barry, don't mention Barry…'

I stopped by the great man, and declared: 'Ladies and gentlemen, one of the world's most successful singers ever, Mr…*Barry Gibb*!'

I looked down to see a stony-faced Robin. And the next noise I heard was that of 1,000 people hooting with derisive laughter, led by Botham and Clapton, who were guffawing so hard I thought they might actually explode all over the top table.

The penny dropped like a large machete in my neck.

'Oh God…sorry…erm…of course, what I meant to say, ladies and gentle-men, was *Mr…Robin Gibb*!' But the damage was horrifically done.

I wanted to be instantly transported to Planet Tharg at a trillion miles an hour.

'As you may know from my time at the *Daily Mirror*, accuracy was never my strong point,' I told the still-chortling audience.

My misery was compounded by guest speaker Stephen Fry, who came on and repeated his favourite joke: 'What's the definition of countryside? The murder of Piers Morgan.'

Bill Wyman tried to cheer me up later.

'Don't worry about it – I got called Keith Moon the other day, and he's been dead 30 years.'

FRIDAY, 11 MAY 2007

Tony Blair has announced his departure date: June 27.

His 'hand-on-heart, I did what I thought was right' speech yesterday was slick, well choreographed, pressed all the right PR buttons, immaculately presented and a veritable masterclass in media-friendly populist oratory.

The only problem was that I didn't believe a word he said.

By contrast, Gordon Brown's first 'I want to be the next prime minister' speech today was a bit of a mess – half an hour late, autocue hiding his face, media all furious. And yet I thought what he actually said was powerful, passionate, honest and inspiring.

SATURDAY, 12 MAY 2007

There are various things that I have curiously avoided doing in my life: meeting David Beckham, skiing and going to Las Vegas.

Today I removed Vegas from the list by flying to the great desert gambling oasis for the bootcamp stage of *America's Got Talent*.

As I sat in my Virgin seat, I spotted an enormous fat bloke waddling towards me and thought: Please, God, not him. There's nothing worse than sitting next to a heaving heffalump on an 11-hour flight, not least because they eat all the best food.

To my delight he swerved right at the last minute, and a radiantly beautiful brunette arrived at my side instead.

I nodded and said hello, she smiled sweetly and did the same – revealing a world-class set of gnashers to go with the obviously expensive clothes and stunning array of jewellery.

She was, I guessed, in her mid-thirties, extremely friendly, and we chatted away about the kind of trivial stuff you talk about to strangers on planes.

After a couple of hours she went to sleep and I went to the bar, where one of the stewardesses said: 'You seem to be getting on well with Shania.'

'Shania?' There's only one Shania I know in the entire world – and that's singing and songwriting superstar Ms Twain, who has five Grammies and the biggest-selling album ever by a female artist to her credit.

'It's not…' I asked.

'It is…' the stewardess replied. 'She's going to the big country music awards in Vegas.'

When she woke, I affected casual nonchalance, as if I had known all along. And then bombarded her with all the questions a crazed fan would ask.

'So, Shania, tell me – how do you write your best stuff, when you're happy or miserable?'

'Oh, miserable definitely. Or bored. When I'm happy I can't write at all because I just fill my days with other stuff.'

'Do you prefer writing or performing?'

'I love my concerts. It's like I'm a mum feeding her hungry children, there's so much emotion out there.'

'What's your favourite of your own songs?'

'"Jealous".'

'And were you?'

'Very.'

'What's your husband's?'

'"You're Still The One".'

'And is he?'

'Yes.'

'Favourite other artists?'

'Sting. And Supertramp…'

'Oh my God,' I interrupted, '*Breakfast in America* is one of my all-time favourite albums.'

We looked at each other with new mutual admiration.

'Don't you hate being so squeaky-clean?'

'I'm not.' Big naughty grin.

'I see.' I turned to the stewardess. 'More wine, please. For both of us.'

'What's the most boring question people ask you?'

'When's your new album out.'

'When is it out?'

'I'm not telling you.'

Eventually, she turned the inquisition on to me.

'So what do you do?'

'Oh, I judge dancing cows and rapping grannies with David Hasselhoff.'

She giggled.

'No, I really do. On a show called *America's Got Talent.*'

'Oh, hang on, I know that show. You're the mean Brit, right?'

'The very same.'

The plane landed.

'Where are your awards?' I asked, as we queued with other passengers for the exit.

'Oh, I keep them all in a box at home,' she replied.

'No, I meant where is the awards ceremony you're attending in Vegas.'

Everyone around us burst out laughing, including an embarrassed Shania. 'Ah, I see, sorry…'

'I keep my awards on the loo wall,' I said, to ease her blushes.

'What have you won?'

'Oh, I used to edit newspapers, and I once got an award for The Least Constructive Contribution to Anglo-German Relations when I printed a front page headline entitled "Achtung Surrender!" in the middle of a soccer tournament.'

Shania stared at me, utterly bemused.

'Well…congratulations. My husband is half-German.'

SUNDAY, 13 MAY 2007

I walked up and down the four-mile Vegas strip today, and it is truly the Neon Kingdom – an intense conglomeration of skyscrapers, hotels and casinos, all with giant signs flashing their wares, designed to titillate, entice and, ultimately, to deprive you of your hard-earned cash, like a hooker in an Amsterdam shop window.

It's brash beyond belief, hideously smoky, incredibly noisy, and yet undeniably exciting.

Money is the only currency that matters here, and as I walked, I was constantly reminded of this by a stream of hustlers, buskers, hookers, drug-dealers and other general irritants.

'You want a girl?' said one slathering, greasy, sleazeball.

'No, thanks.'

'We've got white girls, black girls, Asian girls, small girls, big girls, whatever girl you want.'

I walked on, but he followed me, keeping up a constant sales chatter.

'A hundred dollars for an hour?'

'No.'

'OK, $60?'

I stopped.

'I don't want a girl, OK?'

He laughed, almost maniacally.

'Why, you gay? I got guys…big guys, small guys…'

He eventually gave up, but others moved in, all scrabbling for my business.

'You want coke?' whispered a tall, thin Latino.

'No.'

'Ecstasy?'

'No.'

He pulled out a large black purse.

'I got some good dope, some really good dope, man.'

'I already work with one of those,' I replied, knowing my Hoff gag would pass straight over his head, but feeling the need to crack it anyway.

I don't mind all this kind of nonsense usually. You get it in some parts of most cities, from London to Bogota.

But this seemed especially soulless.

The whole ethos of Vegas is built on a false premise – that you can come here and make your dreams come true.

Wrong.

Sure, you can snort cocaine, sleep with prostitutes, drink yourself into a stupor and spend a lot of money watching a little ball race around a roulette wheel.

But what very few people do is go home feeling their real dreams have come true.

Usually, it's the complete opposite.

Everywhere I went, I saw human zombies. Dead-eyed, sweating, badly dressed, drug-crazed, vile people, who only care about you if you can do something for them.

I got in a taxi, and there was no respite.

'Wanna see a show? Wanna girl? Wanna dope?'

Hustle, hustle, hustle. Beggars line the streets, aggressive and with a masterful patter in patriotic blackmail.

'Hey man, I lost my leg in 'Nam protecting your freedom, give me some money if you love your country.'

Every 500 yards another strip club, wedding chapel or Elvis impersonator looms in front of you.

And it's so hot. We're only in mid-May but it's over 100 degrees already, and the heat is unbearably oppressive in that way only real desert heat can be. It bores into you, suffocating and drenching as it does.

I rounded one corner to see a huge replica of the Eiffel Tower staring at me, and hundreds of tourists staring at it.

And there, right before me, was the real Vegas. A towering monument to excess and fakery that has three times the national average for suicide, mental illness and depression.

It was all so dispiriting. The Vegas of my dreams was so romantic; the Vegas I have found is a Bermuda Triangle of sleaze and sin.

But at least I'm not losing all my money. Then, it must be even worse.

As Hunter S. Thompson put it: 'For a loser, Vegas is the meanest town on earth.'

TUESDAY, 15 MAY 2007

My future as a global talent judge nearly came to an abrupt halt today. The worst nightmare for anyone involved in a show where people do crazy acts is that something goes hideously wrong.

Today, an acrobat called Ivan placed a load of chairs on the stage, walked back into the wings, then sprinted on to a small trampoline, jumped and smashed head first straight into the chairs and on to the floor, where he then lay motionless.

We all laughed, assuming it was part of his act. But when he continued to lie without moving for a full minute, we realised it wasn't. The trampoline had accidentally caved in on impact.

'Oh my God,' said Sharon, 'he's unconscious!'

Paramedics raced to him, the theatre fell silent and I began to feel distinctly queasy. After five minutes he was still out cold, an ambulance had been called and everyone was getting distinctly twitchy.

Then The Hoff marched over to where Ivan was lying and began loudly cajoling him. To my astonishment, Ivan promptly sprang to his feet like he'd been shot with an electric dart and began jabbering away nine to the dozen. Another life, and my career, saved by Mr Baywatch.

WEDNESDAY, 16 MAY 2007

We've been filming incredibly long hours in Vegas, and to while away the often tedious waiting time Sharon and I started playing her favourite game – Who Would You Rather?

It involves your opponent naming two famous people, and you have to choose which one you would sleep with if you were at gunpoint.

It was all going fine until Sharon turned with a mischievous grin and said: 'Hillary Clinton or Cherie Blair?'

At which point I felt so ill I had to go and have a quick lie down.

Tonight, I ventured back out on to the fabled Vegas strip, and endured another gruesome experience.

The restaurants were dull, the bars full of idiots, the shows unwatchable (Barry Manilow anyone?), and as for the casinos – they were ten times worse than I ever feared: huge, sprawling brightly lit, air-conditioned hangars chock-full of obese, unsmiling people pumping money they can't afford to lose into slot machines that always win in the end.

It was ghastly, like watching a financial version of crack addicts. I guess I'd always had this fanciful notion that people who gamble in Vegas are having fun, but they're not.

Every single face I looked at was miserable. And most of the bodies on the end of the faces were fat.

I walked around Caesar's Palace for half an hour, and felt sickened by the end of it.

How can anyone like this place? It's not a fun-loving playground as they claim, it's a parasitical blot on humanity.

For many Americans, this is the personification of the true American dream.

For me, sadly, it's the personification of the American nightmare – a big, brash, gaudy, money-obsessed, breathtakingly vulgar, concrete, glass and marble jungle, full of tattooed hookers and fat, sweating, 'high-rollers'.

It's always awake, always light, always loud and always 'WINNING!'

Only, very few people actually win.

Most of them lose their shirt, and traipse home empty-pocketed, with their dreams shattered.

Vegas is a dump.

SUNDAY, 20 MAY 2007

Back to the UK for the BAFTA awards, where the after-show party at the Natural History Museum was splendidly drunken and bitchy.

General consensus was that sour-faced Catherine Tate was the worst loser ever (was she bovvered? I think she was very very bovvered…), though I loved the horrified forced smirk on Stephen Fry's face when he discovered that Ross Kemp had beaten him in the Best Factual Series category.

Ross was regally hammered by the time I reached him for a celebratory hug.

'I have dreamed of this moment since I was a kid at drama school,' he told me, tears welling up in his eyes.

My own award went to Janet Street-Porter for Worst Outfit Of All Time. Janet, my darling, you have to be 15 to get away with a studded toga, purple leggings and flip-flops.

TUESDAY, 22 MAY 2007

Richard Branson is one of those guys that you hope to interview when nobody else is around to put a gag in his mouth. He just can't stop himself blurting out that most deadly of vices for any famous person – the truth.

I arrived at his daughter's house in Holland Park this morning, and Richard's right-hand woman, a splendidly feisty Northern Irish lady called Jackie McQuillan, was waiting like the school matron.

'Now you two just behave yourselves!' she warned.

'Yes, miss,' we replied in unison.

Jackie left, looking concerned, Richard poured me a coffee and I got stuck in.

'Apparently scientists have discovered Viagra is the new cure for jetlag.'

'Oh, that sounds good! Presumably it works because it keeps you up all night…' (Laughs loudly.) 'I'm certainly going to try it. And I'm sure my wife will be very grateful and will have a very big smile on her face for weeks to come.'

'Have you ever taken Viagra?'

'Um… er…As my wife says, I don't need it!' (Bursts out laughing.)

'Sorry, the pause was too long there. You have, haven't you?'

'Yes…to be honest I've tried just about everything in my life! And that includes Viagra. I tried a variant of it in Japan that someone said was a lot better than Viagra and that definitely worked very well. I had to tie something up around my trousers for the rest of the next day to make sure nothing showed…We're talking bandage round the ankles here…' (Roars with laughter.)

'Talking of which, are you a member of the Mile High Club?'

'I am, yes.'

'Details?'

'I was sitting in economy on an old Freddie Laker flight, next to this very attractive lady, as we headed to LA. We got chatting, and it went a bit further. And it was every man's dream, to be honest. I was about 19, I think. I remember getting off the plane, and she turned to me and said, "Look, it's slightly embarrassing but I am meeting my husband at arrivals, would you mind holding back a bit…" But it was a memorable flight.

'How did you find the gymnastic challenge?'

'The problem with plane loos generally is that they are very small, and the acrobatics can't take too long because there's no room and people start banging on the door. What I remember most vividly is seeing these four hand prints on the mirror as we finished, and thinking I'd better wipe them off…'

'Did it last long?'

'No…it was a brief encounter, definitely!' (Laughs loudly.)

'Do you think she knows who that 19-year-old young man turned into?'

'I am absolutely certain she doesn't. It was quite nice being anonymous then, now I think about it.'

Branson burst out laughing again. I'd only been with him for ten minutes, and already he'd given me three front-page headlines and nearly burst his spleen.

I tried a more serious line of questioning.

'What do you think of Tony Blair?'

'Iraq will overshadow everything else he's done. It was the worst foreign policy decision in recent modern history, far worse than Suez. The invasion was obviously wrong, but what we did next was almost worse. We laid off the army, the civil service and the police, dumped them all on the streets, gave them no money and let the schools, hospitals, museums and libraries be ransacked. And yet Blair supported Bush throughout all this.'

'Why was Blair so slavish to Bush, given their completely different political backgrounds?'

'Well, it is right that Britain supports America generally. But the Bush administration is the worst for centuries, and it is a great pity that it was there at the time Blair was our prime minister. I do believe that without Blair's unflinching support for Bush, the Iraq war would never have happened. Blair came across so honestly and with such conviction that he let Bush get his way. And that is a tragedy.'

'What effect has the war had on Britain's reputation abroad?'

'Remarkably, not much. If you travel round the world with an American, you can tell they are embarrassed to be an American at the moment. Whereas the British are still well received. Having said that, the world is a much less safe place now because of the Iraq war. If we had concentrated on Al Qaeda and Afghanistan, we might have been on top of the situation. But now America is seen as the big bad wolf in Iraq and the whole place has become a fantastic recruiting ground for terrorists. The world is more dangerous.'

'How much of that is down to Bush?'

'I think he and the people around him are the worst administration ever, just dreadful. I met him once, and he was very affable and had his cigar and was joking about dropping the ash into a saucer at Buckingham Palace and so on. It was all very jolly. Like meeting a friendly mid-West cowboy. But the problem is that he is so weak that he allowed himself to be surrounded by incredibly dangerous people.'

'Who would you like to be the next president?'

'I think Hillary would be good, or Al Gore. And Obama might be, it's too early to say. McCain on the Republican side is OK.'

'Who are the most impressive public figures you've ever met?'

'Nelson Mandela is amazing.'

'Anyone a bit more…'

'Fun? Keith Richards, will he do? He was the first person to teach me how to roll a joint. I mean, how cool is that? I remember it mostly for this enormous black guy arriving at the door one afternoon armed with a gun and looking for his wife who was upstairs in bed with Keith. So I had to keep him talking and after about two minutes I saw, to my great relief, Keith and this guy's wife legging it naked across the garden...'

'You might have saved Keith's life...?'

'Yes! Quite possibly.'

'Didn't you get accused of having sex with Kate Moss on Necker Island while Keith was snorting cocaine off her stomach?'

(Laughs hysterically for 20 seconds.) 'Yes! Unfortunately it was completely untrue but I did ponder whether I should really be denying it, because it's quite a good rumour to be out there...'

'Normally at this stage of the interview, I would ask you what drugs you had tried yourself. But in your case it might be quicker to ask if there are any you haven't had...'

(Laughs.) 'Erm, I haven't tried skunk...I have smoked cannabis, though. I mean, I went with my son on his gap year, for God's sake! We learned to surf and had some nights where we laughed our heads off for eight hours...'

'Clinton never inhaled, would the Branson line be drawn at injecting?'

'I've never injected myself with drugs, no! I took LSD once, and I wouldn't recommend that to anyone. I took ecstasy once, too, but it didn't have a massive effect on me.'

'Cocaine?'

'I suspect I've tried it, yes...' (Laughs.) 'When I first went to America, flogging *Tubular Bells*, I was offered what I thought was Coca-Cola by a music business executive, and this enormous white bowl arrived...! So I did find out what it was all about.'

'What have you been like with your own kids about drugs?'

'When Sam was 17, I found him smoking a cigarette, and got really upset, and I said to him, "Look, I don't mind you smoking the occasional joint, but for God's sake don't smoke nicotine." And he took my advice. But he sees his friends being fucked up on skunk, so he won't touch it.'

'Are you good in bed?'

'You'll have to ask my wife.'

'People would love to have an image of you as a five times a night Lothario...'

'Well, if you could keep that image going, I'd be absolutely delighted! I won't sue... And you'd better make it six times a night, because Sting does five, doesn't he?'

'Are you a tantric man, too?'

'Not really, and I don't think Sting is either – I think it was a joke. But I have read a book on tantric and I'd recommend it, definitely.'

'Have you tried it?'

'I have, yeah. It's hard work!'

'Are you any good at it?'

'Well, I would be, but I keep dropping the book.' (More hysterical laughter.)

'Are you a good husband?'

'Erm…' (smiles) '…I think I've become a good husband.'

'Where were you, how can I put this delicately, weak where you're now strong, as a husband?'

'I suppose my head turns less as we walk down a street together, which does tend to help a relationship a bit.'

'You are an outrageous flirt, aren't you…?'

'Erm, I love women, definitely. And have had a lifetime of flirting with them. But fortunately I've known where to draw the line, which has also helped in our relationship! Temptation has certainly crossed my path. But while fame has probably brought that temptation my way, certainly not my looks, fame has also been a very good – what's the opposite of aphrodisiac? It makes sure you don't misbehave, that's for sure.'

'Fame has been a useful barrier to infidelity?'

'Exactly. Yes, thank you.' (Chuckles.)

'What makes you laugh?'

'I heard a story about Bono being on stage recently and starting clapping very slowly. And after ten minutes of this, he went: "Every time I clap, another child dies of AIDS in Africa." And this guy apparently shouted back from the crowd: "Well, stop fucking clapping then!"' (Laughs so hard, I fear he might be expiring…) 'That made me laugh. Life tends to make me laugh.'

'Do you know how rich you are?'

'Oh, God, I have no fucking idea. Sorry.'

At this point, Jackie McQuillan arrived back.

'Oh no, Jackie told me not to say "fuck" because you'd print it.'

'Relax, Jackie, you haven't missed much…just a long, tedious chat about business.'

Richard burst out laughing: 'It's all been sex, drugs and fucking rock 'n' roll!'

Jackie rolled her eyes in fake horror. 'I could have guessed!'

As we said goodbye, I asked him to sign a message for Stanley, a fellow dyslexic.

'Stanley,' he wrote, 'all the best people have Dys, Diss, Dys, Dysley, whatever the fuck it is! Richard Branson.'

SUNDAY, 27 MAY 2007

Only Simon Cowell could be the star of two *This Is Your Life* specials within the space of just four years.

I headed down to the ITV Studios to take part in the show with a heavy heart. Spending several hours fawning over Mr Cowell's genius is not exactly my idea of a great Sunday night.

Amanda arrived at the same time as me, and we posed together on the red carpet for the paparazzi.

'You look rough,' I whispered through fixed fake grin.

'Not as rough as you, you ugly old bastard,' she whispered back, through equally gritted teeth.

American Idol host Ryan Seacrest was standing in the lobby.

'This is going to be the worst night of my life,' he groaned.

'Couldn't agree more,' I said, as we trudged disconsolately together to the green room, where we met Fergie and her daughters Beatrice and Eugenie.

The duchess was on sparkling form, slapping me firmly on the back and shouting: 'How the devil are you, Morgan?' to general raised eyebrows.

Her girls were delightful – beautiful, polite, clever and amusing. A real credit to their much-maligned mum. Though I could have done without Eugenie blushing when I introduced her to Jerry Springer (the host of *America's Got Talent*).

'Why did you go red?' I asked, when he moved on.

'Because he's so...cool,' replied the 17-year-old Princess.

'What? And I'm not?'

'Erm...well...erm...I'm sure you are...'

The show itself was as we all feared – a lengthy nauseating eulogy to Cowell's all-round brilliance as a superstar and human being.

'You enjoying yourself?' I asked Cowell, as Amanda and I went on to add our spoonful of saccharine.

'I'm LOVING it,' he replied.

One person who definitely wasn't loving it was Robson Green, who got moved to the back row after originally sitting next to Ant and Dec.

'That's Siberia on this show,' I told him during a break. 'Further away from the subject, the less important you are...'

'Tell me about it,' he replied, grim-faced. 'My career's obviously over!'

Paula Abdul saved the day with a sustained verbal assault on Cowell's nocturnal habits.

'Simon's the only man I know who calls out his own name during sex,' she said. 'And he's so vain he uses condoms ribbed on the inside...'

TUESDAY, 29 MAY 2007
Barack Obama has announced a radical new health-care plan, which he claims will 'bring health care to all, and save the average consumer $2500 each.'

Obama's plan retains the private insurance system but injects additional money into it to pay for expanding coverage. Those who can't afford the plan would get a subsidy on a sliding scale depending on their income, and virtually all businesses would have to share in the cost for their workers.

His package would also prohibit insurance companies from refusing coverage because of pre-existing conditions.

'The time has come for universal, affordable health care in America,' he said. And if this package is as good as it seems to be, he may just have tapped into the one thing that most Americans care most about – their health, and their ability to pay for it.

WEDNESDAY, 30 MAY 2007
Took the boys to watch Sussex play Lancashire at cricket. Unfortunately, it rained all day and there was no play.

As we sat in one of the hospitality tents, wet and cold, a familiar figure lumbered miserably into view: Freddie Flintoff. He'd just been told that he needs another ankle operation that will leave him out of action for further months. 'I'm gutted,' he admitted.

His benefit manager, Paul Beck, suggested a race meeting at nearby

Brighton might raise his spirits. Freddie readily agreed, and half an hour later we were all in a sumptuous private box.

'Glass of champagne, Fred?' I asked.

He shook his head. 'Water please, mate.'

'Still off the booze, mate?'

'Yep, this pedalo-itis just won't go away! I haven't had a drink since that night.'

Freddie was charming and patient with the boys all afternoon. He really is as nice as you'd imagine. But he made a fatal error when he tried to steal some of Bertie's crisps in a Lineker-esque style swoop.

'Oi, get off,' snarled Bertie, menacingly.

'Oops, sorry Bertie!' he grovelled.

Bertie eyed him with naked fury in his eyes.

'Say please.'

'Could I have a crisp, please?'

Bertie dug his hand into the bag and produced one, small, solitary crisp. 'There.'

Freddie took it, savoured it, swallowed it and sighed with joy.

'Thank you Bertie.'

'That's all right.'

Peace had been restored.

'You got any tips?' asked the chastened all-rounder.

There was a horse in the next race called Showbusiness. 'Has to be this one,' I said.

Freddie cackled. 'You daft prat.'

But we both had a go at it.

Showbusiness came third from last.

We had another big bet, and lost again.

'I've got just the nag to save our day,' I announced.

'What is it?' asked Freddie.

'Flashing Floozie.'

He grinned, and we flashed yet more cash.

It came second to last.

'Morgan?'

'Yes, Fred?'

'You were supposed to be fucking cheering me up, not making things worse.'

I looked at the next race and saw a horse called Vegas Boys. It had to be an omen, I've only just got back from my first trip there.

'I don't want to hear it...' said Freddie, fingers in his ears. 'I'm going.'

At which point the boys said they wanted to go home, too, so we all left.

Obviously, Vegas Boys won.

THURSDAY, 31 MAY 2007

Andy Coulson has become David Cameron's new spindoctor, which is a bit like discovering that your brother is dating Heather Mills.

Gordon Brown called me this evening to discuss the appointment.

'What do you think?' he growled.

'I think that disgraced ex-tabloid editors are suddenly hot political property and you're missing out...' I replied.

'Are you offering your services as my PR man then?' asked the prime minister elect.

'Not exactly, Gordon. I have rather loftier ambitions given my current global megastar status.'

He scoffed, with unnecessary derision in his voice.

'What did you have in mind then?'

'Well, you'll be needing a new Foreign Secretary, and I'm your man.'

Silence.

'At least I'd stop us invading any more countries like Iraq for a while.'

More silence.

'Piers,' he said eventually.

'Yes Gordon?'

'I'll get back to you...'

TUESDAY, 5 JUNE 2007

Glamour magazine asked me to present an award at their annual party in Berkeley Square tonight, which had two enormous bonuses: 1) I was presenting to Teri Hatcher, arguably the sexiest *Desperate Housewife* in the world, and 2) For this gruelling task, I've been sent a goodie bag containing a new Nokia mobile phone, an Armani watch, a £250 Harvey Nichols spa voucher, a silver necklace, a John Smedley jumper, a Lacoste shirt, a leather belt, a suede travelling bag and a veritable abundance of gloriously expensive candles, aftershaves and totally unnecessary anti-ageing creams.

Seconds after I arrived, a huge eruption of flashbulbs erupted around me signalling the entrance of one Posh Spice. I haven't seen Victoria for several years, but it was like we'd never been apart as she mwah-mwahed me in front of the snappers.

She was wearing the tiniest pair of hotpants I've ever seen, but looked great. I keep reading how's she dying from various eating disorders, but trust me – in the flesh, she radiates health and vitality.

'Nice pins,' I remarked. 'I'd be careful wearing that in LA though, they might arrest you...'

'You cheeky little sod,' she cackled. She's got the mouth of a sewer rat.

I've always liked Victoria though, mainly because she doesn't take herself nearly as seriously as other people take her, and I could tell she was genuinely chuffed to be getting the Woman of the Year award.

'It means a lot to me,' she said. 'It's not like I exactly win loads of awards, now is it!'

We talked about Los Angeles, where we're both headed in a month's time.

'You can take me shopping,' she suggested.

'I'd love to, but I'd get mobbed,' I replied.

She laughed, until she realised I was being deadly serious.

'What's David going to do now he's back in the England team?'

'Commute. I have to all the time, why can't he?'

'Because it will kill him. That 11-hour flight knackers me out for days every time.'

'Yes, but he's a bit fitter than you, Piers...'

'I'm still available if things don't work out between you,' I said.

'How kind, Piers. Unfortunately, we've never been happier.'

'But I'm David with brains,' I persisted.

'No, I'm David with brains,' she retorted.

At which point, I saw Nancy Dell'Olio hurtling towards us at high speed, looking like a garish Christmas tree.

Nancy is delightfully bonkers, but I can't help liking her.

I found my table, and discovered I was sitting near man-eating Kim Cattrall from *Sex and the City*.

'I'm a big fan of your work,' I drooled. 'Are you like Samantha in real life?'

'No,' she replied coldly, then ignored me for the rest of the evening.

Teri Hatcher walked by, and I introduced myself.

'I thought I might maul you onstage if that's OK – just for the publicity.'

'Right,' she replied, with abject indifference. These American sexpots are distinctly hard nuts to crack, I must say.

I had to follow Enrique Iglesias up on stage, which ensured a mass downward turn in the level of screaming.

'Come on,' I begged the audience. 'I may not be Enrique but I'm worth a bit more than that, aren't I?'

To my surprise a few shrieks did then fill the air.

'Thanks, Victoria,' I said. 'We Hollywood stars must stick together.'

Teri arrived onstage with a mischievous grin, kissed me and Jonathan Ross (unfortunately, not in that order) and started her acceptance speech for the unlikely title of Best Writer Of The Year.

Halfway through she stopped, turned to me and said: 'Come on, then, what are you waiting for?' Then bent forward provocatively over the lectern.

I stood paralysed to the spot.

'He promised to maul me onstage,' she told the howling audience. 'But I don't think he's got the courage to do it...'

She was right. I blushed and bottled it.

Afterwards I found her chatting with Enrique backstage.

'Hey mate, hands off my bird.'

He looked bemused, then replied: 'OK, man, sorry,' and shuffled off.

SATURDAY, 9 JUNE 2007

Spent the day in Manchester at the Test Match, and beseeched Kevin Pietersen to entertain me with a big hundred.

'Don't cock it up, mate,' I texted him. 'I've travelled halfway across Britain to see you bat.'

'Shut up, you muppet!' he replied.

Mid-afternoon he was out in utterly ridiculous circumstances when he was hit in the head and his helmet hit the wicket.

'And you call ME a muppet?' I texted him in time for his arrival back in the dressing room.

Britain's Got Talent started airing tonight, and is on for the next nine consecutive nights – or what they call a 'strip' in the TV world.

The stand-out act was an unkempt insurance salesman called Paul Potts who came out with a dodgy suit, crooked teeth and a terrible suit, then sang 'Nessun Dorma' like Pavarotti. Quite amazing.

MONDAY, 11 JUNE 2007

The TV critics have all been having a lot of fun at my expense. I'm at a slight advantage over most 'celebredees' in that I know all these guys personally. Which means if they rip me to pieces, I can reveal where all the coke-snorting, alcoholic, philandering bodies are buried (allegedly). But that would be churlish…for now, anyway. The boys didn't disappoint: the *Star*'s Garry Bushell said: 'Having your performance skills judged by Piers Morgan is like asking Shane McGowan to check out your teeth.'

THURSDAY, 14 JUNE 2007

The first live *Britain's Got Talent* show was tonight, and I knew things were going to be tense when I saw Simon patrolling the corridors silently, chain-smoking and brow furrowed.

'Don't tell me you get nervous too?' I asked him.

'God, yes,' he replied. 'This is where you earn your money.'

Amanda was no better. 'I'm shaking,' she said, and by way of confirmation she grabbed my hand and shoved it to her heaving breast.

The coolest kids on the block were Ant and Dec, who glided around cracking jokes and looking as relaxed as a pair of tortoises in mid-hibernation.

It all passed quickly, and without any real mistakes. And what a buzz!

Ratings got off to a rocky start on Saturday, at just under five million, but they hit the 10 million mark by last night, and it feels like the whole country is watching this week-long event. It's become a mass-market version of the Proms.

Backstage, there was an electrifying atmosphere. It's the nearest thing to being in a rock band that I am ever going to experience, and I love it!

FRIDAY, 15 JUNE 2007

Got an email from Caroline in Los Angeles.

She's having a terrible time fighting her cancer.

'I've been in intensive care with peritonitis for the last week,' she said, 'I've lost a third of my hair, all my eyelashes and my weight's gone down from

125 pounds to 94 pounds. I'm puking all the time, and I feel like shit. But hey, at least the sun's still shining.'

I feel so desperately sorry for her. It all sounds horrific, but I've got to try and keep her spirits up.

'Treat it like you would if you were working on a big story,' I wrote back, 'you're one of the best reporters I've ever worked with, so give it every bit of tenacity, hope, ferocious hard work, dedication, energy and humour you'd use at work.'

SATURDAY, 16 JUNE 2007

Simon had a migraine today, which meant we all got a headache. His mood wasn't helped by news that three members of an act called the Kit Kat Dolls, an exotic group of drag queens from Soho, are being exposed in the papers tomorrow as hookers. Which is the least surprising news I've heard since Boy George admitted he was gay.

Unfortunately, today's papers have already been full of 'BRITAIN'S GOT PERVERTS' headlines about a George Formby impersonator called Richard Bates, who is apparently on the sex offenders list for tickling a 14-year-old boy's feet.

'Well,' I said to Simon. 'We did promise this show would be unpredictable.'

He just grimaced and popped more paracetamol.

SUNDAY, 17 JUNE 2007

The final.

This extraordinary rollercoaster week came to a thrilling end with Paul Potts fighting it out with Connie Talbot, the six-year-old singer with the world's cutest smile. I hoped Paul would win. The show's credibility dictates that it needs to be won by genuine potential superstars, not sweet little girls whose lips tremble when they warble 'Somewhere Over The Rainbow'.

But in a show like this, you are at the mercy of the public and their telephone votes.

Thirty seconds before the result was announced, a producer ran over to tell Simon who had won.

He shook his head in shock, leant over to me and Amanda, and said: 'Connie, by a landslide...'

We gasped out loud.

'NO!'

'Yes.'

Then we heard Ant and Dec preparing to reveal this fact to Britain, and adopted our best fake grins again.

'And the winner of *Britain's Got Talent* is…PAUL POTTS!'

Amanda and I turned straight to Simon, who winked and burst out laughing.

He'd conned us again.

I was thrilled for Paul.

He sums up the essence of the show so well – an ordinary guy doing an ordinary job, but with an extraordinary talent.

Later, I was jumped on air during the ITV2 follow-up show by my 'biggest fan' (in every sense…), called Jodie – who, to the delight of Simon, Amanda and Ant and Dec, read a poem to me live on air:

With all my heart I love you, Piers,
I've been a fan of yours for years,
I've heard Mr Morgan,
That the size of your organ,
Can reduce a young girl to tears.

Suddenly Mr Cowell didn't seem quite so jubilant.

Simon threw a small party at the Dorchester afterwards, where we cracked open the champagne and reflected on a quite amazing week.

'That was the best show I've ever worked on,' he said.

TUESDAY, 19 JUNE 2007

Lord Levy had his leaving party tonight at Lancaster House. There can't have been more than 80 people there, sipping champagne and tiny canapés in one of the grand state rooms.

Almost everywhere I looked I saw someone who doesn't like me – Geoff Hoon, Margaret Beckett, David Blunkett, Peter Hain.

I sought refuge at the bar, and accidentally whacked someone in the back.

'Sorry,' I said.

Then turned to see Tony Blair.

I hadn't spoken to him since I left the *Mirror* three years ago.

'God....' I stumbled. 'I mean, hello Tony.'

To my surprise he shook my hand and smiled.

'Hello, Piers, how are you?'

It was a surreal moment. Just the two of us, standing away from the throng, the ex-editor and the soon to be ex-PM.

'I'm fine,' I replied. 'How are you, more to the point? Demob happy?'

He grimaced slightly.

'I don't know about that. It is all a little strange.'

I know that feeling.

We chatted for a few minutes.

'So you're big in America now,' he said at one point, chuckling at the absurdity of what he was saying.

'Not as big as you – you should come and hang out with me in Hollywood. They love you there.'

Blair laughed, wearily.

He looked tired, and worn down. Such a contrast from the vibrant young man I'd laughed and joked with on his first day in office.

His tribute was kind and generous to Levy, a man to whom he owes a lot. It was also rather sad. One of the last speeches he would ever make as prime minister, to a small coterie of loyalists and favoured media.

At the end, we all applauded politely – as you might to someone like Colin Montgomerie when he retires from golf. He would have got a standing ovation if only he'd won a bloody major.

And then, after a few reciprocal words from Levy, Blair was gone.

WEDNESDAY, 20 JUNE 2007

Met Boris Becker at a Ralph Lauren party tonight, and he was everything I thought he would be – tall, imposing and utterly charming.

'So, come on then, Boris,' I said. 'Which female tennis stars did you fancy the most?'

'Oh God,' he sighed, 'there were so many, I don't think I can name any in particular.'

'Force yourself.'

'OK, OK, well, Gabby Sabatini was beautiful. And I always liked Steffi Graf too. Very sexy.'

I told him that he was my grandmother's pin-up, and he smiled.

'Tell her that I am very flattered.'

I relayed this information to Grande the moment I left the party.

'And you tell Boris,' she replied, 'that the next time he's short of company in a broom cupboard he should give me a call...'

I am torn between extreme consternation and sneaking admiration at Grande's response.

SATURDAY, 23 JUNE 2007

Two months ago Thierry Henry assured me that he was 'a Gooner for life'. He even gave me one of his shirts signed to that effect.

I subsequently told all my fellow Arsenal fans to relax about the endless transfer gossip surrounding our brilliant captain. 'He wouldn't lie to me,' I insisted. 'He's going nowhere.'

Today, Henry signed for Barcelona. The lying little bastard.

SUNDAY, 24 JUNE 2007

The Sunday papers are full of stuff on Harriet Harman, who has been made Deputy Leader of the Labour Party, and is thus now Britain's most powerful woman.

'Not exactly Margaret Thatcher, is she?' said Celia, scathingly.

At 7 p.m. this evening, we were standing in a rain-battered marquee in the grounds of the Goring Hotel, sipping champagne and pondering how awful garden parties are when the heavens open.

Then, by a weird coincidence, my eyes alighted on a familiar tousled mop. It was Lady Thatcher.

I bounded over to my schoolhood heroine, with almost indecent haste.

'Lady Thatcher, how nice to see you again,' I said. 'We last met at the Ivy.'

She smiled her acknowledgement. Well, I think it was a smile. May have been a grimace, come to think of it.

'Anyway, I just had to ask you something of vital importance.'

'Very well,' she replied. 'What is it?'

'I wondered what you thought of Harriet Harman now running the country?'

There was a long pause, as she pondered the enormity of the question.

Then she leant forward and responded with slow, emphatic staccato: 'Stuff. And. Nonsense.'

I burst out laughing, just as I had this morning.

'Will that do?' she added.

'It will, Lady Thatcher, thank you.'

She nodded, and strode away. Marbles, and stature, most definitely intact.

WEDNESDAY, 27 JUNE 2007

Tony Blair finally resigned today. And as he left Downing Street with his family, Cherie shrieked, 'We won't miss you!' at photographers as they drove off.

And in that moment, I realised how desperately I would miss Blair after all – not Tony, but his wife.

Cherie has been quite wonderfully awful. A rude, grasping, self-deluded Scouse banshee prone to relentless hypocrisy, shocking manners and High Office greed on a scale rarely seen since Imelda Marcos went shoe-shopping.

Sarah Brown, by contrast, is almost shamefully nice and normal. It's just not going to be the same.

As for Tony, he made a good farewell speech in the Commons, touching all the emotional nerves you'd expect from a great orator. 'That's it, The End,' he said at the finish. And it all felt strangely poignant.

I don't think Blair's been a bad prime minister, if you take the catastrophe of Iraq out of the equation. But he's been a disappointing one.

I remember standing ten feet away from him, as he made his 5 a.m. election victory speech in 1997, and thinking this man was going to transform Britain in a truly dramatic, positive way.

And he didn't. Simple as that, really.

'Watch it, David, she's getting closer...' Sharon Osbourne
slides towards The Hoff on Jay Leno's chat show in America,
and seconds later was trying to lick him to death.

© REX FEATURES

'There's a gullible side to the American people. They can be easily misled. Religion is the best device used to mislead them.' MICHAEL MOORE

THURSDAY, 28 JUNE 2007

Gordon Brown has officially become prime minister. And I am so pleased for him, and for Sarah. At the same time, it does feel a bit odd seeing two old friends suddenly standing there outside the famous black door. Still, at least I should get back on the No. 10 guestlist again.

Down to Croydon for my fourth *Question Time* appearance in two years, where the other guests were Michael Howard, Ming Campbell and Yvette Cooper.

Howard wasn't happy. 'I vowed never to do this programme again once I stopped being leader,' he said. 'But they persuaded me to do this because it was going to have just heavyweights on it…'

He peered derisively at me.

'Erm…and instead you've got me?' I suggested.

'Yes,' he replied, witheringly, 'that appears to be the case.'

It was the implication that *he* is still a heavyweight that amused me as much as his assessment of my own undeniably lightweight credentials.

We walked out one by one as usual, and I was booed as usual. But not, to my joy, as loudly as Howard. I then amused myself by taunting him throughout the show.

He raced off afterwards, declining to stay for the customary dinner.

But I enjoyed a thoroughly entertaining meal with the others, hosted by David Dimbleby.

At 11 p.m., I got up to leave saying (truthfully) that I had a flight to catch.

'Where to?' asked a production assistant.

'Ibiza,' I replied.

Cue numerous raised eyebrows indicating the phrase, 'middle-aged man in ecstasy, all-night club and illicit sex crisis'.

'Yep, and I'm taking Ming and David with me, come on, lads – let's go raving…'

I swear that Ming was up for it. And who can blame him? Has to be more fun than leading the Liberal Democrats.

FRIDAY, 29 JUNE 2007

I've been invited to take part in the next series of *Dancing On Ice*.

'I think not,' said Celia, emphatically. Hardly surprising really, given that she has spent the last six months watching me careering chaotically across ice rinks all over London.

SATURDAY, 30 JUNE 2007

Spoke to Caroline in Los Angeles, and she said the American media have barely mentioned the change in Britain's prime minister. It merited a few paragraphs in the *LA Times*, but she hadn't seen it once in a TV news report, despite Blair being one of the most popular Brits ever in America.

It just proves, once again, that they are an incredibly insular country, with little or no interest in what goes on abroad.

I've watched the NBC nightly news bulletins a couple of times this week on Sky, and hardly seen a single story covered from outside America. Extraordinary.

SUNDAY, 1 JULY 2007

An email arrived as I sunned my pasty, over-worked, underpaid face on an Ibizan clifftop: 'P. Diddy would like to have dinner with you tomorrow night.'

How odd. We've never met, and I very much doubt Mr Diddy has ever woken up thinking: 'I must have dinner with that cool dude Piers Morgan.'

Luckily, we fly back this evening.

MONDAY, 2 JULY 2007

Celia and I arrived at 50 St James, a flash club in Piccadilly, for the dinner, not knowing what on earth to expect.

The answer was a beautifully prepared private dining room for no more than 30 guests, already including Cat Deeley, Natasha Bedingfield, designer Kelley Hoppen and the Sugababes.

I knew it was going to be a weird night when I strolled to the bar and found Will Young choking on a pistachio nut.

The music lover in me toyed with letting him die on the spot.

But as he began to turn slightly blue and gesticulate for help, the kindly human in me kicked in and I positioned myself behind Mr Young and prepared for a firm Heimlicker clamp on his lower abdominal area. (Not a position I ever thought I'd find myself in...)

Fortunately, for both of us, the nut suddenly spewed out and the crisis was averted.

A flurry of flashblubs indicated our host had arrived, and I expected to see a 100-strong posse charge in with him – armed with guns, drugs, hookers and all the other things mean rappers are supposed to like.

But he was alone, smart-suited and shy.

'Hi, Diddy,' I said. 'I'm Piers.'

'Hey man,' he replied in a soft voice, 'thanks for coming to my party. I hope you have a nice time.'

Behind him was his rap mate Pharrell Williams.

'Pharrell, we've met before,' I announced.

'Really? When?'

'Last summer, in an elevator at the Beverly Wilshire hotel in Los Angeles. We were both descending from the 11th floor.'

He looked completely bemused.

'Look, mate,' I whispered, 'can you just pretend you remember me, it would be good for my image at this party.'

Pharrell reacted magnificently, slapping me on the shoulder and shouting loudly: 'Hey man, I remember YOU. How you doing brother?'

He'd played the Diana concert the day before, so I asked if he enjoyed it.

'It was OK. Could have been edgier...'

'Yes,' I replied. 'Can't be easy for you following Donny Osmond.'

He raised his eyebrow, murderously.

Pharrell and I then discussed world affairs for half an hour, and he was surprisingly articulate and informed.

'Iraq has made everyone hate America,' he said. 'It reminds me of Rome when it just got too big, too powerful and started treating everyone else like it owned them. And we all know what happened to Rome.'

'What's the answer?'

'I don't know if there is one. I think we're fucked.'

'What about Obama becoming president, wouldn't that help?'

'It may be too soon for him. I don't know if America is ready for a man with his name and skin colour. Hillary may be the best bet.'

I am fascinated that even a leading black American star like Pharrell thinks it is too early for Obama. And not because he's not up to the job, but purely because of his skin colour.

Lewis Hamilton and his dad appeared at my side, so I said hello. In many ways, he is the Obama of British sport – a dashing young black man heading to the top of a business that has always been dominated by white men.

First impressions were impressive.

Lewis has an absolutely bonecrushing handshake, and stares you straight in the eye when he talks with a focus and confidence that is quite extraordinary for a man of 22.

'How are you dealing with all the mayhem?' I asked.

'It's fine, no problem,' he grinned. 'I'm enjoying it.'

'I've got to ask, do you do much public road driving now?'

'Yeah, all the time.'

'And do you ever exceed the speed limit?'

He smiled. 'Hmmmm…'

Then his dad interrupted.

'I think you'll find that Lewis always drives within the law,' said Mr Hamilton senior firmly.

Lewis giggled: 'Yes, that's what I was going to say.'

'I only asked because I'm currently banned for speeding, and it just seems cruelly unfair that you've got a clean licence.'

Lewis winked. 'You're obviously not very good at driving are you…'

'No,' I winked back. 'I'm obviously just not as good as you are at not getting caught.'

We were called to dinner, and served with sumptuous wine and food over candlelit tables. It was one of the nicest, most civilised meals I've had in years.

Diddy came over to our table.

'Everything OK?' he asked, solicitously.

'No, it's terrible,' I replied.

He looked mortified.

'Terrible?'

'Yes, terrible. My guest has no water, Diddy.'

I expected to at least be smacked in the face for my impertinence.

But he just said, 'Leave it to me,' and returned a minute later with the water.

'There's a good aura at this table,' he declared.

'Can you say that again, but specifically about me, Diddy,' I replied.

'Why?'

'I just want to be able to tell everyone tomorrow that P. Diddy told a table of dinner guests that I had a good aura.'

He nodded. 'OK. Piers, you have a good aura about you.'

When the time came to leave, I found Diddy deep in discussion with Lewis.

'You're a Gooner, aren't you?' I asked him, recalling that he'd once said he was an Arsenal fan.

'What's a Gooner?' Diddy replied, which said everything I needed to know.

Then Lewis piped up: 'I'm a massive Gooner.' And so – judging by his up-to-date analysis of our fluctuating season – he was raising my enthusiasm for him even higher.

We talked Arsenal for a few minutes, then he asked: 'Want to come to Silverstone?'

I would think that Lewis Hamilton inviting you to go as his personal guest to the British Grand Prix is about as hot as sports tickets get at the moment.

But I had to decline.

'Sorry mate, I'll be in Hollywood. Just make sure you kill Alonso.'

'Don't worry,' he chuckled, 'I will.'

I left without ever discovering quite why I'd been invited.

THURSDAY, 5 JULY 2007

Barack Obama pulled in an astonishing $31 million in the last three months for his campaign to be the Democrat nominee. And Hillary Clinton says it's because he is streets ahead in the 'viral marketing' game.

What is absolutely fascinating is how Obama and his campaign team are going about securing money and potential voters. Because they're doing much of it online, hooking people in through social networking websites like MySpace and Facebook. He raised more than $10 million this way in the last quarter, of which 90 per cent was in increments of $100 or less. And that's why he has got financial support so far from a staggering 258,000 different people. It's ground-breaking, and brilliant. Because each of those people now feels that they have an ownership in Obama, creating a huge fan base that is very likely to not only vote for him but encourage their friends and family to do so, too.

MONDAY, 9 JULY 2007

I've flown to Los Angeles for just two days to film one episode of *America's Got Talent*.

I don't care how fit David Beckham is, commuting from LA to the UK is a killer – constant 11-hour flights with an eight-hour time difference reduce you to a semi-permanent psychedelic daze.

It won't affect his football in America, because the standard is pitiful here. But it will, I'm certain, affect his ability to play at the highest level for England.

The only upside, as I discovered today, is that sometimes you wake up in a first-class cabin and find yourself lying next to Cate Blanchett. A woman who, I can confirm, looks just as good without make-up as she does on screen caked to the eyeballs.

As for *America's Got Talent*, the acts are slowly beginning to do their research on me. One guy, on getting buzzed out, sneered back with inarguable logic: 'You've been fired from every job you've ever had, Piers, what do *you* know about talent?'

Had dinner tonight with John Ferriter.

'How did that idiot George Bush ever get re-elected?' I asked.

'You know, it's funny, I met him a few months after his inauguration, in the summer of 2005, at a meet-and-greet in Bel Air. I was with Ryan Seacrest, and we spent ten minutes alone with the President and the First Lady. Now I never voted for him, I voted for Gore because I liked him, and then Kerry because I wanted change. But I'll say this about Bush – he was one of the nicest people I've met in my entire life.'

'Really?'

'Really. He was so personable and charismatic. He'd done his research and asked personal questions, and held your eye when he did it, making us feel like we were important to him. We had a proper conversation for about ten minutes, and both me and Ryan came away thinking that he was just an amazing guy.'

'But he's done so much damage to America's reputation, hasn't he?'

'Yes, he has. There's no question of that. I travel a lot in Europe and always used to get a really friendly reaction from people when I said I was American. Now, it's very different. There's a lot of hostility, try getting a waiter in Paris to serve you if you have an American accent. And it's happened fast, because in 2001, after 9/11, all I got from Europeans was sympathy and compassion.'

'Is it just because of Iraq?'

'I don't think so, no. I think Iraq was the culmination of a lot of things. I think America got arrogant, and thought it always knew best, and that if we didn't get out there and maintain our position as the world's policeman then the world would do terrible things. We felt increasingly superior, and then 9/11 happened and suddenly we felt vulnerable, and we retreated into ourselves, and stopped being the welcoming melting pot we'd always been before. And Iraq just made us look like bullies.'

'Do the public still support the war?'

'Increasingly not, because they think Bush either made some futile attempt to avenge his father with Saddam, or made a massive miscalculation and went after the wrong guy. But they still support the troops. I'm a fairly typical American on this – my brother is a general, my nieces and nephews are in the army, and as it has gone on, so I've got more concerned for their safety. I wish we weren't at war, but I support the people who have to fight it for us.'

'What does America need now to repair all the damage caused by Bush and his foreign policy?'

'It needs a good press agent.'

Ferriter would be perfect for the job – he's a workaholic who exudes charm and vitality. I've nicknamed him 'The Ferret' because according to my research, ferrets are 'intelligent, lively, youthful, playful carnivores that adjust their sleeping schedule to yours so they are eager and ready to play when you are. They're also quite ferocious when they need to be, with a nasty nip if challenged.'

I think he quite likes it – all Hollywood agents hanker for a mafia-style enforcer moniker.

Tonight, General David Petraeus gave a lengthy interview to the BBC's John Simpson in which he again impressed with his frankness, and rhetorical restraint.

'We are in the first full month of operations following the surge in forces, and it is achieving progress and having some effect on the ground,' he said. 'In Baghdad, for example, June was the lowest month for sectarian deaths in a year.'

TUESDAY, 10 JULY 2007
I checked my own entries in Alastair Campbell's diaries this morning, and was bitterly disappointed to discover that there were only eight of them – and even worse, they were all accurate. It amused me to see him confirm that Cherie Blair deliberately leaked the story of her pregnancy to the *Sun* after hearing we had the scoop at the *Mirror*. Just to annoy us.

And people wonder why I loathe the woman.

WEDNESDAY, 11 JULY 2007
I have acquired many great celebrity souvenirs in my time – a signed packet of Marlboro Lights that nearly blinded David Bowie during a Brixton concert, Pete Sampras's grass-stained tennis shoes (he stayed at a mate's house in Wimbledon), Camilla Parker Bowles' watercolour painting of a rhinoceros and a quite spectacularly hideous yellow tie emblazoned with spiders that Gordon Brown once wore on Budget Day. But today I think I topped the lot when I interviewed *Coronation Street* legend Julie 'Bet Lynch' Goodyear for BBC1, and she solemnly presented me at the end with her fake eyelashes, with the immortal words: 'There you go, pet.'

THURSDAY, 12 JULY 2007
The Beckhams arrived in Hollywood today, to scenes of complete pandemonium.

There were hundreds of TV crews and photographers waiting for them at the airport, and even screaming fans too.

If their game plan is to become big stars in America, then this is a bloody good start.

The Ferret rang me. 'Nobody cares about the soccer, but they're going to care about the Beckhams.'

FRIDAY, 13 JULY 2007

BBC1 Controller Peter Fincham is in big trouble after showing journalists video footage of a forthcoming documentary on the Queen which he claimed showed her having a 'hissy fit' towards celebrity photographer Annie Leibovitz.

From what I can make out, the Queen does have a hissy fit, just not when Fincham said she does. A minor error, and not his fault because it was the production company RDF who cocked up, but nothing involving the Queen is ever minor – and everyone's now calling for his head.

I sent him an email:

Dear Peter,

Don't resign.

This was a bloody awful cock-up, but that is what it is.

Having dropped many a clanger in my time, some involving the Royals, I know how febrile the atmosphere can get. And it is totally exasperating when it's not even your fault to start with. But you've done everything you could to rectify the damage, nobody has died, and the storm will subside in 24 hours. (Well, unless the BBC1 News run a fake video of Prince Philip snogging Posh Spice.)

So keep your chin up, your head calm, and remember that Friday is always a great day for things like this to just fizzle out. By Monday you may even be ready to laugh about it.

Kind regards, Piers

PS: Of course, if you do lose your job, then the good news is that I'd like to interview you for the next series of You Can't Fire Me, I'm Famous. Which I know will be of massive solace to you...

'Thanks, Piers,' he replied. 'If I do have to resign I dare say my successor will cancel You Can't Fire Me, so it's in both our interests for me to hang on!'

SATURDAY, 14 JULY 2007

Celia and I sat outside a Twickenham bar for half an hour tonight, during which time three separate groups of women walked past, clocked me and returned to say: 'You're nowhere near as fat in real life, are you?'

Celia listened to all this in dignified silence, and then calmly cancelled my doughnut order.

MONDAY, 16 JULY 2007

Boris Johnson is to stand for London Mayor.

In a suitably chaotic press conference, he said: 'I intend to put a smile back on London's face.'

Which is, undeniably, true. The only question is how, exactly?

WEDNESDAY, 18 JULY 2007

Most men would probably imagine that being incarcerated with Miss Cheryl Cole (formerly Tweedy) for an hour in a dimly lit restaurant might be a rather pleasurable experience.

And I'd readily agree.

Having worked with her on *Comic Relief: The Apprentice*, I can safely say she is one of the prettiest, and wittiest, pop stars I've met.

Unfortunately, though, she is married to one Ashley Cole, the biggest traitor in the history of professional sport. Not that we Arsenal fans are bitter or anything.

So I arrived for our *GQ* interview in an East London bar this afternoon feeling a mixture of excitement and bitter revulsion, depending on whether my mind focused on delightful Cheryl or her despicable husband.

As we sat down, I was nearly blinded by her enormous diamond wedding ring.

'That's obscene,' I laughed.

'Nice, isn't it…'

'Well, yes, if you like great hulking slabs of jewel-encrusted bling then I suppose it is.'

'I just like the fact that it's heart-shaped.'

'Very touching.'

'Don't start.'

'You like big rocks then?'

'I do, the bigger the better for me, and a wedding ring is special. It was my anniversary two days ago.'

'How's it going?'

'Really well, thank you.'

'How disappointing. I keep reading that things aren't going that well.'

'I know. But you can't believe what you read in the press, Piers. You should know that.'

'Apart from the fact that you chose Ashley Cole as your husband, my main problem with your marriage was that you sold it to a magazine for one million pounds. Do you have any right to complain if people now write intrusive stuff about your private life?'

'No, definitely not. But I guess I was so naïve early on about this fame game. I thought if you give the media a little bit then they won't delve as much, or try and ruin you as much. You can say I sold my soul by selling my wedding…'

'I didn't say that, you just did…'

'You implied it. I just wasn't prepared to stand there on my wedding day and pose for pictures for the same little paparazzi shits who take photos of my knickers and private parts when I get out of a car. I wanted to control it, and do it my way, and let my fans see what I want them to see.'

'Yes, I can understand that. But it's the fact you took one million pounds to do it that bothers me.'

'We didn't make money from the day, we didn't earn one million pounds, we just didn't pay for very many things…'

'Well, it's the same thing, isn't it? And your day looked very extravagant…'

'It was very extravagant…I had the wedding of my dreams.'

'That cost one million pounds, right?'

'I don't discuss things like that.'

'Why, because it's a bit tacky to talk about it?'

'Yeah….is there any sugar for this tea? I'm suddenly getting a rather bitter taste in my mouth.'

'I would never sell something as private as a wedding. I'd just invite all the press down to the church and let them have their pictures for free.'

'Why should I let some little shit who's sold pictures of my bum for loads of money make another packet from my wedding day, the most personal day of my life?'

'Yes, but if you're prepared to profit from your most personal day ever, then you have no right to expect privacy from these "shits", do you?'

'I have not profited.'

'You did, you got a free million-pound wedding out of it. Most people pay for their weddings, Cheryl.'

'I suppose…'

'Right, let's turn to Ashley. What's it like being married to Judas Iscariot's half-brother?'

(Laughs.) 'Oh, you're pulling them out today, aren't you… Look, I can understand why you Arsenal fans feel the way you do about Ashley.'

'An apology wouldn't go amiss on behalf of the Cole family.'

'No, I'm not prepared to make an apology for him because I don't think he's completely to blame for what happened. It wasn't about the money; it was about the principle. If Simon Cowell promised you a new deal for the next series of *Britain's Got Talent*, and told you what the amount was going to be, and you went away happy with that, and then you start work and he sidles up to you and says: "You know that little deal we made, well I'm going to cut five grand off it." Then you would be annoyed.'

'Did you ever imagine when you were young Cheryl Tweedy growing up on a council estate in Newcastle that you would one day be married to someone who, when they heard they were only going to be paid £55,000 a week, nearly crashed his car in fury and screamed at his agent, "THEY'RE TAKING THE FUCKING PISS!"?'

'That does sound ludicrous, I totally agree.'

Pause.

'I'm going to tell you something now that Ashley has always told me not to say. But sod it, people should know the truth. I don't care. He was offered a hell of a lot of money to go to a foreign team.'

'Barcelona?'

'I'm not saying.' (Shakes her head.)

'Real Madrid?'

(Smiles.)

'Of course. To go and play with his mate, Becks.'

'But it would have meant that I would have had to give up my career, which I wasn't prepared to do. I've worked just as hard as he has to get where I am, and we spoke about it at length. Either I would have had to move out there with him and commute, or give up my career at a time when we're finally being accepted as a band and it's almost cool to like Girls Aloud. So there was a lot of conversation about it, and a lot of tears. And I almost begged Ashley to sign for Chelsea. Not really knowing what that would mean. I know a bit about football, growing up in Newcastle, and I know it would be difficult for a player to go from Newcastle to Sunderland, for instance. But I didn't realise the extent to which moving from Arsenal to Chelsea would cause so much hurt between the two of us, and to Arsenal fans. And for that I do apologise.'

'What do you mean "between the two of us"?'

'Because I stopped him living his dream playing out there for that team. And he wouldn't have got half as much shit if he had gone there rather than Chelsea. And I blame myself for a lot of that.'

'So you basically caused Ashley to be the most hated man in football?'

'Maybe. He has always told me never to talk about this, but I think people should know. For him to give up his dream, for me, was a big deal.'

'Do you wish he had gone to Real Madrid now?'

'For the hurt it has caused him and his family, yes. For me and my career – selfish reasons, I know – then no. But it would have been equally selfish for him to go there, so there had to be some sort of compromise. Why should all my dreams and aspirations be shattered for the sake of his career? I wasn't prepared to give up everything I had worked so hard for just so Ashley could realise his dream.'

'So you put your own happiness before your husband's?'

'No, there was a compromise there. I'd have been miserable out there so he moved to Chelsea where we could both be happier than if he had stayed at Arsenal or gone to Madrid.'

'Was he offered more money to go to Madrid than Chelsea?'

'A lot more.'

'So you not only made him the most reviled man in football, you also cost him a load of money. Nice work, Mrs Cole.'

'But he loves me and I love him…and that's what love is about…'

'What? Making your husband reviled?'

'Well, what about me being miserable? There wasn't just one person in this. We're a unit.'

'How bad was the backlash when Ashley made his move?'

'We knew it was coming. But it was still very hard. A few people could have come out and said more than they did to help him. Looking back, with all the different advice he was getting and me saying don't go abroad, it must have been fucking hard for him. He went through hell, his eyes were dead until recently.'

'It affected him that much?'

'Yes. I had to live with it.'

'Did it cause problems with your marriage?'

'It made things difficult. I've been through a shit horrible relationship before, so I refuse to argue with Ashley. I disagree with him, that's human nature, but I won't get into an abusive relationship again. So there was a lot of disagreement, and there were a lot of tears being shed, but he made that decision for me and I love him for that. But I totally accept from your point of view and other Arsenal fans that the way it was all reported made him out to be the villain. I don't know what we can do about that to make things better.'

'A public flogging?'

'What do you mean by that?'

'I mean we take Ashley to the Emirates Stadium on a Saturday afternoon and we publicly flog him in front of all the Arsenal fans. That might help. I know when I put him in the stocks for the Comic Relief *Apprentice* show, it made me feel miles better.'

'It made me feel better sticking you in the stocks too...'

'Did you never worry about becoming a footballer's wife, with all the WAGs stigma that entails?'

'I don't mind the WAGs themselves, they are always very nice to me, but I hate the way they are portrayed in the media. As women with nannies, chefs, all the latest handbags, everything they could ever dream of, but who have never had to work for any of it. Now I have never been the kind of girl who has to have the latest Chloé handbag. And I never will be. If I see a nice bag for 30 pounds, I will get it.'

'Yes, but hang on a second, what about that rock on your finger? What's that worth?'

'That's worth Ashley's heart.'

'Hmmmm...not much then.'

'Ha ha. It's white gold and yellow diamond, and it's worth a lot of money, yes. But it is a once-in-a-lifetime wedding ring. And anyway, I am absolutely sick to death of feeling guilty about stuff like this. I work long hours, why shouldn't I spend my money how the hell I like? Ashley trains for three hours a day, I work a lot harder than that. And if I can afford the nice things in life then why can't I have them? I am sick of feeling guilty about it, sick! I liked the ring, we could afford it, so we bought it – big fucking deal.'

'There speaks a WAG if ever I heard one...'

'Piss off. I'm nothing like the kind of women I'm talking about. The kind who make a beeline for my husband even when I'm standing there with him. The ones who do kiss and tells for loads of money. It's disgusting and degrading to women. I am all for traditional old-fashioned ways. If a woman wants to stay at home with three kids and do all the washing and ironing and cooking and stuff like that then that's their right. I just want more than that...'

'Will you be married to him for life?'

'Yes, I wouldn't have said my vows otherwise.'

'I only ask because I interviewed Thierry Henry two months ago and he said he'd never leave Arsenal or his wife, and now he's left both of them.'

'You never know what's going on behind closed doors. But I know what it's like to be in a rock-bottom relationship – I was with a heroin addict for two years...that is rock bottom.'

'And then you married Ashley Cole...'

'And then I married Ashley Cole.'

'Do you trust him to be faithful?'

'I've been cheated on in the past, but I do not believe Ashley would ever do that to me.'

'What would you do if he did?'

'I'd leave him. I wouldn't argue, or try and make it work – I'd just go. For better or worse my arse, I'd be out of there.'

'Are you a good wife?'

'I like to think so. Ashley says I am. I don't know what a good wife involves.'

'Jerry Hall said it involved being a "maid in the living room, a cook in the kitchen and a whore in bed".'

(Gasps, loudly.) 'Oh my God. Fucking hell.'

'Any of them?'

'I'm a maid in the bedroom...'

'Really?'

'No, don't put that...'

'Are you good in bed?'

'I don't talk about stuff like that.'

'Why not?'

'Because I'm a lady.'

'Do you ever get any complaints?'

'Never. Funnily enough.' (Laughs.)

'Speaking as an Arsenal fan it would be quite comforting to think that Ashley is crap in bed.'

'I'm not talking about this, this is awful.'

'What do you think your public image is?'

'That I'm an absolute bitch who slags everyone off all the time. But I'm just a Geordie lass who was brought up to stick up for myself or I'd get picked on and bullied. I learned early to defend myself.'

'Have you ever taken drugs?'

'I've seen what drugs do to people. I went out with a heroin addict, my little brother got into drugs, I've lost friends to drugs. To see a family go through the shit that comes with a drug like heroin is just...'

At this point, Cheryl suddenly started crying, and held her head in her hands for over 30 seconds without speaking.

'I'm sorry, it just broke my heart to see friends and family going through drugs. It put me off for life. I saw people change overnight. I can't stand it when the papers print photos of people like Pete Doherty because it glorifies everything I hate – being a smackhead. Heroin is devil's dust, it ruins lives and families, and everything it touches. I went out with a smackhead and they tell so many lies. You just convince yourself they are going to change, you're blinded by love. And yet the man you love is gouged out and monging in bed all day. It's horrible, and so destructive for everyone around them.'

'You're not such a bitch after all, are you?'

'I don't think so, and Ashley doesn't think so...'

Cheryl kissed me goodbye, and left with tears still streaming down her face.

And I left thinking that Ashley Cole can't be that bad if someone as beautiful, warm, funny and smart as Cheryl loves him.

THURSDAY, 19 JULY 2007

At 4 p.m. this afternoon, after a lengthy BBC1 interview, Donny Osmond was sitting on my knee, in tears, singing 'Puppy Love', while staring deep into my eyes.

And yes, I did feel slightly uncomfortable.

Tonight, the Dow Jones Industrial Average closed over 14,000 for the first time ever, and people are beginning to wonder aloud whether this huge stocks and shares bubble is ever going to burst. History says it has to, that financial booms are cyclical.

But there seems no sign of it at the moment, and everyone's filling their boots.

SUNDAY, 22 JULY 2007

Back to LA. I arrived on the set of *America's Got Talent* and got chatting backstage to Jerry Springer and The Hoff.

'I met Muhammad Ali recently,' said Jerry. 'And it was extraordinary. His wife told me that he loves my show and watches it all the time, and then introduced us. It was one of the most surreal and wonderful moments of my life. To think of Muhammad Ali watching *The Jerry Springer Show* – too crazy for words!'

The Hoff nodded. 'When I met him he said I was pretty, but he was prettier.'

I found it hard to believe that Muhammad Ali watches the *Springer Show* all the time, but didn't say anything.

After the recording, Jerry and I retired to Mr Chow's for dinner. Springer really is a fascinating guy – born inside East Finchley tube station during the Second World War, the son of Jewish refugees from the Nazis, in his twenties he was a presidential campaign aide to Bobby Kennedy ('The greatest politician I ever met, he knew instinctively what needed to be done.'), got appointed Mayor of Cincinnati aged 30, then became a serious news anchorman for 10 years, before stumbling almost by accident into the signature human car-crash show that's now delighted Americans for 17 years, and which he still gleefully calls 'the worst TV programme in the world'.

He barely drinks, has never taken drugs and has been happily married for 34 years. 'I'm the luckiest guy I know,' he told me. 'I've got absolutely no talent but have had a fabulous career and a family I love.'

Jerry's fiercely smart, warm, funny and passionate about life, politics and TV – in that order.

If he ever stood for president he is so popular that he could probably win. And you know what? Hearing him superbly dissect the current American political scene over platefuls of Peking duck, I think that's exactly what he might one day actually do.

'The thing that makes America unique,' he said, 'is that it was founded on an idea. And that idea was that everyone gets the same shot, whatever their religion, colour, sex, birthplace, parentage, anything. That's why I love this show that we do, because anyone can enter and they all get a shot. It's the American dream at its purest.'

'Do you think America can get itself out of the current image problem it has around the world?'

'Yes. America has a built-in self-correcting device that kicks in when things are tough, and we are straying in the wrong direction. We saw that after 9/11, and we will see it again in this election. We need to work with other nations on peace, poverty, climate change, or the economy. Not against them, acting as a big bully.'

'Who do you think will win?'

'I think Hillary should win, because I think she is a brilliant woman. But I wouldn't mind if Obama won either, because an African-American winning the presidency would prove once again that anything is possible here, and that there is hope amid all this current despair.'

We strolled back to the Beverly Wilshire, and as we reached the valet parking area a huge stretch limousine pulled up – out of which emerged Muhammad and Lonnie Ali. Jerry and I looked at each other and he winked.

'Jerry, how nice to see you again,' said Lonnie. 'He's still watching the show!'

She turned to her husband: 'Hey, it's Jerry Springer!'

I will never doubt Jerry's word again about anything.

Ali smiled and stretched out his giant paw to greet him.

Jerry then endeared himself to me for life by saying: 'Muhammad Ali, meet Piers Morgan.'

I shook Ali's hand, mine trembling even more than his.

At which point Mrs Ali exclaimed: 'Oh, I know you, you're in *America's Got Talent* with Jerry! We watch that, too!'

MONDAY, 23 JULY 2007

Another day, another collision with a superstar in my LA hotel foyer. This time it was a glammed-up Demi Moore, 44, holding hands with a long-haired pimply yeti who looked barely out of his school shorts.

It was, a bellman informed me, her toyboy husband Ashton Kutcher, 29.

I'm all for the modern older woman exerting her right to behave exactly how men have behaved for centuries in taking a younger member of the opposite sex as her lover. But as a long-time fan of Ms Moore (particularly during her bald *GI Jane* phase) I'd like to exert my own right to say that they make an absolutely absurd-looking couple.

Tonight, news broke back in Britain that Lord Levy has been cleared over the cash-for-honours scandal. I'm thrilled for him.

TUESDAY, 24 JULY 2007

The boys have come out for ten days, and tonight we watched *America's Got Talent* together when I got back from filming a live semi-final. The beauty of LA is that it's three hours behind the East Coast, so you can watch all your own 'live' shows three hours after you filmed them...

The two-hour programme was interrupted every five or six minutes with adverts – there must have 100 different commercials and promos in total. Quite extraordinary.

As was the nature of many of them.

Because Americans are so health-obsessed, one in three ads seems to be about bodily issues – from diarrhoea tablets and haemorrhoid creams to vaginal yeast infections and wonderfully explicit ones for Viagra tackling 'penile dysfunction'.

All of which can be quite embarrassing if your three young sons are sitting there watching them with you.

Particularly when the final words are usually: 'If you have an erection for more than four hours, please see your doctor immediately...'

All this advertising makes it very hard to watch television here in the same way you would back home.

There's no ad-free BBC to turn to on a prime-time network, no respite from the unrelenting onslaught of aggressive hard selling.

You might think the networks should be less greedy, and allow their shows to air in a less-fragmented, cluttered way.

But when you hear that the final of *American Idol* attracted 70 advertisers prepared to pay $1.2 million for each 30-second commercial, then you understand why they don't.

WEDNESDAY, 25 JULY 2007

I took Spencer to the world premiere of *The Bourne Ultimatum* in Hollywood tonight to belatedly celebrate his fourteenth birthday last week.

America does entertainment, and cinema in particular, so much better than anywhere else. The screens are bigger, the picture and sound quality better, the seats more comfortable, even the popcorn is tastier. Little wonder that it exports 25 times as many movies and TV shows than any other country.

The film was great, superbly directed by a Brit, Paul Greengrass.

The highlight, though, isn't Matt Damon's brilliant performance in the lead role, but the moment when a *Guardian* investigative reporter gets shot in the head at Waterloo station.

It's not the cold-blooded murder of a fellow (albeit fictitious) hack that amused me, obviously. It was the fact that he was unshaven, terribly dressed and behaving like a pathetic limp-wristed sweating goon at the time. Which is exactly how I'd expect a *Guardian* reporter to look and act seconds before their assassination.

When I got back to my hotel, I decided to drop Alan Rusbridger an email, pointing this out, and suggesting we might meet up for a bite to eat and put the *GQ* encounter behind us. All hell broke loose when it was published, and he became a bit of a laughing stock.

'It was honestly not intended as a hatchet job,' I wrote. 'It was the kind of conversation you and I had for years in various guises over a crispy duck salad at the Ivy. Perhaps we should put it behind us when I get back in the autumn over a bottle or two at my expense. But I'll leave it to you as to whether that would be appropriate, or whether you'd rather stick a machete in my head.'

THURSDAY, 26 JULY 2007

Muhammad Ali last week, today I found myself in a lift with George Foreman – his opponent in that all-time great fight: The Rumble In The Jungle.

'Hi George,' I said. 'I've got one of your low-fat grills at home.'

He looked up and down my 'well-nourished' torso for several seconds before growling: 'You turned it on yet?'

Spent the afternoon by the pool with the boys, who were offered – and accepted – an invitation to have their feet massaged in chocolate ice cream inside their luxurious private cabana.

As I watched this ludicrous scene unfurl, I have to confess that a certain 'discomfort' overcame me about the parental direction I am exerting on my children.

SUNDAY, 29 JULY 2007

My second Hollywood world premiere of the week; this time for *Stardust*, a fun fantasy film in which Robert De Niro plays a gay pirate opposite Michelle Pfeiffer.

The after-show party was splendidly decadent – spread over two venues, the Beverly Hills Hotel bar and the infamous Chateau Marmont.

And in a neat twist, there was a member of Take That in each one: Mark Owen at the Beverly Hills, Gary Barlow at the Chateau. Both came over and gave me a hug, which would have embarrassed me in Britain, but which feels perfectly acceptable in LA, where touchy-feely behaviour is not just encouraged, but mandatory.

In the Beverly Hills bar, a large-framed figure emerged from the shadows and slapped me hard on the shoulder.

''Allo old son, what you doing in my town?'

I turned, in pain, to find the beaming visage of Vinnie Jones.

'I've just bought a big house in the Hollywood hills next to my mate Quentin,' he announced proudly.

'Quentin?' I replied.

'Tarantino,' he clarified. 'We're doing a movie together and he thinks it's going to be my best yet.'

There are few more extraordinary life stories than the former hod-carrier turned football Mr Nasty who now earns $1 million a movie out here as a bona fide actor.

Vinnie's new life is beyond parody. 'I've had Pete Sampras round for tennis, Brad Pitt for cards, Claudia Schiffer for a cup of tea and Bobby Duvall's always on the blower.'

He won't be having anything to do with the Beckhams, though.

'I don't know them,' he said. 'And I don't really want to. I'm not into all that red-carpet celebrity stuff they love.

'I'm much calmer now,' he admitted. 'All this sunshine has taken out the aggression…'

Just to be on the safe side, I decamped to the Chateau – where I found David Walliams lurking at a corner table where he was cuddling a tiny but very pretty young Liverpudlian lady he'd 'met last night'.

The last time I'd seen the swine was when we filmed *Dame Edna* together, and he and Matt Lucas conspired to ensure I went down like an even bigger sack of congealed spuds than normal.

'You were dead the moment you told Edna that if you interviewed us you would wind us up by saying who you thought was funnier,' he gloated. 'I replied that whoever you chose we'd both always be funnier than you, the audience roared and you were finished.'

He was almost melting with smuggery. 'So many friends rang to congratulate me on nailing you,' he chortled.

Walliams has been linked to just about every famous woman on God's earth in the last year, so I decided to clarify his nocturnal arrangements.

'Denise Van Outen?'

'Just a great mate.'

'Martine McCutcheon?'

'Not true.'

'Definitely?'

'Fairly definitely – I've never actually met the woman.'

'Lisa Snowden?'

'Ah, well, now she is lovely…'

He looked all wistful, so I seized the moment to return the *Dame Edna* favour.

'…But George Clooney is better looking, richer and more famous?'

'Yes. You bastard. He is.'

MONDAY, 30 JULY 2007

'Dear Piers,' the email began. 'Would you like to come to Hugh Hefner's Midsummer Night's Dream party at the Playboy Mansion on Saturday?'

Oh, I most definitely would, yes.

I accepted the invitation, but then got a further rather worrying email:

'The theme is Arabian Nights and the dress code is very strict: pyjamas and lingerie.'

TUESDAY, 31 JULY 2007
Alan Rusbridger emailed me back.

'I don't quite know how to respond. If you're offering a genuine apology, then it's churlish to spurn it. I did find it a weird, extremely hostile interview, which was why I effectively clammed up. It felt very different from our lunches, which were always good natured and enjoyable. Most people who have mentioned it to me – not all of them friends – wondered what on earth I had ever done to you to merit such a piece. I couldn't really help them. So, yes, if the aim was to re-create the badinage of the Ivy then it really failed. I know better than to whinge, and haven't whinged to you, or anyone. But I'm happy to pocket your apology if it's genuine and to hope that we can return to our bantering ways one day.'

This indignant hurt and anger doesn't seem to tally very well with Rusbridger's first email after I did the interview, which started: 'Big Boy, I enjoyed our little joust.'

Nor is his claim not to have whinged to anyone true – from what I'm hearing, he has been whingeing to EVERYONE.

But I replied: 'OK, look, I'm not apologising for giving you a good grilling – you're a high-profile editor whose staff put very tricky questions to other people all the time (me included!), and none of my questioning (in my humble opinion) was necessarily outrageous considering you are the editor of the *Guardian* with all the "leader of the Socialist free world" mantra that entails. Nor do I think the atmosphere was hostile during the interview, I just found your answers quite surprising and occasionally inconsistent, which is why I pressed you.

'But I have heard from lots of people, too, that I must have had some "agenda" before doing the interview, which is just absurd.

'I am, though, genuinely sorry for all the aggro it seemed to have caused you. We've never been exactly best mates, but I've always enjoyed your company and consider you to be a good journalistic mucker. And I would like to think we could perhaps repair some of the damage over a glass or two in the autumn.'

I suspect he'd rather shoot himself to be honest, but I've tried.

WEDNESDAY, 1 AUGUST 2007

Working on a big American TV show is very different to working on a British one.

There is a far more structured sense of hierarchy about it over here.

The 'stars' are godlike figures, their every whim catered for in seconds, however selfish, crazy or unnecessary.

For instance, today I arrived at noon to be met by two security guards in a golf cart who then drove me 50 yards to the studio.

I could have walked, obviously, but they prefer you to do things properly here. They don't like the 'stars' to behave like normal human beings, whereas on *Britain's Got Talent* I'd be laughed out of the studio if I asked for a golf buggy to ferry me around.

The way you look is also treated in very different ways.

In Britain, I can sit there for an hour with my collar flopping, my hair looking like Jack Nicholson's in *The Shining*, and my forehead pouring out more water than Amanda Holden's tearducts and nobody will bat an eyelid.

In America, a whole team of incredibly efficient make-up girls, hairdressers and wardrobe 'operatives' fusses around the 'stars' all day long on the lot, making sure there is never a hair, bead of sweat or shirt crease out of place.

Perfection is the name of the game on American TV, whatever it costs. And that's why the whole feel of what ends up on screen is so much glossier, and more glamorous, than British television. Even their soap operas only contain 'perfect people'. In contrast to *EastEnders* and *Coronation Street*, where ugliness is considered 'realism'.

Tonight, I took the boys to the baseball, a sport that I've always considered to be cricket without the brains.

Like all American sports, it is fast, furious and very high scoring.

And simple.

No LBW or hit-ball-twice dismissals here. The batters get caught, run out or 'struck out' if they miss three times. And that's about it.

The LA Dodgers were playing the San Francisco Giants at the famous Dodgers Stadium this evening. But the match was of secondary importance to the presence of one man, a batter called Barry Bonds who is currently the most controversial figure in American sport.

He is within one home run (a hit that clears the boundary wall) of breaking the legendary Hank Aaron's major league baseball career home-run record of 755. An achievement that would normally mean Bonds becoming a feted legend for the rest of his life. Except that many people think he's a drugs cheat – his trainer Greg Anderson was indicted in 2003 for supplying steroids to his clients.

So there are a lot of Americans praying he doesn't break the record, and tarnish the memory of the great, clean, Aaron.

The boys and me took our seats, right near the batter's plate, and when Bonds walked out to have a hit, the whole stadium started roaring their fury – a long, howling, intensely loud booing cacophony.

'You cheat, Bonds!' yelled an old lady in the next seat, nearly knocking herself over with the sheer force of her anger.

'You should be ashamed of yourself!' screeched another fan nearby, a middle-aged man in a baseball cap.

The boys loved it, despite having no real idea what was going on.

Then, as Bonds prepared to bat, everyone in the crowd started pulling out gloves.

'What's going on?' I asked a guy in front.

'A million bucks is what's going on!' he yelled excitedly.

'What do you mean?'

'I mean that if Bonds breaks the record tonight, then the ball he hits is gonna be worth a million bucks.'

(This was true: a Dallas-based auction house called Sports Auction Heritage had offered that sum in May to the fan who catches the historic ball.)

'Dad,' said Spencer, urgently, 'go and buy us some gloves!'

Actually catching the ball could prove very dangerous. When Bonds broke the season home-run record in 2001, one man caught it, only to be swallowed instantly by a mob, and for another man to emerge with the ball. The two battled in court for a year and were eventually ordered to split the money 50–50.

To avoid this tonight, there were armed security guards all round the stadium waiting to pounce on the winning catcher themselves and remove him to safety in seconds.

In the end, Bonds failed to hit the ball anywhere and the evening fizzled out.

But it had been a very enjoyable night.

The crowd was large, but behaved very well with no drunkenness or violence. You didn't have to queue up for food and drinks – a whole army of stewards brought hot dogs, pizza and Cokes to our seats and took credit card payment.

The atmosphere, though hostile to Bonds, never got nasty. Everyone was just having a good time.

It made a nice change from going to the football in Britain, where the filthy chants, and violence between opposing fans, can be as depressing as it is unsettling.

American sports fans don't really do hooliganism, which surprises me given how aggressive they can be about life in general. But then I'm beginning to realise that the views I held of Americans before coming here may have been a little clichéd.

THURSDAY, 2 AUGUST 2007

A typically weird day in LA: the seven-foot-two-inch basketball superstar Shaq O'Neal trod on my foot in the lift (and yes, of course it still hurts), I passed a small (genuine) office that boasted the title 'Neurotics Anonymous' and, this afternoon, I ambled down to the Century City shopping mall to buy some books, and found Stevie Wonder sitting in the square singing 'Superstition' at a piano. Now you don't get that at Bluewater, do you?

FRIDAY, 3 AUGUST 2007

Recorded the *Tonight* show with my fellow *America's Got Talent* judges, The Hoff and Sharon Osbourne. The host, Jay Leno, is the most famous chat-show star in America.

'Do you get on with Sharon?' he asked me at the start of a chaotic but amusing three-way interview.

'Yes,' I replied, 'but she's a bit like her dog Minnie, small and ferocious.'

The Hoff laughed a little too loudly. So Sharon turned and started frenziedly licking his cheek.

'I was going to bite him,' she admitted afterwards. 'But I wasn't sure what I'd be eating.'

SATURDAY, 4 AUGUST 2007

During a break from filming, I told The Hoff that I was going to the *Playboy* party tonight.

'You'll have fun there, man,' he said. 'It's pretty crazy! The chicks will be throwing themselves at you now the show's No. 1.'

'I'm going with my girlfriend,' I pointed out.

The Hoff looked totally bemused, then shook his head slowly.

'Man, don't you know the golden rule? Never take sand to the beach!'

I fell about laughing. The Hoff can be very funny when he's on form. And since he recently got custody of his children he has been on great form.

Security for the party was extraordinary. Celia and I were instructed to drive to an underground car park two miles from the Mansion, where we found huge ticket check-in lines of pouting, scantily clad young 'ladies' with peroxide hair, tattoos and pneumatic breasts – interspersed with the occasional middle-aged blokes in bathrobes with huge grins on their faces.

I eventually reached the front of the line, where a severe-faced woman gave me a long, frowning once-over.

'You're not wearing pyjamas,' she growled.

Which was technically true as I'd bottled it and gone for some stripy strides and a white cheesecloth shirt.

'I wear this in bed,' I lied.

'Those pants got a zipper?' she said.

'Erm…yes,' I admitted.

'Then they ain't pyjamas, and you ain't going to the party.'

Disaster was averted by the arrival of Hefner's equally elderly PA – who took pity on me.

'Get him a robe, and let him in,' she declared.

Ms Sourface reluctantly went to her car, fetched me a white bathrobe and flung it at me. 'Wear this, and don't even think about taking it off.'

A shuttle bus took us to the mansion, but only after we'd been inspected by four more security guards.

We arrived at a large mock Tudor house, which was flanked by yet more guards. Nobody was gate-crashing *this* party, and we soon found out why.

A six-foot model in a bikini greeted us with a tray of very strong vodka jellies. Closer inspection revealed she was naked, and the bikini had been painted on.

We passed through into the main party room – and came across what I can only describe as a scene that even Caligula might have baulked at.

Hundreds of naked or semi-naked girls swarming around a giant marquee. Free bars serving magnums of vintage champagne and bottles of Jack Daniel's. Huge plates of lobster and crab being served by crushingly good-looking waitresses.

And in the centre, the infamous Grotto – surrounded by a vast artificial lake, where some guests were already frolicking in the water.

'I bet it gets lively in there later?' I asked a Playboy PR man.

'Oh yes,' he winked, 'and so do the gardens. These girls know how to party, if you know what I mean…'

I knew what he meant, all right.

A million flashbulbs suddenly exploded.

Paris Hilton had arrived, and was standing two yards away, wearing nothing but Agent Provocateur lingerie.

I interviewed her last year, but was pretty sure she wouldn't remember.

'Hello again,' she purred. 'How are you?'

'I'm fine, thanks, Paris. I wasn't sure you'd remember…'

'Oh, I remember.' Cue much eyelashes fluttering, lips trembling, bottom wiggling. She reminds me of Marilyn Monroe without the talent.

'Enjoying liberty?' I asked.

'Yes,' she sighed. 'Very much.'

'And are you going to behave better in future?'

'Oh definitely, Piers, definitely…' Then she giggled, grabbed a champagne flute and was led away to Hugh Hefner's private Bedouin tent.

I followed in her wake to meet the host. He's 82, looks fit as the proverbial fiddle, has a permanent smirk (as you would) and was surrounded by 20-year-old Playmates.

'Great party, Mr Hefner.'

'Isn't it?' he beamed, smacking me firmly on the back. Say what you like about the man, but he loves his life. Especially, an aide assured me, since Viagra came on the scene.

I went to the 'rest room', and discovered that they were unisex. So I joined a queue with five saucy little minxes wearing Arab veils.

'You're that mean Brit judge from *America's Got Talent*, aren't you?' said one. I nodded.

'Well, now we're gonna see if *you* got any talent!' she squealed, as I realised there were no locks on the doors. I made my excuses, before I had to make my excuses, and left.

SUNDAY, 5 AUGUST 2007

Woke up and turned the TV on, to find my favourite American preacher in full flow.

Joel Osteen, 44, is a slim, handsome, gigantic-toothed, besuited man who seeps 'purity' from every pore of his perfectly coiffured head.

And every Sunday, he addresses 25,000 people at Lakewood Church in Houston, Texas. His homilies are broadcast live to seven million more Americans on television, and an estimated 30 million other non-Americans in the other 100 countries in which it is screened. Which makes Joel the most popular preacher on the planet, and the richest, too.

He's extraordinarily charismatic – eloquent, articulate, emotive, passionate. Watching him perform is like watching a Christian rock star working the audience like Mick Jagger. He speaks for exactly 12 minutes each week, timed perfectly to the needs of TV. And steers well clear of any political allegiance, avoiding the right-wing affiliation of other preachers like Pat Robertson, thus making himself appealing to every single even vaguely religious person in the country.

And yet he lacks any formal theological training whatsoever! He just inherited the gig when his father died. And as a result, he doesn't do much theology either. He just sticks to a tried and tested mantra of how God can directly improve your life.

Joel's mission statement is, hilariously, the 'prosperity gospel'. He explains: 'God is a loving, forgiving God who will reward believers with health, wealth and happiness.'

And there, in a nutshell, is why he is so popular. Because Americans care most about being healthy, wealthy and happy. And God.

And good old Joel promises all of that in one hit – you just have to follow him, either by buying his expensive books and tapes, or attending one of his expensive shows.

'God wants us to prosper financially, to have plenty of money,' he says, in a shamelessly self-serving statement that of course validates his own vast fortune.

'And make changes for your health's sake,' he beseeches, hitting the obesity market, too, 'because if you get the physical side in balance, you will be rewarded by God.' In other words, stick to carrot juice, lard-arse, and you'll get rich.

His delivery style is permanently ecstatic, almost like he's in some sort of Utopian trance. And the punters lap it up.

I watch him most Sundays when I'm here, because I find him so funny.

But Joel's having the last laugh – he's worth $100 million, and that fortune is rising fast.

TUESDAY, 7 AUGUST 2007

Met The Ferret for a drink at the Four Seasons hotel tonight, and as we left I spotted a familiar face waiting outside for his car to be returned by the valet boys.

It was James Gandolfini, or Tony Soprano as he is better known – the world's most famous mafia actor since Brando and Pacino in *The Godfather*.

He was massive, and wearing a face like thunder.

'Where IS it?' he growled, as a poor young valet kept promising his car's imminent arrival.

I moved in to deflect his rage.

'Hi,' I said, stretching out my hand. 'I just wanted to say how sorry I am that *The Sopranos* has finished.'

He stared at me like he wanted to tie my lower abdominal region to an electrode.

'Thank you, sir,' he eventually replied.

The 'sir' under normal circumstances would be rather comforting. But then I remembered that mafia types are always incredibly polite just before they blow your head off.

'Still, better to leave the punters begging for more,' I spluttered.

He stared again, with the kind of look he had in the show when he replied to Bobby Baccalieri's 'To the victor belongs the spoils' line by snarling: 'Why don't you get the fuck out of here before I shove your quotation book up your fat fucking ass.'

'Yuh,' he said. Dead-faced, with just a smidgeon of menace.

'You have a lot of fans back in England,' I continued, with now reckless disregard for my own safety.

'Uh-huh,' he nodded. 'That's nice to hear. Thank you. Sir.'

And then he shook my still-dangling hand. Literally. I mean, this vast swathe of fingered muscle gripped my bony paw and crushed it so hard I thought he'd slipped a knuckle-duster on when I wasn't looking.

He then turned his attentions back to the ashen-faced valet: 'WHERE IS IT?'

'It will be right here, Mr Gandolfini, sir.'

I left them to it, feeling bizarrely intimidated by the encounter.

WEDNESDAY, 8 AUGUST 2007

Barry Bonds broke the home-run record last night against the Washington Nationals in San Francisco.

The fan who gloved it, 22-year-old Matt Murphy from Queens, New York, was promptly rescued, and escorted in glory from the mayhem around him to safety. Matt had a massive grin on his face, which is hardly surprising really. He'd just caught $1 million.

THURSDAY, 9 AUGUST 2007

An email from Jeremy: 'Brother, you've done a lot of dumb things in your life but taking a girlfriend to the *Playboy* party has to be the dumbest. Congratulations.'

FRIDAY, 10 AUGUST 2007

For the last few weeks, I've passed a cosmetic dental centre every morning on my way to pick up the papers.

Rather like a strip club in Soho, it has grown more and more tempting with each passing.

And today I decided to take the plunge and have a 45-minute teeth-whitening course. The way I see it, this isn't any different to brushing your gnashers in the normal way, it just does it quicker and better for you. And if I can get my teeth even remotely glinting, then it might shut up all the denture-obsessed American radio and TV interviewers who treat me like I'm bloody Alf Garnett. 'Does it hurt?' I asked the receptionist. 'Oh no,' she replied. And the actual procedure was fine. But four hours later, I was lying on the floor of my hotel room, dosed with Tylenol, trying to stem the ferocious onslaught of vicious shooting pains in my mouth. It was absolute bloody agony. On a positive note, my teeth were so white they could blind a dog from 100 yards. I'm not allowed to eat or drink anything non-white for 48 hours, so ordered a plate of fish with a glass of low-fat milk.

I fear that my LA conversion is now irreversible.

How to nearly kill yourself in the most embarrassing
manner possible: the manufacturers say that Segways
are 'idiot-proof', which may still be factually correct,
given that only me and George Bush are ever
known to have publicly fallen off one.

5

'Everything I have, my career, my success, my family, I owe to America.'
ARNOLD SCHWARZENEGGER

SATURDAY, 11 AUGUST 2007

Woke at 8 a.m., and the pain had subsided, though I still got a few 'zingers' sweeping in through the morning just to remind me of my vanity. My teeth are less gleaming today – apparently the shading goes up and down until it settles somewhere a few notches up from where you started. But it definitely works, and my teeth look exactly the same as they always did, only a bit whiter.

One of my favourite acts in *America's Got Talent* has been a bunch of penniless, homeless, West Indian guys called the Calypso Tumblers, who perform quite extraordinary acrobatic stunts.

The great thing about them is that for 20 years they've played purely in public parks and beaches, living off a few hundred dollars a week. And now they were performing in front of 25 million viewers, for a prize of $1 million.

On Tuesday, to my great dismay, they were knocked out in the semi-final, so desperately close to the win that would have changed their lives for ever.

This afternoon I was cycling along Venice Beach when I came across a large crowd of people cheering. In their midst were the Calypso Tumblers, back doing what they love.

I waited until they had finished and then said hello – prompting high fives and much whooping and hollering.

'You know,' said the group's leader, 'we set out to achieve three things on the show: to do our best, to make America proud of us and to win $1 million. And two out of three isn't bad.'

I laughed. 'No, but the third bit would have been nice...'

He laughed back. 'I agree.' Then he leant forward and whispered. But business has trebled since we got on TV!'

SUNDAY, 12 AUGUST 2007

Gordon Brown has led the Labour Party to its biggest lead over the Tories since before the Iraq War, a new YouGov poll has revealed.

His shrewd, calm handling of various mini-crises since becoming prime minister, including a foot-and-mouth breakout, bizarre unseasonal flooding, and car bombs in London and Glasgow, have given him a huge 10-point advantage.

And there is even talk of him calling a snap election to secure a proper mandate from the public.

I'd go for it if I was him – Cameron looks like a busted flush right now. And politics is all about timing.

My gut feeling that Britain was ready for a more serious prime minister is looking like it was right.

There is another, possibly more pressing, reason why he should consider an early poll, and that's the looming threat of a downturn in the economy.

A huge mortgage scandal has erupted here in America, where trillions of dollars of loans have been made to homeowners with poor credit ratings. The issuing banks that made them then got third parties to effectively bankroll them, in return for higher than usual interest rates. These investors included other banks, hedge funds and wealthy individuals.

What's happened is that the housing market has suddenly collapsed in the States, causing many of these 'sub-prime' homeowners to go bankrupt, and starting a terrible domino effect that is causing havoc in the financial world. How bad it will get is anybody's guess. But today the Federal Reserve injected $43 *billion* into the American financial system to try and prop it up, the highest since 9/11. It all sounds pretty scary to me.

MONDAY, 13 AUGUST 2007

The Internet has been ablaze with The Hoff's denunciation of me on the last *America's Got Talent* show as a 'Brit wanker'.

I was sure that NBC would cut this vile slur out of the final edit, given American television's notoriously prudish view of this kind of thing.

But to my astonishment, and The Hoff's absolute delight, it went out exactly as he said it. Apparently it was OK because no American viewers would understand what it meant.

'Oh man,' chuckled The Hoff backstage, 'everywhere I go I get people coming up to me saying, "Piers *is* a wanker." I have finally got it out there!'

'Well, it takes a wanker to know a wanker,' I replied.

He laughed again. 'Yeah, whatever man. But I got you and you know it.'

And infuriatingly, he has. For now.

Later it emerged that he is going to sing on the live finale. All the TV crews asked me what I thought of this development. 'Well, I think we can safely say that it will be fairly obvious who the wanker really is by the end of his performance.'

During tonight's penultimate show, notable for a genius ventriloquist called Terry Fator singing Roy Orbison's 'Crying' through a puppet turtle, Sharon and David got into a uniquely showbiz debate about which was the best rehab facility in the world – Ozzy and The Hoff having tried most of them at some stage between them.

'Oh man, it has to be the Betty Ford Clinic,' he declared. 'When I was there it was full of all these beautiful young women who were sexaholics.'

America sometimes seems like a country in perpetual therapy.

Going to a rehab centre for any form of addiction, be it sex, drugs or alcohol, is almost considered a badge of honour.

I've seen members of the audience on the show congratulating David for 'dealing with his problems', and some even thanking him for helping them deal with theirs by being so open about his own.

The curious thing is why Americans feel the need for all this psychiatric help.

It's not like they have a particularly tough life. America's astonishing economic growth has meant that the majority of them lead relatively comfortable existences, certainly compared to any third world country.

But perhaps that's the point. Because their lives are quite sheltered, the slightest disruption can be more traumatic than it should be.

A few too many bottles of wine in a month makes them 'chronic alcoholics', the odd line of coke at a party 'drug addicts', and so on. They tend to exaggerate everything that happens to them.

And so when a major disaster occurs, like 9/11, it can have a catastrophic effect on their mental wellbeing.

As The Ferret put it: 'Nobody ever thought we'd be attacked in our own country, so when we were, that whole collective comfort zone we felt as all-powerful Americans went out the window.'

TUESDAY, 14 AUGUST 2007

Even the normally rather placid US TV critics are piling into me now. One wrote today: '*America's Got Talent* airs its penultimate episode as viewer votes halve the remaining eight acts to a final four. The ultimate prize? One million dollars. And, yes, bragging rights as "the most talented person in America". Of course, when you realise this honour was partially determined by David Hasselhoff, Sharon Osbourne and Piers Morgan, well, it loses some cachet. It's a bit like being hailed "the most intelligent person in America" by Paris Hilton, Britney Spears and Andy Dick.'

I have no idea who Andy Dick actually is, but I suspect this is not intended as a compliment.

WEDNESDAY, 15 AUGUST 2007

The front page of today's *Daily Telegraph* contains a large promotional blurb saying: 'CELIA WALDEN: WHY A PORTLY MAN CAN STILL BE ATTRACTIVE.'

And yes, this has caused considerable merriment to just about every single person I know.

THURSDAY, 16 AUGUST 2007

I've just got back from interviewing Arnold Schwarzenegger, and am still buzzing with excitement. If ever a man sums up the American dream, then surely it's Arnie – a guy who came here from Austria with nothing, then turned himself into a world-class body-builder, movie star and now politician.

I'd found him this morning sitting in a large tent inside the grounds of his governor's mansion in Sacramento. He was puffing one of his beloved Cuban cigars and barking into a phone.

'Today is quite a historic day for me, Governor,' I said, as he gripped my hand so strongly I thought my fingers were going to snap off.

'Oh? Why?'

'Because I broke my personal best for bench-pressing in the gym this morning: 185 pounds.'

'That's not your bodyweight,' he scoffed, eyeing me with withering derision. 'If you press your own bodyweight, that is a really good feat of strength.'

'OK, so what advice would you give me to reach that goal?'

'It's all about training. Doing something every day, and being determined to achieve your goal. If you are serious about it then you will succeed quickly.'

'I actually have an Austrian personal trainer over here, who idolises you, and he just chants "BURN! BURN!" at me in the gym.'

'What he means is "no pain, no gain". But exercising is good, and lifting weight in particular. In my bodybuilding days, people thought it was just a cosmetic thing and not good for your health. But as time has gone on, all the research has shown that weightlifting is good for just about everything – for old people, for women, for firemen, for athletes, golfers, tennis players. Everyone. Weight-training alternated with stretching exercises will make you healthy.'

'How much training do you do now?'

'About an hour a day. Cardio-vascular every day, and some weight-training, though not a lot.'

'And what are you bench-pressing these days?'

'I don't bench-press. In fact I don't lift any heavy weights, I just do lots of repetitions with lighter weights. Condition training.'

'So just to clarify, I am actually bench-pressing bigger weights than you at the moment?'

He looked at me, with incredulity.

'I doubt it.'

'Well, if you're not bench-pressing at all, and I am doing 185 pounds, then I must be, right?'

He laughed. 'Look, if it makes you happy to say that in this article then go for it.'

'Have your kids had much trouble being the offspring of Arnold Schwarzenegger?'

'Not really. They enjoy some advantages, and some disadvantages. They get preferential treatment occasionally, but they also have to deal with the pressure of having to live up to the success of their parents, wondering if we are going to be disappointed in them. But we reassure them that if they study hard then we will support them in whatever they want to do. If they want to be a nurse or a billionaire, that's great either way and they will get the support from us just the same.'

'You were abused by your father as a child, weren't you?'

'Not abused, no. He would beat us because that was the tradition then. In those days parents would go to the classroom on parents' days and smack you in front of all the other kids and walk out again if they weren't happy with what the teacher was saying about you. It was not considered abuse then.'

'Have you ever physically punished your kids?'

'Never. Those days have gone because parents today have learned there are more effective ways to deal with kids who behave badly – like communicating with them.'

'And if you did smack them, they'd end up in Orange County…'

(Bursts out laughing.) 'Yes…ha ha! Luckily my kids have always been pretty well behaved. I've had no problems with alcohol or drugs. I have a daughter of 16, and one of 18, and so far they have caused me no problems.'

'I wouldn't like to be one of your daughters' boyfriends to be perfectly honest…'

'It's funny, I thought when my daughters got to the age of dating that I would be very strict. And I could imagine how scared the boys would be opening the door at my home to find The Terminator staring back at them! But the truth is that when my daughters have brought back male friends from good families that I know, and they hang out and watch TV and movies together, or swim and so on, I have reacted in quite the opposite way to how I thought I would. It must be because the reality is very different to the thought… There are so many things I have seen myself do as a parent that I never thought I would do ten years ago. Bringing up kids, you have to be good at improvising because they all have to be treated differently.'

'What have you said to them about drugs?'

'We have let them know there will be drugs in their schools. Because all LA schools have drugs. And we explain that if they get involved in drugs then everything they work for could be gone in a flash.'

'Have you told them that you took drugs?'

'No. I didn't take any drugs.'

'I thought you'd admitted that you had?'

'Which one?'

'Marijuana.'

'That is not a drug. It's a leaf.'

I was stunned by that answer. For the governor of California to call marijuana a leaf not a drug is going to make big news when this comes out. But Arnie didn't seem to realise what he'd done.

'Right, so you've had a few "leaves" in your time... Have you ever tried cocaine?'

'No. Some bodybuilders did, some didn't. I didn't. I got my high from working out, and winning competitions.'

'What has given you the biggest thrill – winning a bodybuilding contest, having a number one movie for the first time, or becoming governor of California?'

'I would say 35 years ago it was winning my first bodybuilding title, 20 years ago it was being number one at the box office, and then becoming governor took over. Each time my goal changed, so the thrill of achieving my new dream was the same.'

'Do you think the law will be changed in your lifetime to allow people born outside of America to become president?'

'This is just a wild guess – I have no idea!' (Lights up another cigar.) 'It is very complicated because the constitution has to be changed. I don't give it very much thought because it is not possible for me to become president as the law stands, and this country has allowed me to achieve everything I have ever wanted to achieve apart from this one thing. So I feel incredibly lucky and grateful.'

'Part of you must yearn for the chance to be president, though?'

'I spend most of my time thinking about how I can do my best for this state.'

'That's a typical politician's answer, though, and you're not a typical politician.'

'I am a public servant.'

'Yes, but you are also someone who has always wanted to be the biggest and the best at whatever you do – whether it be bodybuilding or movies. And to be the biggest and best as a politician, you have to be president don't you?'

'I don't dream about things that are not available.'

'But if the law was changed, and it was available, you'd go for it, right?'

'Then I could think about it, yes. And go after it. I am always interested in challenges and risk. The risk of losing always makes you perform better. When you come from an athletic, competitive background then you learn to enjoy taking risks to reach your goals. And it gives you great satisfaction to then achieve them. Other people prefer not taking risks, and having calmer lives. That is not for me.'

'How do you feel as a Republican about the damaging effects that the Bush presidency has had on America's reputation around the world, and in particular as a result of the disastrous war with Iraq?'

'First of all, you should never confuse what Washington does with what the rest of the country does. Washington, for example, is not as aggressive about the environment, and we feel here that they haven't done enough in that area. So we pick up the slack and show the rest of the world that America is not just Washington. There are 600 mayors in America that have joined the Kyoto treaty. For us, it is very important that America goes and gets back again the great reputation that it once had. And important for us to finish the war, which has been very tough on the country. Just as it has been for Britain and for Tony Blair.'

'You said that after you voted for Bush the second time around, your wife banned you from sex for two weeks.'

(Gives me long, hard stare.) 'You liked that joke?'

'Oh, it was a joke? I see. Well yes, I did in that case.'

'Good. As long as *the joke* worked, then that's fine.'

'You have a reputation for having a bit of an eye for the ladies. Would you deny that?'

'I appreciate women, they are the greatest thing that has ever been put on earth. Without them I couldn't live. And I am so lucky to have found the greatest woman in the world to be MY WIFE.'

Arnie emphasised the last two words with slow deliberation.

'You once said that the best way to stay healthy was "humping and pumping". Do you still think that?'

'It was a great sales tool! People found it very fascinating...'

'But just to reassure all your fans, there has been no deterioration in your ability to "hump and pump"?'

'As I said, it was a great sales tool.'

'What scares you?'

(Pause.) 'Erm...I think...death.'

'Really? Have you thought about dying?'

'Yes.'

'What do you think it will be like?'

'I have no idea. I wish I did! Then perhaps I wouldn't be so scared of it.'

'How often do you think about it?'

'Not often. But when I do, I hate it. I think I should be around for another thousand years at least.'

'Who have been the most impressive leaders in history?'

'I think Mandela, Kennedy, Ronald Reagan, Teddy and Franklin Roosevelt, Tony Blair, and Gorbachev, a man who grew up a communist and then dismantled communism, that is the mark of a great leader.'

'President Bush?'

'I would say that I was...very fond of his father. I worked for President Bush senior and he was a great man.'

'But not his son...?'

'I think his son does some great things and there are some other things I don't agree with.'

'Has Bush damaged America's reputation abroad?'

'As I said before, I think we have to do everything we can as a country to get out of the Iraq War, and to take a lead on the environment. Then we can get our reputation back again. Because people all over the world like Americans, and they like our products. We have to make commitments to get into a carbon-free economy, and I have not seen those goals on a national level.'

'What would you like your epitaph to be?'

'Wow. I don't know...' (long pause) '...I spend very little time thinking about this because I would rather be known for what I am achieving while I'm alive than after I'm dead.'

'There must be some historical legacy you would like to have for yourself, though?'

'No specific thing. I always thought I was put in this world to make an impact and improve things, and to have a hell of a time doing it.'

'What about: "He made an impact and enjoyed himself"?'

'Perfect, I like that. Thank you for writing my epitaph.'

'Any time, Governor.'

I left the cigar tent feeling enthused, if not slightly intoxicated, by Governor Schwarzenegger. It's a shame that the current American constitution does not allow someone born outside the country to run for office.

He would make a fabulous president.

FRIDAY, 17 AUGUST 2007

Ellis Watson is in town, and announced today that he wanted to 'play'.

This almost always means that someone somewhere is going to wake up regretting they ever met the man.

'Here's the itinerary, petal,' he declared, excitedly, 'go-karts, power-boats, Segways and parascending.'

'Forget it, Ellis,' I replied, 'I'm not flying anywhere without an engine, or going near water, with you.'

'All right, go-karts and Segways it is then.'

'What *is* a Segway?'

'They're those things you stand on, and use to whizz up and down the promenade. Old grannies ride them – they're easy peasy, Japanese.'

The go-karts went fine, though Ellis was enraged that they were speed restricted so we couldn't actually get airborne, or feel our eye sockets start to pop.

'Come on, let's go,' he whined, 'even Segways move faster than this.'

We headed down to Santa Monica, and found the shop where they rented these machines. For 15 minutes they made us parade around inside until we got 'the feel' of them, and then the instructor led us off to the promenade.

I found the Segway itself surprisingly tricky to control. To brake you have to lean backwards like a jockey, while pushing the handlebar forward. It's the complete opposite action to what your instincts tell you to do.

But Ellis, of course, loved it. 'This is *fantastic*!' he shrieked, as we sped along, causing pedestrians to dive out of the way.

My Segway suddenly ran off quicker than I wanted, and I struggled to calm it down again. It was a panicky moment, and unnerved me slightly. They only go 12mph, but that seems pretty damn fast as you shoot along the hard tarmac.

I got going again, and lost control again. And this time, I completely lost control. All I could hear behind me was Ellis shouting, 'This is better than sex!' as the instructor who was supposed to be showing us what to do video-taped us with Ellis's camera instead.

He suddenly spotted me racing ahead like a stallion that's just been shot up the backside with an air pellet. 'Slow down!' he cried. 'SLOW DOWN!'

I was trying to bloody slow down, but couldn't. Not for the first time, my technique was letting me down badly.

And then I clipped the kerb, the Segway flew into the air and I flew up with it, before crashing on my side hard into the pavement.

I knew I'd hurt myself, but I didn't think it was too bad. I mean, how bad can you hurt yourself falling off a Segway, for God's sake?

But as I lay on the floor, I suddenly felt a searing pain in my side, and could see blood spurting out of various parts of my hands, knees and ankles.

Ellis arrived, still laughing.

'You all right, petal? Ha ha ha ha ha.'

I tried to speak but words were not forthcoming.

'That was *so* funny!'

I now wanted to punch him, but my fists were too mangled to even think about it.

'Oh dear, oh dear, ha ha ha ha ha!'

I could feel the 95-degree sun burning straight into my gaping wounds, and knew I had to somehow get to the shade.

So I staggered up, and stumbled as fast as I could to a nearby tree.

The penny finally dropped with Ellis that I wasn't in the rudest of health, and he went into Emergency Ward 10 mode – shouting over to some life-guards, who really were wearing the classic Baywatch red shorts.

They ran over, and by now I was having serious trouble breathing.

'Ellis, I'm in trouble here, mate,' I managed to splutter.

The red-short boys agreed, and called an ambulance. By the time it got to me just ten minutes later, I began to slip in and out of consciousness.

I was taken at high speed to the nearby UCLA Hospital, where I was treated quickly and diagnosed with three broken ribs, a partially collapsed lung and a psychedelic array of deep cuts, grazes and bruises.

Not quite the Arnie poster boy any more.

Ellis looked like a choirboy who's just been caught stealing from the donation tin.

'I knew one day you'd fucking kill me,' I whispered.

The hospital care I received was swift, and excellent. Like most things in America, they do 'service' very well, even if your order is for two bandages, a sling and five shots of morphine.

It was exactly how Caroline had told me it would be – aggressive, ruthlessly efficient and carried out by a small army of highly trained staff.

But there was no room for sentimentality.

I was patched up, dosed up and sent back to my hotel – feeling like a large sledgehammer had crashed on to my side.

Three days to the season finale of *America's Got Talent*, and I can barely move, breathe or talk. Great.

SUNDAY, 19 AUGUST 2007

Pain, pain, pain…oh, and more pain. I'm on morphine, extra-strength Vicodin and anything else the docs can throw at me. And nothing is making any difference. It's just mind-numbingly agonising, and broken ribs can't be treated. 'Can you do the show?' asked one of the producers this afternoon.

'I honestly don't know,' I said. And I don't.

MONDAY, 20 AUGUST 2007

Ellis has had to fly back to Britain, but has fixed it for me to have a 24-hour nurse in my suite. She's called Corinne, and looks 60 but is in fact 78. She's cared for many, much bigger, stars than me and was unequivocal: 'Piers, honey, this is Hollywood – you're doing the show.'

Jeremy, perhaps understandably given that he's served on army frontlines in Iraq and Northern Ireland, concurred by succinct email: 'The show must go on.'

My co-judges were touchingly solicitous. Sharon sent a dazzling hamper of rare cheeses, pickles, biscuits and wine with the message: 'We hope this helps with the pain – feel better soon, love Sharon and Ozzy.'

The Hoff sent some flowers and a basket of muffins, which Corinne assured me were 'the best in LA'. His message read: 'Hey Piers, sorry, mate, I've been through this too. Hang in there, all the best, your Hoff Brother.'

By contrast I then took a phone call from Simon Cowell at 1 a.m., punctuated by endless heaving, guffawing laughter.

'I just want to reassure you that I've ordered six extra cameras to capture you screaming in pain,' he cackled, almost hysterically.

'Thank you, Simon…'

'Oh, and if you do have to pull out don't worry because I've got Louis Walsh on stand-by to take over…'

'How kind, Simon…'

'Oh, this is so *funny*!' he yelped. 'Only last week you were telling me how you hoped I might die so you could get all my jobs, and now this – what a *delicious* irony!'

I started to laugh myself, causing another surge of pain.

'It's killing you to laugh, isn't it! *Hilarious*!'

TUESDAY, 21 AUGUST 2007

Caroline came to see me today, with various tubes and bandages on her arms from cancer treatment.

'Look at the bloody state of us,' she laughed, 'what a pair.'

I tried to laugh but it was too painful.

'I bet you're glad this happened in America, right?' she said.

And I was. They take health very, very seriously here. And all the treatment I've received has been first class.

This morning, for example, I had to have an X-ray – which, incidentally, revealed I broke five ribs in total, all in a cluster around my left side where I'd landed on the concrete – and was whisked straight into a room, had the photos taken and was whisked out again, all within 15 minutes. And for just $60, covered by my insurance.

The service was not just efficient, either. It was courteous, kindly and highly professional. I was incredibly impressed.

'The best NHS facility for me back home would have been in

Basingstoke,' said Caroline, peering out of my window over a sun-kissed Beverly Hills. 'Not much contest really, is it!'

I was in such pain that I seriously didn't think I could make it to the studio, but Corinne was having none of it.

'Come on now, Piers,' she said, hauling me gently out of bed, 'you're doing this.'

That American positivity again. It's infectious.

I gritted my teeth and, with Corinne's help, dragged myself to the studio, where The Ferret was waiting for me with a large bag of…spare ribs.

When the producers saw the state of me, hunched in a wheelchair, wincing in agony and sweating in mild delirium from all the drugs, I think even they began to feel just the slightest twinge of sympathy.

It was agreed that I wouldn't say anything during the two-hour show, which was just as well because my speech is severely limited.

But after The Hoff performed a live version of 'This Is the Moment', I signalled that I wanted to speak.

'I didn't think anything could be more painful than five broken ribs,' I said, 'but that was, David. Congratulations.'

The Hoff didn't wait long to retaliate. When the show ended, and Corinne started wheeling me back to my ambulance, I heard him telling *Access Hollywood*: 'When I found out how Piers had his accident, I said to him, "Come on man, at least I wrecked the Harley [Davidson] on the 405 [freeway], going 100 miles an hour! Not on a stupid Segway going at 15!"

To further cement my humiliation, *Entertainment Tonight* aired the actual video of my accident, gleefully passed on to them by Ellis with the shameless collusion of NBC executives.

So my Segway hell is now a national laughing matter.

WEDNESDAY, 22 AUGUST 2007

Day five of my torment, and my punctured lung is making my voice sound like Bonnie Tyler with a bad cold.

Corinne had the deep misfortune to aid me in a shower this morning.

As I stood, naked and hunched against the rail, suppressing yelps of agony, she laughed: 'So Piers, when was the last time you took a shower with a fully clothed grandmother?'

A few minutes later, my doctor, a splendidly no-nonsense man called Myron Shapero, arrived and handed me a printed leaflet with a series of suggestions on how to improve my life. These included:

1) Stay grateful and humble
2) Take 15 minutes a day to sit quietly and aim for 'mindlessness'
3) Decrease TV watching, especially the evening news
4) Develop a sense of humour
5) Occasionally, take off all your clothes and stand in front of the mirror. You will clearly know how much weight you need to lose

What I loved about this was that it was a joke. A great big, sarcastic, ironic joke. From an inhabitant of a country that isn't supposed to understand those.

Meanwhile, back in England, journalists have unfortunately been researching exactly what the *Daily Mirror* (under my editorship) said about President Bush when he, too, famously fell off a motorised Segway in 2003.

'You'd have to be an idiot to fall off, wouldn't you, Mr President?' ran our headline on that occasion, adding underneath: 'If anyone can make a pig's ear of riding a sophisticated, self-balancing machine like this, Dubya can.'

Since only he and I appear to have ever fallen off one, I think the manufacturers of Segway can probably still justifiably claim that the machines are 'idiot-proof'.

Every American who visits me says I must sue the people who hired me the Segway, and especially the instructor who was video-taping me as I fell off and nearly killed myself.

This is an expected, cultural reaction to any accident or injury in the States.

It's never, ever your own fault – always somebody else's.

'You could get millions for this…' said The Ferret this morning, with an agent's glint in his eye.

But you know what? I'm just too damn embarrassed.

FRIDAY, 24 AUGUST 2007
I woke up to find my mobile phone vibrating off the bed with messages from people telling me stupid jokes.

I was totally bemused, until further investigation revealed that Simon Cowell had gone on Steve Wright's Radio 2 show today and urged everyone to try and make me laugh because 'it causes Piers absolute agony'.

SATURDAY, 25 AUGUST 2007

I tried to call The Ferret this morning, but was told he was tied up filming.

'Really? What's he doing?' I asked his assistant.

'Oh, he's judging *Miss Teen America* live,' came the reply.

So as I lie in agony, my *agent* gets to judge a bunch of nubile 19-year-olds in bikinis.

This seems horrifically the wrong way round to me.

SUNDAY, 26 AUGUST 2007

The final indignity. I flew back to London today, and needed 'wheelchair assistance' to get me to and from the plane. This involved me wearing a large yellow sticker on my chest at LAX, sporting the word 'WHEELCHAIR' just to reinforce the fact that I was severely disabled.

It's at moments like this that you just hope and pray you don't see anyone you know – so, of course, I bumped straight into two of the top TV executives from the *America's Got Talent* production company.

'We must get a photo for Simon,' said one, giggling as I ordered my 'special assistant' to make a mad forlorn wheeled dash to the lift.

FLASH! He got me, withered and angst-faced.

'Oh, Mr Cowell will LOVE this!'

And I'm sure he will.

I was then dropped by the gate 40 minutes before boarding, and left to sit on my own – helpless and at the mercy of the Great British Public, which is never a great thing even when able-bodied.

Sure enough, within five minutes I was encircled by a large family from Scotland.

The mother went straight to the point: 'We're big Robbie Williams fans, and we saw that nasty thing you wrote about him recently. So we should really kick you off your seat!'

I felt like James Caan being tortured by Kathy Bates in *Misery*.

MONDAY, 27 AUGUST 2007

I got back home, and showed the boys the video of my accident.

There was a lengthy pause.

'Dad, that is *so* embarrassing,' said Spencer, shaking his head.

And the day got worse.

A new survey released by Travelodge has revealed that *Don't You Know Who I Am?* is second on a list of books discarded in rooms by its customers – behind Alastair Campbell's diaries, but ahead of Katie Price, Jilly Cooper, Gordon Ramsay and J.K. Rowling.

My first thought was mild bemusement that anyone using a Travelodge would actually be able to read my book, obviously.

My second was horror at losing to Campbell at anything.

And my third, after a brief exchange of texts with him, was an absolute certainty (in both our minds) that the only reason our books had been left behind in such vast numbers was because the punters enjoyed them so much they felt an overwhelming public duty to allow others to share their joy.

An assessment which, I believe, is called 'the art of spin'.

THURSDAY, 30 AUGUST 2007

Dinner with Andy and Rebekah.

The former has been working for David Cameron as his communications chief for less than two months now, and appears to have inadvertently accepted one of the biggest hospital passes in political history.

But he hasn't lost his sense of humour yet. Nor his resolve.

'One thing I've learned about politics is that things can change very quickly in this game,' he smiled, ruefully.

I'm torn between wanting Andy to succeed on a personal level, but fail spectacularly on a professional one.

FRIDAY, 31 AUGUST 2007

Had a meeting about the next series of *Britain's Got Talent* at Simon Cowell's massive house in Notting Hill.

I hobbled out afterwards into the street, through his car park of Lamborghinis, and walked past a group of builders.

'Oi, it's 'im!' I heard one cry. 'Let's make 'im laugh like Simon said on the radio...'

At which point all six of them began whooping and hollering until I eventually laughed, causing instant horrendous pain to my ribs, which in turn caused them to fall on the floor in hysterics.

It's at moments like this that you realise Cowell really does enjoy inflicting pain and suffering on the more vulnerable and defenceless members of society.

SUNDAY, 2 SEPTEMBER 2007

News of my injury has inevitably reached the highest echelons of power.

'Hope your ribs are OK,' texted Sarah Brown. 'There's a Segway at Chequers if you need to practise...'

I thought she was joking, but apparently there is – it was given to the Blairs as a gift and they wisely left it behind.

Mum and Dad had a party to celebrate their fortieth wedding anniversary today, and it was a wonderful all-day affair for close family and friends.

Dad eventually got up to make a speech, told a few jokes, thanked everyone for coming, but clean forgot to thank Mum for her decades of devoted, selfless, service.

'You'd better make it up to her,' warned Charlotte.

MONDAY, 3 SEPTEMBER 2007

Mum woke up this morning and found a gift-wrapped Mercedes convertible waiting outside for her.

Dad had definitely made amends.

My mobile rang when I got back to London tonight.

'Piers, it's Gordon. I'm just ringing to see how your ribs are?'

'Well, they're a bit Cameron-esque, Prime Minister. Battered, broken and nobody can tell me when they might improve.'

There was a long, raucous laugh.

We chatted for 20 minutes or so, and I have never heard him sound more positive and relaxed.

His approval ratings are through the roof, Cameron is getting kicked all over the place and the public seem to be loving this new, serious, kind of PM.

'You're having fun, aren't you?' I said at one stage.

'I wouldn't go as far as that,' he chuckled. 'I don't think being prime minister is supposed to be fun...but I am enjoying the challenge.'

I don't think it matters when Brown goes to the polls, he'll make mince-meat of Cameron.

TUESDAY, 4 SEPTEMBER 2007

I was just settling down for my usual rib-healing afternoon nap in front of another execrable True Movies love drama when the phone rang.

'Hello, Mr Morgan, it's the No. 10 switchboard here, I have the prime minister for you...'

What, again? Does the man not understand the meaning of the word 'rehabilitation'?

I quickly remembered my manners, though. 'Prime Minister! How lovely to hear from you again so soon.'

We discussed a brief matter of state before a sudden stroke of genius floated into my brain.

'Erm, Prime Minister...I don't suppose you're free tonight between 7 and 8 p.m.?'

'What for?'

'Well, I'm doing *Celebrity Who Wants To Be A Millionaire?* and I need one more name for my phone-a-friend list.'

He laughed.

'Well, I'm not doing it if you ask me about economics....and definitely not politics!'

'Right...silly me for assuming they might be two of your strong points, Prime Minister. What *are* you good at?'

'Sport. I'm good at sport. Who are you doing it with?'

'Emily Maitlis.'

'Oh, you'll do well then.'

'Well, we'll look good anyway... So, you're up for being my friend then?'

There was a long pause.

'Piers, I think these shows have a potential for acute embarrassment, so I'll leave it to an expert in that area. All I would say is keep smiling, whatever happens. I watched it last week and whoever the celebrities were forgot to smile when they lost all their money. That's a big mistake!'

I arrived at the Elstree studio where *Millionaire* is filmed to find a miserable-looking Sir Steve Redgrave waiting to leave with his wife, indicating things hadn't gone too well for them.

Chris Tarrant did nothing to calm my nerves.

'Oh no, not you again, Morgan…you were hopelessly thick last time.'

Which was cruel but fair – I'd limped to £16,000 with Ann Widdecombe before we bottled it and took the cash.

But Emily's as brainy as she's beautiful, so I had high hopes of doing much better.

'Your chosen charity tonight is Wellbeing For Women, Piers,' Tarrant added, 'which seems a rather inappropriate choice…'

'Pretty rich coming from you!' I retorted, knowing this exchange would not appear but would amuse the hell out of the audience (Tarrant's wife recently left him after it was revealed he's had a lengthy affair).

We got to £50,000 before stumbling over what part of a plant jojoba oil comes from. We asked the audience, they said 'root', and the answer was 'seed'.

Backstage afterwards, Tarrant was amusingly frustrated about his year of tabloid hell.

'Why is everyone so fascinated by my sex life?' he asked.

'Because we're all just amazed at how an old goat like you is still getting so much action,' I replied.

'*You're* amazed,' he chuckled.

THURSDAY, 6 SEPTEMBER 2007

One of NBC's top executives, Meredith Ahr, called me today.

She oversees *America's Got Talent* with another great guy called Craig Plestis, and had a new show for me to consider.

'We're making a celebrity version of *The Apprentice* with Donald Trump, and want you in it.'

Wow. Now this is tempting.

Trump started the original *Apprentice* format in the States, and it's been a huge success. But ratings began to dip in the last series, so they've clearly decided to sling a bit of stardust into the mix and see what happens.

Meredith confirmed that they got the idea, both for the series and my involvement, from the Comic Relief show that we did back in Britain.

'Who else is doing it?' I asked.

'Gene Simmons has signed up, Lennox Lewis, and a load of others. It's going to be crazy.'

I spent the rest of the day mulling it over, and eventually emailed The Ferret:

'The only point of me doing it would be from the humour standpoint of being a "smart, snarky Brit" having to endure these ghastly celebs, and rising effortlessly above it all. The potential upside is I get to raise my profile further in the States, have a bit of fun, refuse to take it too seriously, take the piss out of the other celebs and Trump a bit, do NBC a favour and escape with my reputation enhanced.

'The potential downside is if I emerge as a talentless, thick Brit twat, no better than a bloke who stuck his tongue out onstage for 20 years, and a bunch of reality losers.

'Your advice would be valuable.'

His response was rather less tortuous: 'Do it.'

SATURDAY, 8 SEPTEMBER 2007

To Lords for the one-day cricket international.

I was greeted in a hospitality box by our host, Ian Botham's lawyer Naynesh Desai, with an immediate jab to my broken ribs.

'That's from Beefy,' he chuckled, as I writhed in pain. 'He asked me to hit them as soon as you arrived.'

By 3 p.m., it was hard to imagine a more idyllic scene: England winning, the sun out, legends of the game like Allan Lamb popping in to regale us with hilarious tales, the champagne flowing.

And then I detected a sudden *froideur* in the box, of the kind that once caused the original Ice Age.

It was Jude Law.

He'd arrived with Gary Kemp, the common link being they had both been married to Sadie Frost, and for an hour Jude and I just ignored each other.

Then he stopped me by the bar.

'You're an LA man aren't you?'

'Yes,' I replied, assuming this was some Hollywood in-set thing.

'I thought so – I went to school there, too.'

Now I was confused.

'Where?'

'Alleyns.' (A private school in South London – and no, I didn't go there.)

'Oh, sorry, I thought you said LA.'

It was Jude's turn to look perplexed.

We chatted for a while, mainly about how absurd Madonna is, and then a truly disturbing thing happened: I began to think he was quite a nice bloke.

Still reeling from this revelation, I stumbled down to Michael Parkinson's box, where the great man was relaxing with umpiring legend Dickie Bird, actor Anthony Andrews and comedian Sanjeev Bhaskar, before the start of his last-ever chat-show series.

'Come on then, Parky, what was the greatest moment of them all?' I asked.

He thought for a few seconds, before replying: 'The Ali interviews were brilliant, but it's hard to get past the opening line I once had to say: "Ladies and gentlemen, Fred Astaire..."'

An excited young man suddenly appeared.

'Hi, sorry to interrupt you but I've got a mate outside who you may want to meet.'

'Oh really, why?'

'Because his name is Piers Morgan.'

I laughed. I've heard of three other unfortunate (for them) namesakes over the years but never actually met one.

Piers Morgan 2 arrived, burly, bald as a coot, and with a beaming grin.

I shook his hand. 'I can only apologise...'

'Don't worry about it,' he chuckled. 'It's been a bit of a nightmare, but at least I get good tables in restaurants...'

THURSDAY, 13 SEPTEMBER 2007

Northern Rock, one of Britain's biggest banks, is on the verge of going bust, a development that has caused instant panic for obvious reasons.

It's all a result of this ongoing sub-prime mortgage scandal in America, and an indicator of just how serious the situation really is.

I rang my own bank Coutts and asked how much of my money is safe if they were ever to go bust, too.

'£35,000,' came the terrifying reply.

I'm not a financial expert, but even I can tell that something very bad is going down here. And like everyone else, I feel totally powerless. Banks are supposed to be the last genuinely safe haven for our money. If they can no longer be trusted, then who CAN we trust? And if the banks are going down, where will all this end?

FRIDAY, 21 SEPTEMBER 2007

When I get a suntan, like now, a small but prominent scar emerges above my right eye – a permanent delightful remnant of my fisticuffs with Jeremy Clarkson. Well, his fisties in my cuffs anyway, via three right hooks.

Although we recently made up over a 3 a.m. bottle of red wine, I think we both feel a slight residual tension in the relationship.

Today, though, there has been a stunning development. I sent Jeremy a formal request to be my official Facebook 'friend'. And after a few days' deliberation he has accepted the invitation. Indeed, he has gone one step further and now invited me to confirm a further detail.

'Jeremy Clarkson says you "hooked up" – please confirm to Facebook that this is true,' came the message.

SUNDAY, 23 SEPTEMBER 2007

Celia and I are in the South of France on a long weekend, and found ourselves at the gloriously extravagant Hôtel du Cap in Antibes today.

As we lounged by the pool in the afternoon, a group of young American bankers and their wives arrived. And for the next two hours, the men stood by the diving board that lips out over the ocean, and noisily competed to see who could do the most outrageous triple tow-loop.

As the beer flowed, so their voices grew ever louder and more obnoxious.

These were the worst kind of Americans, the brash, cocky types from Wall Street. The very epitome of capitalist bullshit, who couldn't give a damn about anyone else around them. The ones whose greed has brought America's economy crashing down, and its reputation with it.

'YEE-HAH!' screamed one, as he flung himself into the ether, the girls all shrieking with over-excitement.

'GO GET 'EM, TIGER!' hollered another, as his mate careered backwards off the board.

This lot used to be the only type of American I ever met. Which is why I had such a ghastly opinion of them all.

Thankfully, since I've spent so much time over there, I've now grown to realise that these hideous braggarts are the exception, not the rule. In the same way that our repulsive football hooligans don't represent the average Briton.

WEDNESDAY, 26 SEPTEMBER 2007

Sir Alan Sugar texts: 'Started filming new series of *Apprentice* this week. Sixteen people shitting themselves! Of course I made them all feel very welcome...'

I can perfectly understand why they would feel apprehensive. Filming just one episode of *The Apprentice* for Sir Alan was one of the most gruelling experiences of my life. I can't imagine how hellish a whole series must be...which reminds me that it's only three weeks until I start filming *Celebrity Apprentice* in New York.

Half of me is looking forward to it. The other half is thinking: 'What the hell are you doing, you idiot?'

If I'm slung out by Trump in the first couple of rounds, then I'll look like a useless failure, a washed-up celebrity has-been, and my whole American TV career could quite quickly come to a shuddering halt.

But if I do well, or even win it, then it could be a fantastic experience and a brilliant platform to really establish myself in the States.

It's a hell of a gamble though, and as the days draw nearer, my confidence is receding.

THURSDAY, 27 SEPTEMBER 2007

Alastair Campbell has agreed to be interviewed by me for *GQ*, which both astonishes and excites me.

Short of getting Tony Blair sitting in front of me, I can't think of anyone I'd like to pin to the floor about Iraq and the gruesome art of political spin – or 'lying' as we laymen prefer to call it – more than Mr Campbell.

I don't know why he's willing to expose himself like this, but I'm delighted he has.

This is going to be fun!

FRIDAY, 28 SEPTEMBER 2007

If there are two words guaranteed to send even the most confident celebrity into spasms of panic, then it's these: Red Carpet.

Most parties I attend have a smattering of photographers outside, but dealing with them is quite easy: a nod here, a cheesy grin there, a quick wave to your adoring fan, a deaf ear to the cries of 'Morgan, you're a twat'.

The whole thing lasts 30 seconds, and then you're safe inside and guzzling a complimentary glass of champagne.

But the Red Carpet is a very different proposition.

Tonight, for example, it was the inaugural National Movie Awards in London. And the Red Carpet was so long Paula Radcliffe would have been crouching by the side before she reached the end.

For me, still hobbling with the remnants of my battered ribs, it yawned ahead like a vast cavernous never-ending tunnel of potential humiliation.

My journey into hell started OK. At least five people amid the throng of a thousand members of the public, 100 photographers and 50 TV crews shouted 'Piers! Piers!', allowing me to stop and preen like the proverbial Cheshire cat for a few seconds.

And things improved as the showbiz man from Sky beckoned me over to address the nation.

But just as I started to speak, he was suddenly distracted.

'Judi! Judi!' he bellowed over my shoulder.

I turned to find the great Dame Dench gliding into view.

For the man from Sky, it was a no brainer.

'Sorry, Piers, but…'

'Someone more important has arrived?'

He nodded, and I shuffled on – desperately hoping nobody had noticed my shameful snub.

I was rescued by a portly, slightly mad-looking autograph-hunter.

'You're a celebrity now!' he shrieked, excitedly.

'No he's fucking not!' shouted another 'fan' with a cheerful grin. 'He's a twat!'

Before I could remonstrate with him, a PR woman grabbed my arm and pulled me towards the wall of paparazzi on the other side of the Red Carpet.

The bulbs exploded pleasingly all over the place as I put my best 'I'm a massive global phenomenon' face on.

Then the same PR grabbed me again and hurriedly pulled me out of the way. I tried to resist but the grip was firm and determined, as the sound of 'DANIEL! DANIEL!' filled the air.

I was consoled – no man could ever complain about being upstaged by James Bond. But no, it wasn't Daniel Craig as I had thought.

It was Daniel Radcliffe. Meaning I had just suffered the indignity of being shoved out of the limelight for Harry bloody Potter.

I retired to the bar, still glowering with embarrassment, and found Dame Judi waiting with some friends. A few minutes later, another sea of flashes signalled the arrival of another major star – this time Dame Judi's No. 1 rival for the title of Britain's movie queen, Dame Helen Mirren, who looked absolutely fabulous.

Judi turned and gave Helen a long, lingering, head-to-toe stare.

I can't read minds. But if I could, I reckon that judging by her stony expression, Dame Judi's thought process was something along the lines of: 'Damn it, Mirren's pulled it out of the bag again.'

TUESDAY, 2 OCTOBER 2007

General Election talk is reaching fever pitch in the papers, fuelled quite deliberately by Gordon Brown's aides indicating that it is very much on the prime minister's mind.

Most Westminster people think Brown should go for it, and so do I.

He's in a very powerful position, Cameron looks dead and buried, and anyway, to rein back now might look weak.

WEDNESDAY, 3 OCTOBER 2007

Matthew Vaughan and his wife Claudia Schiffer threw a fantastically lavish party at their Notting Hill home tonight, to celebrate Matthew's latest hit film *Stardust*.

I arrived first, having skipped the premiere, and the second person through the door was Jeremy Clarkson.

'Ah…my Facebook friend,' I said, trying to break the ice before he broke my head again.

'It was a mistake,' he snarled. 'I pressed the wrong button.'

I escaped to the bar where I found Clare Staples, who has the dubious privilege of being Robbie Williams' latest squeeze.

'He's lovely,' she said, 'but he'll kill me if I am seen talking to you.'

Pause.

'After he's killed you.'

By coincidence, Jemima Khan then shimmied past. She is dating someone else who wants to kill me – serial whinger Hugh Grant, who has never forgiven me for buying up the story of his Los Angeles prostitute friend Divine Brown when I was editing the *News of the World*.

I stopped her in her tracks.

'Hi, Jemima.'

She stared at me in total horror. 'Oh my God, you're too scary. I can't…'

'…be seen talking to me, I know – it's becoming a familiar theme tonight.'

Jemima giggled, the ice thawed and we chatted for 15 minutes. She's more attractive in the flesh than I thought she'd be, and funnier too.

'If it's any consolation, Hugh can't hate you that much because he hasn't even chucked baked beans over you yet. Jeremy Clarkson definitely hates you more than Hugh does.'

'No, no…Jeremy and I are best friends now. Ask him – he's right behind you.'

She turned and there was Clarkson, guffawing at one of his own jokes.

'We're friends, aren't we, Jezza?' I said.

'NO!' he shouted, furiously. 'I just hit the wrong button on Facebook.'

Jemima laughed. 'I'm on that too.'

'Perhaps we could be friends, then?' I suggested.

'But how can I be friends with a journalist?' she sighed.

FRIDAY, 5 OCTOBER 2007

Peter Fincham has been forced to resign from the BBC over Queengate. Absurd. There's an increasingly ridiculous culture in Britain that demands a resignation following every so-called scandal, however small and insignificant.

Football managers, politicians, TV stars, and now even BBC1 controllers, all have to leave their jobs if the media say so, even if such a punishment far outweighs the crime.

If I'd been running the BBC, I'd have said: 'Mr Fincham made a mistake, nobody died, so he's going nowhere. Now, let's all get over ourselves shall we?'

SATURDAY, 6 OCTOBER 2007

Right, well don't say I haven't tried…

After all my efforts to restore peace to our tempestuous relationship, Jeremy Clarkson writes in his *Sun* column today: 'I received an invitation to be Piers Morgan's [Facebook] friend. Desperately looking for a box that said "I'd rather eat my own testicles", I accidentally hit "Confirm".'

He adds: 'I see there's a box inviting me to "poke" Piers. I did that once and broke my damn finger.'

On a more positive note, Jemima Khan has become my Facebook friend, saying: 'I am a little nervy around you – it's true – but I was amused to meet you all the same. X.'

It's a weird thing this Facebook lark. But quite fun.

I'm now 'friends' with 265 people, many of whom I've never met before in my entire life. My criteria for accepting friends are a) I actually know and like them, b) I don't know them but they say something nice about something I've done professionally, or c) I know them and don't like them, but it's just too embarrassing to decline.

All sorts of people have popped out of the woodwork – ex-schoolmates, ex-girlfriends, work colleagues, long-lost cousins. Unfortunately, it's also attracted an array of people who want to kill me, abuse me, or date me (and unfortunately the accompanying photos in this last category make even the thought of this quite unthinkable…).

My celebrity 'friends' so far include Clarkson, Jemima, Dom Joly, Nick Ferrari, Victoria Hervey, Toby Young, Andrew Neil and Yoko Ono (though that may be a spoof entry!)

Which probably just confirms why no sensible human being should go anywhere near it.

SUNDAY, 7 OCTOBER 2007

Gordon Brown is *not* going to the polls, explaining: 'The easiest thing I could have done was call an election, which we would win on competence, whether we had it today, next week, or weeks after. But I want the chance in the next phase of my premiership to develop and show people the policies that are going to make a huge difference and make a change in the whole country itself.'

Predictably, the Tories, Lib Dems and the media are already hammering him as a ditherer, a bottler and a coward.

The mistake was not necessarily deciding against it, though I think that it is a mistake. It was leading everyone up the garden path into thinking he was going to call one. That's just bad politics.

MONDAY, 8 OCTOBER 2007

Sat with Sarah Brown at an NSPCC fund-raising dinner tonight, and she was on sparkling form despite all the aggro now engulfing her husband.

'I didn't think you'd turn up,' I said.

'Why not?'

'Because I assumed you'd bottle it...'

Sarah fixed me with the kind of look a wise carer gives a hyperactive idiot savant.

'Oh, very amusing, Piers. I see what you did there.'

'Rough week?'

'Gordon has done the right thing, and it will all blow over,' she said firmly. Sarah's always been extraordinarily calm under pressure, which must be a huge asset to him.

'I'd have gone for it,' I replied. 'But then I'm the guy who once looked at a set of photos of British soldiers abusing Iraqis and declared: "They look good to me, chaps..."'

She laughed. 'Exactly!'

David Cameron has suddenly gone from halfwit to genius, with Brown heading the other way just as fast. But I've always believed in the maxim that form is temporary, class is permanent. And when push comes to shove, are we really going to vote for another smooth-talking, fresh-faced, old Etonian snake-oil salesman so soon after Bomber Blair shuffled off to laughably 'bring peace' to a region he personally helped destroy? I think not.

TUESDAY, 9 OCTOBER 2007

My mobile rang and I saw that it was Sarah Brown.

'Hi,' I answered.

Silence.

'Sarah?'

More silence, followed by a slight gurgling noise and the phone went dead.

God…has all the pressure turned the First Lady to the bottle, I thought?

I called back, concerned.

'Ah, sorry about that,' giggled Sarah.

'It was John [her four-year-old son]. He has started randomly ringing people on my phone.'

WEDNESDAY, 10 OCTOBER 2007

I woke up quite literally licking my lips with anticipation at the thought of interviewing Alastair Campbell.

'There is a café in Regent's Park called the Honest Sausage,' he suggested.

'That sounds an appropriate place for this encounter.'

A minute later came a second text: 'I may be wearing Lycra.'

We met at the Honest Sausage and ordered two cups of coffee.

He was indeed wearing Lycra and sweating profusely from a long bike ride.

'So, Alastair…'

'Yes, Piers…'

The bizarreness of this was not lost on either of us.

'I suppose my first question has to be whether you consider yourself to be an Honest Sausage?'

'Well, I'm definitely not a sausage. But I think I'm honest, yeah. And I think one of the reasons why I have such bad relations with the press is that the papers spend their entire time demanding politicians tell the truth, but when they are confronted with people in politics who do that, and say what they really think, then we get a bad press.'

'Did you ever lie to the press?'

'Look, you and I both know that there were times when you would ask me a direct question and I would know the answer, but for political or strategic reasons you don't want to give it…'

'So you lied?'

'No, I don't think that is lying. I would not answer the question in this case, and you would know what I was doing. I did not see it from my first day in office as a case of me having to help the press do their job. It was the other way round – they had to help me do mine. And sometimes it meant you couldn't tell people things you knew.'

'There were times though when you would deliberately mislead journalists...'

'Such as?'

'Such as when you gave an article by Bill Clinton on the Ulster peace refer-endum that we had organised at the *Mirror* to the *Sun* – and then lied to me about doing that all night until you eventually broke down and admitted it...'

'I didn't break down...'

'You did. And then said you had "done it for peace".'

'I didn't say that.'

'You did.'

(Laughing uncontrollably.) 'God, did I?'

'Yes. You handed our exclusive article to our main competitor and lied about it.'

'I didn't hand it to them...'

'You did.'

'Piers, I didn't.'

'Alastair, you did.'

'I did not. I arranged for a better version to be written and gave that to the *Sun* – it wasn't word for word the same.'

'Oh, bollocks. You stiffed us and you know you did. Why are you denying it?'

'I'm not denying it...'

'You are. And in the Honest Sausage, too. Come on, just admit it.'

'OK, I'm not denying I stiffed you, and that's unfortunate. But both the *Mirror* and the *Sun* felt they were entitled to special treatment and it was a fucking pain in the arse, to be honest.'

'Does Tony regret being so closely aligned to Bush? Would it have been easier if Clinton had still been president?'

'Oh yeah, of course it would.'

'People found it hard to stomach a Labour prime minister being so supportive of a right-wing president who gave every impression of being a complete idiot.'

'Yes, but again to give Tony some credit, in full knowledge of that image problem he stayed focused on what he thought was the reality of our own national interest. People seem quite surprised that I am supportive about

Bush, but I find it totally dumb to think that we should have marched round slagging off the leader of the most powerful country in the world. If Tony was doing a guidebook to a future prime minister about what were the most important aspects to the job, then I reckon that he would put "getting on with the American president" pretty high on the list. He got on very well with Clinton, personally and politically, and strategically. And he started out strategically with Bush, but I think what he got out of Bush – and this is what I liked about him, too – is that Bush is very, very plain speaking. He is just a bit like Prescott in that he mangles his words.'

'Well, that's the problem, isn't it? He comes across as an inarticulate very right-wing, Texan redneck.'

'Yeah, but if you're prime minister you can't choose who the American president is going to be. I think you've got to think long and hard about whether the relationship with America really matters – and I think it does.'

'Having fought the war specifically on the assumption that Saddam had WMD, would it not have been the honourable thing for Tony to have resigned when the weapons didn't turn up?'

'No. Because that would have meant Tony accepting the main charge against him which is that he took the country to war under a false premise.'

'Well, he did. That's inarguable. The only argument is whether he did it deliberately dishonestly.'

'He certainly wasn't dishonest, and what he presented to parliament is what he believed. We all have to accept that the WMD haven't turned up yet, but I subscribe to the theory that they were there but must have gone somewhere. Not all the intelligence can have been wrong.'

'If you had known then what you know now, would Tony have sanctioned war?'

'It's not as easy as that.'

'Yes it is. It's absolutely as easy as that. If you had known that WMD didn't exist, then what would you have done?'

'OK, well if we had known that Saddam did not have any WMD then clearly we could not have made the case for going to war that we did, on the basis of WMD. We would have to have done it on the grounds of policy regime change.'

'And would you have done that?'

'I don't know. Government is not done in hindsight.'

I was curious what he thought of the furore over Brown supposedly 'bottling' the election.

'If you were still there during this recent party conference, would you have allowed the election talk to get as out of hand as it did?'

'I hope not, no. I arrived at the Bournemouth conference and everyone was talking about the election, and I thought it was just a media thing. But then I was talking to Alan Milburn and John Reid and they were both quite keen on the idea, and I said, "I don't understand this – why are we talking about the election?" The reason Gordon had done well at the start was that his strengths were based on long-term stability and then suddenly there is all this stuff about a snap election and that became the narrative for the Tory conference rather than whether Cameron could hold his party together. I just couldn't see the point of ratcheting up the election talk unless you were definitely going to have an election. Just don't do it unless you mean it.'

'Do you believe Tony was always honest about the succession issue with Gordon, or did events just change things?'

'I know there was a point at which Tony thought about it, and clearly Gordon was in the mix. But I think Tony lost his nerve…'

'And so a guy who thinks he is about to become prime minister gets shafted.'

'Look, the idea that two guys could sit around in 1995 and one of them says to the other, "Right, I'll be leader then you take over after the next election" – I mean, the world doesn't work like that.'

'Of course it does. That's exactly how it works.'

'Tony is very, very good at…er…politics.'

'You mean lying?'

'Tony doesn't lie.'

'Well, one of them lied. You can sit there and look me in the eye and say that Gordon was never ever led to believe that Tony might be going and he might be taking over?'

(Laughs louder.) 'I would ask Tony if he had done a deal with Gordon and he would say no.'

'So he lied to you, then.'

(Laughs even louder, for so long he can barely speak.)

I pressed harder. 'When I hear you say you never heard Tony say he'd told Gordon he might be going, I know you're lying.'

'Right, were there periods where Gordon might have thought that Tony might be leaving, there might well have been.'

'Did Tony ever lie to you?'

'I think sometimes when you are managing certain people and certain events then you might leave different impressions with different people.'

'So he lied to you then!'

Alastair laughed again, so I determined to try even harder to embarrass him.

'When I became editor of the *News of the World* I actually broke the story of your shameful past as a gigolo on the French Riviera and porn writer for *Forum* magazine.'

'That's right. It was soon after I first met you, an event I remember oddly well. Probably because I couldn't believe what a twat you were.'

'Oh, the feeling was mutual, don't worry. But just to clarify, you were a gigolo?'

'Erm…no, not really.'

'Not really? Did you or did you not look after wealthy older ladies for money in return for giving them sexual favours?'

'Not in the way it was described in…' (Bursts out laughing.)

'You were fairly explicit, mate.'

'This is quite difficult for me because I was forced to admit that some of what I wrote wasn't true. There was a grain of truth in it but it was exaggerated a bit.'

'Right, so not for the first time, you sexed things up a bit.'

(Shakes his head.)

'If you were writing your epitaph, what would you like it to say?'

'Erm…'

'How about: "HERE LIES ALASTAIR CAMPBELL. AGAIN".'

(Laughs loudly.) 'No, what about "HERE LIES AN HONEST SAUSAGE".'

THURSDAY, 11 OCTOBER 2007

Alastair Campbell had his photo taken by the legendary David Bailey today, to go with our interview – and he sent me a gleeful text detailing the following exchange that took place during the shoot:

BAILEY: Who did the words for this then?

CAMPBELL: Piers Morgan.

BAILEY: Who the fuck is that?

BAILEY'S WIFE CATHERINE: Isn't he a celebrity chef?

Hmm. If I don't do well in this *Celebrity Apprentice* thing, I might as well be.

Me dressed as King Arthur on the streets of New York for *Celebrity Apprentice*. As one British passer-by put it: 'Piers, what *are* you doing?'

'I have made the tough decisions, always with an eye toward the bottom line. Perhaps it's time America was run like a business.' DONALD TRUMP

TUESDAY, 16 OCTOBER 2007

I've flown into New York to start filming *Celebrity Apprentice*. I have no idea what to expect, other than a lot of hard work (they've warned me that the hours are horrendous the longer you stay in). The other contestants include Gene Simmons, Vinny 'Big Pussy' Pastore from *The Sopranos*, Stephen *Usual Suspects* Baldwin, gymnastic legend Nadia Comaneci, Ultimate Fighting Champion Tito Ortiz, country singer Trace Adkins, and Lennox Lewis. An eclectic mix!

We all gathered today at Trump Towers to meet the great man and have some publicity photos done. It was a weird afternoon, 14 massive egos circling each other like suspicious sharks in a small pond. And I could feel the testosterone surging from every pore of the men, most of whom were huge. Simmons and Lennox both stand at six foot five, Ortiz is six foot four and Adkins six foot seven.

As we posed for a group picture, I was told by the photographer to move closer to the woman in front of me, who turned out to be Marilu Henner, one of my teenage pin-ups from the hit American comedy series, *Taxi*.

'This is strange, isn't it?' she whispered.

'Very,' I whispered back. 'I used to have you on my bedroom wall.'

I knew from my experience on the Comic Relief episode that everyone is always terribly nice to each other before the challenges start, but then adrenaline, tiredness, ego and personality clashes kick in, and all hell breaks loose.

What was clear after this afternoon's 'getting to know each other' session is that Gene Simmons has a self-esteem of astronomical proportions, and clearly just assumes he is going to win; Trace Adkins doesn't speak, he just sits there like some giant gun-toting cowboy in a bar, staring everyone out; Stephen Baldwin already seems very bossy and irritating, and most of them are only vaguely aware of who I am.

Unlike the usual *Apprentice* series, the winner won't be getting a job with Trump, obviously. Instead, we will all be competing to raise money for individual charities.

I've had to choose an American charity under the rules of the show, so I've gone for the Intrepid Fallen Heroes Fund, which supports seriously wounded soldiers. It has helped British soldiers in the past, and seems a very worthy cause, particularly given the large volume of troops returning badly hurt from Iraq and Afghanistan at the moment.

I'd met Lennox Lewis a few times in the old newspaper days, and suggested we grab a coffee somewhere later.

After the photos, we strolled off to find a Starbucks near Central Park, and in the three blocks we walked together I discovered what it is like to be a REAL global phenomenon, rather than just tell everyone you're one like I do.

Every step we took, someone shouted 'Champ!' at him. Hotdog sellers, newspaper vendors, construction workers, students, a series of highly attractive women...it didn't seem to matter what age, colour, IQ or religion they were, everybody knew The Champ.

'Is it like this for you everywhere you go?' I asked.

'Yeah, pretty much,' he replied. 'Boxing is such a global sport now that even when I think I'm somewhere that nobody would know me, a voice will shout "Hey, champ" at me.'

'Yes,' I concurred, 'I know the problem.'

Lennox stopped, looked at me and shook his head with pity in his eyes. And then laughed, loudly.

I think we're going to get along well. He's a Londoner, like me.

WEDNESDAY, 17 OCTOBER 2007

Donald Trump set us our first challenge today – to run a hotdog stall on a street of our choosing in Manhattan. We all laughed loudly when he revealed what it was, thinking this would be an easy start. But the devil with *The Apprentice* is always in the detail, and the rulebook for this apparently simple challenge was about five pages long.

As we walked through New York's Mercantile Exchange, where we'd been taken to hear the challenge being announced, one of the contestants, a woman called Omarosa Manigault-Stallworth, sidled up to me. The only thing I knew about her was that she was voted 'Biggest Bitch on TV' after her performance on the first-ever series of *The Apprentice*.

'Do you want a showmance?' she purred.

'A what?'

'A showmance…you know, we get it on together. Happens all the time on *Apprentice*, everyone has sex together.'

I stared at her grasping, ferociously ambitious little eyes, and laughed. 'You must be joking.'

She didn't take it well. 'What are you? Gay?'

It was an extraordinary, and rather unsettling encounter, the kind of thing the public assume probably goes on but which my cynical media head told me was just a load of hype.

Both teams – we'd been split into men and women – were driven back to our respective 'war rooms' inside Trump Tower; these are specially built areas where most of our planning for the next few weeks will take place, and come equipped with computers, food and drink, phones and other basic essentials.

As we sat waiting to start, Lennox pointed to a chess set in the corner.

'You play?'

I was my school chess champion two years running.

'Oh, I play all right, Lennox.'

We laid out the board, and started. Now chess is supposed to be a slow game, with the players spending several minutes pondering each move.

But Lennox plays it like he boxed. Jab. Jab. Jab. Jab. WHACK. Jab. Jab. Jab. WHACK.

He moved so fast and furiously that within five minutes the board resembled *The Texas Chainsaw Massacre*.

Lennox was good, very, very good. In fact, he is the best chess player I have come up against, bar none. And far more physically imposing.

I decided the only way to counter him was to go on the attack.

'Even been smacked in the solar plexus?' I sneered as I took his knight with my pawn.

Lennox said nothing.

'Ooh baby, this is gonna *hurt*,' I cackled, as my bishop out-smarted his castle.

Lennox said nothing.

'Wham, bam, thank you, Ma'am...' I giggled, as I moved my queen into what I thought was a match-winning position.

Lennox said nothing.

After exactly 13 minutes, he suddenly stood up and walked away.

'Where are you going?'

He stopped and grinned.

'It's over, man.'

'What do you mean, "It's over"? Sit down and stop being so ridiculous.'

'No man, it's *over*. I've knocked you out.'

I stared back at the board, panic rising.

'How?'

Lennox returned to the crime scene, and slowly moved his queen towards my king. My eyes helplessly flitted around the board like a rat caught in the headlights of a two-ton Hummer.

It *was* over. He had indeed knocked me out.

I'd been beaten at chess by a boxer.

Lennox chortled and slapped me across the back, so hard I thought my shoulder blades were going to snap on the spot.

'Better luck next time, sunshine.'

The first thing we had to do was come up with a name for our team, and then choose our first project manager. That role is a dangerous one early on, because if you lose then Trump often blames the project manager, and you can get fired straight away. I'd already decided to keep my head down for a few challenges, until I'd settled into the rhythm of the show. That attitude, though, can also be dangerous – because Trump might single you out for shirking leadership, and that in his book is a despicable crime.

After half an hour of scrabbling around for a name, Gene, who had immediately insisted on being the first project manager, suddenly raised his arm.

'I have it. We should be called "Hydra".'

'Why?' asked Tito.

'Because it was a mythical savage three-headed dog that guarded the gates of hell.'

(To which Vinny Pastore observed: 'No, that was my ex-wife.')

'No, it wasn't,' I said.

Six heads turned towards me.

'That was Cerberus. But Hydra is more appropriate because it was a seven-headed monster, and we are seven-strong.'

Gene looked at me coldly. He doesn't like being upstaged, and he certainly doesn't like being wrong.

But I'll say this about him; he is a good businessman.

As we quibbled about whether to charge $10 or $100 for our hotdogs, Gene just calmly picked up a phone, called a rich mate and asked him to come and buy one for $5,000.

'It's not the vacuum cleaner that gets sold,' he explained, as we reeled with shock, 'it's the way the salesman sells the cleaner.'

Which, when you consider that he has sold 13 million Kiss musical toothbrushes, is probably true.

By making that call, Simmons changed the whole game right then and there.

I had no idea that we would be required to tap friends to raise such big sums of cash, and I don't think anyone else did either. Mentally, I resolved to email everyone I knew when I got back to the hotel tonight, asking them if they would consider helping me with a future challenge. As Jeremy's unofficial regimental motto goes, 'Prior Planning and Preparation Prevents Piss-poor Performance.'

By weird irony, our selected pitch was right outside Rupert Murdoch's News Corporation HQ in Manhattan, and according to this morning's *New York Post*, he is there today with Tony Blair.

I was praying they'd walk out halfway through the challenge to find me standing there, shouting: 'Hotdog, gentlemen?'

We had three hours to sell our dogs, and it was controlled chaos throughout. The rules stated that we had to take either cash, cheques or credit cards, running those through the machines ourselves.

My job on the task was to deploy a megaphone and encourage grim-faced New Yorkers to buy the dogs, matching their 'get outta my freakin' way' rudeness with my own – 'There goes the meanest man in New York, ladies and gentlemen.' Which nearly got me several smacks, but was very satisfying.

'How much?' snarled back one builder.

'Fifty dollars?' I suggested.

'You gotta be kidding me!' he replied, walking off at high speed.

But we did start to shift a lot of dogs at that kind of price, while Gene's mates kept turning up clutching cheques for $5,000 or $10,000. Quite extraordinary.

As was the sudden arrival of first New York's Mayor, Michael Bloomberg, and Donald Trump, closely followed by the infamous porn star Jenna Jameson.

'What's she doing here?' I asked, bemused.

'She's my girlfriend,' bristled Tito.

'Like a hot British sausage, Jenna?' I asked.

'Love one,' she sniggered. 'With extra relish please...'

What surprised me was that she was treated like a proper celebrity by passers-by. The adult entertainment game is pretty mainstream over here, and doesn't carry anything like the stigma that it does back in Britain.

We finished just as the heavens opened, and rain crashed down on our stand. Any earlier, and we'd have been completely drenched and all our punters would have stayed inside.

'Thank the Lord!' said Stephen Baldwin, eyeing the skies. He's a born-again Christian of pronounced zealotry, having previously been one of Hollywood's biggest hellraisers. I get the feeling that The Lord will be making numerous appearances in days to come...

We got taken back to our hotel, Trump International. Unlike the contestants in the usual *Apprentice*, we don't have to sleep together, which would have been a dealbreaker for me. We each have our own room in the same hotel instead, which is much more civilised.

I got straight on to my laptop and began firing off emails to potential donors.

THURSDAY, 18 OCTOBER 2007

We were driven to our first boardroom confrontation this morning in a small-ish van, seven large men confined to a space more suitable to an under-14 hockey team.

And thanks to the shocking nature of New York's traffic, which is miles worse even than London's, we were stuck in there for over 45 minutes while we travelled just a few blocks.

'This is shit,' observed Trace, in what was virtually his first public utterance. He's a massive man who exudes an air of silent menace. I checked him out on the Internet last night, and he recently wrote a book called *A Personal Stand: Observations and Opinions from a Freethinking Roughneck*.

These opinions included the following: 'If anybody wonders who the good guys are and who the bad guys are in the world, just look at the way we teach our children as opposed to the way the fundamentalist Muslims teach their children.'

Global warming? 'Americans always want to take on the sins for the entire world, this time for the damned planet warming up. They says Mars is getting warmer, and nobody lives there.'

On Americans: 'We won't mess with you or bother you, but just know that when you kill innocent Americans, you've opened that can and we're gonna come for you. Like the Romans did.'

On 9/11: 'If I'd been president then, I'd have... let's not go there.'

Further investigation revealed a rather colourful life in which he was stabbed and beaten in numerous bar-room brawls, got shot in the heart and lungs by his ex-wife and had been a raging alcoholic until he quit the booze after a drink/drive conviction.

Quite a character!

Once the boardroom got under way, Trump revealed that we had absolutely murdered the girls' team by raising $52,000 for charity to their $17,000. An astonishing sum for a few sausages.

Unedifying scenes then followed as the ghastly Omarosa (I like to think of her as an African-American version of Jade Goody) fought to avoid being fired by Trump by abusing everyone else.

Eventually I decided to intervene.

'I know you're a celebrity, Omarosa, I've just never heard of you,' I said.

'Well, I've heard of you, you're known as an asshole back in Britain, and you've been fired from every job you've ever had,' she shouted back. 'What have *you* have ever done?'

'Well, I am currently starring in America's No. 1 television show, so I'm relatively happy with that.'

Trump loved it. I knew from watching a few previous episodes that there's nothing he likes more than conflict, and your chances of staying in the show definitely improve if you can regularly provide it.

The Hydra team retired to our war room, where we were allowed to watch the firing scene on a TV screen.

Omarosa was vicious to her colleagues, ripping them all to shreds.

Eventually the axe fell on Tiffany Fallon, a *Playboy* pet. She'd done nothing wrong, but just didn't stand up for herself enough.

Afterwards, the two teams were encouraged to share a drink with each other.

As I tucked into a large glass of celebratory wine, Omarosa screeched: 'You're a disgusting drunk!' (All Brits are automatically deemed drunks in America if they consume more than two glasses of wine.)

I just laughed, and replied: 'As Churchill said, "Madam, I may be drunk but you are very ugly, and tomorrow morning I shall be sober."'

Gene Simmons loved that, he is big on his historical quotes.

Tonight, the Hydra team had dinner together, and I couldn't help bringing up the subject of Iraq.

Trace listened to me banging on about what a mistake it was for a few minutes, and then slammed his fist down on the table. 'You're just talkin' bullshit, dude.'

The table fell quiet.

'Oh really, why?'

'Because Saddam should have been fucking nuked, that's why. You mess with America, then you're gonna get your ass busted.'

'Do you not think it's time America stopped being the world's policeman?'

'We don't wanna be, man, but someone has to do it. And we should be respected for it. And if you don't, and you kill innocent Americans, then we're gonna kill 1,000 of you for every one of us. If you think you have enough Monopoly money to stay in the game, then keep on and know that every time you land on Boardwalk, we're gonna collect.'

The unnerving aspect to this rant was that nobody else at the table seemed remotely perturbed by it, and once Trace had warmed up there was no stopping him.

'This thing with the Islamics is gonna come down to a scrap, and it's gonna be a big scrap, and we have to settle this once and for all.'

'How?'

'We're gonna have to take care of Afghanistan, incinerate it if we have to, and if Pakistan doesn't like it then we thump their ass, too. That's what America does to people that take us on. The only way to fight Islamic terrorism is to crack skulls. We need to flush them out of their caves and kill them. And then Americans can be like the Romans, and if we're ever confronted with trouble anywhere in the world then we just have to say "Civis Americanis". And that will be the end of it.'

Even Gene Simmons, who I thought might be rather more liberal, agreed with most of what he was hearing.

'You have to stand up to injustice,' said Gene, 'whether it's stopping the Germans and Japanese in the Second World War, or the Albanian Serbs in Bosnia, or the Viet Cong, or Africa, or the North Koreans...it's always America that has to do it. Others think the bad guys will just decide one day to lay down their weapons and we'll all be OK, but they won't. It's such an idiotic mindset to think they will. So America has to be the world's policeman, because if it's not then who will do it? The French?'

At which point, the whole table rocked with laughter. Americans absolutely loathe the French, and everything about them.

I went to bed feeling that if the majority of Americans feel the way Trace Adkins does, and I suspect they do, then this country is going nowhere fast. And like his beloved Romans, they will wake up one day and discover that the rest of the world has taken over, and their reign of power is finished.

FRIDAY, 19 OCTOBER 2007

The second challenge is to make a TV commercial promoting dog adoption for Pedigree.

My research was slightly distracted by going to wardrobe, and finding myself confronted by Nadia Comaneci in her underwear.

She was the Romanian gymnast who scored the first ever perfect 10 at the 1976 Montreal Olympics (I was 11 at the time, and recall experiencing strange stirrings at the sight of Nadia flinging her 14-year-old torso around the parallel bars...). And judging by the expansive cleavage she now sports, her plastic surgeon deserves a gold medal too.

'Oops,' she giggled, 'I 'ope you don't mind, Piers...'

'Not at all, Nadia,' I replied. 'I've waited 31 years for this.'

Gene Simmons and I clashed later after he started pompously quoting from *The Art of War* in our presentation, pronouncing the author Sun Tzu's name as 'sun shoe'. When I corrected him (it's 'sun sue'), he insisted: 'Oh, I was using the more traditional Mandarin.'

Which is complete nonsense, but was a good answer.

Gene was project manager again, and started bossing us all around like we were junior shelf-packers at the Kiss Organisation.

To be fair to him, he and Stephen Baldwin should know about making videos – they've been in that kind of business for 80 years between them.

So I happily left them to the technical stuff, and sat down with Trace to write the script. For an apparently dumb redneck he was surprisingly poetic, and despite being at very different ends of the political and social spectrum, we actually worked very well together. He also has a magnificently deep, cowboy voice.

Halfway through the afternoon, Ivanka Trump – Donald's daughter, who, with her brother Donald Junior, plays the role of 'eyes-and-ears' assistant to Trump – arrived unexpectedly to see how we were getting on.

She's beautiful, very smart and vitally important to our chances of success on this challenge given its subjective judging criteria.

But Gene just ignored her, so I started enthusiastically explaining our plans to Ivanka, only to then be cut off in mid-stream by Gene.

'It's terrific that you're here, Ivanka, but we've got work to do,' he said, dismissively.

Ivanka, unsurprisingly, wasn't amused.

'I don't think it's great that you've made me wait,' she said.

Gene then dug himself even deeper into the large hole he had created.

'Being the female of the species, does that mean you're going to be talking to your sisters about what we've talked about?'

I was stunned. Being a sexist pig to Ivanka is like telling Trump his hair's weird; it just isn't going to help...

Ivanka pursed her lips. 'To the women because I'm a woman? No,' she replied, tersely, 'I have no interest in doing that.' And with that she left.

Gene was unrepentant. 'She was wasting our time,' he insisted.

'You were bloody rude,' I responded. 'And that's just dumb.'

Despite this, though, the video was very strong – showing Lennox cuddling a rescue dog, with Trace's Nashville baritone as the soundtrack.

At 9 p.m., Gene announced that everyone but he and Stephen could go back to the hotel, so we did, and went to sleep. I, like everyone, was already exhausted from the relentless and gruelling nature of the work. But at 11 p.m., Tito woke me up again.

'I don't trust Gene,' he said. 'I think he's setting us up so that if we lose he can say we abandoned him. Let's go back.'

I wanted to go back to sleep, but there was method to his madness, and so I got back in my suit and we took the van back to the video suite, where Gene and Stephen greeted us like aliens from outer space.

'What are you doing here?' Gene said, with obvious irritation.

'Checking you two are not stiffing us,' I replied.

'*Stiffing* you?' snorted Baldwin. 'What the hell does that mean?'

'It means that a little tiny part of us thought you might be setting us up for a very large fall, Stephen. Now, show us the video.'

We watched it together in silence. And it was brilliant.

They may be bloody annoying, but they know how to make a video.

SATURDAY, 20 OCTOBER 2007

We showed the video to the Pedigree boss this morning, and he seemed to like it. But then, nobody gives much away at this stage.

In the ensuing boardroom, Gene was predictably held to account for his treatment of Ivanka.

'Did you insult my daughter?' demanded Trump. 'Nobody insults my daughter!'

'I sincerely apologise for any short-sightedness I may have had,' Gene replied, looking like he didn't give a damn.

Our team won the challenge despite his behaviour, which was hardly surprising when I heard that the girls' team had stood around holding hands, and 'imagining white light coming in' to inspire positivity.

Nadia Comaneci was fired, to my intense disappointment. The morning wardrobe session is not going to be anything like as much fun now.

Back to the war room this afternoon, and I got into another fascinating discussion with Gene, this time about business.

'The key to being a successful businessman is not to be arrogant in the way you do business. I am arrogant onstage, and in interviews, but not when it comes to business. Because if you get all full of yourself, and actually believe it, then you'll get killed. It's like Mike Tyson when he got knocked out by Buster Douglas in Japan. He thought he couldn't lose, and the moment you think that, you lose. I work hard, and that is the American dream – work hard, be a success and you will be rewarded and celebrated for it.'

He's right. Everywhere I go, I see this engrained in the American psyche. They do work hard, they only have three weeks' holiday a year. And they do applaud each other if they're successful. Their class system is based on it.

But Gene, and Trump for that matter, are also the prime examples of how Americans love their success stories to have big egos, and show off their success and wealth. Nowhere is that phrase 'if you've got it, flaunt it' more appropriate than in modern-day America.

As if to emphasise the rather different way that egotistical celebrities are treated in Britain, today's *Guardian* contains two separate whacks at me.

Francis Wheen describes David Cameron as 'the bastard child of Piers Morgan and Mr Bean' – which struck me as pretty rich coming from some-one who is the dead spit of Iain Duncan-Smith, only uglier and more stupid.

And their TV critic Charlie Brooker sneered: 'If I was compiling a list of things I wouldn't want to happen to me, "losing my ears in an accident" would rank pretty highly, just below "accidentally coating my own eyeballs with hot melted cheese" and three slots above "sharing a sleeping bag with Piers Morgan" (which comes one place higher than "being force-fed live mice").'

I should hate them for it, obviously. But I actually prefer the British way of dealing with success to the American way. Over-inflated balloons should be pricked.

MONDAY, 22 OCTOBER 2007

Our *Apprentice* van was driving through Manhattan this afternoon when I suddenly spotted Jeremy Paxman.

I pointed this fact out to Lennox.

'Who's he?' he asked.

'He presents *Newsnight*.'

'What's that?'

'It's a very serious political TV show in which he takes great delight in embarrassing people.'

Lennox nodded, digested this information, smiled, then leant his large dreadlocked head out of the window.

'OI! JEREMY! HOW YOU DOING, MAN?'

Paxo almost jumped out of his skin, then desperately started craning his neck to see who was shouting at him.

But we sped off before his eyes alighted on the culprits.

The third task was to create a mobile advertising campaign trailer for Kodak, and Trump threw an instant surprise by asking Gene if he fancied going over to the women's side as their project manager.

'It's a roll I was born for,' he declared, 'I'm the king of women.' Which given that he claims to have slept with 4,800 of them is not far from the truth. Simmons is in many ways an appalling human being, but I can't help liking him.

The Hydra team spent the afternoon working hard on the creative artwork for the trailer, which I suggested should involve Lennox and Tito in fight mode, selling Kodak's latest ink deal as a 'knockout punch' to the consumer.

Stephen Baldwin continues to be very annoying, but has lots of ideas, and is a useful addition to the team. But at 4 p.m., with just an hour to the deadline for handing in the artwork, disaster struck. As Tito and Lennox lay on a table for the photos, Stephen stood up on it to take the pictures and they fell off – flipping one cup of coffee high in the air and straight on to our iMac computer.

I've got Macs, so I know what happens when liquid gets inside them – they die. But you have a window of about two minutes to save stuff before it does.

We missed it by a few seconds. And lost everything.

'Congratulations, Stephen,' I observed, perhaps rather churlishly. 'You've just single-handedly ruined everything.'

At which point Trace erupted with anger. 'Just everybody CALM DOWN! We can still fix this.'

He doesn't say much but when he does, we listen.

And he was right. We managed to knock out some quick new artwork and get it printed up in time.

We finished at 1 a.m., again. And have a call-time of 6 a.m. tomorrow morning. The producers' strategy is obvious – wear us all out, get tempers flaring and make fantastic TV. I just have to try and keep a lid on my fuse, because it's getting ready to blow…

TUESDAY, 23 OCTOBER 2007

Our trailer looked terrible, because the artwork was poor, but our sales pitch was great – and I could tell that the Kodak executive loved it when he came round to inspect our proposition.

We sold quite a few printers too, literally flogging them out of the side of the trailer. Including one to Alec Baldwin, Stephen's older and more successful brother.

'Ah, thank God,' I said, when he appeared, 'at last we have a real Baldwin.'

Stephen stared at me with pure loathing in his face. 'Be careful how you use the name of the Lord,' he warned.

Tensions are beginning to creep into my relationships with almost every other contestant apart from Lennox and Tito, the Ultimate Fighter. (I'm not completely stupid…)

The main problem I have is that most of them are drama queens. Like most American stars, they are obsessed with their image, and how they are coming across on TV. So everything becomes an act.

Baldwin, the former hellraiser turned teetotal preacher, drinks around 20 cans of Red Bull a day which causes him to leap around like a demented rhino with a spear in its back. He also insists on calling everyone 'bro', using the word 'freakin'' as a form of safe expletive punctuation, and preaching to me on an hourly basis about my numerous moral shortcomings.

'I've been in 20 freakin' movies, bro,' he boasted during one heated exchange in the trailer today.

'You have?' I replied, eyebrow raised.

The old Stephen Baldwin would have whacked me then and there. The new one isn't allowed to, so instead he held his hands together like a priest, smiled beatifically and walked away.

Gene committed suicide in the boardroom tonight by arrogantly insisting his idea ('It's a Kodak world') was better than ours, and that Kodak were wrong. And then compounded things by refusing to bring back colleagues into the boardroom who Trump had made very clear that he preferred to fire than him.

'I'm a benevolent dictator, and we will win,' he announced.

'You're fired, Gene,' replied Trump, reluctantly.

And so Gene is gone, which is a massive shock to us, and I suspect an even more massive shock to him. But regardless of that, my chances of winning just doubled because the man with the biggest Rolodex just left the building and I reckon I've probably got more contacts than anyone still in the competition.

Kevin Pietersen is in New York with his fiancée Jess and brother Bryan, so we met up for dinner tonight in a fun Italian restaurant in Manhattan.

The best thing about being with a cricketer in this city, especially one with an ego almost as big as mine, is that no American is going to recognise them in a million light years.

They think 'cricket' is an insect you hear chirping on your Caribbean holidays.

Unfortunately, however, nobody recognised me either throughout our meal, which was highly embarrassing given that I'd spent the previous two weeks assuring Mr Pietersen that I was so famous out here I would need bodyguards at the table.

'Morgan,' he observed as the Chianti arrived, 'you're full of shit.'

I got back to the hotel and discovered that Rupert Everett has finally broken his whimpering silence on our now infamous *Comic Relief Apprentice* collaboration.

'It was ghastly,' he wails in *Now* magazine. 'Piers and Alastair Campbell had so much testosterone. It was very emasculating. It made me feel like I wanted to throw myself out of the window…'

WEDNESDAY, 24 OCTOBER 2007

The fourth challenge was to sell tickets to Broadway musicals.

And Baldwin and I went toe-to-toe again as we argued about strategy.

'We've got to hit the high-rollers and get them to buy tickets for lots of money,' I said.

'No, we need to sell every ticket, that should be our priority,' he snapped back.

'If you're now going to refuse to hit your high-roller contacts just to spite me then you are a shallow little man,' I replied.

He leant forward, nearly touching my nose with his.

'Boomerang.'

'Sorry?'

'When you're full of bullshit, and you spew it out, it's gonna come right back and hit you in the face,' he explained.

I laughed, which irritated him even more.

Then I called Richard Branson, putting the phone on loudspeaker, and asked him to buy some tickets for $10,000.

'OK,' he said, with a chuckle.

The others looked astonished.

'You know him?' asked Tito.

'Yep. And a lot of people like him, too.'

It was time to apply a bit of mental pressure.

Vinny, who has starred on Broadway, was an obvious choice as project manager.

And I wholeheartedly endorsed this decision until 2.15 p.m. when he came up to me at our stall halfway down Broadway itself, clutching a King Arthur suit and a white toy rabbit, and announced: 'Put these on, you English bastard, you're going to sell us some *Spamalot* tickets.'

I toyed with refusing, but then remembered we're making a TV show, and this would be very funny TV. And if it's funny TV, then it will make the final edit, and that means I get more airtime. You need to be that calculating in this kind of show, it's the only way to progress.

So for the next two hours, I patrolled Broadway in my Knight's chainmail, clutching the rabbit, loudly selling *Spamalot* tickets.

There were hundreds of tourists there, many of them British.

'Are you Piers Morgan?' asked one middle-aged Irish lady.

'Yes,' I replied.

'If you don't mind me asking, what on earth are you doing dressed like that?'

'I can't tell you. I'm afraid.' (We're not allowed to say we are filming *Celebrity Apprentice* at any stage.)

She shook her head, smiled at me and walked off, muttering to her friend: 'Sad, isn't it?'

With two minutes to the end of the challenge, Branson's representative still hadn't turned up. And if she didn't make it in time, the money would be deemed invalid and we might lose. With 30 seconds left, two Virgin stewardesses ran up with his cheque.

'Never in doubt,' I said, sweating profusely.

It turned out to be crucial, because we won the challenge by just $2,000.

And as a result, Vinny declared me his MVP, or Most Valuable Player – the ultimate accolade in American sport or business.

In the boardroom, Omarosa scorned my outfit, calling me a 'clown'.

Vinny sprang to my defence.

'He did what my dad used to do – he got out his sandwich board, and he sold tickets. That's not being a clown, that's being a star.'

I was more succinct. 'Arthur was not a clown, Omarosa. He was a king.'

Jennie Finch, a famous softball player in the States, was fired, for being 'too nice'.

She agreed with the assessment.

'It's such a nasty environment,' she said. 'It's all boom, boom, boom, with everyone attacking you, and it just wipes you out. I'm not used to that.'

'And you shouldn't get used to it,' said Trump.

'I don't want to!' she replied.

'Jennie, stay the way you are. This is not your world, and I like your world better. So you're fired.'

I watched all this with intense fascination.

Trump likes it competitive and nasty, that's the world he works in every day of his working life. So long as you play by the rules, you can be as ruthless and hard as you like, because that's the way he thinks you get to win in business. And I agree with him.

Later in the war room, Vinny had a bout of palpitations.

He's a great character, a short, amply proportioned, loud and funny Italian, but he's also prone to severe bouts of hypochondria. Barely a day passes without him claiming he is 'about to have a heart attack'. He lies, sweating and panting, on the sofa in our strategy room, groaning: 'Guys, guys, I can't take this much longer, it's gonna kill me.'

This evening, I suggested it might be time to seek a professional medical opinion to confirm his impending departure from Earth. So a doctor was called in, prodded Vinny's torso for an hour and then made a formal statement to the rest of us: 'Gentlemen, I have given Vincent a thorough examination, and I am very pleased to report that his heart is absolutely fine. He's just stressed from the challenges, and not getting enough sleep, and...'

'Excuse me,' I interrupted, 'but if he's not dying after all, then can he please just stop whining and get on with some bloody work.'

The Americans in the room looked at me in appalled astonishment. They just don't talk to each other like this, especially about health matters – which they take very very seriously.

Vinny was incensed. 'YOU'RE A HEARTLESS, NASTY BRITISH ASSHOLE,' he yelled.

'Thank you,' I replied. 'And my bad points?'

FRIDAY, 26 OCTOBER 2007

For the fifth *Celebrity Apprentice* challenge, I decided it was time I was project manager for the first time. 'You've been a star for the men so I think that's right,' said Trump. I think he's starting to like me, perhaps recognising a kindred spirit.

The task was to design an advertising campaign for Crocs shoes.

And to stir things up a bit, Trump mischievously placed my team's makeshift 'war room' right next to the girls' team, which was a bit like leaving a large Chinese meal-for-six yards from Johnny Vegas and not expecting him to devour it.

Sensing a good opportunity, I staged a row with Vinny and threw him out of our team, so that he could defect to the opposition and leak their secrets.

'You are my Luca Brasi,' I told him, in honour of the infamous *Godfather* enforcer-turned-rat.

Vinny played his role to perfection, inveigling his way into their team, and then emerging after half an hour to chuck a piece of paper at our door containing all the other team's plans.

This, though, sparked a furious ethical debate between me and Baldwin, who first brought the note to my attention but then refused to touch it.

'I won't compromise who I am,' he declared, 'I think God is watching us all.'

'Why did you tell me about it then?' I asked. 'You're just a flaming hypocrite.'

The 'h' word is the worst thing you can say to a born-again zealot, and he reacted with predictable fury, but I ignored him. What we had done was perfectly within the rules. A fact confirmed when Ivanka came to visit us, and laughed when I told her about it.

'I don't support this because it's sabotage,' said Baldwin, pompously.

'I'm sort of into sabotage,' Ivanka replied, with a mischievous smile.

When she left, I rounded on Baldwin. 'You treacherous weasel. But it backfired, didn't it? The Trumps will now think you're a weak sneak.'

Armed with the other team's information, I led Lennox out to say hello to the ladies and sing their planned slogan 'Share the love' to them.

'Oh my God!' squealed Nelly Gahan, a very successful Latino television executive. 'Those assholes know what we're doing! Vinny must be telling them!'

Vinny, who was with Marilu Henner in a van at the time, was fired on the spot – and returned to us in a distinctly unamused state of mind.

'You don't turn in your informers,' he whined when he got back, 'it ain't funny, because watch what happens to a rat...'

'Settle down, Vinny,' I replied, laughing, 'we're not dealing with the mafia here, Marilu Henner's not going to whack you.'

He didn't laugh. Vinny was now having a massive sense of humour failure.

SATURDAY, 27 OCTOBER 2007

We reconvened to prepare for our presentations to the Crocs executives, and Vinny looked murderous.

After a few minutes circling each other warily, it suddenly erupted into a vicious slanging match.

'You're an arrogant British FART!' he yelled. 'And I've had enough.'

'Well quit then, that's what you're good at, Vinny.' (He had recently provoked scorn by quitting another reality show *Dancing With The Stars.*)

'Fuck you,' he responded. 'I hope the girls win because their concept is better than yours anyway. And I hope you lose and get fired!' And with that, Vinny announced he was going to tell Trump he was quitting the show.

When we were shown each other's presentations in the boardroom later, I realised to my horror that he was right – their one, designed like a crocodile, was better than ours, designed like a conventional box, although our slogan 'wear them, share them' was miles more powerful (and had been dreamed up by Trace, who is quietly going about his business in a very effective way). For the first time, I knew we were going to lose, and since I was project manager there was a very real risk of me getting fired. I started to feel rather flushed. I've been enjoying the show, and I must admit I've started to have thoughts about how it could give my American TV career another huge boost. I really didn't want to get fired now I'd come so far.

Trump confirmed we lost, and then, sensing my rising physical discomfort, asked my teammates who they thought should be fired.

'Piers,' said Baldwin, obviously.

'Piers,' agreed Trace.

Only Lennox stood up for me. 'He's savvy,' he said, loyally.

But just as I feared the axe was falling on my head, Vinny suddenly threw the towel in. 'I'd rather go back to my family than have conflict like this,' he sighed. 'Pierce called me a fat Italian.'

(None of them can pronounce my name properly.)

'Did you?' Trump asked me.

'No,' I replied. 'I called him a very fat Italian.'

Trump smirked, and then asked him: 'Vinny, if I fire Piers, will you stay in the show?'

'Oh yeah,' replied Vinny, suddenly perking up.

I could feel my face reddening and sweating even more.

'You OK, Piers?' he asked. 'You're looking a little hot there…'

'Well, I don't like getting fired,' I replied.

Trump eyed me and then Vinny, the tension mounting with every second. And then he reached his verdict.

'Vinny, you can't just quit and then take it back, you can't do that. A winner fights to the end, right, Lennox?'

Lennox nodded. Trump watched all his big fights, and loves him, which is why Lennox is feeling increasingly confident.

'I'm not quitting, I'm walking away,' said Vinny. 'Piers has more determination and desire to be *The Apprentice* than me. Let me resign.'

So Trump did. And we all walked out knowing another thing about him. He doesn't like quitters, or people who even think of quitting.

As I celebrated later in the war room, Omarosa came in and we quickly started bickering, culminating in me saying to her: 'Is it true you once worked in the White House under Clinton?'

'Yes,' she replied.

'As what, a cleaner?'

She stood up, walked over and poured a glass of champagne over my head.

I think it's fair to say we've crossed the point of no return in our relationship.

I walked out, drenched, to be confronted by Stephen Baldwin.

'I can't work with you any more,' he said. 'I'm going to ask Mr Trump if I can resign.'

Trump called us all into the boardroom.

'Don't tell me you want to quit too, Stephen?'

'If I may respectfully, sir…'

'Don't go home a loser!'

'I'm going home for the same reasons as Vinny.'

'Whether you like it or not, Vinny got beaten up by Piers...'

'I've been beaten up by Piers, too, Mr Trump.'

In the end, he was persuaded to stay by Trump's suggestion that he join the girls' team.

But he is dead man walking now – a spineless quitter. The worst kind of man in Trump's eyes.

Back in the war room, Lennox and I pulled out the chess set again. We've played 33 games so far and he's won all of them.

But tonight, at the thirty-fourth attempt, I finally won – with a devastatingly aggressive counter-attack involving two knights, three pawns and a queen.

He took it well, smashing his king to the floor and growling: 'You didn't beat me, I resigned.'

'Ah,' I replied. 'So you're a quitter as well as a loser. Congratulations, champ.'

At which point, Lennox gave me that stare he gave Mike Tyson seconds before he started beating him to a pulp. And I instantly began to regret my jibe. Particularly when I watched him and Tito spend the next hour sparring around the war room, landing increasingly violent blows on each other.

'Who'd win in a fight?' I asked them.

'If it was boxing, Lennox,' said Tito, 'but if it was ultimate fighting, then I would.'

'How do you figure that one, dude?' scoffed Lennox derisively.

'Because, dude, I'd get you straight down in a wrestling hold, and you'd never escape.'

Lennox laughed. 'Yes, dude, but you'd have to get me down first.'

I'd pay serious money to watch these two go at it.

SUNDAY, 28 OCTOBER 2007

A day off, and I am so tired I've decided to just stay in bed all day, watching terrible films and sleeping. This is so much harder than I thought, but incredibly stimulating at the same time. I am enjoying the mental and physical agility required for the challenges, the feuding with other contestants and the sparring with Trump in the boardroom. It reminds me of running newspapers, battling other editors and having to defend myself to Rupert Murdoch.

Enthralling, but knackering!

MONDAY, 29 OCTOBER 2007

The sixth *Celebrity Apprentice* challenge today involved creating a live shop window display for the world-famous bridal-wear designer Vera Wang. Which given that my team consisted of Lennox, Tito and Trace, and the other team had four women, was going to be rather tricky to put it mildly.

Things weren't helped by the dictatorial antics of our project manager, Mr Lewis, who insisted we all raise our hands before speaking and say, 'Permission to speak.'

He then put all decisions to a vote, thereby avoiding any personal responsibility for anything.

And to compound our irritation, when we finally confronted him about all this nonsense, he started laughing so hard he loudly broke wind on camera.

'Lennox, that sums it up,' I observed. 'As a project manager, you stink.'

Incredibly, we still won the task, thanks to Trace coming up with another brilliant idea, to do our window with an Anthony and Cleopatra theme.

'The world's greatest romance deserves the world's greatest mattress,' he said, which was a superb slogan. For a man of few words, he is extraordinarily good with them.

'See,' said Lennox, chuckling, as we left the boardroom, 'my tactics worked.'

Nelly Gahan was fired, and Trump had harsh words for Omarosa too: 'You need to step it up, Omarosa,' he warned, 'because Piers is killing you, and I'm a little surprised to see that.'

My hardball 'killing' tactics appear to be working with the American audiences as well as with Trump.

One comment on the NBC website today read: 'Piers is an evil, arrogant, childish, ruthless bastard…and I love him SO MUCH.'

Trump called us all back into the boardroom just before we left, and said he was sick of the girls losing all the time.

'I'm going to mix things up a bit,' he said, with a glint in his eye.

And promptly stuck me and Omarosa on the same team.

'I don't think I can do this,' I said.

'You'll have to try,' retorted Trump. 'The task is to sell horse and carriage rides around Central Park. The team that raises the most money wins.'

In the war room later, I dealt with the situation head on.

'Omarosa, you don't like me and I don't like you, but let's be professional about this.'

'OK,' she said, extending a hand, which I shook.

I was elected project manager, and announced what I wanted from the team. 'This is about getting rich friends to buy rides for lots of money,' I said, 'as simple as that. So hit all your contacts and get the cash because if we lose then the person I'm taking into the boardroom will be the one who brought in the least amount of money.'

I looked at Omarosa, who had distinct panic in her eyes. I know from previous challenges that she doesn't have any rich friends, so can't bring any money in. I also know that when cornered, she turns things into a fight, believing that Trump will keep her in if she's abusive enough. Tomorrow will be interesting...

Back at the hotel tonight, I've found that the *GQ* interview with Arnold Schwarzenegger has made headlines around the world thanks to his controversial claim that 'marijuana is not a drug, it's a leaf'.

But you have to hand it to him for how he's handled the revelation.

Arnie's press secretary Aaron McLear has told the media by way of explanation: 'The governor was doing an interview with Piers Morgan, the host of *America's Got Talent*, the newest version of *The Gong Show*,' he said. 'I think it's important to keep that quote in the context of the environment where it was said.'

I see. So what he's basically saying is that I'm a shallow little reality TV twerp, so whatever the governor said to me doesn't count.

TUESDAY, 30 OCTOBER 2007

I got into the van with my team – Omarosa, Lennox and Carol Alt, a former supermodel who seems a little neurotic but is nice enough.

I'd asked Omarosa last night to prepare a sheet of paper detailing every ride we had to sell so we could tick them off as we did.

She handed it to me, and I noticed she had spelt my name 'Pierce'.

'That's not how you spell my name,' I said, handing it back to her.

'So?' she reacted, defensively.

'So it's unprofessional. If you spelt Trump's name wrong on a note like this he'd probably fire you.'

'He's my boss, not you,' she snarled, screwing the paper into a ball and throwing it on to the floor.

'That's just stupid,' I replied.

And that triggered a mini explosion in her.

'You're a fucking joke,' she said, 'everyone hates you, your teammates, your wife, even your kids hate you!'

That was so random, and outrageous, that I just erupted.

'Don't you mention my children, you disgusting little tramp!' I shouted back at her. 'You're just a pointless celebrity wannabe who can't raise any money because nobody knows you, so you're no use to me and I'm firing you.'

'You can't fire me motherfucker, you're not Donald Trump. You're a cocksucker who everyone hates, including your OWN KIDS.'

I'm afraid I could feel pure venom seeping out from every pore of my flesh.

'I told you, don't mention my fucking children.'

The van pulled up at Central Park, and we got out.

'Man, I've been in some crazy fights but nothing like that,' said Lennox, shaking his head.

I was raging inside. I was tired, fractious, and she'd hit the one nerve that could really get to me – the boys.

As I marched down the road, I wondered to myself what the hell I was doing in this situation. Why am I even in this stupid show? I don't need the profile, I'm already in the No. 1 rated show here. It's not for the money, because we're only getting $24,000 each. There's the charity, obviously, and that is very important. But the harsh truth is that the main reason I'm doing this is for vanity. And now I'm trapped in a horrific scenario with this ghastly woman abusing me through the boys on national TV. I hate it.

As the afternoon wore on, I tried to focus on getting big donors to come down and buy rides, which I did pretty successfully. Nick Jones from Soho House gave me $5,000, Dylan Jones $5,000 and Gerard Greaves from the *Mail on Sunday* $5,000. Paul Beck, Freddie Flintoff's benefit manager, even sent his wife down to buy one for $2,500!

But throughout it all, Omarosa just stood there, abusing me.

'You're fucking gay, you faggot,' she spat at one stage. 'How are your kids going to feel when they find out their daddy's a fag? You're a terrible father, no wonder they hate you.' And so on, hour after hour.

I tried to ignore her, but the constant references to the boys was really getting to me and occasionally I'd react, shouting at her to shut up. It was unedifying and horrible to experience. I just wanted the day over with as soon as possible.

Lennox tried to stop her. 'This is ghetto stuff, pack it in,' he said. But she was like a woman possessed.

By the time I got to the boardroom that evening, I was contemplating quitting.

'I don't think anyone should ever have to hear the kind of abuse I was subjected to today,' I told Trump. 'I wouldn't mind if she aimed it at me, but she kept bringing my kids into it, and I will do anything to protect them.'

'As you should,' he nodded.

'I can tell you now I'm not working with her again, so if you try and make me you will have to fire me. She's a low-life piece of trash.'

Astonishingly, we still won the challenge, though Omarosa brought no money in.

Trump said he was so upset by the fact that the team abusing each other had beaten the team that was united, that he didn't have the heart to fire any of the losers.

So for the first time ever, nobody got fired.

Trump then switched Omarosa back to the girls' team for the next challenge, and we were sent back to the hotel.

I got back to my room feeling disgusted with Omarosa, the producers and most of all myself for losing my cool.

I poured a large Jack Daniel's, and rang The Ferret. 'It was awful,' I said, 'Omarosa was screaming at me, I was screaming back. I just lost it.'

'Who won?' he asked, calmly.

'We did,' I replied.

'Then relax. All Trump, and America, care about is who wins.'

'Does it matter that I called Omarosa a piece of low-life trash?'

'No, that's just a fact.'

Reassuring though The Ferret was, I don't feel at all comfortable about what happened today. Rule one of reality TV is never lose your rag, and I lost mine big time. I'm tired, really, really tired. The 18-hour days are getting to everyone, and making us all fractious, which is of course the production team's intention.

I rang Celia to tell her what had happened, and she was distinctly unimpressed.

'Why do you have to do these things?' she asked, wearily.

'I'm not really sure,' I replied.

I called the boys.

'How did filming go, Dad?' asked Stanley.

'Not great. This terrible woman kept telling me that my sons hate me!'

'But we don't hate you, Dad, we love you,' replied Stan.

WEDNESDAY, 31 OCTOBER 2007

Today's challenge involved a helicopter flight to the QVC network in Pennsylvania, where we had to plan and carry out a ten-minute live segment on the shopping channel.

It was all fairly uneventful after the fireworks of yesterday, and I felt rather disengaged all day.

We ended up losing, and Marilu Henner got fired because she had been project manager and also decided to star in the segment herself, so there was nobody else to blame.

On the way back, I saw Lennox lean over and have a quiet word with the helicopter pilot, who for the next 15 minutes embarked on an unbelievably terrifying series of 100-metre death drops, scissor dives, high-speed surges and sideways manoeuvres.

Lennox screamed with delight, as I screamed in horror – and repeatedly begged the pilot to stop.

We finally landed, me sweating like a dog and wanting to vomit, Lennox laughing so hard I thought he might rupture a stomach muscle.

'Who is the quitter now?' he chuckled.

THURSDAY, 1 NOVEMBER 2007

We're down to just seven contestants now, and everyone is beginning to feel a new surge of energy as the finishing line draws closer.

The whole ugly business with Omarosa has fired me up beyond belief, and I now feel very, very focused.

Today's challenge involved creating a four-page advertorial for *Redbook* magazine on a Dial body lotion product.

Given that publishing is my trade, and Carol used to be one of the world's top models, I was very confident we would win.

And we did, easily, with a stunning piece of work that delighted the Dial and *Redbook* executives.

Tito was fired, after stammering his way through the other side's dismal presentation. I'll miss him because he's a nice guy. Tough, but always polite and respectful, hard-working, and surprisingly sensitive too.

FRIDAY, 2 NOVEMBER 2007

The next challenge was to sell art in a gallery and Omarosa said she wanted to be project manager for her team.

Trump looked at Hydra.

'Who wants to lead you guys this time?'

'I do,' I said.

Trump smiled, a long, slow, delicious smile.

'Excellent.'

I felt a steely surge of determination well up inside me as we walked out, to not just beat her, but to pulverise her.

The challenge was to sell art in a gallery, and my plan was simple: to hit every contact I know to try and finish her off. I was so pumped up, I would have fancied my chances against the entire Russian army, never mind a Bible-basher, country singer and reality TV wastrel.

Just before the evening started, I caught Baldwin trying to sneak a look at our pictures, and the prices.

'Stop cheating,' I said.

'I wasn't cheating, I was on my way to the rest room,' he spluttered.

'You're a liar as well as a cheat then, the Lord isn't going to be very happy with you now, is he Stephen...'

He tried to continue walking, but I put my arm up and stopped him.

'What are you going to do next?' he squealed.

'The next step is that I'm going to hit you.'

'You're going to *hit* me? For going to the rest room?'

'No, I'm going to hit you for cheating and lying,' I replied.

Baldwin considered his options, and retreated back to his side of the gallery, telling his team, 'Man, he's nuts...'

The generosity of my contacts was incredible.

Sir Philip Green paid $25,000 over the phone for a painting he couldn't even see; Gordon Ramsay gave $5,000 ('I fucking love art,' he lied); Nick Jones sent one of his managers down with another $10,000 in cash, my godfather Simon and former Arsenal boss David Dein did the same with $10,000 donations, and Ioan Gruffudd stumped up $5,000.

As the evening wore on, I could tell we had buried them. It wasn't even close, in fact they seemed to barely sell one piece of art. I caught Omarosa's eye once, and winked. She was going home after tonight, surely. There was no escape.

When we entered the boardroom, Donald Trump revealed that I'd raised $170,000 to her $7,000.

'This isn't just a beating,' he declared, 'this is the biggest slaughter in the history of *The Apprentice*.'

Oh, the sweet joy.

I was ushered out into the victory room, and watched the losing team's inquest on TV in our war room.

At one point, Omarosa alleged I was 'in the closet'.

'You're calling Piers a HOMOSEXUAL?' roared Trump, with an incredulous look on his face. 'I wonder what he thinks of that? Does Piers want to come back in here and defend himself?'

I stood up and charged into the boardroom – with absolutely no idea what I was going to do until I got there.

On arrival, I saw Omarosa, and next to her the unreconstructed Trace Adkins, all six foot seven inches of him.

There was only one thing for it; I raced over, leant down and kissed Trace firmly on the right cheek, telling him: 'I've always loved a beautiful cowboy.'

Trace recoiled in horror, Trump recoiled in laughter and I ran back to my room where Lennox was waiting in hysterics to high-five me.

'Dude,' he chortled, 'that was *crazy*!'

Trump, still chuckling, said: 'That was a pretty good defence, and I fully understand why he did that.'

'I don't!' said Trace, clearly furious.

'He was kidding,' assured Trump.

And then came the words I'd been waiting for:

'Omarosa, you were the project manager and you didn't just lose, you got creamed. It wasn't even close. Omarosa, you're fired.'

The camera panned in on her face, and I thought I detected just the glimmer of a tear in her left eye.

MONDAY, 5 NOVEMBER 2007

Celebrity Apprentice exploded today, with three of the remaining five contestants fired in a brutal Donald Trump bloodbath.

First to go was Baldwin, who was axed after his team lost the penultimate challenge, which involved selling Quizno sandwiches.

'People think I'm crazy,' he squealed at one point during the task, 'and I am...I'm crazy for JESUS!'

After Baldwin was sent back to spend more time with his Lord, Trump called the last four candidates into his boardroom – me, Lennox, Carol Alt and Trace Adkins. And announced that two more of us would be fired that night after interviews with two of his business chums, Jim Cramer and Erin Burnett from CNBC.

As we sat outside, waiting to go into the boardroom, I felt a sudden rush of doom enveloping me.

Trump loves Lennox, and he's comfortably the biggest star left in the show, which makes him good box office. Trump also loves Carol Alt, who is as smart as she is beautiful.

So putting my Trump head on, they should be the two finalists.

My fears were confirmed when the interviewers reported back to Trump, and both of them hammered me for being 'edgy, harsh and too aggressive'.

Trump asked me for my response, so I went for it, thinking I had nothing to lose.

'Mr Trump, if I am to lose because of my lack of diplomatic tact in a game which is led by a man who is renowned around the world for being a ruthless, tough businessman, then I happily accept that.'

Lennox and I had worked together on every task, winning nine out of eleven, and we both wanted to beat each other desperately.

'Who would have won more challenges if you'd been apart?' Trump asked.

'I would,' I replied instantly.

And to my amazement, Lennox agreed. 'Piers is a great asset to the team, one of the greatest assets.'

Trump looked as surprised as I was, but said: 'Lennox, you're a really smart guy but you just said you wouldn't have won so much if it weren't for Piers. I don't really like that statement, so Lennox, you're fantastic, but you're fired.'

I winked at a disconsolate Lennox: 'See ya, champ.'

Trump stared at the three remaining contestants, and said: 'You're probably the least nice person, Piers...'

'Wait a minute...' I tried to interrupt, but he cut me off.

'I'm getting ready to exonerate you, so shut up... I'm not going to fire you!'

He'd said it. I am in the final. Huge relief flooded through me, and excitement too.

This is now the most important thing in my life for the next few days. I have to win.

'Trace, do you like Piers?' Trump then asked the cowboy, knowing the answer.

'He's ruthless, and merciless,' wailed Trace, whose permanent 'I'm a living saint' impression doesn't sit too easily with the fact that his ex-wife shot him. 'He doesn't stab you in the back, he'll stab you in the forehead.'

'What do you say to that, Piers?' asked Trump.

'Yep, that's about right,' I replied.

Trump chuckled. 'I want to see these two guys slug it out...sorry, Carol, but you're fired.'

So the final was to be me against the cowboy. Or as Trump put it: 'This is good versus evil. It's the United States versus the UK. It's a clash of civilisations.'

I turned to Trace. 'You're going down, cowboy.'

'And I'm gonna bust your British butt,' he growled back.

The Ferret brought things sharply into focus when I called him with the news.

'Remember the words of Vince Lombardi, the great NFL coach,' he said. 'Winning is not the most important thing...it's the ONLY thing.'

I rang the boys.

'I made the final!' I yelped excitedly.

'Dad,' said Bertie, 'when are you coming home?'

I've been away nearly a month now, and they no longer care if I win my silly little TV game, they just want their dad back.

TUESDAY, 6 NOVEMBER 2007

Trump set the final task – to hold a charity auction for a star-studded audience, with the Backstreet Boys as the entertainment. There are three criteria for winning: money raised from selling 50 tickets each, proceeds from our own unique auction prizes and how we managed our management roles on the night. I was responsible for the auction itself and the food (with my helpers Stephen Baldwin and Carol Alt), and Trace (backed by Marilu Henner and Lennox Lewis) for the Backstreet Boys and the bar.

I needed some big help, and immediately called Fergie's office.

'Where is the Duchess?'

'New York, but only for two hours.'

I jumped in a cab, and 20 minutes later arrived at the twenty-seventh floor of a sumptuously extravagant tower off Broadway, and found a doorway embossed with what appeared to be a small royal crest.

The door suddenly flung open, and there was the Duchess – looking fabulous.

'Hello, you old devil!' she cried, smacking me heartily on the back. 'Come and see my empire.'

She led me inside, and I found row after row of smartly dressed assistants beaming up at me.

'These are my girls,' she shrieked excitedly, then pulled my hand towards a large glass-fronted corner room.

'And *this* is my office...'

The décor was luxurious, the views extraordinary. The whole place smacked of power, achievement and money. Donald Trump would have been proud of it.

'Blimey!' was all I could think to say. 'Haven't you done well...'

'Not bad is it?' she cackled, sitting down at her regal desk. Behind her were two giant photos of her and Prince Andrew (how many divorced women keep big photos of themselves and their ex behind their desk like that? Answer: not many) and – of course – dozens more snaps of their two girls Beatrice and Eugenie.

'I've worked very hard to get to where I am today, and I'm quite proud of myself.'

'So you should be. I'm proud of you too, your Majesty.'

'Piers?'

'Yes, Ma'am?'

'Do piss off.'

It was time to get down to business...and I explained the challenge.

'Your Majesty...help me!'

She laughed, and quickly agreed to offer a royal tea with herself. I was ecstatic: the Americans love Fergie.

'Who's the most generous person you know in this city?' I asked.

'Howard Lutnick.'

'Who's he?'

'He's the boss of Cantor Fitzgerald, who had the top four floors of One World Trade Center when it went down – killing over 650 employees, including his brother.'

I called Howard and, after 15 minutes of relentless badgering, he said he'd come down to the auction.

I returned to the venue and spent the next two hours making over 100 calls and sending emails to every star, PR, tycoon and friend I could think of.

'Will you help me win?' I asked Simon Cowell.

'But that will only make you more famous in America, and therefore more obnoxious, so why would I want to do that?' he answered.

'Because the charity is great – it raises money for wounded soldiers.'

Silence.

'OK, I'll help, but only because I like that charity, not you...'

My phone kept ringing with more offers of help. 'Piers, Ronnie Wood 'ere mate, I 'ear you're flying the flag for Britain -- count me in for three of my paintings.'

Five minutes later, Roger Daltrey gave me the microphone he used at his last Who concert.

Sharon Osbourne called from Hollywood. 'Right, revolting though you are, Ozzy and I are going to offer dinner at our house here, and if you get at least $50,000 for it then Ozzy will take his band anywhere in America and play for free.'

A text arrived from Sarah Brown: 'We can offer tea at No. 10, with me definitely and GB too if he is in town. Am on the case for other stuff too, good luck!'

I tracked down Andrew Lloyd-Webber in London, and he suggested two priceless VIP tickets to the opening night of his sequel to *Phantom of the Opera*, including dinner with him and the stars afterwards. 'Win it for Britain!' he cajoled.

Then Richard Curtis rang to throw in a walk-on part in his next movie plus two first-class tickets to the premiere in London.

The willingness of all these people to help astounded me.

A representative of my charity, the Intrepid Fallen Heroes Fund, turned up. 'They say I'm being too mean,' I told her. 'Does that bother you?'

'No way! Be as mean as you like...go get 'em Piers.'

An hour from the auction starting, I overheard Lennox Lewis saying he had Don King coming down – the wealthiest man in boxing. There was only one thing to do...

I called Sir Philip Green.

'I might be in trouble tonight...can I call you if I am?'

He chuckled.

'Of course...relax.'

There must be more reassuring things than hearing Britain's richest and most generous retailer saying 'relax' at that precise moment, but I can't think of any.

The auction started, with our items being sold off alternately.

Trace went first, raising $20,000 for an Opus book on the Superbowl.

My first prize came next.

'And what am I bid for tea with the Duchess of York?'

The bidding reached $10,000 before a middle-aged balding guy stepped forward and declared: '$100,000.'

It was Howard Lutnick.

The room erupted into shocked gasps, then loud cheers.

Trace's next item, a Marilu Henner jacket, went for just $4,000.

Mine was dinner with the Osbournes.

'I'll go another $100,000,' said Howard Lutnick again, winking at me as he did so.

Trace looked like someone had just garrotted him.

By the time my fourth lot had gone for $50,000, courtesy of a phone bid from Mohamed Al Fayed, I knew it was game over.

Particularly when it became clear that Don King wasn't going to show.

Donald Trump passed by, smiling.

'All over by the seventh,' I crowed, knowing he loves his boxing.

'Nice work, Piers...really nice work.'

I could see Trace slumped towards the back of the room, being consoled by his team.

This had to be the worst day for a cowboy since Gary Cooper met a gang of them head-on at *High Noon*.

My last item was a shopping trip with Ivanka Trump, and bidding reached $20,000 before I grabbed the microphone and announced a special phone bidder from London.

'Mr Cowell...how lovely to hear from you.'

We exchanged some typically acerbic banter before he made his bid: 'One hundred thousand dollars.'

I turned to see Lennox ask Trace: 'How much?'

'Another hundred grand man,' he sighed wearily. 'Jeez.'

The auction ended, and as the Backstreet Boys came onstage, I noticed a voice message on my phone.

'Hi, Piers,' it said, 'this is Jo Rowling. Sarah Brown asked me to help with your auction, and I'd like to offer a signed Harry Potter book if it's not too late...'

Tragically, it was.

At midnight, I crawled back to my hotel, mentally and physically exhausted.

The auction had raised over $500,000, and I knew I'd brought in at least three-quarters of that sum.

But Trace had sold more tickets, and run his side of the event well.

So I hadn't necessarily won.

It's all down to Trump now, and the final boardroom drama.

THURSDAY, 8 NOVEMBER 2007

Woke today feeling incredibly tense.

I know it's only a reality TV show, but I also know that if I win then it's going to give huge impetus to my career in America.

Americans love winners, period.

It won't matter a stuff to them how I've played the game, if I win.

And anyway, the fact that I've been a ruthless, egotistical bastard will surely appeal to Donald Trump?

We got to the boardroom, only to find one last twist to the tale was being sprung on us.

'The finale is going to be live, in April,' said Trump, with a huge mischie-vous grin. 'And I will reveal my winner then.'

So I've got to wait six months.

Fuck.

'His name's Simon Cowell, Your Majesty, he's a legend in his own mirror.'

7

'America is an idea, but it's an idea that brings with it some baggage, like power brings responsibility. It's an idea that brings with it equality, but equality, even though it's the highest calling, is the hardest to reach. The idea that anything is possible, that's one of the reasons why I'm a fan of America. It's like hey, look there's the moon up there, let's take a walk on it, bring back a piece of it. That's the kind of America that I'm a fan of.' BONO

MONDAY, 12 NOVEMBER 2007

My phone vibrated with sensational news this morning.

'I've got a big shock for you,' texted Amanda, 'I was out jogging this morning, training for the London marathon…and I found a dead man!'

'What?' I texted back immediately.

'He had kind of hung himself from a tree,' she explained. 'Looked like some form of self-strangulation. Brandy and Night Nurse lying there. Dressed warm, with socks and shoes, which I found really sad. Thought he was a tramp but he wasn't. It's weird, but I wasn't surprised to find him even if it was a million to one chance. And I wasn't fazed, I just ran around trying to get people to help.'

WEDNESDAY, 14 NOVEMBER 2007

News of Amanda's bombshell discovery is all over the papers. But she is not happy.

'They all said I'm 30-fucking-9, darling! I am more shocked by that!'

For the record, Ms Holden was born on 16 February 1971. Which makes her just 36. Give or take a bit of Botox.

THURSDAY, 15 NOVEMBER 2007

Peter Fincham emailed me today, asking me to sponsor him on a bike ride through Vietnam and Cambodia for charity.

I gave £100 through his fundraising website, then noticed that Rowan Atkinson had given £1500. I hope he doesn't think I'm being mean. The problem is that everyone I know seems to be doing some sort of charity ride, walk or run at the moment. The world's going fitness barmy.

SATURDAY, 17 NOVEMBER 2007

I've been voted the twenty-ninth 'Sexiest Brain in Britain' by *Psychologies* magazine.

The criterion for voting was apparently: 'Men who combine wit, intelligence and natural charm.'

But as with all these ridiculous lists, the real joy comes from seeing who I beat.

AA Gill, for example, stutters in two places behind me, at No. 31, which will utterly enrage the little chump. But spare a thought for Sebastian Faulks (40), Melvyn Bragg (41), John Humphrys (42), Andrew Neil and Martin Amis (joint 45) and Clive Anderson (50).

MONDAY, 19 NOVEMBER 2007

Lewis Hamilton is a great racing driver but he's got a lot to learn about public relations.

He announced this week that he is emigrating to Switzerland, because he can't stand all the 'intrusion' he gets from fans on the streets of Britain.

What utter bilge. He's going to the world's most boring place for one reason – to avoid paying millions of pounds in tax.

Lewis, my friend, never bite the hand that feeds you. Especially when you haven't actually won anything yet.

TUESDAY, 20 NOVEMBER 2007

'Stevie Wonder will be playing at Selfridges this afternoon,' claimed the world's most unlikely invitation.

Curiosity got the better of my jet-lagged cynicism, though, and I headed down there.

The first person I saw as I walked down a convincingly luxurious red carpet was Matthew Freud.

· 'This is all a wind-up, right?' I asked.

Matthew just winked.

I walked inside and found around 400 A, B, C and Z-list people, including Kate Hudson, Cilla Black, Kimberly Stewart and Joan Collins, all standing around wondering if we were the victims of a hideous practical joke.

An excited squeal signified the presence of David Beckham's alleged former mistress Rebecca Loos, whose only saving grace is that she is also my cousin.

'Ah,' I said, 'it's the black sheep of the family.'

'Oh, bugger off,' she giggled. 'I'm nowhere near as bad as you.' Which is probably true.

And then, at 8.30 p.m., a man from Selfridges stood up, made a short speech, and uttered the immortal words: 'Ladies and gentlemen, it gives me great pleasure to introduce Mr Stevie Wonder.'

A giant curtain fell away and there was the great man, sitting at a piano, with his band behind him.

'Hi everyone,' said Stevie, as 400 human beings fought to break the land-speed record to the front of the tiny stage.

What can I say about what happened next? Other than Stevie played a 45-minute set including 'My Cherie Amour', 'You Are The Sunshine Of My Life' and 'Superstition'. And most of the celeb-fuelled audience behaved like teeny-bopper pop fans, shrieking with excitement, dancing like loons, calling mates on phones and generally letting themselves down very badly.

Well, I did anyway.

At one stage I looked over and saw Trinny Woodall grooving a few yards away. We hadn't met since our infamous *Comic Relief Apprentice* clash.

Our eyes met, a mutual half-smile was grimaced, and I felt the ice thaw slightly.

The most memorable thing about the whole amazing experience was his voice. So few performers sound anything like as good in real life as they do on record. But Stevie's rich, soulful singing was if anything even better. The guy is a musical genius.

An hour later I was in Aspinalls casino, standing at the roulette table with Matthew, and I was on a bit of a winning streak.

But as always, boredom set in and I wanted to go home.

'Right, stick it all on red,' I asked the croupier, who raised an eyebrow as if to suggest, 'Oh dear, another day another sucker.'

'No, it's black,' said Matthew firmly, pushing my chips as he did so.

'Nope,' I insisted, pushing them back. 'It's red, definitely.'

'BLACK.'

'RED.'

The whole room went silent as the wheel started whirring.

Matthew shook his head in despair. 'It's black, I can feel it.'

I stared dementedly at the wheel, reciting 'Red, red, red' like a robot.

All eyes turned to the ball, which was rattling around in the final death throes of the wheel spin.

Black, red, black, red, black…RED.

I looked at Matthew, who looked more crushed than if I had just won his house, yacht, plane and wife off him.

WEDNESDAY, 21 NOVEMBER 2007

Elle magazine have asked me to be the subject of their first-ever male makeover. Its editor, Lorraine Candy, used to work with me on the *Wimbledon News*.

And for four hours this morning, I was paraded in increasingly garish outfits by Ozwald Boateng.

Eventually he slicked my hair back like Gordon Gekko, and forced me into a bright gold lamé shirt and red suit.

'THAT'S IT, BABY!' he shouted. 'THAT'S THE LOOK!'

I stared at myself in the full-length mirror, and saw Huggy Bear from *Starsky and Hutch* staring back at me.

Proof, once again, that me and high fashion should give each other a very wide berth.

Tonight, I was just settling down to watch the England/Croatia match when my mobile rang with a voicemail message.

'Hi, Piers darling, it's Naomi. I'm at the match, where *are* you? I thought you'd be here? Call me!'

What is it about these supermodels? When will they learn that I'm just not going to succumb to their endless efforts to lure me into their seedy worlds of sex, drugs, fine wine and glamour?

At 8.15 p.m., seconds after a shell-shocked Scott Carson committed hari kari (ironically, given I now want to murder him), I sent her a text: 'Did you sleep with our goalkeeper last night?'

'I should have...' Naomi replied, slightly misunderstanding what I was getting at. 'Would it have made a difference?'

SATURDAY, 24 NOVEMBER 2007

Book-signings are always ghastly affairs, but mine today at Harrods was even more surreal than usual; the first person in the queue suddenly produced a bunch of flowers, put on a white veil and proposed marriage to me. The second asked me to sign a copy of Jeremy Clarkson's latest self-congratulatory tedious tome.

And then I found myself being strangled from behind by a chortling Mohamed Al Fayed.

TUESDAY, 27 NOVEMBER 2007

It was either the British Fashion Awards tonight, or watching Christopher Biggins and Janice Dickinson scrap it out in the *I'm A Celebrity* jungle over who has the biggest breasts and most annoying laugh.

So I opted for the Awards, which turned out to be surprisingly good fun.

Sarah Brown won the unofficial Bravest Woman of the Night award for turning up at all, given all the continued flak her husband's getting at the moment. His approval ratings have bombed since he supposedly 'bottled' calling an election, and the shortest honeymoon in history has exploded into bitter acrimony.

'How are you bearing up?' I asked.

'Oh, it's just a storm,' she replied. 'And storms always pass.'

'Maybe, but this one has a hurricane feel to it at the moment...'

'It's fine. In fact, it doesn't seem that different to the last job really, it's just that the highs seem a bit higher and the lows a bit lower. Gordon is handling it all remarkably calmly.'

And he probably is. When you've nearly gone blind as a teenager, and lost a child as a father, then a few rough headlines probably aren't going to depress you too much. Particularly when they are written by people who called him a washed-up has-been in June, the greatest new prime minister of the century by September, and now a useless dud again.

When the awards started, Vivienne Westwood – whose hair is so shockingly red it genuinely looks like someone has just set fire to it – made an endearingly barking speech, confirming her status as Britain's Maddest Fashion Icon; a series of tiny, very camp male designers then trotted up on stage to tearfully thank the world and receive their awards from gigantically tall models like Erin O'Connor (Little and Large had nothing on this lot) and presenter Zoe Ball managed to skilfully avoid making me laugh once.

The dreary procession was saved by Stella McCartney, winner of the top award of 'Designer of the Year', who made a rather moving and gracious speech, thanking among others her 'mum and dad' for all their support.

No mention of her delightful stepmother, I was pleased to note.

Afterwards, I spotted Stella walking down some stairs to the ladies' cloakroom.

I'd never met her, but felt a sudden burning urge to do so – and ran down after her, stopping her by the arm.

'Excuse me, Stella.'

She turned in her tracks, looking strikingly like her mother.

'Yes?'

'I'm Piers Morgan, and since I am one of the few people in the world who loathes Heather Mills more than you do, I thought it was time I said hello.'

She smiled.

'Oh yes, I know all about you... Dad always says you tried to warn him about Heather!'

'Well, that's true, but unfortunately it was a bit late given that I introduced them in the first place.'

Stella shook her head slowly, then laughed: 'Yes, thanks very much...'

'I think you have all been very dignified in your silence,' I said. 'There is nothing more powerful than saying nothing when someone goes on a global rant like that.'

'Well, silence is always the most dignified way of dealing with something like this,' she replied.

'Yes, especially when that something is a raving bloody lunatic.'

Stella stifled a giggle. 'You might say that Piers, I couldn't possibly comment...'

WEDNESDAY, 28 NOVEMBER 2007

If there's one thing worse than ice-skating, it's trying to ice-skate with recently broken ribs.

I edged precariously around the Natural History Museum rink with Celia this afternoon, feeling about as fluently mobile as a one-legged armadillo.

Eventually, and predictably, I tumbled to the ground, right on the area where the ribs had been decimated. And felt a new surge of pain shuddering through my battered old torso. A few youngsters by the side of the rink started laughing as I remained facedown in the freezing ice.

'Get up,' snapped Celia, whose elegant gliding had made Jayne Torvill look amateurish.

'No,' I replied, with absolute certainty.

And that was it. The end of my ice-skating career.

THURSDAY, 29 NOVEMBER 2007

Marion and I have spent the best part of this year now trying to complete the divorce.

I think we both assumed it would all be quite a simple procedure given that we have remained friends, and the financial situation is fairly straightforward.

But the legal process has conspired to string it out for as long, and there-fore as expensively, as possible. And as a result things have got rather fractious.

Today we had a second court hearing, during which I exchanged some heated 'differences of opinion' with Marion's counsel – a posh twit called Mark Saunders. He's young, arrogant and extremely condescending.

And I made my feelings very clear to him outside court afterwards, in what quickly became a heated debate focused on what I considered to be his numerous character failings.

FRIDAY, 30 NOVEMBER 2007

There are very few things in life that cause me to instantly lose control of a car; Eva Mendez strutting across a pelican crossing in a leopard-skin bikini might do it, or finding Nelson Mandela as a lollipop man outside my sons' school perhaps.

But this afternoon, I was subjected to perhaps the greatest motoring chal-lenge of my life – how to continue moving in a straight line down the M40 when I'd just heard Simon Mayo announce on his Radio Five Live show: 'My special guests today are Jeremy Clarkson and Ian Hislop…'

The Maserati went into spontaneous careering mode, swerving from lane to lane like a Tour de France cyclist trying to evade a dope-tester.

And, sure enough, Mayo's very first question was: 'So, gentlemen, here is a road test idea for you. You're both in supercars and we set Piers Morgan off like a fox, running as fast as he can, and we see which of you can get to him first...'

I waited for the inevitable torrent of abuse, but was pleasantly surprised.

'I think Piers is tremendous,' said Jeremy.

'Yes, you mustn't be fooled by this media idea that we all hate each other,' said Ian.

'No...he's terrific fun. He's round my house all the time...' agreed Jeremy.

'And his career has gone from strength to strength,' added Ian. Who could begrudge him all his international success and money? I am really happy for him.'

At which point I unfortunately hit a bad signal area of Oxfordshire, and so didn't get to hear the rest of their extraordinary eulogy.

Now, mean-spirited cynics have suggested it may not have been entirely sincere, particularly after I lost reception, but I personally can't think of two more sincere men in the world than Jezza and Moonface.

I'm touched.

MONDAY, 3 DECEMBER 2007

I performed in front of the Queen at the Royal Variety Show tonight.

Well, when I say perform, that might be slightly stretching things. I was there tonight to introduce *Britain's Got Talent* winner Paul Potts to Her Majesty.

But I did appear onstage, I did address the audience and I even got an ovation – albeit for admitting I was wrong about thinking a balding, badly dressed, broken-toothed mobile phone salesman couldn't possibly sing opera.

I knew it was going to be a memorable day when I boarded the train to Liverpool at 7 a.m. and found myself sitting next to Al Murray, TV's pub landlord.

Within a few minutes, a woman bustled past us and entered the loo, where she began singing at the top of her voice.

Al and I exchanged raised eyebrows, and then began to snigger, swiftly joined by most of the carriage. By the time the mystery voice got round to murdering 'Let It Be' and 'Lady Madonna', we were in fits.

Eventually, after an increasingly angry queue had formed, a stewardess banged on the door and ordered her to vacate. At which point we discovered our verbal assailant was none other than Cathy Tyson, star of the movie *Mona Lisa* and hit TV show *Band of Gold*.

As everyone else shuffled with embarrassment in their seats, I gave her a rousing clap.

'Oh, thanks!' she said. 'Hope it wasn't too loud...?'

'Nooooooo,' I replied. 'Just what we needed at 7.15 a.m. on a Monday morning.'

On arrival at the famous Empire Theatre, I was hit by another shattering female spectacle – Amanda Holden in her curlers.

'Just call me the new Hilda Ogden,' she cackled, posing proudly for photos outside a door with the words BOILER ROOM on it.

Rehearsals for the grand finale started promisingly when I was told I was going to be standing bang in the middle of the front row for the curtain call, next to Bon Jovi and Seal, while we all sang 'Let It Be'.

Pole position.

Within 20 minutes though, I'd been shoved further and further away from the centre by the likes of Dame Kiri Te Kawana, James Blunt, Russell Brand and even Al bloody Murray – until I eventually ended up offstage altogether, stuck behind a large camera.

'What a shame...' whispered Amanda, gleefully.

'Yes, well watch my elbows when the real action starts,' I hissed back.

Russell Brand was still seething about our *GQ* interview last year, in which he boasted of sleeping with 2,000 women.

'You tricked me into admitting that,' he wailed.

'No, I didn't,' I replied. 'I just asked if you'd had more than Bill Wyman and your stupendous ego refused to let you say no.'

He nodded slowly. 'True, very true. You're still a slippery bastard, though.'

Simon Cowell arrived at 6.30 p.m. for a last-minute run-through of our script, looking unusually twitchy.

'Have you ever actually met the Queen?' I asked.

'Erm...no.'

'Nervous...?'

'No, of course not.'

'But what if she doesn't recognise you?'

'Piers, don't be ridiculous.'

An even more worrying problem arose when he suddenly exclaimed: 'Slight problem. I can't read autocue.'

It was like that moment when the Sundance Kid admits to Butch Cassidy that he can't swim.

'You're joking?'

'No, I'm not. My long sight is terrible.'

As worried producers raced to increase the typeface to a size even David Blunkett could read, Amanda and I pondered the possibility of total disaster on stage if he still couldn't.

'On the one hand, it would be awful,' I said. 'But on the other, the idea of Simon dying on his backside in front of the Queen is too wonderful to contemplate.'

'Oh don't,' she panicked, 'I'm feeling sick enough as it is!' At which point she did her usual trick of pulling my hand firmly to her frantically beating chest. I never complain...

Tragically, Cowell pulled it off – and we retired to watch the rest of the show in a tiny green room with Bon Jovi, Joan Rivers, Michael Ball (dressed as a drag queen) and a scantily clad Darcy Bussell.

Variety ain't the word for it.

We returned to the stage for the finale (I squeezed myself firmly back into the camera-line), then all lined up to meet the Queen and Prince Philip.

And it was quite clear when they reached us that neither had a clue who Cowell was.

The Queen just shook his hand with a bemused half-smile on her face and moved swiftly on to me with an expression of familiar relief.

'Hello again, Your Majesty,' I said. It was, after all, the fourth time we've met.

'Hello,' she replied, deliberately looking vague to avoid charges of favouritism.

'Did you enjoy Paul Potts' performance?' I asked, breaching all the ridiculous protocol. (If you ever meet The Queen by the way, just ignore all the rules and talk to her, she doesn't bite and never seems to mind.)

'Oh yes,' she smiled, turning to him. 'You were very good.'

What a moment for a guy who this time last year was flogging Nokias in Carphone Warehouse.

'You're judges, is that right?' asked Philip.

'Yes, sir,' I replied.

'So,' he chuckled, looking back at Cowell before pointing to Paul Potts, 'you sponge off him then?'

An hour later I was sitting in Cowell's sumptuous private jet heading back to London with Amanda. (A new Rolls-Royce Phantom was waiting on the tarmac to complete our tortuous journey.)

'Perfect night,' I said. 'The Queen didn't know you, and Philip called you a sponger.'

Cowell ignored my jibe, leaving a giggling Amanda (it was her first-ever private jet flight and she was literally quivering with excitement) to observe: 'That would be the same Queen and Prince Philip who are getting the slow train home?'

SATURDAY, 8 DECEMBER 2007

Oprah Winfrey has come out and publicly endorsed Barack Obama to be the official Democrat candidate for the presidential race. It is hard to overestimate the significance of this, because until now everyone has just assumed Hillary Clinton will walk it, given that she's been miles ahead in the polls for most of the year.

And Hillary may have assumed that Oprah would support *her*, given that they have been friends for 20 years.

But at a rally in Columbia, Oprah told a huge, excited crowd: 'Barack Obama speaks to the potential inside every one of us. Dr Martin Luther King dreamt the dream, but we don't just have to dream the dream any more. We get to vote that dream into reality by supporting a man who knows not just who we are, but who we can be.'

In a later interview with Larry King, Oprah explained her decision in more detail. 'I know Barack personally. I think that what he stands for, and what he has proven he can stand for, is worth me going out on a limb for him. I haven't done this in the past, I felt that I knew anybody well enough to be able to say I believe in this person. I have nothing negative to say about Hillary, and I am not against her in any way. I have great respect for her. But I believe Barack can be president, I believe that is possible.'

Oprah said she hadn't given any money to Obama's campaign.

'My money is not going to make any difference to him. I think my value to him, my support of him, is worth more than any cheque that I could write.'

And she's right, it is.

Fox News are already suggesting that Oprah's endorsement could be worth 'millions of votes' to Obama.

Aside from this momentous development, Obama's campaign looks increasingly slick, well organised and oozingly professional. And most importantly, his image just seems perfect for the time.

As The Ferret said this evening: 'It's all about presentation in modern politics. Franklin Roosevelt was one of the greatest presidents who ever lived, but if he tried to run now in a wheelchair, he wouldn't win a single state. Obama looks the part, he's tall, youthful, dynamic. If I was up against him, I'd have to go straight to the gym and lose a ton of weight. Because otherwise he'd just look better on TV.

'Look at you – you didn't care how you looked before you did *America's Got Talent*, but now you've had your teeth whitened, you go to the gym all the time, you watch what you eat and drink. That's the pressure of image, and the Internet. Because if you look fat on TV, then everyone's going to talk about it online all day long, whether you're a politician or a movie star.'

The polls suggest Obama is now closing in on Clinton in the race for the first proper election vote, the Iowa caucus on 3 January.

And with Oprah intending to speak with him at several more rallies before then, I'd say Hillary's got real problems.

THURSDAY, 13 DECEMBER 2007

Doing *Question Time* in London is always a double-edged sword. It's great to appear in your own town, but London audiences tend to be much tougher and more cynical than other parts of the country.

I walked on after Charles Kennedy, receiving as many boos to his cheers. It was like appearing on stage as Captain Hook in a panto, seconds after Peter Pan. But I'd have it no other way.

Kennedy, incidentally, was on hilarious form in the green room beforehand – very funny and self-deprecating about his little local difficulty with various vats of whisky.

He was still recovering from chickenpox, given to him by his son Donald, and when I asked if he'd ever consider running for the Lib Dem leadership again, he laughed: 'I don't think so, unless it was on a "pox and booze" ticket.'

He then went outside for a cigarette, saying: 'It's the only bloody vice I'm allowed these days, so I may be some time…'

The show was a good laugh – notable for Kirstie Allsopp calling Hazel Blears 'Heather', David Dimbleby telling me to 'go to Panama and stay there' and my joke about David Cameron being Mr Has-been (while defending Brown against recent 'Mr Bean' jibes) going down like a tin of mouldy tuna.

'One for the midnight oil, Piers,' chortled Chris Patten as the studio was deafened by silence. The irony being that I had burned most of the bloody midnight oil trying to come up with that useless gag in the first place.

Kennedy shook my hand at the end. 'Congratulations. That was the best arse-licking to a serving prime minister I've ever heard in my life. Hope you get a knighthood out of it.'

I don't know about that, but I have got lunch at Chequers coming up.

I dashed off straight after the show to Matthew Freud and Elisabeth Murdoch's house in Notting Hill, where they were hosting their annual Christmas party. On arrival, I walked upstairs to find Tony Blair talking to Mick Jagger. (It was that kind of party – I later spotted Sting sipping wine next to Ken Livingstone, and Peter Gabriel frowning as he marched past Alastair Campbell and Peter Mandelson.)

'Two old rockers together then, Tony?' I asked.

'Well, Piers, one is a rather more distinguished old rocker than the other,' Blair replied.

'Which one?'

Blair rolled his eyes and moved on. So I'm none the wiser. He still shakes my hand, though, even if it is with gritted teeth.

I hadn't seen Jagger since a Rolling Stones tour of Japan in the early nineties, when he gave me the runaround in Tokyo for two weeks before finally doing an agreed interview with me on the phone once I'd left town.

'That was just to annoy me, wasn't it?' I asked, as he fended off a bevy of over-excited blondes.

'Yes,' he laughed. 'Of course it was. You were working for the *Sun* then, what d'you expect?'

'Well, it's not too late to apologise...'

'Piers, I am truly sorry...'

'Thank you, Mick. I forgive you.'

Blair, by now, was on his knees talking to Ash Atalla. 'What did you talk about?' I asked Ash later.

'Oh, he said his kids love *The Office*, and that he sympathised with me for my disability. I said it was worse than that, I was gay too...'

Which Mr Atalla is most definitely not...

George Osborne, who was there with David Cameron, sauntered past. He's just slam-dunked Labour with a surprise announcement to increase the inheritance tax threshold to £1 million.

'Hi George, good move on the inheritance tax.'

'Thanks, Morgan.'

'Yes, you're doing really well.'

He eyed me suspiciously.

'Thanks again, what's the catch?'

'Nothing. I really do think you're doing well, it's just Cameron who is cocking it up for you...'

Osborne stared at me so menacingly I sought refuge in a side room, where Sharon Osbourne and Louis Walsh were giggling in the corner like naughty schoolkids.

'What have you done now?' I asked.

'Erm, well, I did this interview with Graham Norton tonight,' said Sharon, barely able to talk through tears of laughter, 'and I said a few bad things about Dannii Minogue (her replacement on *X Factor*), and I think I'm going to be in big trouble with Simon...'

'Did you mean them?'

'Well, yes. She's had a few pops at me, so I'm having a few pops back.'

It takes a brave woman to go pop-swapping with Sharon Osbourne. I wish Ms Minogue well...

SUNDAY, 16 DECEMBER 2007

The Browns invited Celia and me to lunch at Chequers today. I'd been there once before, for tea with Tony Blair, and it's a fascinating old place – jammed with priceless works of art, and historical documents that the public never get to see.

Celia and I walked in to be greeted by the PM himself, a tray of champagne glasses and ten other guests including Kirsty Young and Ruth Kelly.

Gordon was on remarkably good form considering the fearful hammering he's been taking.

'I've had better months,' he admitted, 'but then I've spent the last decade getting thumped around by the media from time to time, so it's nothing new really.'

'Blair must be loving it,' I said.

Gordon looked bemused.

'Tony? No, no. We talk all the time. In fact, I spoke to him this morning.'

Interesting.

We debated various matters of state before getting down to the really serious stuff – like how the hell Leon won *X Factor*. Gordon, as a Scot, was naturally delighted. But something else had caught his eye more.

'Those Minogue sisters are quite something, aren't they?' observed the prime minister. 'Kylie, especially. I met her the other day and she knows exactly who she is, what she's about and where she's going. I thought she was very impressive.'

The dining room was stunning: a long, deep mahogany table, the finest silver, and cut-glass crystal everywhere – with amazing views out over the countryside.

'Hey, Gordon, where did it all go wrong?' I joked, as we sat down.

'Not bad, is it?' he replied.

A small army of waiters served us vegetable soup, roast pork with apricot and sage stuffing, and Chequers apple crumble with cinnamon ice cream. All washed down with delicious bottles of Château Sénéjac 1990 and Chassagne-Montrachet 2000.

I sat next to Kirsty, who was feisty and funny. And opposite Ruth Kelly, who was much warmer than you'd ever imagine from her rather serious public image.

Quite glam, too, with her new *Dynasty*-style hairdo.

Our end of the table got into a discussion about how to improve Labour's standing in the polls.

'Invade Zimbabwe,' I said firmly.

The table went strangely quiet. Like the audience on *Wogan* when David Icke walked out in purple and said he was the son of God.

'I'm serious – take out Mugabe, and not just Britain but the whole world will support and thank you. The man's totally evil, much worse than even Milosevic or Saddam. But we just sit there doing nothing.'

'Any other thoughts?' Gordon asked, uneasily twiddling the pepper pot.

'Yes, abandon collective cabinet responsibility. It's absurd you all pretending to agree all the time. Imagine Ruth and Jack Straw on *Question Time* disagreeing with each other about a big issue – it would be great to watch, and the public would respect it.'

Ms Kelly nearly choked on her vegetable soup.

'Well, I'm not going to be the first one to test that...' she laughed.

This morning's *Mail On Sunday* has revealed that Admiral West, Brown's new minister for security, had developed a 'close friendship' with Abba star Anna-Frid Lyngstad.

'I was there when they first met,' said Gordon.

Blimey, this was more like it...

'Yes,' I said, 'I heard she had her eyes on you first?'

'NOOO, Piers, she did not.'

'So she didn't sing "Gimme gimme gimme a Brown after midnight" into your ear then?'

'No. She did not. And it's all perfectly innocent anyway.'

Towards the end, I got into a noisy argument with Indra Nooyi – the worldwide boss of Pepsi, who has been named the world's No. 1 businesswoman for the last two years by *Fortune* magazine – over who will be the Democrat candidate in the next US election.

'It will be Hillary,' she said, firmly.

And everyone else seemed to agree – she is, after all, ahead in the polls.

'No, it won't,' I insisted. 'Obama is the one with the momentum. And he should win.'

'Why should he?' asked Indra.

'Well, because he's fresh, untainted, charismatic, eloquent, and I can't think of a better way for America to rebuild its terrible image than by having a black president whose middle name is "Hussein".'

Gordon sensibly kept quiet, as Indra – who is a delightfully smart and funny woman – and I exchanged increasingly heated banter.

Eventually, she brought the debate to an abrupt end.

'Piers,' she smiled. 'Let me put this as politely as possible. You are FOS.' Which I don't think meant, 'Full of Sense.'

'That may be so,' I rejoined. 'But I'm right – Obama's going to win the nomination, and become president.'

I don't think anyone else agreed with me.

After lunch, Sarah took us on a tour of the house.

And what a place it is...endless creaking corridors laden mainly with Oliver Cromwell's private art collection, a secret dungeon (no sign of Cherie down there, sadly), a large indoor swimming pool, the tiny bedroom where Elizabeth kept Lady Mary Grey prisoner (her graffiti pleading for clemency still adorns the walls) and the famous 'Long Room' which contains an astonishing treasure trove of books and memorabilia.

I spent a few extraordinary minutes reading Nelson's handwritten diaries, and Napoleon's original love letters to Josephine, which lie on a desk next to his leather briefcase.

'Now that is how a man should woo a woman,' said Celia, wistfully.

'He was five foot three,' I replied. 'Not a man.'

I even made it back in time for the second half of the Arsenal match.

As the final whistle sounded, Sarah Brown texted me: 'All that, and the right result too.'

MONDAY, 17 DECEMBER 2007

I was guest speaker at *GQ*'s annual Christmas lunch today. Dylan Jones had given me strict instructions not to insult the celebrity guests in the audience.

So, naturally, I did the complete opposite, announcing a mock Kofi Annan Award For Diplomacy to Lily Allen, for calling Bob Geldof a 'sanctimonious prat', President Bush a 'fucking knob', Cheryl Cole a 'stupid bitch' and saying that 'anyone who buys Paris Hilton's new album should be shot dead'.

Far from being offended, young Lily took a deep bow of pride and got a huge ovation.

I sat next to the splendidly entertaining Sharlene Spiteri, who has been one of my favourite people since nearly punching Paris Hilton at a *Vanity Fair* party earlier this year.

'Paris thought I'd thrown ice cubes at her, which I hadn't,' Sharlene explained. 'So she came marching over and started shouting "Who the fuck do you think you are?" at me. So I just looked her straight in the eye and said: "Fuck off you little twat before I smack you one in the face." So she did.'

TUESDAY, 18 DECEMBER 2007

Janet Street-Porter has a new book out on beauty. Which, when I'd stopped laughing, prompted me to ring my publishers immediately and suggest three new books to them. Simon Cowell On Modesty, Amy Winehouse On Sobriety, and Steve McClaren On Management.

Any takers?

Celia interviewed Calum Best in Chelsea this afternoon, and I waited downstairs for her to finish. Well, you can't be too careful with him, can you?

An hour later, they both walked past me and off down the King's Road together. She'd forgotten I was there.

This created a certain 'tension' over dinner tonight.

MONDAY, 24 DECEMBER 2007

I took Stanley to the dentist today to remove an abscess-afflicted tooth, a trip that was never going to be easy because he has a phobia about the place. As we walked inside, Stan stopped at the door saying 'BATTERSEA RISE DENTAL PRACTICE' and observed solemnly: 'Dad, I would feel a lot more confident about the situation if the dentist wasn't still "practising".'

Afterwards, we stopped by the chemists to get him some medicine, and he begged me for some sweets.

'Sorry, Stanley, but no. And before you ask, the answer will be no to everything else you ask me while we're in here, too.'

He thought about this for several seconds, and then replied, very loudly: 'Dad?'

'Yes, Stanley?'

'Do you love me?'

THURSDAY, 3 JANUARY 2008

Celebrity Apprentice launched on air in America tonight, and any doubts I had about taking part were instantly dispelled by Trump's opening line:

'We've brought together 14 of the most successful celebrities in the world...' Well, if you say so, Mr Trump.

More importantly (but only just), Barack Obama has sensationally won the Iowa caucus vote. Given that Iowa is a predominantly white state, this represents an extraordinary moment in American politics, and a stunning blow to Hillary Clinton.

She's suddenly on the ropes, looking rattled, and, in my view, there for the taking. And if Obama can beat Hillary, then he can surely beat anyone.

I'm in Antigua on holiday with the boys, and they are showing surprising interest in the story, as well as the simple insightfulness of young minds.

'It would be a great thing for America and the world if a black man became president,' I said.

'He shouldn't win just because he's black though, should he?' replied Spencer.

'No,' I said, 'but nor should he lose just because he's black.'

And there lies the great unanswered question again: is America ready to take that giant leap?

FRIDAY, 4 JANUARY 2008

The Apprentice ratings were huge, making it the night's No. 1 show. Reviews were equally pleasing.

'Piers Morgan is fantastically obnoxious,' said one.

'The biggest Brit asshole since Simon Cowell,' snorted another.

Sir Alan Sugar, who plays the Trump role in the UK, was his usual concise self: 'Watched it, you're the only one with a bit about you,' he emailed from his Florida home. Which, coming from him, is about the biggest compliment imaginable.

Later, a series of texts arrived from Amanda:

1) 'Happy New Year, darling, I'm learning to ski and loving it!'
2) 'Don't forget to watch my show tommorow [sic] "When Britain First Had Talent".'
3) 'Spelling error. Tomorrow. Alittude [sic] affecting brain.'
4) 'Is it one T in altitude?'

SUNDAY, 6 JANUARY 2008

Two of my favourite celebrity goons are in the news today, both offering further proof that they've lost all touch with reality.

First up is Robbie Williams, who is threatening to go on strike but hasn't explained from what, exactly.

EMI responded to his 'threat' by calmly announcing that one million unsold copies of his last album *Rudebox* are being destroyed and used (genuinely) to pave roads in China.

As for Tom Cruise and the leaked video in which he claims that scientologists have some form of higher calling which means they are the only people who can 'really help' if they see someone have a car accident, I only have one thing to say: Can you imagine anything worse if you're lying seriously injured in mangled wreckage than suddenly seeing Cruise's mad-eyed, wild-grinned head gurning down at you?

I would literally rather die.

MONDAY, 7 JANUARY 2008

It's the New Hampshire vote tomorrow, the first of the crucial primaries. And the candidates read like a snapshot of modern America – a woman (Hillary Clinton), a black African-American (Obama), a Mormon (Mitt Romney), a Vietnam vet (John McCain), an Italian-American catholic (Rudy Giuliani), a Baptist minister (Mike Huckabee) and a Hollywood actor (Fred Thompson).

It reminds me of that great old *News of the World* slogan: 'All human life is there.'

TUESDAY, 8 JANUARY 2008

Obama narrowly lost the New Hampshire primary to Hillary Clinton, tossing the Democrat nominee race up on its head again.

But it was close, and Obama's speech afterwards was stunning in its eloquence and power.

'We know the battle ahead will be long,' he said, 'but always remember that no matter what obstacles stand in our way, nothing can withstand the power of millions of voices calling for change. We have been told we cannot do this by a chorus of cynics who will only grow louder and more dissonant in the weeks to come. We've been asked to pause for a reality check. We've been warned against offering the people of this nation false hope. But in the unlikely story that is America, there has never been anything false about hope. For when we have faced down impossible odds; when we've been told that we're not ready, or that we shouldn't try, or that we can't, generations of Americans have responded with a simple creed that sums up the spirit of a people: YES. WE. CAN.'

Obama repeated this last phrase numerous more times, building excitement in the crowd as he did so. I even started mouthing the words myself! It's a great slogan for a country built on the 'Yes, we can' philosophy but which is currently feeling, 'No, we can't.'

I watched Obama, and the crowd, closely on TV as he made the speech, and it was extraordinary. For the sheer power of his rhetoric and oration, he has a bit of JFK, Martin Luther King and Bill Clinton about him, and that unteachable ability to take people to him with words.

He is seizing the moment, and brilliantly articulating the hopes, and fears, of a nation cowed by what has happened to it.

Obama may not win the Democrat nomination. But he is re-energising world politics. And his mantra of 'change' is definitely gathering momentum.

In the Republican race, John McCain won the vote. So we could end up with a black man or a woman taking on a Vietnam veteran for the White House. A battle that might split America right down its spine.

THURSDAY, 10 JANUARY 2008
Celia is interviewing Simon Cowell tomorrow for *Glamour* magazine, and we sat in a Kensington pub tonight for two hilarious hours, plotting embarrassing questions for him.

FRIDAY, 11 JANUARY 2008
The interview went as well as we could possibly have hoped for...

Highlights included:

CW: Do you wear platform heels?

SC: We're not going there, an inch high maybe...

CW: Who would be better in bed, Amanda or Dannii?

SC: Well, Amanda is the definition of naughty and she's very flirty with guys. Dannii is much more closed and less trusting, so it takes longer to get to know her. So I'm going to guess here that it would be Dannii.

CW: Who would you have a threesome with?

SC: Well, this might sound a bit odd, but you – and whoever you choose.

CW: Ooo – can we have Cindy Crawford pre-tummy tuck?

SC: Sure.

[Sir David Frost comes up to the table: 'Simon – how are you?']

SC: I'm brilliant – Celia and I are going to have a threesome and everything's great.

[Frost, looking baffled, 'Jolly Good.' Wanders off.]

But the best line from it came when Simon revealed he was recently offered £1 million to be the new face of Viagra.

His response? 'I just said: sorry, but that has to be a fucking insult.'

SATURDAY, 12 JANUARY 2008

Britain's Got Talent starts up again tomorrow, with the first auditions being filmed up in Blackpool.

As I toyed with the concept of a hideous five-hour cab/train/cab slog through driving cold rain to get there, Cowell rang and invited me to jump on his private jet instead, which took precisely 42 minutes.

We were both hugely excited about what the unofficial 'Home of British variety' might bring us. 'It's going to be utterly brilliant,' said Simon, confidently.

In the bar of our hotel, we met a distraught Ant and Dec returning from a local pub, where they had watched their beloved Newcastle lose 6–0 to Manchester United.

'It was a bloody nightmare,' said Dec. 'There were about ten people in there when the match started, but they all started texting their mates and by the end the place was packed – all of them taking the mickey out of us as each goal went in...'

Cowell's make-up artist Julia joined us late for dinner, still shaking after her taxi hit another car on the way up, bruising her arm. The table fell silent as we all contemplated the enormity of this revelation.

Eventually, Cowell's PA, Ali, spoke for us all: 'You will....(gulp)...still be OK to..(gulp)...do Simon's make-up....won't you?' All eyes turned nervously to Julia.

'Yes, I will,' she replied, quietly.

The table heaved a collective sigh of relief.

SUNDAY, 13 JANUARY 2008

I didn't think anything could possibly be more grim than Blackpool's weather in January, but its 'talent' most definitely was...

We sat through eight hours of what I can only describe as less an 'end-of-the-pier' show, more a 'chuck-yourself-off-the-end-of-the-pier' show.

TUESDAY, 15 JANUARY 2008

Flew to Manchester in Simon's private jet again for the second leg of our

Britain's Got Talent auditions tour. As I got into the lift to go up to my room at the Radisson Edwardian Hotel, Sven-Goran Eriksson – who is apparently a long-term resident there – got into the one next to me with a beaming grin on his face, surrounded by pretty girls.

By total coincidence, I'm sure, I was woken at 3 a.m. by a loud, sustained clanking noise.

THURSDAY, 17 JANUARY 2008

People always imagine that the stars of shows like *Britain's Got Talent* must have huge separate dressing rooms, but we don't. Simon, Amanda and I all muck out in the same 'green room' with various make-up artists and production executives, spending the long days bickering, eating and gossiping together.

This morning we were waiting, as usual, for 'God' to arrive when the show's PR, Sara Lee, mentioned that two dodgy characters had been spotted hanging around the stage yesterday with suspicious-looking earpieces.

'They may have been bugging us,' she said, sending Amanda into instant spasms of horror (which was understandable given that she had spent most of the previous 24 hours discussing her prolific bowel movements).

Two minutes later, we discovered a small two-inch grey listening device sellotaped under the table. A sound technician was called to the 'crime scene' and confirmed the device was on, and active.

Amanda began to cackle dementedly (she has a laugh even filthier than Sid James) and shrieked: 'What the hell have we been saying!!??'

I shared her discomfort. If these tapes got out, we'd all have to leave the country given the sheer scale of celebrity 'look at the Botox on that' bitching that goes on as we flick through *OK!* and *Hello!*

But a security check outside the theatre found them in a nearby car, listening equipment everywhere. And they were soon helping Manchester police with their enquiries.

We were, thankfully, dealing with the most stupid buggers in Britain.

WEDNESDAY, 23 JANUARY 2008

Robbie Williams has been hanging out with David Icke in Los Angeles, according to the papers today.

Poor old Icke, has it really come to this?

THURSDAY, 24 JANUARY 2008

The biggest American property agency, the National Association of Realtors, has warned today that house prices dropped by 25 per cent in 2007, and that we could be going back to the Great Depression of the 1930s.

This sub-prime thing has caused complete carnage to the world's economy. The only question now is how much worse it can get.

SATURDAY, 26 JANUARY 2008

Ashley Cole has been caught cheating on his wife Cheryl, which will come as absolutely no surprise to Arsenal fans.

I feel very sorry for her, though. She's a lovely girl and deserves better than him.

MONDAY, 28 JANUARY 2008

The Glasgow auditions were fairly horrific, as were the audiences.

A cocky young rap dancer arrived on stage and announced: 'I'm like Justin Timberlake and Michael Flatley.'

Seconds after his act started, it became clear that he was slightly exaggerating his abilities – and we rewarded him with three quick buzzes.

'Screw you!' he snarled at the judges. To which the crowd reacted by chanting 'cheerio, cheerio, cheerio'.

'And you lot can all fuck off too!' he retorted.

THURSDAY, 31 JANUARY 2008

Tonight, I was the guest speaker at the ITV senior management conference.

'No pressure,' said Cowell helpfully, as I left. 'Just remember that if, God forbid, things don't go that well tonight, then you'll probably never work on TV again.'

I was introduced by Michael Grade, who said: 'Piers is a self-made man…which is just as well because nobody else would actually want to make him, would they?'

FRIDAY, 1 FEBRUARY 2008

We are unearthing some quite amazingly good talent amid the train wreck carnage.

One shy, unassuming, 12-year-old girl called Faryl Smith came on stage this evening and sang 'Ave Maria' so spine-tinglingly beautifully that Cowell's beady commercial eyes nearly exploded with 'Ker-ching' excitement. Britain's definitely got talent...it's just proving quite painful locating it.

SATURDAY, 2 FEBRUARY 2008
Celia found a T-shirt saying 'I LOVE GB' on it, so we sent it to Gordon Brown to cheer him up.

WEDNESDAY, 6 FEBRUARY 2008
A new Gallup poll in America has revealed that a majority (57 per cent) of Americans now believe the Iraq war was a mistake. The significance of this should not be underestimated. Americans are intensely loyal, patriotic and pro-military people. For most of them, condemn the invasion as wrong is an admission of historic proportions, and I applaud them for it.

I can sense the American public waking up to the reality of their current status in the world. They know that everyone seems to hate them, and they know that is largely down to Iraq. And they don't like being hated, they like to be loved.

And the more they realise this, the more I warm to them.

To judge a country by its leader is never a good idea, and I feel rather ashamed of myself for dismissing all yanks as war-mongering Bush clones. They're not, as this poll confirms.

THURSDAY, 7 FEBRUARY 2008
Breakfast at 10 Downing Street.

I haven't officially been back in there since I was fired from the *Mirror* four years ago. But nothing much has changed, though the art seems to have improved.

The prime minister seemed a bit beleaguered, hardly surprising given the ferocity of the media mauling he's received in the last few months. It's been cruel, and unfair, but that's modern politics.

We discussed the US presidential race, which is getting increasingly exciting.

'You'd better hope John McCain wins,' I said.

'Why?'

'Because he's the only one of all the candidates who's older than you. If Obama wins, you'll look like his dad.'

Gordon laughed out loud.

There's actually a rather good precedent for an older British PM and young American president – Harold MacMillan had a terrific relationship with John Kennedy in the early sixties.

The discussion moved on to Fabio Capello's debut as England football manager last night, and we agreed that his strict new 'no WAGS, PlayStations, flip-flops, or golf' regime, coupled with an emphasis on punctuality and formality, was a thoroughly good thing for our pampered, prima-donna star players.

'You should try it with the Cabinet,' I suggested.

Though I suspect the Brown regime makes Capello look like a lightweight.

Gordon walked me through No. 10, which, like the Tardis, is absolutely vast inside, a labyrinth of halls, corridors, staircases and strange secretive rooms.

We bumped into his younger son Fraser, who looked rosy-cheeked and bursting with good health.

'Say hello to Piers,' said Gordon to his 18-month-old boy.

'P—-i—-ers,' came the reply. Followed by a huge cheeky grin.

I'm no doctor, but Fraser looks to be making excellent progress and I detect a cautious optimism from his parents.

As I walked out of the famous black No. 10 front door, a group of people were coming in with some petition.

'God,' said one of them, 'we didn't know you lived here!'

I walked up to New Bond Street, grabbed a coffee and sat outside in the sun when a familiar face walked straight past me. It was, by remarkable coincidence, Fabio Capello, marching grimly along the road, ignoring everyone who stopped to stare, his fierce eyes blazing with determination.

He scared me from 50 yards and I don't even work for him.

WEDNESDAY, 13 FEBRUARY 2008

Back to No. 10 for another meeting with the prime minister. I'm getting more face time with Mr Brown than President Bush at the moment, which feels right given the way our respective careers are going in America. Gordon was a bit testy. He doesn't really understand why it's all gone so badly wrong for him in the polls since he decided not to have an early election.

But he's not a quitter, and he's got time – nearly two years if he wants it – to come back strongly. He just needs a big event to show off his leadership skills.

Even Thatcher was struggling in the polls until the Falklands war came along.

Perhaps this economic crisis, if it worsens, will be his Falklands?

THURSDAY, 14 FEBRUARY 2008

This is getting silly… I returned to No. 10 yet again tonight for a party in honour of Sarah Brown's brilliant PiggyBankKids charity.

'Be easier if you just stayed here, wouldn't it, Mr Morgan?' remarked a policeman at the gates.

Jilly Cooper bounded up and hugged me as I walked in, saying, 'I love you! I've always loved you!' Which was the first time anyone's said that to me in this building.

I had my arms around Joanna Lumley and Nigella Lawson when Gordon appeared. 'Happy Valentine's Day, Prime Minister,' I said.

Sarah Brown looked amazing – she's lost a ton of weight recently. 'I had to,' she explained. 'I launched London Fashion Week, so the pressure was on.'

I spied Norman Tebbit and introduced myself. 'Mr Tebbit, I've always been a massive fan.'

'Thank you. Who are you?'

'I'm Piers Morgan.'

He looked blank. 'I used to edit newspapers…'

Still blank.

Anyway, I wish you were back running the country,' I stammered.

'Funnily enough, I was just talking about that with Ronnie Corbett,' he said. 'We couldn't decide if I should be PM and he my chancellor, or whether he should be PM, and me his straight man.'

And on that surreal note, I went home.

The two women in my life – Celia and Naomi.

8

'Do not yield. Do not flinch. Stand up. Stand up with our President and fight. We're Americans. We're Americans, and we'll never surrender. They will.'
JOHN MCCAIN

TUESDAY, 19 FEBRUARY 2008

As the Pub Landlord, Al Murray interviewed me on his pre-recorded show tonight, and made me sing a duet of 'My Way' with him, while wearing a large pointy Oliver Cromwell hat and a blue spangly silver jacket.

I approached the front of the stage like a lemming nearing the edge of a cliff and launched into a rasping Ray Winstone-style cockney baritone version of Sinatra's classic.

It was exactly as it sounds. Appalling.

WEDNESDAY, 20 FEBRUARY 2008

'Can you interview the Liberal Democrat leader, Nick Clegg, for us?' asked Dylan Jones a few days ago.

'God, do I have to?' I groaned. 'He won't say anything.'

'Well, try your best,' said Dylan.

All I know about Clegg is that he looks and dresses like David Cameron, speaks like Alastair Campbell, is married (with two young children) to a beautiful Spanish lady called Miriam, refuses to say if he ever took drugs, claims to be 'a Liberal by temperament, instinct and upbringing' and once got arrested for burning rare cacti in Germany.

I arrived at his Westminster office this afternoon to find two young female assistants waiting, too.

'Are you joining us?' I asked.

'Yes,' they replied in unison.

My heart sank.

It's so boring when people insist on aides being present through interviews, because it usually means every tricky question is slyly passed to them with a flick of an eye to see if the Boss should answer it.

But their presence irritated me enough to want to try and have some fun with him.

After an hour of fairly tedious political chatter, I decided to liven things up a bit.

'Would you say your wife is the love of your life?'

'Oh yeah. Definitely.'

'How many times had you been in love before?'

'Properly? Twice. Once was unrequited. And I'd better not name her because she doesn't know who she is to this day. And the other was a childhood sweetheart and we broke up after a few years. It was a mutual thing.'

'It's never mutual.'

'OK, well I think I was probably a lot keener than she was...'

'So you had your heart broken?'

'Yes, I was like any adolescent for whom the great romantic ideal didn't work out. You must have experienced the same, Piers?'

'Never happened to me, mate... Do you think you're good in bed?'

The two aides gasped in mutual shock, but then, to my astonishment, just sat there giggling – leaving Clegg thrashing helplessly, like a mouse snared in a trap.

'Um...er...I don't think I am particularly brilliant or particularly bad, actually!'

He laughed nervously, and stared at the two aides for support. They just carried on giggling. So I carried on digging.

'What a typical Liberal Democrat answer, sitting on the fence, neither one thing nor the other.'

'Oh, God, look since the only judge of that is my wife...'

'Not the only judge, surely. We've already established there is at least one other out there.'

'Yes, OK, well, not for a very long time anyway.'

'How many women would actually know for a fact if you're good in bed?'

He turned desperately again to his aides, who didn't seem to know what to do to stem the tide of this particular line of interrogation.

(Spluttering.) 'Erm…not a…not a list as long as yours I'm sure…'

'Well, how many are we talking, 10, 20, 30?'

'No more than 30.'

'So there are 30 women out there who could answer the question?'

'There are not 30 women…it's a lot less than that.'

'And what would the general consensus be, do you think?'

'You'd have to ask them!'

'Ever had any complaints?'

'Oh God, yes, of course.'

'Many?'

'No.'

'What would your wife say?'

'I think she'd be very content and happy.'

'Positive?'

'We are very positive about each other, physically and emotionally.'

'Would you ever be unfaithful to her?'

'I certainly hope not.'

I ended the interview.

'That was fun!' he said. 'Nice to talk about things other than just politics for a change.'

'Yes,' I concurred. 'It certainly was.'

I walked back into the streets of Westminster and rang Dylan.

'I apologise.'

'What for?'

'You were right about Clegg.'

'Go on…'

'He shagged 30 women.'

'*What*?'

'Clegg admitted to me he's had sex with up to 30 women. And I suspect by the time he tells Mrs Clegg this, he's going to wish he hadn't!'

Dylan howled with laughter.

'Genius!'

THURSDAY, 21 FEBRUARY 2008

You can tell a lot about people by how they behave in airports. Björk, for example, seems a sweet, innocent Icelandic lady until she gets near a terminal – and then she habitually turns into a rabid monster, attacking anything on sight. But I've never seen anyone quite as unhinged as Javier 'Volcano' Bardem, the notoriously fiery Spanish actor and boyfriend of Penélope Cruz.

Shortly before boarding my plane to LA for the Oscars, I witnessed Volcano ranting, raving and hurling abuse at the official airside agency photographers for daring to take a picture of him and Penélope.

His mood further deteriorated when he was taken to one side at Heathrow for an extra examination of his carry-on bags.

Penélope stood, head bowed and sighing heavily, as Volcano continued to spew his verbal lava.

I took my seat in first class, and discovered they were right behind me. Volcano stomped on, eyes blazing, and I waited for further eruptions. But some soothing neck nibbles from Penélope calmed him down, and the moment we were airborne he went to sleep.

When he woke four hours later, Volcano morphed into a love-struck teenager, spending the rest of the flight kissing, fondling and giggling with his lover.

On landing, though, he was off again – chuntering loudly about the paparazzi and refusing to walk out of the airport with Penélope, leaving her to run the gauntlet of the sole photographer waiting for them.

Volcano is up for Best Supporting Actor at the Oscars for his portrayal of a crazed maniac in *No Country For Old Men*, but judging by this performance he was clearly just playing himself.

I arrived at the Beverly Wilshire, and bumped into a gurning Tom Hanks in the lobby – which is all you need after a long flight. So I fled to Soho House (the club chain has come to LA for Oscar week), where I found Drew Barrymore celebrating her thirty-third birthday.

'I was watching you in bed this afternoon,' I said.

'I'm sorry?'

'*Fever Pitch*. They had it on the plane.'

'Oh,' she laughed. 'You had me worried there.'

'Relax – you were wonderful. But the British version is much better.'

'Is it? I've read the book, but haven't seen the British film.'

'The book is about my soccer team, Arsenal. So is the British film. It doesn't work with baseball, because Arsenal are ten times sexier than the Boston Red Sox.'

'I don't know about that…'

'Take my word for it. Why don't we remake it? I can play Colin Firth and you can be my love interest.'

'Well, your accent is quite cute,' she admitted.

At which delicately poised point in the negotiation, her mate Cameron Diaz arrived to drag her away.

I wandered further in, observing the wonderfully decadent scene: plush sofas, ornately decorated tables, waiters bearing huge slabs of lobster and gargantuan bottles of Grey Goose vodka, and celebrities lurking in every corner. Anna Friel was by the bar, looking hot. As was Quentin Tarantino, though in a different way. I don't know what he was on, but his face was a pulsating red and he seemed extremely excited to be there.

Minutes later, I was chatting to photographer-to-the-stars Richard Young when Madonna bustled in, gave him a kiss and then threw me a filthy look that said, 'Behave, or I'll induct you into Kabbalah.'

David Furnish arrived. And for some bizarre reason we got round to discussing underwear. 'I'm a boxers man myself,' I said.

'Oh nooooo,' he replied. 'Has to be tighty whiteys for me. Otherwise everything dangles around, doesn't it?'

I was still mulling this over as I went back to my hotel.

FRIDAY, 22 FEBRUARY 2008

I headed back to Soho House, where Ben Silverman, the maverick young boss of NBC, was throwing a surprise birthday party for Ozwald Boateng.

'So, are you in the business?' I asked one guest.

'Piers, he's Chris Tucker…' said Ozwald, cackling with unnecessary glee at my failure to recognise the *Rush Hour* star.

At midnight, Elton arrived with David Furnish and came straight over to shake my hand – which at a Hollywood party is like having the Queen knighting you on the spot.

'Boxer shorts?' he asked, eyebrow raised.

SUNDAY, 24 FEBRUARY 2008

God, the Oscars were dull. I've spent more exciting evenings watching logs float down the river. The only real highlight was Gary Busey's red-carpet assault on a severely affronted Jennifer Garner.

I did enjoy the Europeans thrashing the Americans, though, and host Jon Stewart's acerbic performance. Especially when he revealed his porn name, which you calculate by taking the names of your first pet and the street you grew up in. Mine, I'm proud to announce, is therefore Rocky Oxbottom.

As for Volcano Bardem, he won his Oscar. And posed endlessly, and with delirious happiness, for all the photographers. Amazing what a gong can do for a moody thespian, isn't it?

TUESDAY, 26 FEBRUARY 2008

America's Got Talent starts up again this week, and this time we're taking the auditions all over the country, starting with Atlanta, Georgia.

It was the first time I've been down South since I once toured around with New Kids On The Block (they hated me and I hated them – it was a mutually miserable relationship that ended with Donnie Wahlberg walking on stage at a later Wembley show wearing a T-shirt emblazoned with the words 'PIERS MORGAN SUCKS').

They couldn't be more different from the LA or New York crowd down here.

Very conservative, very family orientated, very religious and very opposed to anything that even remotely resembles 'pinko liberalism'.

I asked The Ferret what the difference is between places like Atlanta and LA, and he replied: 'If I call my friends or family anywhere outside of LA or New York on a Sunday morning, they will be in church. If I call my business associates in LA or New York on a Sunday morning, they'll be on the golf course.'

Spend time in a place like Atlanta, and you quickly understand why someone like George Bush got re-elected.

Everywhere I went today, I met people who speak like him, think like him and behave like him.

Southern Americans are respectful (they all call you 'sir'), welcoming, kind and fun to be around.

But get them on to politics, and with many of them it's scary. Think of the most right-wing person you know in Britain, and double it.

I spoke to one guy in the hotel bar this lunchtime, an oil worker, and asked him what he thought of Bush.

'He's done a great job for America,' he drawled. 'Europeans may think he's dumb, but he knows what he's doing. This country's under attack from terrorists and we gotta defend ourselves. And if that means blowing up everyone in Afghanistan and Iraq, then that's fine by me.'

A big dinner was thrown tonight for the stars of the show, and Sharon was still excited from hosting the Brits last week. 'Presenting an award to Paul McCartney was one of the best moments of Ozzy's life, it was worth it just for that,' she said. 'He loved the Beatles, and couldn't believe he was there sharing a stage with one of them.'

The Hoff was on splendid form, too. Papers leaked to the TV celebrity shows today – we've decided his new nickname should be 'Breaking News Hoff' due to the number of times he is just that – claim he wants back some treasured possessions from his former marital home including a giant elephant tusk, a dolphin statue and a life-size – and apparently unnervingly realistic – prosthetic French maid.

'I should have married the maid,' he chuckled wistfully, 'would have saved me a lot of trouble!'

He was typically supportive of my appearances on *Celebrity Apprentice*.

'I haven't watched it myself,' he lied, 'but my friends have and they all think you're a wanker.'

'That's as maybe,' I replied. 'But it's making me as big a star as you.'

'A *star*? Oh please…' he scoffed.

Five minutes later, Jerry Springer arrived and instantly exclaimed:

'Piers! Congratulations! *The Apprentice* has turned you into such a huge STAR now!'

I turned to The Hoff, whose mouth was frozen in horror, and winked.

But he had the last laugh. After I went to the loo, the restaurant manager apparently produced a book that he always gets celebrity guests to sign.

'He didn't know you were one,' scoffed The Hoff, delightedly.

WEDNESDAY, 27 FEBRUARY 2008

First day of auditions ended with a gargantuanly proportioned Jordan-esque lady called Miss Busty, who wobbled on stage and proceeded to break things with her 30-pound cleavage.

Beer cans first, then planks of wood and finally giant watermelons with my face and The Hoff's attached to them.

'Well,' I said, as the 2,000-strong audience fell about, 'I guess America *does* have talent after all...'

THURSDAY, 28 FEBRUARY 2008

One of the few downsides of working in America so much is that I now have to miss some of the boys' school stuff. And never did I feel that more keenly than tonight when Stanley starred as the Artful Dodger in *Oliver!*

A choice of role that came as no surprise to The Hoff, as we compiled a good-luck fax to be sent to the school.

'Yeah, well, his old man's been one of those all his life...'

FRIDAY, 29 FEBRUARY 2008

Peter Fincham has been made the new boss of ITV.

'Congrats. Thank fuck I sponsored you on that bike ride,' I emailed him today.

'How much did you actually give?' he replied, rather sinisterly. 'Must look up my records.'

Shit. Rowan Atkinson's going to get all my work.

SATURDAY, 1 MARCH 2008

I flew down to San Antonio in Texas today, to spend time with some of the wounded soldiers benefitting from the Intrepid Fallen Heroes Fund.

As I walked through the airport, I saw hundreds of people waiting for the return of soldiers and clutching American flags. Many of them, I discovered, had no connection to any of the servicemen and women, but just came along to pay tribute to them.

When I reached the Intrepid Center, I was taken to meet some of the more severely wounded troops.

One 21-year-old soldier called Matthew Bradford had lost both legs and been blinded by a bomb in Iraq.

He was sitting in a wheelchair, with a fake eye flashing a skull and cross bones at me.

I assumed he would be sad, bitter perhaps. (I know I would be.)

But then we talked. 'Do you feel angry?' I asked.

'No, sir,' he replied, quickly, defiantly and with the civility so common in Americans, and so rare in Britain these days.

'Why not?'

'Because I am proud to have served my country, sir.'

'No part of you is resentful of what happened?'

'No, sir. The only thing I resent is being unable to rejoin my unit in Iraq.'

'I find it extraordinary that you could even think of going back, given what happened to you.'

'I'd go back tomorrow if they let me, sir. I want to finish the job.'

During the rest of our conversation, Matthew never once showed even a trace of self-pity.

He was funny, self-deprecating, intelligent, respectful and thoughtful. In fact, about as far removed from the stereotypical John Wayne-style American Marine image as I could imagine.

By his side stood his mother, with tears streaming down her face.

'This place has given my boy a new life,' she said, 'and a new hope.'

Shane Parsons, another double-leg amputee Marine, had not an ounce of self-pity either. 'Hey, look at it this way,' he laughed, 'the good news is that I never have to worry about clipping my toenails again!'

Shane suffered three heart attacks in the aftermath of a roadside bomb in Iraq, and has brain damage that means he can't even read any more.

'What does this centre mean to you?' I asked.

'It means that America cares about me, and that's all I need to know.'

Lillian Benning, a mother of two who had her leg blown off in an Iraq mortar attack, showed similar extraordinary spirit.

'I don't have time to worry about myself because my kids need me,' she said. 'I couldn't let them see that I was scared.'

The trip has definitely altered my view of American troops, which has always been that they are a cold, callous, military machine.

But meeting them today, hearing their stories, their motivations and their love for their country, I felt inspired, not appalled.

It made me realise that whatever you think of the politics of various wars, we should never forget the courage and, yes, heroism of the troops who get sent to do their government's often dirty work.

At the end of my visit, the centre's boss insisted on presenting me with a commemorative coin to thank me for my support. I felt embarrassed to even accept it.

Selling a few hotdogs on the streets of New York, and winding up a few prima-donna American celebrities in the process, is surely the very least any human being can do.

But as I left afterwards, Shane Parsons' mother approached me.

'Piers, I just want to thank you for what you're doing on *The Apprentice* for the troops. It makes such a difference, as you can see.'

Went out for a few drinks in San Antonio in the evening, and found a wonderfully rough redneck bar called Coyote Ugly, where scantily clad and, it has to be said, fairly gruesome-looking cowgirls strut their stuff along the bar.

The sign on the door said it all: 'PLEASE DO NOT BRING LOADED FIREARMS INSIDE.'

Which brings a whole new meaning to the phrase: 'Is that a gun in your pocket, or are you just pleased to see me?'

A lot of people approached me for a chat during the evening, and were, to a man and woman, polite, friendly and naturally warm.

It's a ridiculous generalisation to say all Americans are like that, but then my previously held views that they're all arrogant, obnoxious gits was also a ridiculous generalisation. Americans are bonded by certain key characteristics – a love of their country, an obsession with weather and their health, a genuine love and respect for success and money, and a fear of all things foreign.

But the people I met tonight were otherwise from a different place to the aggressive, ballsy types you find in New York, or the busy-busy entertainment crowd in LA.

It's important to remember just how big America is, and just how many people live in these 'fly-over' states. Not least because they are the ones who quietly, but powerfully, go to the ballot box every four years and decide who runs their country. And judging by the conversations I had this evening, Obama has a long way to go before he wins over these hearts and minds.

'He's too young,' they kept saying, 'and too inexperienced.'

But when I pointed out that Bush had plenty of experience but was cocking things up left, right and centre, they became quickly affronted.

'Our president is a good man,' said one man. 'He may have made some mistakes, but he ain't no fool. And he's done what he's done to protect our country from terrorists. 'Obama just wants to talk to them all, which is the road to disaster.'

SUNDAY, 2 MARCH 2008

I flew into Dallas for the second leg of *America's Got Talent* auditions tonight, and got asked by a customs officer: 'So Piers, I've gotta ask – are you gay?'

I'm used to tricky interrogations at US immigration desks but this was ridiculous.

'I beg your pardon?'

'I didn't mean to offend you, but there's a promo running on NBC for *Celebrity Apprentice* that says you might be…'

I raced to my hotel like a hyperactive greyhound and switched on the TV. Within a few minutes, there indeed was Donald Trump saying: 'You're calling Piers a homosexual?'

Cue dramatic drum roll and a Henry Kissinger-style voice saying: 'How did Piers react? Find out on Thursday…'

I hit the streets of Dallas this afternoon in a T-shirt – it's 72 degrees – expecting to find an exciting, vibrant city like the one we always saw in the TV show.

But God, it's so dull!

Like so many American cities now, it has lost all sense of its own identity, and is just a brand extension of everywhere else. A Starbucks on every corner, a KFC and McDonalds, a Barnes and Noble bookstore, a Gap…

Same old, same old.

There's no real greenery, just a big load of skyscrapers.

And it just seems to lack much soul.

On a positive note, the people, again, were utterly charming.

'I love your British accent,' said a woman in the bookstore. 'It's so… so…like Prince Charles! Do you know him?'

Americans always assume that Britain is so tiny we must all know each other. Which, I think, given the relative size of our two countries is perfectly understandable.

'I do, actually,' I replied.

'Oh my God! Really?! That's amazing!'

She called over her two friends.

'This British guy knows Prince Charles!'

For the next ten minutes I was forced, thanks to my idle boasting, to discuss the Royals.

But it was quite fascinating to see how much they loved them.

'I wish we had a queen,' said one, wistfully.

'Even a prince would be nice,' agreed another.

America puts its presidents on such a pedestal, however obvious their shortcomings, because they don't have anything else. Simple as that.

If we had no royal family, then I suspect Gordon Brown and his family would get treated with a lot more reverence than they do. Every country needs a figurehead to look up to. You just don't always get a good one, unfortunately.

Cowboys were everywhere, and looked rather magnificent in their big Stetsons and spurs. And the women were gorgeous, all long-legged blondes with cheeky smiles.

It's just a shame there's nothing to do here.

MONDAY, 3 MARCH 2008

Simon Cowell has done a deal to make a Hollywood movie out of the phones-to-riches life of *Britain's Got Talent* opera-singing winner Paul Potts.

And this has predictably led to a flurry of speculation about who will play the judges on the big screen.

I emailed The Ferret, suggesting that George Clooney might be appropriate for my role.

'Clooney booked,' came his reply an hour later, 'but Stephen Hawking available.'

I asked the concierge at my hotel what I should go and see while I was in Dallas, and he replied: 'The JFK Sixth-Floor Museum.'

Ah, of course. Nothing defines Dallas more than the Kennedy assassination in 1963, with the possible exception of Sue Ellen's drunken pout.

I walked down to the museum, past the famous Grassy Knoll (which is a small, very dull, grassy knoll, with a large white 'X' literally marking the spot on the road where he died).

It's located on the sixth floor (obviously) of the former Texas School Book Depository building from where Lee Harvey Oswald shot his fatal bullets.

There was a big crowd of people when I arrived – apparently over 300,000 people flock there each year.

The stuff inside wasn't that new or interesting, but just standing there looking out on that iconic view was worth the $14 entrance fee alone.

To understand why America became the way it is now, look no further than the day their beloved young president got shot dead.

Millions of hopes and dreams died that day, too. And even now, more than 40 years later, the scars run deep.

'What do you think of Obama?' I asked one man as we watched a video of the shooting.

'I think he's gonna get shot, too,' he said.

And that's a very real fear in America. As the Obama bandwagon grows stronger, so do the doubts about his physical safety. America couldn't stomach another dynamic young president getting assassinated. It would devastate them even more than 9/11.

TUESDAY, 4 MARCH 2008

Tried to get in my hotel lift this afternoon, only to be stopped by a burly security man.

'Sorry,' he growled, 'no entry.'

I was bemused.

'Why? Someone more important using it?'

'Yes, sir,' he said, with no semblance of humour.

Seconds later, a cavalcade of limos swept up to the hotel entrance, and John McCain marched past me and straight into the lift. He looked surprisingly small, and very old.

It turns out that McCain is here to celebrate his expected formal nomination as the Republican candidate tonight, with a huge party in the hotel's official ballroom.

As I stood in the busy lobby bar waiting for a taxi to go to dinner, I received a vivid reminder of the need to have a catchphrase if I want to really make the big time.

Jerry Springer walked by, greeted by raucous chants of 'Jerry! Jerry!'

Then came The Hoff, who received shouts of 'Don't Hassle The Hoff.'

And finally I saw Henry Winkler, aka 'The Fonz', fending off fans cooing 'Aaaaayhh!'

I'd prefer mine, on balance, not to be 'HEY PIERS, ARE YOU GAY?'

Later in the evening, I returned to the hotel and sneaked into the McCain party, which was now in full celebratory swing, just in time to hear his valedictory address.

His speech was like his campaign, heavy on patriotism.

McCain's stump shtick has been to repeatedly call himself a 'maverick', draw on his time as a Vietnam prisoner-of-war, and say he will cut bureaucratic waste from government, while encouraging entrepreneurial capitalism.

'Stand up with me, my friends, stand up and fight for America, her strength, her ideals, her future.'

But the Republican faithful lapped it all up, with whoops and hollers, chants of 'USA, USA' and fist-pumps galore.

Americans love their war heroes, mavericks and comeback kids. McCain is all three of those, and milks each tag like an eager farmer with six juicy cows' udders in front of him.

'There are going to be stark choices between a liberal Democrat and a conservative Republican,' he said, 'and I believe we can prevail in that contest of ideas and vision.'

You can say that again. No election in modern history will be as vital for America as this one – because the nation needs a fresh face, a new image, a re-direction.

And that face is increasingly likely to be female, black or war-battered.

McCain's life has been one long scrap, and he's going to try and scrap his way to the White House now.

The Democrat nominee battle, meanwhile, rages on. Obama has 1,386 of the all-important delegates now, to Hillary's 1,276. The winner needs 2,025, so there is still everything to play for.

WEDNESDAY, 5 MARCH 2008

Tony Blair is, coincidentally, in Dallas too, receiving some Freedom of the City honour for being George Bush's mouthpiece.

It really is quite sickening to see the adulation, and huge amounts of cash, that he is being showered with in America for making fatuous speeches about how desperately he wants peace in the Middle East.

It's like a fox being paid to address the world on why we should be nice to hens. But around town today, I couldn't find anyone to say a bad word about the man.

'What do you think of Tony Blair?' I asked my cab driver this morning.

'I love that man,' he replied, in hushed sincerity. 'He stood shoulder to shoulder with us when it mattered.'

'But wouldn't it have been better for all of us if he'd tried to persuade Bush not to invade Iraq?'

The driver eyed me suspiciously in his rear-view mirror.

I detected an expression of 'I've got one of them left-wing, pinko surrender monkeys in the back of my car'.

'Saddam was gonna blow us to pieces with nukes. We had to take him out, and we did take him out! The president, and Prime Minister Blair, were right!'

Note the respectful titles again – I have been called 'sir' by most people from the moment I arrived in Dallas, and it's not because they think I've been knighted for services to my country.

'But Saddam didn't have any nukes,' I ventured, perhaps unwisely.

Silence.

Then a grimace.

'Yes he did, he just hid 'em where we can't find 'em.'

I wouldn't say that Americans have been brainwashed about Iraq and Saddam, it's more that they desperately want to believe in their president.

And while Bush may sound like an inarticulate dimwit to many Europeans, here in Dallas he sounds just like everyone else, only more articulate than most.

As a waitress put it to me with a big grin over breakfast: 'We're not stupid in Texas, we just sound it.'

And that's completely true. I've met some highly intelligent people down here, but their slow, drawling speech delivery can appear deceptively slow-witted. Particularly when compared to a rapid-fire New Yorker.

I had dinner with Sharon Osbourne tonight, and we both sank our red wine a little too quickly.

At 12.30 a.m., she burst into a self-created song called 'I LOVE MY HUSBAND'S WILLY!' which she proceeded to sing at the top of her voice (and not, it must be said, completely in tune) as her assistants and I hustled her swiftly along various corridors to her room.

I left Sharon at her door, swaying gently from side to side, and with an utterly adoring look on her face, still shrieking her unique anthem to Ozzy.

THURSDAY, 6 MARCH 2008

The weather in Dallas has been extraordinary. When I arrived on Sunday, it was a balmy 72 degrees, and people were sunbathing.

Today, it was 32 degrees, and snowing.

The locals were stunned. 'Goddamn,' I heard one old boy exclaim outside the hotel this morning, as he eyed the tumbling white flakes in wonder, 'I ain't never seen anything like this in March in ma life!'

The TV news channels are running with this climatic phenomenon like it's the biggest crisis since the Bay of Pigs. Flights are being cancelled, people are being told to stay indoors and everyone is talking about little else.

It is hard to overstate the obsession with weather over here. The average American will happily spend a good hour talking about it every single day if you let them.

Whole TV channels are devoted to 24-hour weather reports. There is even one called, simply, The Weather Channel. Which, amusingly, gives hourly updates on the weather changes in hundreds of countries that 90 per cent of Americans will never visit in their lifetimes.

And they have the reverse attitude to Britain – they hate heat.

In Los Angeles, you'll regularly hear the weather presenters announcing in grim tones: 'Bad news for the weekend I'm afraid – it's gonna be a hot one!'

Can you imagine Sian Lloyd on ITN miserably declaring: 'Really sorry to have to break this to you, but it's going to be 90 degrees tomorrow...'

Americans like their weather to be like everything else in their lives – calm, moderate, regular. They don't want to be shocked by their weather, in the same way that they don't want to be shocked by terrorists, or restaurants suddenly changing their usual menu. So when it snows in March, in a place like Dallas, it sparks near end-of-the-world-style panic. Because nobody is expecting it. And Americans don't like surprises.

FRIDAY, 7 MARCH 2008

The 'greatest slaughter in the history of *The Apprentice*' episode aired last night, and America is suitably ecstatic at the destruction and elimination of the ghastly Omarosa.

'Are there enough words in the English language to describe last night's episode of *Apprentice*?' wrote one reviewer. 'It was a rout, beating, cakewalk, clobbering, debacle, disaster, drubbing, shellacking... Omarosa made General Custer look like Alexander the Great.'

Ratings jumped over 10 million viewers, and as I walked through Dallas airport, an endless stream of jubilant people ran up to shake my hand and thank me.

I've gone from panto villain to national hero in America...or as one woman put it to me as I boarded the plane: 'I just love to hate ya!'

Most strikingly, my choice of charity has really hit a nerve with Americans. There is a rising anti-war sentiment about Iraq, but unlike in Britain where the public have been shamefully taking it out on soldiers returning from the battlefield, this has increased, not diminished, their concern for the young men and women fighting for their country. It's like they've all remembered what happened in Vietnam, where the troops got so badly blamed and betrayed for waging a war their political masters made them fight.

Three people came up to me during the flight, to thank me for raising money for the Intrepid. One man was actually in tears. 'I fought in the first Gulf War,' he said, 'and I think what you are doing is a fine thing, sir.'

SUNDAY, 9 MARCH 2008

Amanda burned to death in *Wild At Heart* tonight, and couldn't have been happier if someone had strung her naked from the top of Big Ben.

'I just can't spend another day standing in elephant dung in the African bush,' she explained to me with typical dignity.

Excrement was the running theme of our conversation, as we turned to Amanda's forthcoming debut appearance in the London marathon, in aid of the Born Free charity.

'I'll give you £10 for every minute under five hours,' I said, 'but you have to give me £10 for every minute over five hours. If you die, we'll call it quits.'

'I'm more worried about doing a poo in my pants, like Paula Radcliffe, than dying,' she said. You can take the girl out of Gloucestershire...

SUNDAY, 16 MARCH 2008

Celia and I are in Mexico, enjoying a week of tortillas and tequila, and finishing our marathon four-month re-watching of *The West Wing*, which I've decided is the greatest TV drama series ever made.

It is also remarkably prescient, given that it ends with a handsome, dynamic, young, non-white (in this case Latino) Democrat becoming president, replacing an old, tired, white guy.

The issue of race is dogging Obama every step of his campaign. You just cannot escape from the big question: is America really ready to vote for a black president?

I think it just might be now, but it's still a big might.

MONDAY, 17 MARCH 2008

I read the McCartney divorce settlement revelations today with a mixture of fascination, incredulity, horror and downright hilarity.

'I am not a lying, fantasist, gold-digger,' Heather has repeatedly insisted in her regular mad-eyed global TV rants.

Now a senior judge has confirmed that she is indeed a liar and fantasist. And the disclosure that her original demand was for £125 million confirms she is one of the greatest gold-diggers of all time.

TUESDAY, 18 MARCH 2008

Last time I was in Los Angeles, I broke five ribs falling off a Segway.

Today, I found an even more absurd way to injure myself.

My fitness trainer, a six-foot-six Austrian called Alex, took me to a local gym because the hotel one is being refurbished.

After 20 minutes, the new gym's manager, Mike, informed us that private trainers were not allowed.

'Can we finish the session?' I asked.

'Yes, but your trainer will have to pretend he is a friend working out with you.'

Alex handed me two weights to do some curls, then picked up two considerably larger 40-pound ones himself and began flapping them around with straight arms like they were pieces of plywood.

We did this for eight repetitions before he smacked me straight in the face with one of his weights, causing several buckets of blood to spurt out of my mouth.

'Thanks, Mike,' I grimaced, as we passed the manager on the way out.

'No problem!' he grinned, blissfully oblivious to the sarcasm dripping from my battered lips.

'This may be a good thing,' suggested Alex.

'Oh, thow?' I lisped.

'Well, if you can't eat any food, the weight will fall off.'

We agreed that until the hotel gym is fixed, we'll use the local park instead. It's safer!

TUESDAY, 25 MARCH 2008

Flew to New York for the live *Celebrity Apprentice* finale, and felt like a boxer heading into town for a big fight.

'Knock him out, Piers!' shouted a construction worker outside the airport.

'The cowboy's gonna kill ya!' yelled another.

The media, and public, are all buying into Donald Trump's clever marketing ploy of 'America vs Britain, good vs evil'. And the polls are saying 80 per cent want six-foot-seven country singer Trace Adkins to win.

I called an *Apprentice* expert for some tips on how to turn things around.

'I saw the penultimate show and, knowing edits as I do, I reckon the cowboy's going to win,' said Sir Alan Sugar from his Florida home, helpfully. 'They are all bigging him up, he's American, and I'm sure he will have all his pals in the audience telling Trump what a great guy he is. You need someone to do the same, but I don't think such a person exists...'

'Oh, ha ha. Seriously, what should I do?'

'Challenge Trump on the credibility of the show, and his own credibility,' advised Sir Alan. 'It's based on his business show, and business is about the numbers, not who the nicest bloke is.'

WEDNESDAY, 26 MARCH 2008

Interviewed Mickey Rourke for BBC1 in his favourite New York bar this morning.

He was a magnificent physical specimen – gnarled, beaten up, scarred, scalpelled and calloused.

And an even more magnificent man to talk to. Bright, funny, self-deprecating, ferocious, intense and slightly scary.

Abused as a child, ostracised as an actor, broken-hearted by the only woman he ever really loved (Carrie Otis), he's had to fight his whole life.

'You've had it tough,' I told him.

He paused, and stared me straight in the eye.

'I'm tough.'

He had to be, too. Hollywood, as he so eloquently explained, is an unforgiving place when you fail.

'I had achieved so much success in my career and then had this spectacular fall from grace which left me unemployed and living in a town, Los Angeles, that is built on envy. Once you fall, people don't really root for you to come back again, you know? I'd go to restaurants where I always had the best table and half the time they wouldn't even let me pay. And then when I stopped making movies, the same places wouldn't even give me a fucking lousy table, never mind the best one! It was hard, but that's the way it is. It would have been easier if I had never been as successful, then the fall wouldn't have been so tough. I'd go into stores and people would look at me and say, "Didn't you used to be Mickey Rourke?" And that would really hurt. But there was no quitting in me. If you want to keep me down then stand on top of me and shoot me. Because that's the only way you're going to stop me getting back up.'

Afterwards, we had a coffee together and chatted some more.

On the current state of America, he was fascinating.

'Since 9/11 we've been in total chaos, two wars, anthrax scares, the economy in the toilet, all sorts of shit has happened. I don't know how it all gets resolved, but I do know it's a shame that so many young men and women are dying at the moment and nobody seems to know how to stop it.'

'Are the wars justified?'

'I don't know. What I do know is that after 9/11, I wanted to go over there, you know what I'm saying? I was in London recently and I couldn't believe all these hate-talking fanatics you have over there who are allowed to carry on doing their thing even when a bus full of women and children gets blown to pieces. I know you've deported one or two of them, but it seems crazy. I don't think these fundamentalists should be allowed to talk all this crap, and brainwashing these young kids.'

'Don't you think Bush has seriously damaged America's reputation though?'

'Yeah, that's true. But President Bush was in the wrong place at the wrong time, I don't know how anyone could have handled this situation any different. I don't give a fuck who is in office, Bush or whoever, there is no simple solution to this problem. I mean, look how long we've had the war between Israel and Palestine. There seems to be no answer to that, no end to it all. It's too easy to blame Bush for everything. This shit between the Christians and Muslims goes back to the Crusades, doesn't it? These are unpredictable, dangerous times, and I don't think anyone knows quite what to do. But hey, look, all the great empires have their periods where they rule the world, and then they crumble. And I don't know if that will happen to America in our lifetime, but it's possible.'

THURSDAY, 27 MARCH 2008

I know it's only a TV show, but God I felt nervous today.

I did 30 radio interviews across America from my hotel room this morning, then a round of the big breakfast TV shows.

And everywhere I go, people keep saying 'everyone's a winner tonight'. But that's such garbage. Americans only care about winners; losers are instantly forgotten. I've *got* to win.

Mum and Charlotte have flown out to support me, and they were so excited I thought at one stage they were going to pass out. It was so good to have them, though.

Mum has been, without question, the most important person in my life. An absolute, unequivocal, never-wavering rock of love and support through all the relentless turbulence of my chaotic life and career.

We speak almost every day, and her opinion is the one I value above all others. She's terrified of flying, so it's taken a real effort for her to make the trip, but she's done it, and I really want to win to make her and my little sister proud.

The first hour of the show was the recorded final event, where we had to put on the charity auction. I had raised $380,000 to Trace's $65,000. But there were several other criteria for victory.

Predictably, almost all the other American contestants told Trump they wanted Trace to win, because he's 'so nice'.

We then watched a touching video of him and his six-year-old daughter, whose deadly peanut allergy is why he appeared in the show, before he sang a ballad on stage.

It was all 'Saint' Trace, and the clock was ticking.

I turned to Mum and Charlotte, and they were both looking dejected, but I mouthed the words, 'It ain't over till the fat lady sings.'

But it felt like it might be.

Then, with just 15 minutes left, they finally played the video of the trip I made for the Intrepid Fallen Heroes Fund. When it finished, six of the soldiers I had met in San Antonio came up on stage in uniform, several in wheelchairs. The audience gave them an instant and rousing standing ovation.

We returned to the boardroom debate, and Ivanka Trump confronted me: 'Piers, you've raised an incredible amount of money for your charity, but the problem is your bedside manner.'

'With respect,' I replied, to audience laughter and applause, 'you don't know anything about my bedside manner, Ivanka.'

Trump grinned, then ordered us both to make our final case, and Sir Alan's advice rang loud and clear in my head.

'If this is a likeability contest, then Trace should win,' I said. 'But it's not, it's a business show. And business is about numbers. I won the most tasks, raised more money than the other contestants put together, brought in the most stars and made history with what you called "the biggest slaughter in the history of *The Apprentice*". I also happen to think that there is no more important charity in America right now than the Intrepid Fallen Heroes Fund.'

Trump nodded, and began his verdict.

'Piers, you're vicious, you're smart, you're tough, you're probably brilliant, I'm not sure. You're certainly not diplomatic, but you did an amazing job and you beat the hell out of everybody.'

Which way was he going here, I couldn't tell...

Then he turned to my rival. 'Trace, you have an amazing family, beautiful children. You're a special guy – you're a special human being, a beautiful guy. I'll always love you...but for tonight...'

Oh my God, he's going to fire Trace...

Then he swivelled back to me suddenly. Damn. It was a double bluff.

'Piers...'

The bastard.

'…you're the *Celebrity Apprentice*.'

Cue firecrackers, falling confetti and general mayhem. It was a double double bluff, and I'd won.

I turned back to see Mum and Charlotte in tears, virtually exploding with joy. It was so nice to have them there. God knows they've been through some pretty grim times as my mother and sister over the years.

Trump shook my hand.

'I should hire you…'

'You can't afford me, Mr Trump.'

He laughed. So I pushed my luck.

'Mind if I educate Ivanka about my bedside manner later?'

'Sure,' he replied, 'if you don't mind me killing you…'

My mobile vibrated.

'Well done, good fight,' said the text from Sir Alan.

As I celebrated at the aftershow party with Mum and Charlotte, a lithe and very attractive young blonde grabbed me.

'I love your evil style,' she purred into my ear. 'Take my hand.'

'Why?'

'Because it has my phone number in it. And trust me, I'm no *Apprentice*.'

My first proper bona-fide groupie. Marvellous.

I got back to my hotel at 3 a.m., and a message arrived from the man who brought me to America, Simon Cowell.

'Congratulations from Dr Frankenstein.'

FRIDAY, 28 MARCH 2008

Sir Alan was quickly back in touch: 'The MSNBC website says, "RELATIVE UNKNOWN WINS CELEBRITY APPRENTICE…BUT HE WILL SOON BE FORGOTTEN BY THE PUBLIC." How sad, after all your effort. But how true! Ha ha.'

And they call *me* obnoxious…

The ratings were amazing, over 14 million saw the moment I won, which was NBC's biggest audience for a non-sports event since 2006.

Most of the TV and press headlines are screaming 'Vicious Piers wins *Apprentice*', though my favourite just says: 'PIERS MORGAN WINS *APPRENTICE* DESPITE BEING PIERS MORGAN.'

I've received over 200 texts and 150 emails since I won, the biggest reaction I've had to anything I've done since, ironically, getting fired from the *Mirror*.

Even heads of state are clamouring to honour me.

'Piers,' read one phone message this morning. 'Well done on your TV success, Gordon.' It's the first text I've ever received from the prime minister. I didn't even know he knew how.

'Thanks,' I replied. 'Try being more evil, it seems to work...'

Brimming with self-satisfaction, I called the boys, expecting them to be beside themselves with excitement over their father's international triumph.

'I won!' I half-shouted down the phone.

'Erm, Dad,' said Bertie, 'the thing is that we're having a really good game of football, so can you call back in an hour or something...'

SATURDAY, 29 MARCH 2008

Alex and I have been using the local park near my hotel in Beverly Hills for our work-outs while the gym's being fixed. Today, photographs of one of those sessions appeared over two pages in the *Mail on Sunday*, taken by a sneaky paparazzi who yet again I had failed to spot.

To describe them as embarrassing is to massively understate the matter. In one, I appear to be groaning under the weight of dumb-bells so small they are barely visible to the naked eye.

Others show me in various ludicrous positions, huffing and puffing like a dying man – while Alex towers over me, muscle-bound and magnificent, resembling some sort of Greek god.

I can just imagine how these will be going down back in the UK.

They'll all think I've now completely disappeared up my vain, self-obsessed, Hollywood backside.

SUNDAY, 30 MARCH 2008

My forty-third birthday, and I found a card in my *America's Got Talent* trailer from David Hasselhoff. 'You're the nicest wanker I've ever met,' it read, 'Hoffy Birthday.'

I celebrated with a small dinner party at Robert De Niro's restaurant, Ago, in Beverly Hills, with 12 guests including Ioan Gruffudd, Simon Cowell, Ian

Royce, who is also the warm-up guy on *America's Got Talent*, and Caroline, who finally went back to work for the first time yesterday after more than a year battling her cancer. She looks fabulous.

'It's the non-drinking,' she said. 'Every cloud, etc.'

'Some people think this *Apprentice* win will make you even more unbearable,' Cowell observed as the treble amarettos arrived, 'but I have assured them that is literally impossible.'

To his delight, my stupendously expanded ego didn't take long to be demolished.

As we reeled into the 4 a.m. light, we were confronted by LA's paparazzi video kings TMZ – who, to my horror, incorrectly identified Roycey as me.

'So how does it feel to win *The Apprentice*, Piers?' they asked him. And for the next five minutes he pretended to be me, revealing such gems as: 'Donald Trump is a bit odd to be honest…and as for his hair, my God…'

Eventually the penny dropped, and they realised their mistake. But by then, as a chortling Mr Cowell gleefully reminded me, 'the damage has been done'.

MONDAY, 31 MARCH 2008

This morning I spent the first five minutes in the breakfast restaurant of the Beverly Wilshire hotel signing autographs for *Apprentice* fans, posing for photographs and generally feeling even more pleased with myself than usual – if that's possible.

And then Oscar-winning legend Sidney Poitier walked in, and I was dumped by my 'fans' faster than Boris Johnson drops his trousers.

I looked over and waved at Sidney – who looks astonishing youthful and fit for 81 – hoping that if he responded it would at least look like he knew who I was.

He didn't.

TUESDAY, 1 APRIL 2008

I interviewed Pamela Anderson for BBC1 in Malibu today. And it was everything I'd hoped, and feared, it would be.

She's an extraordinary whirlwind of flesh and energy, speaks at 100mph and knows, and joyfully exploits, the devastating effect she has on the male gender.

The chat ended with my head planted between her infamous breasts as she sat on my knee.

'I've waited my entire life for this moment,' I drooled, slightly embarrassingly.

Afterwards, we tried to get her to pose for some publicity photos, but she refused.

'Oh, come on, Pammie, just one?' I pleaded.

She looked at my pathetic, forlorn eyes, ran over and threw her arms around me in what can only be described as an extravagant grope.

FLASH!

The desperate photographer got just one frame away, but it was enough.

It looks like she's all over me, and I'm trying to resist.

WEDNESDAY, 2 APRIL 2008

An extraordinary CBS/*New York Times* poll has been published revealing that 81 per cent of Americans think their country is 'on the wrong track'.

And nearly as many believe the country is worse than it was five years ago, and heading for recession.

Approval ratings for Bush continue to plummet. He's now at 28 per cent, with even fewer, 21 per cent, approving of his handling of the economy.

I can't remember a time in my lifetime when America was in such a state about itself.

Meanwhile, back in Britain, my *GQ* interview with Nick 'I've slept with up to 30 women' Clegg has hit the headlines.

His instant new nickname is 'Cleggover', and other Lib Dem MPs are apparently being chased all around Westminster being asked: 'Are you good in bed?'

THURSDAY, 3 APRIL 2008

Hugh Laurie has given a fascinating interview to *The Times*.

He gets paid £300,000 an episode to star in *House*, which is huge in the US. The downside is that he has to spend nine months of the year living in LA, working six long days a week.

But after moaning a lot about this in the past, he now seems to be coming to terms with it.

'It's taken a long time to adjust to the permanence of it,' he says. 'The first year I was in a hotel. And I did feel very foreign there, as if I'm on safari, looking at exotic animals and the way they behave. Then again, America is made up of people who don't feel American until they do, so I'm not alone in that. There is also real sensuous pleasure in riding to work on my Triumph motorbike at half past five in the morning.

'I'm a huge admirer of the openness, energy, optimism and dynamism of Americans. And this idea that Americans have no sense of irony – I mean, Americans hardly do anything unironically these days. If you want a drink of water, you have to say, "I really don't want a drink of water."'

FRIDAY, 4 APRIL 2008

Had dinner with Jerry Springer back at the Beverly Wilshire last night, and within a few minutes Roseanne Barr came over to say hello.

'You know Piers, right?' he asked her.

She shook her head.

'He just won *Celebrity Apprentice*...?'

'Didn't see it.'

'He's a judge on my show *America's Got Talent* too, you must know him?'

She peered closer at me.

'Nope.'

Then Roseanne leant down and stared intently at my face over her small librarian-like black glasses – for several long seconds.

'Wait a minute...yes...I know him...the mean one, right?'

'Right,' said Jerry.

'Sorry,' explained Roseanne, 'but I am completely blind these days.'

Ten minutes later, Lionel Richie also popped over to pay homage to Jerry. He didn't have a clue who I was, either.

First TMZ, then Sidney, now Roseanne and Lionel – my post-*Apprentice* euphoria is fading fast into a vat of horrific Z-list obscurity.

As pudding arrived, Jerry suddenly revealed he has just bought a 280-pound pig called Bella for $2,000.

'I just liked the look of her,' he explained, pulling out a photo of his hideous new pet. 'She'll live longer than me, and I want to have her leading my funeral cortege when I die.'

'Well, I hope you'll be very happy together,' I said.

SUNDAY, 6 APRIL 2008

I've flown back to New York for *America's Got Talent* auditions and, on the phone, Spencer couldn't wait to tell me about Rory Bremner's new *Spitting Image*-style ITV show, *Headcases*.

Apparently, I appear, with Lord Falconer-sized double chins, presenting something called *The Piers Morgan Show* (what a fantastic name for a TV series, incidentally...)

'Hi, I'm Piers Morgan...' I say, before a giant anvil falls on my head and squashes me.

In the second half, I'm miraculously brought back from the dead, saying: 'Earlier you may have seen me senselessly killed by a falling anvil. Well, the emails have been flooding in – "brilliant", "fabulous", "well done, ITV, you have restored my faith in public service broadcasting". And this from a Mrs G in Luton – "I'm afraid I missed it because I was in the loo, could you show it again?" Well, Mrs G, I've never knowingly disappointed a lady, so...'

At which point a grand piano lands on my head, and squashes me again.

'It's hilarious, Dad,' said Spencer, with shocking disloyalty.

Jeremy then rang to say it was quite an accolade to be one of only 62 people chosen as puppets for the series, a list that also includes Robert Mugabe.

'That seems particularly appropriate,' he said. 'Two globally reviled chancers whose luck is just about to run out.'

MONDAY, 7 APRIL 2008

Sir Alan Sugar has been named as a new gay icon and, to my surprise, he is taking it rather well.

'It doesn't make me a bad person,' he emailed me today, before adding: 'Ooooh...you are awful!'

I'm getting worried about the old growler.

TUESDAY, 8 APRIL 2008

General David Petraeus is appearing at congressional hearings in America, and once again seems to be saying all the right things.

As idiots like Bush boast that 'the surge is winning us the war', Petraeus hits a completely different, far more measured and realistic tone.

'We haven't seen any lights at the end of the tunnel,' he said, 'the champagne bottle has been pushed to the back of the refrigerator, and the progress, while real, is fragile and reversible.'

To hear an American military leader talk in such honest, modest language about something that he could easily ramp up as a triumph is both startling and such a relief.

This man has single-handedly given Iraqis hope that their country might genuinely come through this nightmare, Americans hope that the unrelenting hell of this war might one day be over and the world hopes that the United States might be finally learning that killing everyone isn't always the right way to instil democracy.

In a fascinating exchange with Ted Kennedy, who suggested that Iraqi forces were deserting their units (a view propagated by Fox News and others, always keen to bill the 'enemy' as a bunch of losers), Petraeus snapped back: 'Senator, they are fighting and dying for their country in substantial numbers. Their losses are three times our losses of late.'

Empathy for the Iraqis, solidarity even.

Extraordinary, and surely, in the end, so much more likely to succeed than just bombing the place to smithereens?

THURSDAY, 10 APRIL 2008

Sugar emailed again this morning.

'I'm in Florida among the young and trendy. I keep asking everyone (once they hear my English accent) if they have seen the winner of *Celebrity Apprentice*, my pal Piers Morgan. They say, "Piers who? The only Pier we know is Delray Pier." Can you imagine how frustrated I am, I am trying to big you up out here…'

'Trust me,' I replied, 'I'm bigger than Obama at the moment.'

'Yes,' he agreed, 'by about two stone.'

FRIDAY, 11 APRIL 2008

The last day of *America's Got Talent* auditions in New York finished in typically surreal style, when a shrieking Sharon Osbourne physically wrestled me off my chair.

My crime? An Ozzy impersonator had just come on and performed a horrific tribute to her husband. To which I commented: 'Well, I thought you were not only better-looking than the real thing...'

Cue absolute mayhem as an enraged Sharon launched herself at me like a banshee on steroids. 'You disgusting little creep!' she yelled, jumping on me and smacking me with both hands.

As I dived for cover, I managed to grab the microphone and finish my critique: '...but a much better singer too!'

Sharon exploded: 'WHAAATTTTTT!?!...how DARE you, you horrible little man!'

By now I was being violently shoved to the ground, as the audience howled with laughter.

Later, as I recovered from my mauling in my dressing room, the door suddenly flung open and there was Sharon, armed with a fire extinguisher.

'Sharon, don't...' I pleaded, knowing she would show me about as much clemency as Saddam Hussein on a bad hair day.

BLAST!

SATURDAY, 12 APRIL 2008

As soon as I got home, I raced straight to Sainsbury's to buy some proper tea.

Standing at the check-out, an attractive young woman came up, said 'Hello, Piers!' and kissed me on the cheek.

As this kind of encounter is now an occupational hazard of being a global phenomenon, I smiled, said thank you in the manner of the Pope bestowing his beatification on nuns in St Peter's Square and turned back to pay my bill.

'I'm cooking Kevin a roast!' she added.

'Oh right,' I replied, not having a clue what she was on about – and giving her my firmest 'OK, you've had your fun with a celebrity, now please move along' face.

Half an hour later, a text arrived.

'You are a knob for not acknowledging Jess in the supermarket!'

It was from Kevin Pietersen. And Jess is Jessica Taylor, now his delightful wife, who I have met many times.

And yes, I did feel a complete and utter tool.

TUESDAY, 22 APRIL 2008

What is it with these Liberal Democrats?

Just two weeks after Nick Clegg suffered national humiliation for his 'I slept with up to 30 women' confession, Lembit Opik virtually begged me to interview him as well.

Lembit, 43, bought me a coffee, sat back in the chair of his Westminster office and waited for my first question with that eager lopsided grin on his face.

'OK then, Lembit, how many women have you slept with?'

'I am fascinated by your interest in Liberal Democrat sex lives, but this is something I will pass on.'

'But in your case, Lembit, your sex life is in the public domain because you never stop banging on about it. You give interviews about your private life to magazines and newspapers all the time.'

'Yes.'

'And been paid for them?'

'Erm…yes. I give the money away to charity…some of the time, anyway.'

'All of it?'

'Sometimes.'

'How much do you get paid?'

'I'm not going to tell you.'

'Do you declare it?'

'Yeah.'

'So why not tell me, if it's a matter of public record?'

'I am not going to discuss it, sorry.'

'Are you embarrassed about taking money to talk about your private life?'

'No. Lord Carlyle told me once never to negotiate my salary with the public.'

'But this is not your salary. It is about payments you have received for talking about your love life in celebrity magazines. You seem very edgy and embarrassed about this – do you regret doing it now?'

'No,' (looks very red-faced) 'why would I?'

'I don't know, you just seem very twitchy about it.'

'I always try to answer your questions precisely.'

'No, you don't. You just refused to say how much you got paid. Would you sell your private life to a magazine like *Hello!* again?'

'No, I wouldn't sell my private life at all.'

'You recently described your relationship with Gabriela as a meeting of intellects not lust, and said she challenges you intellectually. How?'

'We have great conversations about everything from science to philosophy, and value structure. One evening for instance we discussed the concept of a perfect circle, as a geometric challenge. And we spend a lot of time talking about science, and astronomy in particular.'

'Is it true that your Westminster nickname is "Tripod"?'

'I've got Stephen Pound to thank for that.'

'Is it true?'

'There are people who insist on using that nickname for me, yes.'

'True then?'

'That's an unanswerable question because confirmation would mean arrogance, and a denial would lead to disappointment.'

'What would Gabi say?'

'You'd have to ask her.'

'Do you think you'll marry her? I noticed you declined to propose when invited to on *Mr and Mrs*?'

'I thought it was very cheeky of Fern and Philip to try and get me to propose – not everything in my private life has to happen on television.'

'You go on a show called *Mr and Mrs* but don't want them trying to get you to propose…come off it, Lembit. Anyway, just to clarify, you are not planning to propose in the near future?'

'Let me be very precise about that. I am delighted by your interest in my physique, and in my relationship with Gabi, but there are some things that must remain private. And one of them has to be the personal stuff in life, like that.'

'What absolute bollocks. You sell every part of your private life to magazines. And you will almost certainly sell the announcement of your engagement to *Hello!*, won't you?'

'Ha ha ha ha. I'd love to live in a *Hello!* world…now come on, it's getting late. Fancy a pint?'

Two hours later (I had rejected the offer of a pint, there's only so much Lembit a man can take in one day), my phone rang at home. 'Piers, it's Lembit, I need to come clean about something.'

'What?'

'I'm getting married. To Gabriela.'

'But you told me you weren't.'

'I know, but I had a reason for that, and I just thought I couldn't mislead you because it is actually going to come out in the newspapers tomorrow.'

'Don't tell me...you sold it to *Hello!* magazine?'

'Ha ha ha ha ha ha ha. Yes.'

And indeed, that's exactly what he had done. In fact *Hello!* was already on sale boasting details of his exclusive marriage proposal, at the precise moment he was telling me the complete opposite.

'Well, congratulations,' I said.

'Thanks. Do you want me to put in a good word with Monica? We'd make a good foursome.'

In time-honoured journalistic fashion, I made my excuses and hung up.

THURSDAY, 24 APRIL 2008

I finally got divorced today. And yes, the process has been just as repulsive, expensive, enraging, depressing and tiring as everyone always says it is.

I'm sure all lawyers could settle these things in ten minutes if they wanted to.

But why would they want to do that when they can rack up £100,000 in fees first by tacitly encouraging loads of unnecessary conflict?

I found the whole experience horrifically, indefensibly, parasitical.

But Marion and I talked today, and concluded that the only sensible way to move on is to forget everything that's happened in the past year, and be the friends that we were before the greedy, grasping legal profession stuck their claws into us.

MONDAY, 28 APRIL 2008

I've spent most of my life dreaming of seeing Joanna Lumley at 8.20 a.m., with a coffee in her hand, smiling at me.

And today that dream was finally realised.

We were both guests on the BBC *Breakfast* show, and I sat in my dressing room watching Joanna talking about something (I've no idea what, because I had the sound turned down so it wouldn't ruin the view) and thinking how fabulous she looks for a woman of 62.

In mid-drool, I was summoned to replace my heroine on the sofa, and passed her in the green room chatting to Roy Hudd (not quite such a pretty sight at 8.20 a.m., it must be said).

I tapped Joanna on the shoulder.

'You were MAGNIFICENT, dahling!'

She turned slowly, almost regally, eyeing me up and down with a half smile.

'And you, Piers…'

I waited for the inevitable return compliment, mouth slightly agape with prescient excitement.

'…are a very silly little man.'

WEDNESDAY, 30 APRIL 2008

One of the most dreaded words in the TV language lexicon is 'clearance'. You wouldn't believe the time and effort that goes into legally 'clearing' everything that appears on your screen. Literally anything with a logo, or a copyright, has to have specific permission granted before it can be broadcast. And to give you some idea how painful this process can be, take what happened to me this morning.

I'm hosting ITV's *Best of British* show next week, and had to film a short promo for it today, which involved me sitting in a small room, with the only props being a teapot, teacup, saucer and sugarbowl.

I had to say about ten lines into the camera about why Britain is so great, then take a sip of tea. Easy, right?

Wrong.

Things didn't start well when the cameraman stopped after a few seconds and said firmly: 'The head is wrong.'

Everyone turned to me.

'What, my head?'

'Yes.'

'What's wrong with it?'

'Too sweaty.'

'OK, well could you at least refer to it as "Piers' head", please.'

An hour later, we had finally finished the twentieth take, and my will to live had receded to the point of near death – think Bill Murray doing that *Lost in Translation* whisky advert in Tokyo and you'll get the general drift.

Then I spotted the director talking urgently and anxiously to two of her assistants.

'What's the problem?'

'The teapot.'

'What about it?'

'Hasn't been cleared.'

I stared at the offending pot, which was emblazoned in union jacks.

'Don't tell me we have to start again?'

'Uh-huh. With a white teapot.'

THURSDAY, 1 MAY 2008

The London mayoral election took place today, and the *Los Angeles Times* summed it up perfectly with the headline: 'LOONY vs LOONIER.'

I love Boris. But the idea of him standing in the rubble of some future terrorist attack, scratching his foppish blond mop with that permanent buffoon-like half-smirk, while trying to deliver some serious message of defiance to al Qaeda, is where I stop enjoying the joke, I'm afraid.

FRIDAY, 2 MAY 2008

Boris won. Batten down the hatches everyone.

© CAROLINE BETTANY

One of the best moments of my life – opening the batting on my
village cricket pitch with England superstar Kevin Pietersen.

9

'Americanism means the virtues of courage, honour, justice, truth, sincerity and hardihood – the virtues that made America. The things that will destroy America are prosperity-at-any-price, peace-at-any-price, safety-first instead of duty-first, the love of soft living and the get-rich-quick theory of life.' THEODORE ROOSEVELT

SUNDAY, 4 MAY 2008

Sir Alan Sugar threw a huge bash to celebrate his fortieth wedding anniversary tonight.

Celia and I arrived at the sprawling Sugar mansion in Chigwell, Essex, to find a long tarpaulin tunnel patrolled by a small army of security men, leading through to an absolutely enormous marquee teaming with over 250 people in smart black tie, standing around several large bars and gleefully guzzling vintage champagne.

It was spectacularly lavish, like a scene from a Corleone family wedding in *The Godfather*. The centrepiece being two giant digitally enhanced photos of the happy couple on their wedding day.

Sir Alan bounded towards me, looking horribly slim and tanned after a month in Miami.

'Nice place,' I said.

'This?' he replied, with mock disdain, 'it's just a small tent in my back garden.'

'So is this going to be fun, then?' I asked.

'Wait and see,' he said, with what I thought was a slight twinkle in his beady eye.

I found my table, one of at least 25 spread around the marquee on two levels, all decorated with a sumptuous array of flowers and the finest silver, cut-glass and china.

Seconds later Bruce Forsyth walked on to a big stage in front of me to announce that there would be 'a series of surprises'.

Brucey worked the crowd for a bit, but we were all too sober to let our hair down yet. In a desperate bid to raise the atmosphere, he grabbed Maureen Lipman and whisked her around in a fast foxtrot, not once realising who she was.

'Is that really you, Maureen?' he gasped in embarrassment, when he returned to the stage and the penny finally dropped. 'Oh my God, I'm so sorry!'

Things got worse for the great man when one of Sir Alan's young grandsons came up and sang a hilarious adapted version of Elton John's 'Daniel' to his father of the same name and his grandfather (including lyrics like 'Whoa oh, oh, Daniel and papa, you're both as old as can be, you moan about aches and pains, now it's rubbed off on me.') and got a standing ovation.

Brucey threw his hands in the air in mock exasperation. 'Sixty years in show-business,' he wailed, 'and I end up being the warm-up for a seven-year-old!'

Sensing the great man needed a bit of support, I laughed deliberately over-loudly at one joke, and he stopped and peered down to where I was sitting.

'Piers, is that you? Thank God you're here, at least I've got one laugh.'

Which, of course, brought the house down.

The first surprise was Jackie Mason, the best and most outrageous Jewish comic in the world, who had flown in from New York just for the occasion. And who, to my joy, instantly launched into an offensive verbal bombardment at our host.

'I don't know why I'm here,' he said, 'or who for. Other than he's a billionaire with a big head and short legs.'

I turned to Sir Alan, whose face was frozen in a fixed, horrified grin.

'I understand he has lots of friends, none of whom could be here tonight... He is such a humble, modest, private man – that's why he's on TV all the time.'

I would have paid a considerable amount of money for this.

The second surprise was a stunning and incredibly rare private performance by the cast of the current West End musical smash *The Jersey Boys* – based on the story of Frankie Valli and the Four Seasons. (Apparently they have never done, and will never do again, a private gig like this.)

I was beginning to wonder how much all this party was costing, and thinking somewhere north of a million pounds.

Then came the speeches. First up was Sir Alan's *Apprentice* sidekick Nick Hewer, who revealed how the couple first met.

'Alan was 17, Ann was 16, and she said it was his sense of humour that she was attracted to...' Cue an explosion of laughter from everyone who knows them.

Not sure why, though. It was hardly going to be for his looks, was it?

Sir Alan himself then took the podium. 'I can honestly say I have never ever heard anyone say a bad word about Ann,' he said. 'As you know you can't say the same about me...talk about chalk and cheese. She always says the day she met me she knew she had met Mr Right; what she didn't know my first name was Always.'

He then addressed the shameful birthday card incident.

'It was a busy day in the office...' he explained, to guffaws of ridicule. 'Ann was not a happy bunny,' he admitted. 'So I apologised and then ran through loads of things I could buy her to make up for my mistake.

'"Do you want a new dress?" I asked.

'"No."

'"A new watch?"

'"No."

'"A car?"

'"No."

'"OK, well just tell me what I can get you."

'To which she angrily replied, "A bloody divorce."

'I said, "Sorry, I wasn't thinking of spending that much." She ended up the next day buying me something that she said went from 0–20 in three seconds...a bloody set of bathroom scales.'

By now the whole room was heaving with laughter, including Lady Ann. But Sir Alan was only just getting started.

'Last week, we were driving home from the airport, and Ann commented that it was 40 years to the day since we got a married. To which I nodded, as you do when driving, and muttered: "Yeah amazing, eh."

'Then there was a silence, as there is when you are driving along. A few moments later she said to me, "Do I see a tear in your eyes? Don't tell me you are going soft and feeling sentimental."

'I said, "I am going to tell you something now that I have never told you before. Forty years ago, your father took out his old army pistol and held it to my head and told me if I didn't marry you he would make sure I was banged up in jail for 40 years. So yeah, I am being sentimental – the thing is, I would be getting out tomorrow…'"

On a roll now, Sir Alan rattled through a whole stand-up routine of jokes. Then, an amazing thing happened. Sir Alan suddenly did turn all soft and sentimental.

'Now here is a message to those young aspiring men here tonight: I would remind you what it is to be a successful man, and what is one's prize possession in life. It has absolutely nothing at all to do with money, academic achievement, or any material things.

'A real successful man puts the love of his wife and children first, a real successful man's greatest position in life is to have a great family.

'I am lucky enough to have had a wife for 40 years, who gave me three great children, who in turn have given us seven wonderful grandchildren. Everything I have today is because of the love of that lady and the respect my three children have for the both of us.'

I felt the merest suggestion of a lump developing in my throat. It was as moving as it was surprising.

As Sir Alan stepped down, and the audience erupted into wild applause, I turned to see Lady Ann blushing with pride. It may have taken 40 years, but the old devil had finally come good.

And not just with his words either. The food and wine were magnificent. Who would have thought Sir Alan Sugar would ever lay on a menu containing such delights as 'amuse bouche', and 'baked Arctic black cod with bok choy'. All washed down with that fine Italian wine, Amarone Classico 2004 Masi Costasera?

Oh, and if you're wondering what on earth you give a man who has £500 million in the bank, the answer in my case was a pair of Arsenal shirts emblazoned with 'Sir Alan, 40' and 'Lady Ann, 40'. He, of course, is a lifelong Spurs fan.

Bruce Forsyth reappeared, tapdancing, singing and cracking gags like a man a quarter of his age – and, by now, going down a storm. For a man of 80, he is really quite astonishing. 'Our final surprise,' he declared, 'is really something special.'

I looked at Sir Alan, who just winked.

'Ladies and gentlemen, I give you Sir Elton John!'

Blimey, this was turning into some party.

Elton came out with his band, wished the happy couple a very happy anniversary and performed some of his greatest hits for over 45 minutes.

As 'Saturday Night's Alright For Fighting' filled the air, I walked over to Sir Alan's table.

'They're playing our song, fancy a dance?'

TUESDAY, 6 MAY 2008

A young barrister has been shot dead by police in Chelsea, after apparently shooting at neighbours. Nobody seems to have a clue why the whole thing happened, other than he appears to have lost it after an all-day drinking session. All a bit odd.

WEDNESDAY, 7 MAY 2008

I was playing golf with Rob McGibbon today when Marion called.

'That lawyer who was shot dead by the police...'

'Yes?'

'...was Mark Saunders, my divorce counsel.'

God almighty. That was the posh twit who I shouted at in court last November. How utterly extraordinary.

First News, the children's newspaper that I helped create, celebrated its second birthday today with a party at Downing Street. It now has over 750,000 readers according to a recent YouGuv poll, which is pretty amazing given the general state of the newspaper industry.

Gordon Brown popped in to congratulate us.

'I can't stay long,' he said.

'Hope you've got a good excuse?' I replied.

'I've got to go and see the Queen.'

Which wasn't a bad one.

Alistair Darling and I made speeches.

'Welcome to my little home,' I joked, before eyeing the extensive scaffolding outside our No. 11 reception room. 'Actually, it's very encouraging to see the chancellor expanding his abode during the credit crunch.'

He didn't take long to retaliate.

'This is the first time so many cabinet ministers have actually been pleased to come and share a room with Piers Morgan,' he said, to loud cheers. 'And it's very good of him to welcome you to *my* home...'

'Your current home, Chancellor,' I retorted.

'Well, Piers,' he said, turning slowly, 'you of all people should know all about the perils of job insecurity...' Cue more cheers. Darling may have the charisma of a stuffed aardvark, but he's quick, I'll give him that.

I moved on to the *Spectator* magazine's 180th anniversary party, a star-studded affair that quickly turned into another celebratory thrash for Boris Johnson – who got noticeably more attention from the photographers than his boss David Cameron, after marching into the room with his entourage like a Roman emperor marching into an orgy.

'I don't know how the hell you did it, Boris, but God help us,' I said, patting him on the back.

'Oh, bugger off, Morgan,' he snarled, jabbing me hard in the ribs with his granite-like elbow.

'I'm doing *Question Time* with your sister tomorrow,' I said, undeterred.

His eyes swivelled away from the ravishing blonde he was chatting up. 'Really? Well, just behave.'

'Oh, I will, don't worry. I think I'll just stir things up by saying you told me you want Cameron's job...'

Another hard elbow rocked into my side.

'You're a scoundrel, Morgan, an absolute scoundrel.'

I met Jon Snow by the bar. 'I'll give Boris six months,' he said. 'By then he'll be bored and fed up with earning so little money, and he'll blow.'

I think he's being optimistic. I'll give it three months.

Later, I caught David Cameron's eye.

'I want to talk to you,' he said, urging me forward with his index finger.

I walked through the throng and shook his hand. (Cameron, like Blair, has impeccable manners – even to those in enemy camps.)

'What's up?'

'I just want to look you in the eye and promise you one thing...'

'Blimey, this sounds fun. OK, what is it?'

'After what you did to Nick Clegg, I will never, ever, do an interview with you in my entire life...'

THURSDAY, 8 MAY 2008

Shared a taxi to *Question Time* in Dorking with Rachel Johnson. 'What is the secret of the Johnson family success?' I asked at one point.

'Well,' she giggled, 'all the men are incredibly well-hung.'

'Really?'

'Really. I know because we all used to go skinny-dipping together. I think that's what gives them so much confidence.'

We met up with fellow panellists Michael Heseltine and Ming Campbell – the third time I've appeared with them in three years.

'This is getting ridiculous,' said Ming. 'We'll have to start calling ourselves the Three Oldies or something.'

'THREE oldies?' I spluttered indignantly.

When we walked out to the desk, a weird thing happened. I didn't get booed. Which was so historic that David Dimbleby made a point of mentioning it, at which point the audience immediately all booed me. Obviously.

I raced from the studio afterwards into a waiting taxi, which whisked to a tribute dinner for Ian Botham at the Grosvenor House hotel in London.

As I arrived, I heard the host, Rory Bremner, announce: 'And I'd now like to invite some of the famous faces here tonight to join me onstage. From the world of cricket...Sir Viv Richards, Mike Gatting, David Gower...(the castlist of legendary players was incredible). From the world of music, Bill Wyman, Charlie Watts, Eric Clapton...from the world of showbiz...Sam Fox, Max Boyce...and from the world of...well, from the world of Piers Morgan...Piers Morgan.'

'I've spent the afternoon made up as you,' he said, as I reached the stage. 'But I still can't get the bloody voice right.'

Jeffrey Archer started the fund-raising part of the evening, and I wasn't really paying attention until he suddenly said: 'And now a really special prize, the chance to spend the day at the *Daily Mirror* and help the editor produce his paper.' Lord Archer turned slowly to me. 'I can think of one person who might rather enjoy this experience.'

Everyone laughed, so I bid £1,000 and kept bidding until it reached £6,000. Which seemed quite enough for a day at a place I spent ten years as editor until I was fired, and turfed unceremoniously into the street.

Then a new bidder entered the ring – the *Mirror*'s current editor, Richard Wallace, an old friend who had clearly just realised the full horror of what was unfurling.

Ian Botham, a columnist for the paper, was in hysterics – and goaded us both on until eventually I won at a ridiculous price of £12,000.

By now, though, I could see the potential hilarity of my prize which includes breakfast with the editor, attending his morning editorial conference, lunch with him and a 'celebrity', and then back to the newsroom for the afternoon to, and I quote from the auction brochure, 'put the finishing touches to the paper'.

Oh, I'm going to enjoy this...

SUNDAY, 11 MAY 2008

I'm on a quick five-day trip to Las Vegas for the bootcamp stage of *America's Got Talent*, and Sharon Osbourne invited me to go and see the new Cher show at Caesar's Palace last night. We were both quite excited, until the act actually started that is.

Cher makes 18 costume changes in 90 minutes, which means she spends most of the show...changing. Leaving us to 'enjoy' a series of tedious videos and dreadful dance routines by her support company. When she did grace us with her presence to actually sing, her deep masculine monotone voice rang out like a particularly maudlin funeral director.

After an hour of this, Sharon – who, like me, has the attention span of a lobotomised newt – nudged me in the ribs. 'Look behind you, quick.'

I turned to see a small Chinese man, fast asleep, snoring contentedly.

'I feel like him,' I told Sharon.

'So do I!' she giggled back.

And ten minutes later, we were in a nearby Italian restaurant opening a bottle of fine red wine.

'If I Could Turn Back Time' is Cher's biggest hit.

And trust me, luv, I now know exactly what you mean.

MONDAY, 12 MAY 2008

Sat by the pool this morning, reading a brilliant article by Fareed Zakaria, the editor of *Newsweek International*.

'Americans are really glum at the moment,' he writes. 'No, I mean really glum. There are reasons to be pessimistic – a financial panic, and looming recession, a seemingly endless war in Iraq, and the ongoing threat of terrorism. But none of this is dire enough to explain the present atmosphere of malaise. American anxiety springs from something much deeper, a sense that large and disruptive forces are coursing through the world. And for the first time in living memory, the United States does not seem to be leading the charge. Americans see a new world is coming into being, but fear it is one being shaped in distant lands and foreign people.'

He then cites examples.

'Look around. The world's tallest building is in Taipei and will soon be in Dubai. Its largest public traded company is in Beijing. Its biggest refinery is being constructed in India. Its largest passenger airplane is built in Europe. The largest investment fund is in Abu Dhabi; the biggest movie industry is now Bollywood not Hollywod. Once quintessentially American icons have been usurped by the natives. The largest Ferris wheel is in Singapore. The largest casino is in Macao, which overtook Vegas in gambling revenues last year. The Mall of America in Minnesota once boasted that it was the largest shopping mall in the world. Today, it wouldn't make the top ten. Only two of the world's richest ten people are American. Ten years ago, the United States would have topped almost every one of these categories.'

And he reaches a shattering conclusion: 'In every dimension, industrial, social, financial and cultural, the power is shifting. The world itself has shifted from "anti-Americanism" to "post-Americanism".'

But it's not all doom and gloom. Zakaria says that this expanding globalisation could be a good thing for America in the long run.

Namely, as more and more countries develop a strong economic investment in the future, they will realise that peace is much more profitable than war. And that working with, rather than against, America would be of significant benefit to their own prosperity.

'This new world could be thrilling – billions of people escaping from abject poverty and becoming consumers, producers, inventors, thinkers, dreamers, doers. All because of American ideas and actions. For 60 years, the United States has pushed countries to open their markets, free up their politics, and embrace trade and technology.

'Generations from now, when historians write about these times, they might note that by the turn of the twenty-first century, the United States had succeeded in its great historical mission – globalising the world. We don't want them to write that along the way they forgot to globalise themselves.'

It's the most brilliant, coherent and accurate assessment of modern America that I've read.

TUESDAY, 13 MAY 2008

After the amazing success of Leona Lewis and Paul Potts, the claim that TV talent shows don't produce real talent has borne substantially less credence.

But their two stories pale into insignificance compared to what has just happened to the winner of last year's *AGT* – the singing impressionist and ventriloquist, Terry Fator.

A year ago, he played to just one person in a theatre and nearly packed in his showbusiness career after 30 years. Only his wife's encouragement made him carry on.

Today, Terry was named as the new headline act at the Mirage Casino here in Vegas, on a five-year deal worth (and this figure is a fact) an unbelievable $100 *million*.

Terry came to see me in my dressing room this afternoon, and was still shaking with excitement.

'I am living my dream,' he said.

'What are you going to do with the money?' I asked.

'Well, when I proposed to my wife I was so poor I could only afford a cheap ten-dollar ring. So yesterday I took her to a very expensive jeweller's and told her to take her pick.'

WEDNESDAY, 14 MAY 2008

The more I work with Sharon, the more I like her. She's as tough as nails, and explosive if you challenge her, especially on her family. But once she trusts you, she's a kind, warm and often utterly hilarious friend.

I went down with the flu today, and 100-degree Vegas is not a place to have a high temperature. But Sharon fussed over me like a mother hen all day, constantly soothing my fevered brow, feeding me endless fruit and sweets to keep my energy up and finally ordering the producers to take pity on my pathetic burning torso at 10 p.m., with the screeching command: 'Piers is going to bed. NOW!'

And trust me, when Sharon screeches, everybody obeys. 'OK,' said one executive producer who shall remain nameless (Georgie Hurford-Jones), 'but we will need to film you being attended to by a doctor, and going to bed.'

'But I'm dying,' I wailed. 'Surely you don't need that on camera?'

There was a long, uncomfortable pause.

'Piers, that's *exactly* what we need on camera.'

THURSDAY, 15 MAY 2008

Shania Twain has split from her husband, Robert Lange.

The man who inspired her smash-hit song, 'You're Still The One'.

If I'd known things were that rocky when we met on last summer's Vegas flight, I'd have never gone to sleep.

MONDAY, 19 MAY 2008

Warren Buffett, the world's richest man, and the most successful businessman in American history, today endorsed Obama.

'I will be very happy if Obama is elected president,' he said, 'he is my choice.'

This is a massive moment. Buffett is known as the 'Oracle of Omaha'. in recognition of his astonishing ability to read stock markets and make a killing. But what Americans love about him most is that despite his $62 billion fortune, he has never left the smallish five-bedroom house in Omaha that he bought in 1958 for $31,000. He's also recently announced plans to give away 83 per cent of his money to charity. Buffett's genius comes from his simplicity. He only ever invests in companies that he believes are well run, but undervalued. 'It is far better to buy a wonderful company at a fair price than a fair company at a wonderful price,' he says. 'The business schools reward difficult complex behaviour more than simple behaviour, but simple behaviour is more effective.' And his views on money are just as shrewd. 'Money just brings out the basic traits in billionaires; if they were jerks before they had money, they are simply jerks with a billion dollars.'

For Buffett to back Obama, amid the backdrop of this increasingly serious economic crisis, is about as strong a support for the candidate's so-called lack of experience imaginable. The average American will hear this, and think Obama can be trusted on the economy, because Buffett is the man they most trust on the economy. And if this global credit crunch bites much harder before November, then the economy could well be the deciding factor in who wins.

Obama's now got Oprah, Buffett, the youth vote (via the Internet), an expanding support coming from the vast Hispanic community and he's on the right side of the increasingly febrile Iraq debate.

I'd say his chances of not just becoming Democratic nominee, but also president, are getting better every day.

WEDNESDAY, 21 MAY 2008

I had to speak to 300 Jewish ladies today over lunch, and turned to Sir Alan Sugar for help.

'I need a good Jewish joke to end my speech with.'

Within an hour, he'd sent over a selection of gags.

I chose one, and stuck it on the end of my speech.

Everything went swimmingly, and as I reached the end, I announced that I had received help from Sir Alan for my finale.

The room gasped with delighted surprise.

Then I started the joke.

'Sir Alan invited the fiancé of his daughter to his study for a drink. "So what are your plans?" he asked the young man.

'"I am a Torah scholar," he replied.

'"That's admirable, but what will you do to provide a nice house for my daughter to live in, as she's accustomed to?"

'"I will study," the young man replies, "and God will provide for us."'

As I said the words 'God will provide for us', I could hear an instant loud murmur of discontent fill the room.

I stopped. 'You've all heard this, haven't you?'

'Yes!' came the firm reply from many of the 300 guests. Sir Alan had clearly sold me the oldest Jewish joke in the world (probably deliberately).

I decided to finish it anyway:

'"And how will you buy her a beautiful engagement ring, such as she deserves?" asked Sir Alan.

'"I will concentrate on my studies," he replied. "God will provide for us."

'"And children?" I asked. "How will you support children?"

'"Don't worry, sir, God will provide."

'Sir Alan was quite pleased with this, and raced back to tell his wife the good news: "He said he has no job and no plans, but the good news is he thinks I'm God."'

As I reached the punchline, the whole room fell about laughing.

Sir Alan, by total default, had pulled it out of the bag again.

SATURDAY, 24 MAY 2008

Jonathan Ross started his chat show tonight by saying it was 'National be nice to nettles day'. Then he added: 'Nettles are unpleasant and painful and no one likes them, or to give them their Latin name – Vulgaris Piers Morganus.'

Ross, of course, is currently paid £18 million to ask his celebrity mates like Ricky Gervais such penetrating questions as: 'So, Wicky, how long have you been this brilliant?'

Or to give him his Latin name: 'Sycophanticus Smarmitus Jonathan Rossus.'

I don't know what's got into Ross. We used to be quite good mates, but lately he's started whacking me all over the airwaves.

MONDAY, 26 MAY 2008

The live *Britain's Got Talent* semi-finals start tonight, so I got to the Wembley studio nice and early – only to find that Simon was already there. A truly historic moment, the world's worst timekeeper had finally beaten me into work.

The first show had a dancing dog, a belly dancer and a bloke who sticks lighted barbecues on his head.

My favourite moment had to be Michael, a barmy *Star Wars* keyboard player, who reacted to Simon's barbs by snarling: 'What you know about music can be written on the back of a postage stamp.'

WEDNESDAY, 28 MAY 2008

Kevin Pietersen and Michael Vaughan came to the show tonight, and KP was, to my intense dismay, almost shaking with excitement about the prospect of meeting Cowell.

'He's a legend,' he drooled.

'Well, I can arrange an audience,' I replied, 'but then you'll owe me one, right?'

'If you fix that, I'll do anything for you, china!' he said.

Twenty minutes later, Cowell was posing for photos with KP in his dressing-room.

'Remember you owe me one,' I said, as he left, beaming from ear to diamond-studded ear.

'Whatever you want, china! Whatever!'

FRIDAY, 30 MAY 2008

Peter Fincham has offered me a very good two-year exclusive deal at ITV, thanks to some skilful negotiating by Peter Powell and his team, and I've accepted it.

Strange how things work in the modern media.

I got fired from the *Mirror*, Peter commissioned me to do a series for BBC1 called *You Can't Fire Me, I'm Famous*, he then had to resign from the BBC over Queengate and now he signs me for ITV.

As if my day couldn't get any better, I walked into Amanda's dressing room at 7.04 p.m. tonight, to find her standing completely starkers by the door.

'Oh my God!' she yelped, desperately trying to cover herself up.

'Oh my God!' I replied, throwing my hands over my eyes.

I have nothing further to add, other than to say that all those who accuse Ms Holden of having no talent fit to judge a show like this...well, you're wrong.

SATURDAY, 31 MAY 2008

The final had everything. Drama, tension, excitement and a shock result that split families and friends all over the country.

The winner, 15-year-old dancer George Sampson, is, as Simon said, our Rocky and Billy Elliott all rolled into one.

But he nearly blew it, by wanting to try a new, not very exciting, routine for the final.

It was Simon who persuaded him, during a tense last-minute meeting, to re-perform the 'Singing In The Rain' number.

When we walked offstage at the end, George came running up and threw himself into Simon's arms. 'Thank you so much,' he cried.

'What is the first thing you're going to do with the money?' asked Simon.

'I'm going to pay off my mum's mortgage,' he replied instantly.

And that's why Britain fell in love with George Sampson. He's a fighter with a heart.

Simon, of course, hit the airwaves immediately, pointing out that Amanda and I had rejected George last year.

'Only I spotted his talent,' he crowed, revoltingly.

'We were right to do it,' I retorted. 'He wasn't ready.'

'Rubbish,' snorted Simon.

At midnight, we headed to the Dorchester Hotel for a party. Simon was as happy as I've ever seen him. 'I think that was the best TV show I've ever been involved with,' he said, as we tucked into a large magnum of Krug.

As the hours wore on, I have vague recollections of Amanda ripping my shirt open to stroke my chest, Holly Willoughby gamely preventing me doing the same to her, and getting into an ill-advised Jack Daniel's drinking contest with Ant and Dec.

Simon and I stumbled into the street at 5 a.m. He was still smiling.

SUNDAY, 1 JUNE 2008

Emily Maitlis invited me to be her walker tonight at the final of Heston Blumenthal's BBC2 cookery show *Great British Menu*.

We met Tom Parker Bowles at the entrance, who revealed that his mother Camilla had been gripped all week by *Britain's Got Talent*. 'Who did she want to win?' I asked.

'Well, put it this way, she's a very big dog lover!'

So the future queen voted for Gin, the moonwalking border collie. Extraordinary.

Upstairs, I was waylaid by an agitated Ronnie Corbett.

'I can't believe that young dancer won!' he exclaimed. 'It should have been those girl violinists!'

MONDAY, 2 JUNE 2008

George Sampson appeared on *This Morning* today and said: 'Piers was quite right not to put me through last year, I wasn't ready and would never have beaten Paul Potts. And it just made me work even harder to come back and win it this time.'

That's my boy.

TUESDAY, 3 JUNE 2008

I attended *Glamour*'s annual magazine awards this evening, to present the Best TV Performer award to Dannii Minogue.

I sat next to Sarah Brown at dinner, and Lily Allen came over.

'I just want to say that I think it's terrible all the stick your husband's getting,' she told Sarah. 'He seems like a really good bloke, and I'd vote for him. I mean, he's not the same as Tony Blair, but then Blair turned out to be a complete knob anyway, didn't he?'

Sarah burst out laughing.

'I'm off to LA next week,' Lily added, turning to me. 'Know any good places to stay?'

'Yes,' I said, 'there's plenty of room in my suite.'

'Great, how much?' she said, not quite getting the joke.

'Erm, well, let's see now, you can stay for free but there might have to be the odd communal shower involved.'

'Fucking hell. I'd rather pay for somewhere else in that case.' The penny had dropped.

'A wise decision,' nodded the First Lady, approvingly.

Talking of wise decisions, I'd blow your nose next time you talk to the prime minister's wife, Lily.

WEDNESDAY, 4 JUNE 2008

Barack Obama has won the Democrat nomination. He's triumphed against his main rival Hillary Clinton after a 54-contest, five-month fight. There's something incredibly thorough and reassuring about the American electoral process. Yes, it does seem to go on and on. But it also really gets to the heart of the candidates, what they stand for and how good a president they might make.

To deafening applause, Obama told a 20,000-strong crowd in Minnesota: 'Tonight, we mark the end of one historic journey with the beginning of another – a journey that will bring a new and better day to America.'

Hillary, for whom this must be a crushing disappointment given how long she led in the polls, was magnanimous in defeat. 'It has been an honour to contest these primaries with Barack, just as it is an honour to call him my friend.'

The big question now is whether Obama will choose Clinton as his vice-presidential running mate. I would, if I were him. She'd bring the female vote, and counter the enduring argument against him that he has no experience.

I emailed Indra Nooyi, the Pepsi boss who I had the big Obama/Hillary debate with at Chequers.

'I may be FOS,' I wrote, 'but I was right…'

She emailed straight back. 'You were. You're a genius! Any more predictions?'

'Yes, Obama will be president, you will be *Fortune*'s Woman of the Year again, I will become prime minister – and Gordon will become the new judge on *America's Got Talent*.'

THURSDAY, 5 JUNE 2008

Met Michael Heseltine at a drinks party tonight.

'Oh hello Piers, I was reading a really derogatory article about you in the papers yesterday...'

Pause.

'...which, as you can imagine, brought me enormous pleasure!'

FRIDAY, 6 JUNE 2008

Now this fact sometimes surprises me: I've only been punched by one celebrity, ever. Despite 20 years of taunting, exposing and mocking famous people, only Jeremy Clarkson has ever actually landed one on me.

But at 11.31 p.m. tonight, I was fairly sure I was going to receive my second celebrity fist in the kisser, when Robbie Coltrane stood up in the middle of the Ivy restaurant, stared into my eyes with the kind of evil intent that puts Joe Calzaghe to shame and informed me loudly: 'I'll fuckin' do yer, yer fuckin' wanker.'

Quite how things got to this stage remains a mystery, as I have never met Mr Coltrane before in my life, and to the best of my memory have never had any run-ins with him on any of the papers I have previously worked on.

In fact, I've always rather liked the man's 'body of work' – *Cracker* was a brilliant series. My children (we both, coincidentally, have sons called Spencer) are big fans of his Hagrid character in Harry Potter.

And we're even born on the same day – 30 March.

But I feared this admiration society might not be entirely mutual when I was led towards my table, and Mr Coltrane – sitting two feet away, greeted my arrival with the words: 'OH FUCKIN' HELL! NOT THAT FUCKIN' WANKER!'

I turned to see who he was talking about, and then realised his drooping inflamed eyes were looking at me.

I sat down, feeling slightly disconcerted. Mr Coltrane, after all, is now at least 30 stone, has a face like a gnarled warthog and looks like he could 'handle himself' as they say in his native Lanarkshire.

My guests, *Mirror* boss Richard Wallace and Conor Hanna, were – of course – highly amused. But just as perplexed as I was. 'What have you done to him?' they mused. 'Nothing,' I replied, as Mr Coltrane continued to audibly chunter away about me in a disturbingly derogatory manner.

To add to the surreal nature of the proceedings, John Cleese then arrived at an adjoining table and immediately walked over to talk to Mr Coltrane. As he did so, his very attractive young leggy blonde date pulled out a book and started reading it. It was *my* book, *The Insider*.

Weird.

Cleese returned to his table after a few minutes, hurried words were exchanged, his lady put the book straight back in her bag and they were abruptly moved to a window table. An hour later, Mr Coltrane stood up and marched into the kitchen. Presumably to save waiting time before he could start noshing.

Well, when I say 'marched', I mean 'waddled' really. His gigantic frame takes several long seconds to be heaved even a few inches.

When he returned, I stood up and introduced myself.

'I don't think we've met,' I said, offering my hand.

'Don't you fuckin' come near me, you cunt,' he responded, his face contorted into blind, eye-popping fury.

'I'm sorry?'

'I said don't you fuckin' come near me…if you know what's good for you, you cunt.'

'What's your problem?'

'You're my fuckin' problem.'

'Why?'

'Fuck off.'

By now, the fabulous Ivy staff and other diners were becoming aware of the 'problem'.

I pondered Mr Coltrane's behaviour over another bottle of Château Palmer Margaux, and decided to confront my antagonist directly at his table.

'I just want to clarify one thing,' I said, stopping him in mid-bite. 'We've never actually met, right?'

'Fuck off, you cunt,' came the by now predictable reply.

My patience spontaneously evaporated.

'No, I've got a better idea, why don't you fuck off, you rude little man.'

Mr Coltrane's face went puce, and he began to foam at the edges of his mouth.

'WHAT? Don't you tell me to fuck off, you fuckin' cunt.'

'I'll do what I like,' I said, firmly. 'Trust me, I now feel the same way about you as you do about me.'

Mr Coltrane began to sway from side to side, rocking with pure fulminating rage.

'I'll fuckin' do yer,' he roared.

I laughed out loud.

'Come on then, big man. I'm not scared of you. If you've got something you want to do to me, then do it.'

'You fuckin' cunt,' he recited several more times.

'Come. On. Big. Man.' I repeated.

Mr Coltrane staggered to his feet, and the restaurant fell quiet with fevered anticipation, allowing Mr Coltrane to let fly with one last 'you're a fuckin' cunt' outburst – earning him a round of applause from four camp theatrical types nearby.

'Big words, big man,' I said. 'But what are you going to actually *do* about it?'

Mr Coltrane spat more venom like a puff adder rearing for a lethal strike.

'Go on, big man. Make yourself a hero.'

Mr Coltrane bristled, and seethed, and growled, but then he sat down again.

'Fuck off, you cunt,' he said, yet again, but with less authority than his previous 26 versions of the statement.

'Oh, I'm going my friend, don't worry. Now I've established that you're all mouth and no trousers.'

Mr Coltrane stared at me once more, unspeakable loathing emanating from every battered crevice of his gargantuan torso. But rather than exuding the magnificent heroic air of Hagrid the Giant, he more resembled Dobby, the pitiful house-elf.

I've had many memorable moments in The Ivy over the years: poked in the chest by Margaret Thatcher, 'snogged' by Dale Winton and rendered a dribbling, alcoholic, incoherent imbecile by newsgirls Sophie Raworth, Katie Derham, Andrea Catherwood and Emily Maitlis (twice...so far).

But I think this encounter with Mr Coltrane, OBE, beats them all for sheer shock value and enduring mystery.

I got home and checked on the Internet to see if we had ever been linked in any way. We hadn't.

But what I did establish is that Mr Coltrane hates the press, absolutely detests every journalist on the entire planet.

Of course, like every hypocritical old thespian, he continues to do plenty of interviews to promote himself (he was on Jonathan Ross's show tonight), and regularly gorge at the Ivy, the most high-profile media haunt in the world.

TUESDAY, 10 JUNE 2008

'We're holding a tribute dinner for you,' said Dylan Jones a few weeks ago.

'Why?'

'Not sure really,' he replied, 'let's say it's for services to Nick Clegg.'

I knew it would be a strange night when I turned up at the Dorchester Hotel and instantly spied Nancy Dell'Olio. We've only met once, and my sole contribution to her life was exposing Sven's affair with Ulrika.

'I don't know why I'm 'ere,' she said.

'To honour me,' I said.

'Are you crazy?' she exclaimed.

Next through the door was Celia, inexplicably accompanied by the heart-throb star of *Gossip Girl*, Chace Crawford.

'I found him at the bar,' she said, drooling visibly at the mouth. 'It shouldn't be allowed, should it?'

'What shouldn't?'

'To look that good...'

She was interrupted, thankfully, by Amanda, who burst in shouting: 'Why the hell are we honouring you? It should be *me*!'

Other guests included Tracey Emin, Tony Parsons, Emily Maitlis, newspaper editors Roger Alton and Peter Wright, and, of course, Simon Cowell, who was even more succinct with his thoughts on the solemnity of the occasion.

'Can someone please explain to me what the fuck we are all doing here?' he announced, grimly.

MONDAY, 16 JUNE 2008

I rang Kevin Pietersen.

'KP, remember saying you'd do anything for me in return for that Cowell meeting?'

'Yeah...'

'Well, I'm calling in the favour.'

'What is it?'

'I captain a family side in an annual cricket match against my local village team every year...'

Silence.

'...and always bring in a famous ringer...'

Silence.

'…but despite this, I always lose…'

Silence.

'So…it's time to bring in the mother of all ringers…'

Silence.

'Which brings me back to *you*, Kevin…'

Silence. Long sigh…

TUESDAY, 17 JUNE 2008

I'm in New York to promote tonight's premiere of Season 3 of *America's Got Talent*, and finally achieved an all-time career ambition – to appear on the Howard Stern radio show. He's the most infamous, outrageous and brilliant $250 million-a-year shock jock DJ in the world, and even had a hit movie made about him called *Private Parts*.

'How long am I on?' I asked the producer.

'As long as you amuse Howard,' came the unsettling answer. 'Could be five minutes, could be 45 minutes.'

I walked into the studio, and could see Howard staring at me curiously, with an expression that said: 'Come on then, *amuse* me.'

Terrifying!

There was only one thing for it – start gossiping.

Nearly an hour later, I was finally sent packing, after unloading every bit of salacious celebrity tittle-tattle I could think of.

'I had dinner with George Michael and by the end of the first course he told me he'd slept with 500 men in the last seven years,' I said early on, causing Howard to break into a gigantic grin.

'Oh, and I introduced Heather Mills to Paul McCartney, not realising she was a grasping, horrible, gold-digging bimbo…'

The grin got bigger…

'Stephen Baldwin kept preaching to me on *The Apprentice* about my moral and religious deficiencies, then he'd start bragging about how many hookers he'd had in Vegas before he got married and found God…make your mind up, mate.'

The grin became Cherie-like.

'I like you, man,' said Howard afterwards, patting me on the shoulder. Which was like being called holy by the Pope.

WEDNESDAY, 18 JUNE 2008

I appeared on the Regis and Kathy breakfast TV show this morning cooking a meal of my choice, live on air, to try and win their coveted 'Golden Wiener' award.

The only slight problem being that my culinary skills extend to microwaving a baked bean can. And even then the results can be deeply distressing.

I opted for a prime New York steak (I'm not stupid...) with a special Sharon Osbourne sauce ('hot, spicy, unpredictable and with a kick like a mule') and lashings of David Hasselhoff blue Cheddar ('very, very, very cheesy').

To my astonishment, it tasted rather good, and Regis Philbin seemed impressed. 'My coveted wiener's within your grasp,' he chuckled, filthily.

THURSDAY, 19 JUNE 2008

I arrived back at Heathrow at 11 a.m. today, and headed straight to Simon Cowell's box at Ascot.

I'm a terrible gambler, and usually blow everything at race meetings like this. But my confidence rose when Frankie Dettori came into our box and handed out six 'red-hot' tips.

Frankie's a fantastically positive and enthusiastic character, and seemed utterly convinced of his predictive powers. Each tip came with an excited 'that's a sure-fire winner!' or 'put your 'ouse on it!' and so on.

And since he once memorably went through the card at Ascot, who was I to doubt him?

Cowell arrived late, obviously, and I gleefully told him that he'd missed out on Frankie's inside info.

'Hmmm,' he replied, 'rule one of Ascot is never back anything a jockey tells you...'

'You don't want Frankie's tips, then?' I gloated, waving them in front of his face.

'Nooooo, thank you.'

I then had to endure three hours of incessant torture, as Frankie's choices competed for the title of 'Most Incompetent Nag Ever Seen At Ascot' – while Cowell's own selections romped to victory in virtually every race.

'Oops...' he said, as No. 5 roared home, 'looks like I got lucky again.'

By the end of the day, I'd lost £1,000, Amanda and her fiancé Chris £2,000, and Cowell had won at least £5,000.

FRIDAY, 20 JUNE 2008

Stanley and Bertie's prep school asked me a while ago to try and find a celebrity who might be the surprise guest at their 'Musical Soirée' tonight, in which the main performance is going to be *The Sound of Music*.

I knew just who to ask.

'Oh my God, darling, I've played Maria professionally!' screamed Amanda down the phone. 'I'm a wonderful yodeller.'

At which point she burst into a loud rendition of 'The Lonely Goatherd'.

The great thing about Amanda is that she's always up for a laugh.

I've also persuaded fellow parent Michael Grade to take part – me and him are going to be singing nuns!

At 5 p.m., Amanda called.

'Hi, I'm at Richard and Judy doing an interview, and Jerry Springer's here too – want a word?'

'Love to, stick him on.'

Pause.

'Piers, how are you?'

'I'm great Jerry, what are you doing tonight?'

'Not much, just going back to my hotel for dinner.'

'Fancy a bit of fun instead?'

'Of course! What kind of fun?'

'Well, Amanda, Michael Grade and I are all going to be making complete arses of ourselves in my kids' school's rendition of *The Sound of Music* tonight. Want to join us?'

Jerry laughed loudly.

'Sure, why not?'

Two hours later, I walked into the school assembly hall with Jerry Springer, prompting the kind of quiet but tangible furore that you might see if Jade Goody and Jordan walked into Buckingham Palace for a garden party.

Amanda arrived soon afterwards, almost panting with nerves.

'Oh God, why did I agree to do this?' she yelped, placing my hand as usual on pert, beating chest.

'You'll be wonderful, darling,' I encouraged her.

And she was – singing beautifully, yodelling her heart out and bringing the house down.

As for me, Jerry and Michael, well, let's just say that when we strolled out as two singing nuns and a Catholic priest (Jerry), it caused more than a little degree of merriment.

'My rabbi would be so proud,' chuckled Jerry afterwards.

Stanley was pleased with my efforts, but already looking forward. 'Dad, can you get Take That and Justin Timberlake next year, please?'

SATURDAY, 21 JUNE 2008

Definition of pure joy: being called by your Hollywood agent and asked if you want to host the Miss Universe extravaganza in Vietnam on 13 July.

Definition of total despair: checking the diary to see it clashes with the Lord's test match.

Definition of abject bemusement: the Ferret, when I tried to explain that watching cricket comes before spending four days in an Asian hotel with 80 beautiful young women.

WEDNESDAY, 25 JUNE 2008

Coffee with Sarah Brown at No. 10 Downing Street. ('Mandela and me in the same week,' I told her, 'you lucky girl.')

As I waited just inside the famous black door to be taken upstairs to her flat, Geoff Hoon hurried past, then spied me and stopped dead in his tracks.

I once called him BUFF-HOON in a *Mirror* front-page headline following one of his particularly dismal 'Why we must go to war with Iraq' entreaties to the nation. And he hadn't spoken to me since.

Now we stood just inches from each other, and I could see Labour's chief whip was mulling over whether to say anything at all, or just start whipping me.

'Geoffrey, how lovely to see you,' I said, diplomatically.

'Morgan, what the hell are you doing in here?' he replied.

'Just returning to the corridors of power where I belong,' I retorted.

He stared at me for several seconds.

'Don't take this personally,' he said, with a smile, 'but I would really rather you died a long, slow, horrible death instead.'

It had taken him over a decade, but Geoff Hoon, the world's dullest politician, had finally said something spontaneous and funny.

FRIDAY, 27 JUNE 2008

'Dad, can I have all your money if you die?' asked Bertie in the car today.

'No, you can't.'

Pause.

'I would be quite upset if you did die.'

'Glad to hear it.'

Pause.

'But what happens to your money if you do?'

'You won't be getting it, Albert.' (I always call him that when I want to be very serious with him.)

Long, thoughtful pause.

'OK, well how about we go halves then?'

SATURDAY, 28 JUNE 2008

Kevin Pietersen has been captain of England's one-day cricket side today, after a last-minute injury to regular skipper Paul Collingwood.

He is, understandably, jubilant.

'This is one of the best days of my life,' he told me by text, an hour before he was due to walk out at Lord's.

I feel very proud of him. He's come a long way from the cocky Mohican-haired brat who first exploded on to the British sporting scene four years ago. The new KP is calmer, more mature and nicer to be around.

Unfortunately, England lost.

'Sack the captain,' I texted him.

SUNDAY, 29 JUNE 2008

What a day! One of those I'll be boring my great-great-grandchildren about until my false teeth self-implode.

At 1.50 p.m. this afternoon, my annual family cricket match against Newick Village CC was about to start.

Around 40 villagers, including many of my oldest friends, were waiting expectantly to see which 'ringer' I had brought down this time.

'It's the best ringer in the world,' I declared, in a statement that was met with scornful laughter.

Seconds later, a Mercedes S500 pulled up alongside the pavilion.

And out stepped Kevin Pietersen, shades on and bat over his shoulder.

I watched the life physically drain from the villagers' faces.

'Morgan,' said portly surveyor Cameron Jones, 'this is not fair…'

'Fair?' I replied. 'Who the hell said we had to be fair?'

I tossed KP some kit.

'How do you want me to play it?' he asked.

'Simple, china,' I replied. 'Just murder them.'

'Right, let's go boys,' he barked. Surreally, he had, of course, barked the very same instruction to the England team 24 hours ago.

Newick's opening batsman was deli owner, Tim Gill.

'Time to teach the pros how to bat...' he vowed confidently.

Tim was out caught first ball of the match, and departed to the inevitable cry from KP of: 'Quite a lesson that, china! Thanks!'

The other opening batsman, James Hitchings, then started blocking virtually every ball stone dead.

'Are you ill?' bellowed KP.

'No,' said Hitchings.

'Then why are you being so boring?'

Our superstar barely broke sweat until the twelfth over, when antiques restorer Rupert Thacker decided to chance a quick run to him.

Outraged by this grotesque insult to his genius, Pietersen swooped on the ball like a ravenous puma, and threw it at ferocious speed right to the base of the stumps, missing by an inch.

It was a sudden explosive reminder that we were in the presence of someone so far out of our league it was scary.

But to his great credit, KP was constantly supportive and encouraging to his team throughout the two hours we were in the field.

When Stanley bowled one of the home side's top batsmen out LBW, KP instinctively ran up and high-fived him.

'Great bowling, Stan!' he shouted.

What a moment for an 11-year-old boy!

Unfortunately, KP's own bowling was less impressive.

'Just rattle through them, mate,' I ordered, tossing him the ball towards the end of Newick's innings.

There was a definite rattle all right. Of wood from nearby trees. To my utter horror, KP was hit for two huge sixes by inkjet tycoon Miles Caldwell. The second one nearly felling a large oak.

'Erm, no offence, china,' I said, 'but you're paid to do this, he isn't...any chance of actually getting him out?'

KP nodded grimly, took off his sunglasses and fizzed the next ball right in the blockhole.

Hapless Caldwell duly hit it straight up in the air, and KP laughed as he went to take the simple catch, gleefully crying 'Got him!' as the ball fell into his hands.

The problem was that it then promptly fell out again.

He'd dropped it.

'What the hell are you playing at?' I asked.

'Sorry skipper,' he grinned, sheepishly.

Two balls later, a massive-framed student called Mark Symonds smacked him back into the trees for another six.

I caught KP's eye and raised an eyebrow. Words were superfluous.

Newick finished with 266 off 40 overs.

'Right,' I told him as we trudged off, 'you'd better get a lot of bloody runs after that, china.'

'Don't you worry about that,' he laughed, 'that's my business.'

We walked out to bat together, which was the only way I could guarantee I'd bat with him.

And KP was nearly bowled immediately – the ball whistling just over his stumps.

'Relax, china,' he chuckled, 'it's all going to be fine.'

He then hit two balls to the boundary so hard they emitted a noise not dissimilar to Concorde when it used to break the sound barrier.

Several balls later, I also managed to hit a four.

'That's how you play the pull shot, china,' I chortled.

Next ball, I was out, bowled.

'Yeah, and that's how not to play the forward defensive shot, china,' came the withering response.

I was happy, though – I can now have a tombstone that reads: 'Here lies Piers Morgan, who once opened the batting with Kevin Pietersen.'

KP proceeded to smash a brilliant century, then looked to me for further guidance.

'Carry on,' I ordered. So he did, going from 100 to 158 in 32 balls.

At which point, he turned and asked the wicket-keeper: 'Which of your lot can catch?'

'I can,' said Cameron Jones, standing 20 feet away.

So KP deliberately spooned the next ball straight up in the air to Jones, and began to walk off.

Only Jones, of course, dropped it.

Pietersen laughed, and carried on walking anyway.

His work on this village pitch was done.

The crowd, by now over 500 people, roared him off as if he had scored a century in a test match.

It was a wonderful moment, and I could tell he had genuinely enjoyed himself. He also took time through the day to sign hundreds of autographs and pose for endless photos. KP was polite, charming and incredibly patient. And made a lot of new friends.

Unfortunately, we still lost the bloody match – by three runs. Jeremy not helping matters by falling over twice in his brief erratic innings, and then being hit on the chin after insisting that 'helmets are for wimps'.

'If you hadn't bowled so badly, we'd have won,' I told KP in the bar afterwards.

'Yeah, and if you had done anything at all, we might have stood a better chance, too, you MUPPET!' he fired back.

Fair point.

My despair at losing was compensated by the sight of a large touring coach pulling up an hour later outside the house – where I was throwing a party.

It was Freddie Flintoff, and five of his Lancashire colleagues, fresh from their match against Sussex.

On the list of people I'd most like to have at a party, Freddie would be comfortably top.

Especially when 100 of your village friends have come up from watching Kevin Pietersen just smack 158, and are now thinking: 'Top that, Morgan…'

We drank beer, ate fish and chips, talked nonsense about cricket and Freddie showed everyone why he's the most popular player in England by dealing with the throng of excited villagers around him all night with great charm, humour and patience.

At midnight, I finally collapsed to bed.

It had been, and I don't say this lightly, one of the best days of my entire life.

MONDAY, 30 JUNE 2008

I didn't believe the Madonna divorce stories until I read a quote from her notorious American publicist Liz 'Godzilla' Rosenberg formally denying it.

I remember once, when I was *Mirror* editor, phoning Ms Rosenberg in New York to ask her if Madonna was pregnant.

'No, no, no,' she insisted.

'You sure?' I asked, knowing my source was unusually impeccable.

'Piers, listen to my lips: Madonna. Is. Not. Pregnant.'

The very next day, Madonna's pregnancy was announced on the *Sun*'s website, with a confirmatory quote from one Liz Rosenberg.

Godzilla is to the truth what Jeremy Clarkson is to beauty.

And purely on the back of her firm denial, I'm going to have a few quid on a Madonna divorce by Christmas.

Jamaican superstar Usain Bolt storms to victory in the 100m Olympic race – leaving the Americans trailing in his wake. A further symbol of the weakening power of the United States in recent years.

10

'America makes prodigious mistakes, America has colossal faults, but one thing cannot be denied: America is always on the move. She may be going to Hell, of course, but at least she isn't standing still.' E.E. CUMMINGS

WEDNESDAY, 2 JULY 2008

Dinner with Jay-Z. Sounds good, doesn't it?

But then I've got gastronomic form with rappers – counting P. Diddy and Pharell Williams among recent culinary companions.

I think it must be all those hard-core gangsta moves I do on *Britain's Got Talent*. The lads recognise a kindred spirit.

The event was hosted by Dylan Jones.

The most pressing question was, of course, what to wear: ripped jeans and leather jacket? Baseball cap and Air Nike pumps? I eventually plumped for a suit and tie, and was thrilled to see Jay-Z also sporting the same.

'Smart,' said Jay-Z, eyeing my attire approvingly, as poor Dylan sat, open-necked, in fashion Siberia.

Jay-Z, like Diddy and Pharell, was much smarter than I thought he'd be, and funnier, too.

'How's David Beckham doing in America?' I asked.

'Very well,' he smiled, 'as a *celebrity*.'

'Not as a sportsman, then?'

'No, because he isn't playing. He's always injured. Soccer needs an iconic figure like Michael Jordan to make it a big sport in the States, and that person has to play every week and score a lot of goals, not sit on the bench.'

I asked him what he thought of the presidential race.

'It's not so much a case of "Can he do it?" but "He has to do it",' he replied. 'Because if he doesn't, then I don't know where America is going.

Black kids in the ghettos don't have anyone to look up to in the political world. In the absence of their families, their gangs become their families, and they need people to follow. Barack is that man.'

'I'd hardly expect you to say you're voting for McCain,' said Dylan.

'I'm not voting for Obama because he's black,' rejoined Jay-Z. 'I'm voting for him because of what he stands for.'

'Which is?' I asked.

'Change. He stands for change. We didn't have anyone like Obama when I was running around as a kid. I did some crazy shit but I never looked up to a politician, because they never addressed us, or spoke to us. With Obama, you get a sense he's gonna talk to everyone. And for a black man, that's a powerful message.'

'Will you be glad to see the back of Bush?' said Dylan.

'No more than anyone else in America. Look what he did in New Orleans after Hurricane Katrina, nothing. That's how much Bush cares about black people.'

When the conversation drifted more tediously to David Cameron ('Who?' asked a bemused Jay-Z), I decided it was time to turn to more urgent matters of global concern.

'What's it like going out with someone with the best backside in show-business?' I asked, referring to his booty-licious lady, Beyoncé.

There was an uncomfortable silence.

Then he laughed.

'It's nice. I like her "backside" too...'

At which precise point, Simon Cowell texted me to say *America's Got Talent* was No. 1 in the ratings – allowing me to send him the immortal reply: 'Please don't bother me when I'm talking to Jay-Z about Beyoncé's bum.'

You might imagine that rappers gorge on a relentless diet of Cristal and caviar. But the most excited Jay-Z got was when a large bowl of macaroni cheese arrived.

'This is good,' he murmured, 'really, really good.'

He took another huge spoonful.

'Man, this is incredible, the best I've ever tasted.'

SUNDAY, 6 JULY 2008

For the last two years the bane of my life has been Sharon Osbourne's small white Pomeranian dog, Minnie.

Every time I went near this ferocious creature, it would go berserk – snarling, growling and attempting to bite me.

A behavioural pattern, in fact, rather similar to its owner. (Though Sharon assured me it wasn't personal – Minnie sank her fangs into half of Hollywood, including Patrick Swayze and The Hoff.)

Minnie died this week, after a long illness. And I found myself feeling unexpectedly sad.

'I can't believe I'm saying this, but I'll actually miss her,' I told a heart-broken Sharon on the phone tonight, 'she was a real character.'

I don't normally 'do' dogs, but this was no ordinary dog.

Minnie, I salute you.

MONDAY, 7 JULY 2008

There may be a credit crunch infecting the globe but it isn't infecting Russia yet.

I'm in the South of France with Celia and have been been staggered by the sheer volume of Muscovites swaggering around the South of France, and even more staggered by the amount they were spending.

Tonight, for example, we were dining at Elton John's favourite restaurant, La Chaumière near Nice, and had the undivided attention of the enthusiastic waiting staff for approximately one hour, 12 minutes and 54 seconds...at which point a group of boisterous young Russians arrived, and we were instantly ignored.

The reason? The 12-strong group's opening order was for four £1,000 magnums of vintage Dom Perignon champagne, and four magnums of Petrus red wine at £2,000 a pop.

The Russians, comprised of six pasty-faced scowling young men in jeans and T-shirts, and six highly expensively sculptured ladies, guzzled their way through the finest fare the restaurant had to offer – then calmly paid in cash a bill that must have been well over £20,000.

To compound my misery (Celia was by now looking witheringly at our very nice bottle of Puligny-Montrachet like it was cheap rat poison), another table of rich older types started singing raucous songs.

One voice rang out louder than the others, nearly breaking the windows with its power.

Curious, I peered around an obstructive pillar to find Tina Turner belting out 'For He's A Jolly Good Fellow' in German.

WEDNESDAY, 9 JULY 2008

The super-efficient assistant manager from the Wyndham Chelsea Hotel turned to leave my sumptuous harbourside suite, and said: 'I will make sure that you are not bothered, Mr Morgan.'

I looked at the stunning woman sitting on the sofa next to me, shimmering with natural Welsh beauty, and laughed: 'Yes, that would be greatly appreciated. Although if the press call, do feel free to confirm that I am secretly ensconced with Katherine Jenkins.'

'Of course, sir,' he nodded, gravely, 'and would you like a "Do Not Disturb" sign on the door?'

'Most. Definitely.'

He left, and Katherine dissolved into giggles. Of the slightly nervous variety, it must be said.

Of all the onerous jobs that Dylan has ever thrown at me (I still shudder at the day he tried to get me to go to Suffolk and interview Alex James at his cheese farm), this had to rank as the least troublesome.

Ms Jenkins, 28, has a voice like Maria Callas, a body like Marilyn Monroe and the radiant, easy charm of a thoroughly well-brought-up young lady.

But from the few times I've met her, I've always had a sneaking suspicion that lurking beneath this wholesome, uncorrupted, girl-next-door image there may lie a raging tornado of naughtiness.

So my mission was clear: to find, locate and expose the (hopefully) dark side of Katherine Jenkins. The one every *GQ* man prays she has.

I didn't get very far, unfortunately. She doesn't smoke, barely drinks, prefers to keep details of her sex life to herself and has only once broken the law – a speeding offence.

The only slightly curious moment came when I asked her this: 'You've never taken any drugs?'

(Shakes head.)

'Whoa…was that a hesitation there?'

'No! I've never taken drugs.'

There was something about the way she looked at me when she dithered that suggested she wasn't being entirely frank.

After a thoroughly enjoyable, but rather fruitless, 90 minutes, we went back downstairs to meet her assistant, who asked how the interview had gone.

'Not well,' I said.

'No?'

'Nope. She really is too good to be true…'

Katherine looked at me, and winked.

FRIDAY, 11 JULY 2008

The boys' school reports have come in.

Spencer is apparently 'a born-again academic'.

Bertie 'produced a very fine rendition of Picasso's cockerel in oil pastels'.

And Stanley is a 'natural showman'.

I'll settle for that.

What was rather less palatable was Spencer thrashing me at table tennis this afternoon. And I mean 'thrashing'.

By the end he was toying with me, predicting what shot would win the point.

The little (five foot ten and growing) scamp has beaten me at tennis and chess as well in Newick this week, nearly broken my finger bowling a vicious bouncer at me in the cricket net and run rings round me on the football pitch.

I feel old, very, very old.

MONDAY, 14 JULY 2008

Lembit Opik has split from his Cheeky Girl lover. I confidently expect to read about his heartache in next week's *Hello!*

TUESDAY, 15 JULY 2008

I was due to interview Dame Helen Mirren this morning, and woke feeling curiously uncertain of myself.

What to wear? Jeans and smart shirt, or a suit?

I put on the jeans, walked to the door, stopped in my tracks, went back and put a suit on.

Weird. I never do that.

An hour later, I knocked on the door of her suite at the Rookery Hotel in London, and her very first words, hilariously, were: 'Hello Piers, that's a very nice suit. I was wondering what you'd wear for this interview...'

'Really?' I replied. 'I was actually going to wear jeans, but it just didn't seem right to wear jeans for a Dame of the British Empire.'

She smiled. 'I thought you'd either wear jeans or a suit, and I'm sure you'd look great in jeans, too.'

Dame Helen may be 63, but she knows how to melt a man's iron resolve.

'I am in your bedroom at the moment, Dame Helen, should I be starting to feel a little uneasy...'

She laughed. 'Edith Piaf used to go out and get drunk with journalists and take them to bed,' she said, 'not that I've ever done that, of course, I hasten to add. *Ever.* But when I saw this great big double bed, I thought this was not the place I should be doing an interview with Piers Morgan!'

'How do you explain that every man who I told I was interviewing you reacted by saying: "You jammy devil"?'

(Laughs.) 'Perhaps they think I am accessible, friendly...'

'Or sexy?'

'Or sexy....yes, perhaps. I mean, I've always had big tits and blonde hair.'

I burst out laughing. You just don't expect a Dame who has played the Queen to talk like this.

'Every time I look at your tattoo on your hand twinkling in the sunlight, there is a suggestion of inherent naughtiness about you?'

'I've always been a would-be naughty girl, wanting to be bad, desperately, but never quite with the balls to get there and do it properly.'

'What stopped you?'

'Fear. And having to make my own living, although that is a piss-poor excuse, I know. But it meant I had to turn up on time for work, and be a good girl and learn my lines. I was never courageous enough to break the rules. Even now I am incredibly intimidated by anyone in a uniform. I wouldn't dream of getting on a train without a ticket for instance.'

'Have you ever broken the law?'

'I used to shoplift for food when I was younger. But I was very poor.'

'What did you steal?'

'Little bits of ham.' (Laughs.)

'Is that as bad as it gets? "I STOLE LITTLE BITS OF HAM, SAYS DAME HELEN" is not going to set the tabloid world alight, is it?'

'Oh dear…well, I did steal a hat as well one day because I craved it…oh, this is terrible, what are you doing to me, Piers? You're making me confess to all kinds of awful things…. I'll go home tonight and think, "Oh fuck him, he got me, the bastard, he made me say all these things, how did he do it?"'

'Ever taken drugs?'

'Erm, well, a bit of dope when I was younger…'

'Cannabis?'

'Yes, but I hated it. Dope always made me feel miserable and paranoid and unhappy. And I woke up one day and just thought, no more of that, thank you.'

'Anything harder?'

'I did a bit of cocaine…'

'How did you find it?'

'I loved coke. I never did a lot, just a bit at parties. But what ended it for me was when they caught that man Klaus Barbie, the Butcher of Lyons, in the early eighties. He was hiding in South America, had changed his name and was now living off the proceeds of being a cocaine baron. And I read this in the paper, and all the cards fell into place, and I saw how my little sniff of cocaine at a party had an absolute direct route to this fucking horrible man in South America. And from that day I never touched cocaine again.'

'You once famously said you set your alarm clock for early in the morning to ensure you had sex before going to work…so I have to ask, are you good in bed?'

'Shut up, Piers, that's private!'

'But I can invade your privacy, I'm an ex-tabloid editor.'

'I know, but I can stop you as well. It's none of your fucking beeswax, so just bugger off!'

'You're making a movie about a Nevada whorehouse. Could you ever imagine selling your body for sex?'

'Hmmm, when I was younger I could have done.'

'You'd have probably earned a pretty good rate for yourself! Liam Neeson says you taught him how to eat prawns during your romance… how *do* you eat a prawn?'

'You pull the little head off, then the little tail off, then you rip their little legs off, and then you suck them out of their shells and slurp their bodies in your mouth, or very delicately peel them off…'

'And is that what you did to Liam Neeson?'

Dame Helen gave me her most censorious frown.

'No, Piers, I didn't. I cared for him, and about him, and nurtured him, and I loved him.'

'You have hinted at the fact that you were date-raped when you were younger, more than once.'

'I was, yes. A couple of times. Not with excessive violence, or being hit, but rather being locked in a room and made to have sex against my will. I was very innocent when I went to college in London, and was living on my own. And I found that guys were horrible – mean, rude, insulting and so without feeling. And I was looking for love, and for someone who just liked me, made me laugh and was nice to me. And instead I just met all these creeps. And when they weren't date-raping me, I was being bored into bed because these dreary men would drone on and on and on until eventually I just said "Oh for fuck's sake, all right then, get on with it and let me go home."'

'But you didn't report the date-rapes to the police?'

'No, you just couldn't do that in those days. It's such a tricky area, isn't it? Especially if there is no violence. I mean, look at Mike Tyson. I don't think he was a rapist.'

'Do you think if a woman voluntarily ends up in a man's bedroom, takes all her clothes off and engages in sexual activity in bed with him, she should always have the right to say "no" right to the last second, and if the man ignores her then it's rape?'

'Yes. But I don't think she can have that man into court under those circumstances. I don't think that's fair. I guess it is one of the many subtle parts of the men/women relationship that has to be negotiated and worked out between them. Times have changed, definitely. I hate young girls going around beating each other up, and all this happy-slappy crap. But I do love the fierceness of young girls nowadays, and the way they just say "fuck off", because I wish I'd been taught to say "fuck off" when I was younger. If I had ever had a little girl, the first words I would have taught her would have been "fuck off". Say after me darling, "fuck off".'

The interview ended, as it had started, outrageously. I stood up and kissed Dame Helen goodbye.

'You were magnificent!' I said.

'You weren't so bad yourself,' she smiled.

WEDNESDAY, 16 JULY 2008

My membership of Facebook is now getting slightly out of hand, with more than 30 different groups paying tribute to me.

Well, 'tribute' may not be quite the right word judging by some of them.

Here is a brief selection I found this morning:

Largest group: 'I fucking hate Piers Morgan.'

Second largest: 'I fucking love Piers Morgan.'

My favourite: 'Piers Morgan is both funnier and cleverer than Jeremy Clarkson.'

My least favourite: 'Piers Morgan should be taken into the street and shot.'

Most ambiguous: 'Piers Morgan is the mutt's nutts.'

Most woundingly worded: 'I hate Piers Morgan almost as much as Jeremy Kyle.'

Most amusingly worded: 'Piers Morgan is my not-so-secret shouldn't but would.'

Most double-edged sworded: 'I used to think Piers Morgan was a prat but I've changed my mind.'

Closely followed by: 'I like Piers Morgan and I'm not afraid to say it.'

The aren't-you-slightly-overdoing-it-group-given-Mugabe-is-still-alive: 'There isn't a single person more vile than Piers Morgan.'

Most unlikely to succeed: 'Piers Morgan for prime minister.'

THURSDAY, 17 JULY 2008

Celia's written her first novel, a twisted love story of obsession set in Paris, and tonight she had a party to launch it.

I marched confidently to the door of the splendid new Basement House club at Soho House, only to be stopped dead in my tracks.

'Name?'

'Piers Morgan.'

Not a flicker of recognition on the young lady's face as she checked her guest list.

'I'm sorry, but you don't seem to be on the list.'

I grimaced.

'But I helped draw up the list.'

Pause. A slow shake of the head.

'Celia is my...other half...?'

A small crowd of drinkers on the street nearby began to chuckle at my humiliation.

Eventually, another club official arrived to rescue me from social hell, and I was permitted to enter.

My pain only eased when Sarah Brown arrived in a slight fluster later on, having suffered the same non-recognition shame at the door.

But to be fair, the prime minister's wife had come with her brother Sean – an old journalist friend whose new close-shaven haircut and beard make him resemble an escapee from *Prison Break*.

It wouldn't have been quite so bad if Nancy Dell'Olio had not been greeted like the Queen of Sheba and ushered straight inside.

Sarah took her snub in her usual dignified and highly amused manner.

Can you imagine the scene that would have erupted if it had been Cherie left standing on the doorstep? It would have made Baghdad look like Shoreham-by-Sea.

As the evening wore on, Nancy bewitched two handsome young city boys into a cosy corner, and began to dazzle them with her sultry Italian charms.

'Hang on a second!' yelped Emily Maitlis and Andrea Catherwood simultaneously, when I pointed out this smouldering vignette. 'Those are our husbands!'

SATURDAY, 19 JULY 2008

Lunch with the family in Sussex.

I asked Jeremy what he now thought of what was happening in Iraq, and his reply astonished me.

'It has completely changed,' he said. 'And I mean for the better. General Petraeus has transformed both the way the Americans think, and behave. He has been genuinely magnificent in his leadership.'

'Is it a safer place now then?'

'Not necessarily, but he has stabilised things, calmed a lot of people down and stopped all the gung-ho rhetoric that was causing so much trouble. Petraeus realised that the way to try and achieve things in Iraq was not to keep killing everyone, but to talk to the warring factions, and to try and provide the security needed to let freedom and democracy start to develop. And his military have responded superbly well. They re-trained themselves, adapted to the new direction they were being given incredibly fast and became more inclusive than

I thought possible. The American military that I deal with now are so different to what they were like even two years ago. They have learned humility, and the power of talking to people and actually listening to what they are saying. Petraeus has stopped the Americans talking about winning and losing, and put the emphasis now on creating a stable Iraq. I think they just woke up and realised that their isolationist, inward-looking, relentlessly aggressive style was not working, and changed tack. They've also accepted that the average Arab's concept of democracy is rather different to the average Texan's. And they've done a brilliant job recently, since the surge began. They've steered themselves from the abyss, and there is now a real chance of hope, security and a bit of space out there, which Iraq needs so desperately.'

Jeremy seemed as stunned as I was by what he was saying.

'What do the American military guys think of Obama?'

'Ah, well, that's a very different story. They all think he's some sort of dangerous subversive leftie. And that's because they are, at heart, all very right-wing Republicans. Obama is going to have to be very careful how he treats his military.'

SUNDAY, 20 JULY 2008

Sir Alan Sugar's *Apprentice* sidekick Nick Hewer is on some road trip from the UK to Mongolia in his battered old Renault, and has just reached the Russian border.

'He is a bit apprehensive,' Sir Alan told me today, 'but fortunately I was dining tonight in a Spanish restaurant with a load of boozing Russians, so I've been able to help Nick out with some friendly phrases to give the local police or military if he gets into trouble.'

I laughed, knowingly.

'Like?'

'Like "are you gay?" and "would you kiss me if I gave you 100 roubles?"'

WEDNESDAY, 23 JULY 2008

Jonathan Ross and I go back a long way.

We've partied on yachts together at the Cannes film festival, shared a few mojitos on a Malibu beach (while giggling at the sight of David Hasselhoff chasing dementedly after Pamela Anderson) and always had a laugh or two when we've met on the London social scene.

I've also done him some pretty big favours over the years. As editor of the *News of the World*, I once returned him a laptop he'd left in a London taxi that was offered to the paper for £7,000. It contained thousands of words of eye-wateringly graphic erotic prose he had written to his wife, Jane. We paid the money, and never published a word to save his blushes.

I also think that in his day Jonathan was one of the naturally funniest and quickest-witted men in showbusiness. I once saw him rescue a newspaper editor's leaving party, where the speaker was dying horribly on his backside, by jumping onstage and launching into a hilarious 15-minute routine that brought the house down.

But since I left the editing world and started working in television, Jonathan has started behaving rather oddly towards me. Barely a month goes by without him making some snide little dig, either on his own shows or someone else's.

Last night, he was at it again, telling Charlotte Church that he hated *Britain's Got Talent*, thought Amanda and I were 'just a waste', and sneered for good measure: 'Morgan has been sculpted from lard.'

Normally, I'd just laugh this kind of personal abuse off. Particularly as I'm actually pretty trim these days, and jowly Jonathan is tipping the scales rather nearer his good friend Robbie 'I'll do yer' Coltrane.

But I'm bemused as to what is behind all this angst.

Perhaps it's down to all the aggro he's been getting for being paid £18 million by the BBC while thousands of the corporation's staff are being made redundant.

Or perhaps it's because I've just signed an exclusive deal with ITV to present a new chat show, which will pit me right up against…Mr Ross.

Either way, I've written a pretty acerbic riposte to him in my *Mail on Sunday* column. If he wants a public spat, he can have one.

FRIDAY, 25 JULY 2008

Barack Obama is on a tour of Europe, and 200,000 people turned out to see him in Berlin.

It was almost a carbon copy of the mad scenes that greeted JFK's famous 'Ich bin ein Berliner!' speech over 40 years ago.

Obama has got that 'something'. He is, as Rupert Murdoch has put it, a 'rock star'. It doesn't bother me that he's not had much experience running things, because George Bush had, and he has been one of the worst presidents of all time.

What Obama does seem to have is a calm head – his team's motto for the campaign is 'No drama, Obama' – and the ability to take people with him. And that, in politics, is a rare thing.

He also has global appeal. People in other countries like him, from Africa to Europe.

And at a time when America has never been more despised, this could be a massively valuable healing tool if he becomes president. That's still a very big 'if' though. McCain is a street fighter, and early polls suggest he is marginally ahead of Obama.

SATURDAY, 26 JULY 2008

Abi Titmuss has written an autobiography, and during one promotional interview for it described her literary tome thus: 'It's kind of racy, very funny, a lot of surprises – I really don't think that it will be exactly what people expect. It's like Piers Morgan meets Bridget Jones on rocket fuel.'

Of all the compliments I've ever received (not an extensive list, it must be said), this is quite comfortably the least helpful.

MONDAY, 28 JULY 2008

I've flown to Monaco for a week to film an ITV documentary on the billionaires' favourite tax-free playground.

My arduous task this morning was to drive David Coulthard round the famous Grand Prix circuit that snakes right through the streets of the Principality.

I've never met Coulthard before, and on first glimpse he looked a little the worse for wear.

'Blame him,' he groaned, pointing to a shame-faced character lurking in the shadows. It was Amanda's fiancé Chris, who also happens to be Coulthard's best mate. 'We've had a long weekend partying.'

This lengthy binge included a trip to Monaco's top nightspot Sass on Saturday.

'It was a surreal night,' said Coulthard. 'Bono got on the microphone with some mates and sang "Wonderwall" by Oasis. But it was terrible first time, so they did it again. And the second time it was brilliant.'

And that wasn't all.

'Felipe Massa was in there too, and the cheeky bastard sent me over a pot of green tea. So I sent him back a bottle of champagne with a note saying: "You should try getting on a few more podiums then you might drink a bit more of this."'

Later, as we sat in our convertible Mercedes by the harbour, a very attractive and buxom German lady spotted us, and spent the next 15 minutes stripping and writhing around her nearby car in a flagrant display of outrageous flirting.

'Sorry about that, Piers,' laughed Coulthard, 'occupational hazard.'

'What makes you think it was for your benefit?' I replied.

TUESDAY, 29 JULY 2008

Still on the Formula One theme, I dined tonight at Pulcinella, the regular local restaurant of Monaco's most notorious resident, Max 'Spanker' Moseley.

When I grilled the owners about him, they launched a stoic defence of 'a delightful, charming, generous man'.

And then they showed me a copy of a hilarious email doing the rounds that defends the world's oldest profession. It shows two photos, one of Heather Mills-McCartney and the other of disgraced New York governor Eliot Spitzer's high-class hooker, Ashley Dupré.

And it reads:

'One of these women is 38, very ugly, and cost Sir Paul McCartney £25 million for four years of mental torture. The other is 22, very beautiful, and cost Eliot Spitzer just £2,000 for a night of pleasure, which works out at £2.9 million over four years. You do the maths.'

Later, I called Vinnie Jones in Los Angeles.

'Sorry, mate, can't talk now, I'm in the middle of an earthquake.'

'*What?*'

'Yeah, just kicked off. I'm on the fourteenth floor of the Four Seasons hotel and it's rocking all over the place. Call me later!'

Click.

WEDNESDAY, 30 JULY 2008

I found myself sitting two feet away from Leonardo DiCaprio in the Sass bar tonight. The privacy-obsessed actor looked very short, very scruffy, very miserable, and wore an attention-seeking baseball cap tightly clamped over his head, as if to say: 'LEAVE ME ALONE, I AM A MAJOR STAR.' A precaution that proved to be a tad unnecessary as nobody bothered him all night, or took his picture. Monaco has outlawed paparazzi, and the locals are far too rich and cool to bother celebrities.

To my amusement, Leo ended up being 'papped' by his own friends on their mobile phones. Presumably to cheer him up.

THURSDAY, 31 JULY 2008

Dining at the stunning Anjuna beach restaurant down the road from Monaco in Eze tonight, I bored the production crew with tales of my 'good mate Bono' who has a house there.

'We once sang a duet of Charlene's only hit "I've been to Paradise but it's never been to me",' I insisted (truthfully), to six sharply raised eyebrows.

I could see them all thinking, 'I bet the name-dropping little twat has never even met him.'

At 10 p.m., a large group swept past our table.

Bugger me if it wasn't Bono and his mates. Six eyebrows shot excitedly up again, this time conveying the collective sentiment of 'Right, now we'll find out, won't we…'

I stood up and marched over to the U2 superstar, completely unsure as to whether he would even acknowledge my existence.

'Please recognise me,' I begged him telepathically.

'Bono, how are you?'

He stopped dead in his tracks and peered at me through his shades (yes, he does still wear them when it's dark). My credibility hanging in the air like Evel Knievel tottering on a Grand Canyon tightrope when the wind got up.

'Hey…Piers…how are you, man?'

He smiled, shook my hand, patted my shoulder and I almost fell to my knees with pathetic gratitude.

'I'm fine, thanks. Just down here filming a documentary on Monaco.'

'It's a great place.'

'I don't suppose you'd consider saying that on camera?'

Bono looked like I'd just asked him to parascend naked off the roof of the Monte Carlo casino.

'No, I wouldn't!'

'Fair enough. Out of interest, why is it so great?'

'You don't want to hear my answer…'

'Oh, I do…'

'Oh, you don't…'

'Try me…'

'OK. Three words. No. Fucking. Paparazzi.' Then he roared with laughter.

'I heard about your singing in Sass the other night.'

'What did you hear?'

'That you murdered "Wonderwall".'

'That's a myth.'

At which point his long-haired Irish mate interrupted. 'No, it's true. We did.'

Bono shook his head in disbelief.

'We *did*?'

His mate nodded. 'We did.'

'Fuck,' sighed Bono. 'I'd forgotten that…we must have been more drunk than I thought!'

FRIDAY, 1 AUGUST 2008

John McCain has launched a savage TV advertising attack on Obama, branding him a 'celebrity' – as if there could be no greater slur!

'He's the biggest celebrity in the world,' says the commercial, 'but is he ready to lead?'

It's actually quite clever, because Obama's celebrity power could engulf McCain's campaign if he's not careful. But by trivialising it, and using it as another stick to beat him with about his lack of experience, McCain has seized back the baton.

SUNDAY, 3 AUGUST 2008

Jonathan Ross emailed me first thing this morning, raging about my *Mail* column – and furiously denying one specific claim I made about his *Mirror* film reviews.

We had a lengthy, and 'frank', exchange of views for most of the day, with me refusing to back down, until he eventually said if I didn't print an apology then he would pass it all to his lawyers.

How pathetic. He whacks me on the airwaves all year, then squeals like a baby when I finally retaliate and threatens to call in his expensive lawyers to try and make me grovel.

Perhaps I should now sue him, too, for calling me a 'waste of space sculpted from lard' on the Charlotte Church show?

After all, he'd have to prove it, wouldn't he? And how is he going to legally establish that I am both a waste of space, and been sculpted from lard, eh?

MONDAY, 4 AUGUST 2008

Kevin Pietersen has been made England cricket captain.

As I pointed out to him, it must have been playing under my astute leadership in Newick that tipped the balance.

His first press conference was classic KP – passionate, confident, positive, fiercely patriotic and full of hyperbole.

I'm thrilled for him, and think he'll be a terrific skipper.

But I'm also very sad for Michael Vaughan, who was in tears at his own farewell press conference. He has been one of the greatest captains English cricket has known, and one of its most stylish batsmen, too.

TUESDAY, 5 AUGUST 2008

Chris Moyles has hurled himself into my mini-feud with Jonathan Ross.

'Piers Morgan is the most deluded man on the planet,' Moyles raged on his Radio 1 show today. 'Him calling Jonathan Ross simpering is like me calling someone overweight.'

Warming to his task, he added: 'I'm nothing but pleased for your American success, Piers, in fact I'll buy you a one-way first-class ticket to LA, get you a limo, everything. Just make sure you never come back to Britain again because NOBODY LIKES YOU, PIERS.'

This is all getting a bit nasty. I'm endlessly amused by how shockingly two-faced some of these 'celebrities' can be. When I met Moyles recently he couldn't have been friendlier.

THURSDAY, 7 AUGUST 2008

Paris Hilton has released a brilliantly funny spoof presidential campaign video in response to John McCain's jibe that Obama is just a lightweight 'celebrity' like her.

Reclining in a bikini by her pool, Paris says: 'Hey, America, I'm Paris Hilton and I'm a celebrity, too. Only I'm not from the olden days and I'm not promising change like that other guy. I'm just hot!'

Between flipping pages of a travel magazine, the 27-year-old socialite adds: 'But then that wrinkly white-haired guy used me in his campaign ad, which I guess means I'm running for president. So thanks for the endorsement, white-haired dude, and I want America to know I'm, like, totally ready to lead.' Paris then offers a bumbling alternative US energy strategy, suggesting that she plans to combine elements from Mr McCain's and Democratic rival Mr Obama's policy platforms. 'We can do limited offshore drilling with strict environmental oversight while creating tax incentives to get Detroit making hybrid and electric cars... Energy crisis solved, I'll see you at the debates, bitches!'

She signs off the ad by declaring that she is considering pop singer Rihanna as her vice-presidential running mate. 'I'll see you at the White House,' Ms Hilton says. 'Oh, and I might paint it pink. Bye.'

I laughed out loud when I saw it, but I doubt McCain will. It makes him look old, out-of-touch and boring.

FRIDAY, 8 AUGUST 2008
The Beijing Olympics kicked off in spectacular fashion last night, with one of the greatest opening ceremonies ever seen.

The Chinese are clearly going to try and send the world, and America in particular, a firm message with this event – we're the biggest country on earth now, and the best.

WEDNESDAY, 13 AUGUST 2008
Called The Ferret to discuss a TV offer I've received.

He sounded strangely muted.

'You OK?'

'Not really, no. Some guy attacked me in a restaurant.'

'Why?'

'No reason. Seriously. I had never met him before. I just sat down in this restaurant, started looking at the menu and this lunatic came over, started shouting at me and then hit me.'

Random violent crime is worryingly prevalent in America.

The Hoff told me recently that he's heard of Latino gangs in South Los Angeles whose initiation test is to indiscriminately shoot from a bridge at cars on the 405 Freeway.

It's easy to get complacent about crime if you're cocooned somewhere like Beverly Hills. But there are large parts of LA, as in most large American cities, that are seriously violent no-go areas.

And the prisons, as a result, are getting fuller by the day. In 1973, 200,000 Americans were in jail today there are well over a million. And as jail conditions deteriorate due to overcrowding, so does any chance of effective rehabilitation.

The answer, I'm sure, is tougher policing. New York has had tremendous success in tackling serious crime, mainly by flooding the streets with more coppers. It looks, and feels, a massively safer place than it did when I first went out there in the mid-eighties.

THURSDAY, 14 AUGUST 2008

Today, I received a bizarre offer from the police after I was recently caught doing 36mph in a 30mph limit. They said I could either accept the usual three points, or sit through a three-hour lecture on how to drive properly, somewhere in Ealing.

I was pondering the absurdity of this when I decided to nip out and buy a cake.

I parked my gleaming new Maserati Gran Turismo in a quiet Wandsworth side street, and spent approximately five minutes purchasing a very pleasing lemon tart. Then, as I went to leave the shop, it began to rain. Heavily. In fact, I've never known a lashing like it – there were hailstones the size of small rocks cascading down amid the several inches of water. I was forced to stay inside for my own safety.

After 20 minutes, the astonishing downpour began to ease and I returned to my car. Or rather, to where I'd left my car.

It was gone.

As I stood, open-mouthed with horror and fury, a wizened old man approached me. 'Was that your Maserati?'

'Yes.'

'They towed it away.'

'What, in the middle of that storm?'

'Yes.'

I stopped a passing cab and went to the pound, where they charged me a ridiculous £260 to retrieve my vehicle. Turning my cake into one of the most expensive gastronomic treats ever purchased.

My seething mood was not enhanced by one of the pound officials exclaiming: 'Hey – you the guy off *Britain's Got Talent*! Can I show you my dancing skills?'

And then doing a pitiful little jig in the puddles. God, where is a red buzzer when you need one?

SATURDAY, 16 AUGUST 2008

I've fled once again with Celia to the far more civilised and elegant confines of Paris.

The hotel we're staying in, near the Latin Quarter, names all of its rooms after famous French writers like Proust and Stendhal.

But my one left me stumped – it was called simply 'Curnonsky'.

Further investigation revealed this was the pen-name of Maurice Edmond Sailland, the Michael Winner of Paris, only ten times as powerful.

This extraordinary character was known as the 'Prince of Gastronomes', a title he was awarded in a public referendum in 1927, and one that nobody else has been given since. It is said that at the height of Curnonsky's prestige, 80 restaurants around Paris would hold a table every night just in case the great man showed up.

He was loved and loathed in equal measures. And the parallels with our own magnificent Mr Winner don't end there. In his later years Curnonsky was so heavy he was unable to walk and had to be carried by six friends to his favourite restaurants. Rather ominously, though, at the age of 84, Curnonsky leaned too far out of his window and accidentally fell to his death.

SUNDAY, 17 AUGUST 2008

Usain Bolt won the Olympic 100m race today, smashing the world record in the process with a time of just 9.69 seconds.

If he had been an American, the TV coverage would have exceeded that of the moon landing here. But because he's a Jamaican, winning an event usually dominated by Americans, there is a total lack of excitement about it on TV and in the papers.

I watched NBC's news tonight, and it devoted almost wall-to-wall coverage instead to their homegrown hero Michael Phelps, the extraordinary swimmer who later tonight won his eighth gold medal.

Americans, as I've discovered, only really care about their own sportsmen. Much as they only really care about their own news.

WEDNESDAY, 20 AUGUST 2008

Let's be honest, I've led a pretty glamorous life.

Yachts, palaces, Aston Martins, lobsters, private jets, magnums of Krug – you name it, I've either guzzled it, driven it, flown it or just stood in awe and gawped at it (Pamela Anderson's cleavage).

But just as Conrad Black is finding at the moment, gilt-edged privilege can't always spare you the vengeful wrath of that sinister global organisation, 'The Authorities'.

Which is why I found myself entering an office block in Ealing, West London, this morning to receive a three-hour lecture on how to rehabilitate myself from my criminal driving activities.

My heinous offence was to be caught doing 36mph in a 30mph zone. Normally, you'd get three points on your licence. Now, the police are offering an alternative – a 'speed awareness course', conducted by a professional driving instructor.

Curiosity got the better of me, so I took up the offer and arrived at the designated room at 8.30 a.m. to be met with huge smirks from the other inmates.

'Britain's got no driving talent then!' said one.

'Not got that Mr Loophole's number then?' quipped another.

'It happens to the worst of us,' I muttered, uncomfortably.

When the full 20-strong party of offenders had arrived (14 men, five women), we were led into what looked like a school classroom full of desks and computers.

Our lecturer arrived. His name was Dave, he wore a short-sleeved white shirt and tie, and he was extremely keen to establish his headmasterly credentials.

'This is a Highway Code, yeah?' he announced, lovingly holding a copy aloft. 'And you should all buy one because YOU DO NEED TO KNOW THE RULES, yeah?'

The man next to me sighed audibly. This was going to be a long morning.

'You're here to gain a fuller understanding of why people drive above the speed limit, because…'

Dave paused for dramatic effect.

'... bet you've all DONE IT BEFORE, yeah?'

Most of the room nodded gravely, as I tried not to laugh out loud. Dave looked, sounded and behaved exactly like David Brent from *The Office*.

'I want to encourage group interactivity, yeah,' he announced.

One man, sitting in the front row, and wearing a tank top and glasses, stuck his hand up every two minutes.

'Any advanced drivers here?' asked Dave.

'ME!' said The Swot, proudly.

And so on.

Dave then announced that we were all to submit ourselves to a written test on our computers.

The first part was a Q and A containing – and this is not a joke – questions like:

Q. Keeping to the speed limit in the next year would be wise?
A. 1) I agree very strongly 2) I don't know 3) I disagree very strongly.
And:
Q. Breaking the speed limit in the next year would be enjoyable?
Same choice of answers.

Part two involved real virtual situations of road hazards. Most involving wandering lorries and grannies. It was like playing *Grand Theft Auto*, only not quite as exciting.

After 15 minutes, I'd finished.

First.

I felt an odd, slightly disconcerting, flush of pride.

'Well done,' beamed Dave, admiringly, 'go and get yourself a coffee!'

We were handed our results afterwards.

My speed and 'hazard perception' was higher than average, but apparently I kept further away from vehicles in front of me than most.

As for my 'emotional feedback' (i.e. potential road rage), I was 'higher than average'. But Dave dismissed that category with a curt and intriguing: 'I don't want to go there. I really don't...'

Then he added, with the suspicion of a leer: 'Any thrill-seekers here? Because that's a very different workshop...'

Dave pulled himself together, and asked, 'Why did you all come today?' confidently expecting, I think, to hear the answer: 'To hear your brilliant lecture, Dave.'

The class answered loudly as one: 'To save points on our licence.'

Dave shook his head slowly, more in sorrow than anger.

'Would any of you have come anyway,' he pleaded Brent-style, 'even if the points couldn't be saved?'

He couldn't be serious, surely? Why would any of us have voluntarily taken half a day off work to trawl across London to listen to Dave banging on for three hours about how to avoid doing a few miles over the speed limit?

But no, to my astonishment, one hand raised itself. Another front-row teacher's pet. 'I would have, yes.'

'Great,' cooed Dave. 'That's GREAT!'

He then tried to explain the point of the exercise: 'I would tentatively use the word "re-educate" but then you all know it all anyway, don't you, yeah?'

Yes, Dave, we do.

'We have the safest roads in Europe, and safest motorways in the world,' he declared, with a smug look that just screamed 'thanks to people like me'.

He then blasted us with horrifying statistics of injuries and fatalities involving cars, thus rather negating the impact of his previous statement.

''Ow many are caused by bloody cyclists?' said a shaven-haired man in row six, to a rumbling murmur of approval.

Dave, visibly indignant at this outbreak of classroom insolence, ignored him.

'And now we come to my favourite question,' he drooled. 'Do you know all the national speed limits?'

'There are two for carriageways,' interrupted the shaven-haired man.

Dave froze in horror. 'Go and stand in the naughty corner,' he barked, 'you've spoiled my fun.' There was not the faintest glimmer of humour on his stern face.

His mood deteriorated further as general boredom engulfed the class.

'What did I tell you?' admonished Dave as someone asked a question he'd already answered seconds before.

'LISTEN!'

He cupped his hand to his ear menacingly.

'WHAT. DID. I. TELL. YOU?'

And then came the most shocking moment of the morning.

'I have offended,' said Dave, in a new very serious tone. 'I got three points for speeding at 5.30 a.m. a few years ago.'

The room fell silent as the enormity of his confession sank in.

'And as a result, I am now the person who holds everybody else up in traffic, because I WILL NEVER EVER SPEED AGAIN, yeah.'

As fewer and fewer people showed any reaction to anything he was saying, Dave suddenly exploded: 'ENGAGE! COME ON EVERYONE! ENGAGE!'

But I couldn't, Dave. I just couldn't.

You'd sucked the very life out of me, and there was nothing left to give.

He left us with the following stunning conclusion:

'Remember this when you go home today: the faster you go, the MORE CHANCE THERE IS OF HAVING AN ACCIDENT, yeah.'

Thanks, Dave.

Next time I'm taking the points, mate, yeah.

THURSDAY, 21 AUGUST 2008

I'm back off to LA for six weeks tomorrow, so spent last night having a 'Last Supper' with the boys.

We watched the Will Smith movie *The Pursuit of Happyness*, and at the end, I observed solemnly: 'The motto of this film is always live your dreams boys, then you can achieve anything...'

There was a contemplative silence, until Stanley, 11, finally responded, very slowly, on behalf of the group:

'Oh. God. Dad thinks he's Martin Luther King...'

I arrived in the sumptuous first-class BA lounge at Terminal 5 this morning, and bumped into Jemima Khan, who reacted – as she does, oddly, every time we meet – by recoiling in mock horror, going bright red and beginning to palpitate.

'Oh gosh, I'm blushing,' she sighed. 'Why do I always feel so weird when I see you?'

'Settle down,' I laughed, 'I'm not Hannibal Lecter.'

I've no idea what provokes this reaction in the radiant Jemima; I can only assume that having dated Hugh Grant, it must be truly shocking to encounter a genuinely good-looking, witty and intelligent man.

FRIDAY, 22 AUGUST 2008

Arrived in LA to learn that the American sprint relay team dropped the baton both in the men's and women's races last night.

What was fascinating was the way this barely got a mention on the news, or in the papers. And that's purely because it would highlight American failure.

It's the same reason the TV networks never show the planes crashing into the Twin Towers any more.

Americans celebrate success, and hide failure. It's their great strength, and possibly one of their greatest weaknesses, too. Because surely only by embracing failure, and learning from it, can a country truly grow in the modern age.

One of the best shows on American TV is *The Wire*, a hard-edged drama series starring a British actor, Idris Elba – who was recently named one of the 'ten hottest men on the planet'. So my eyes were drawn to a big interview he gave in *The Times* today, and then extended on to stalks of mounting fury when I read the last three paragraphs:

'I ask if he has a girlfriend… "Yeah, I'm dating. I'm not in a full-time relationship, and I like that." In spite of Elba's new-found openness, he declines to tell me any further details about his new female companion. Judging by his glances at our waitress, however, I can't help but wonder how long that'll last. "I should date that girl who interviewed me in New York," he says, turning to his manager. "What was her name again?" As it happens, I have the printout of the article in front of me: the interviewer's name was Celia Walden. "That's her," he says. "She's gorgeous." I tell him there's only one small problem with Ms Walden: she's dating Piers Morgan. Elba gives me a horrified look. And then he confirms what I suspected all along: that when he left England behind along with all those dud Ford Fiestas, he did so without ever looking back. "Piers Morgan?" he says. "Who's that?"'

SATURDAY, 23 AUGUST 2008

Met up with Donald Trump today, at his palatial new home in Beverly Hills, to interview him for GQ. I thought it would be a compelling couple of hours, because nobody embodies modern America more than Trump.

He's tough, ruthless, charming, passionate, patriotic and, above all else, a winner.

As if to emphasise this last fact, he spent the first 15 minutes taking me on a guided tour of the immediate neighbourhood. 'I'm buying the whole street, house by house,' he chuckled. 'And I'll make a ton of money out of it when I'm finished!'

We sat down in his ludicrously extravagant sitting room, and he fired an imaginary starting pistol.

'OK...let's go. Whatever you want to ask. When I heard about this, I figured: what can my man Piers do, kill me?...Can you kill me?'

'I doubt it. Your staff told me the interview would last as long as your attention span did. How long is that normally?'

'It can be long, or short, depending on who I'm with. My attention span with intelligent people can go for ever. I'm sure you'll do OK.'

This was classic Trump, aggressive, challenging, flattering and threatening – all in one sentence.

I was curious about his thoughts on the Olympics, given the way the Chinese powered their way to gold medal triumph by bending most rules sidewise.

'I think all that stuff with them fielding 14-year-old girls and lying about their ages shows that China is a country prepared to bend the rules, whereas America has become so politically correct that it is very, very hard for us to compete with them. We are going against people who don't understand the meaning of political correctness. And at a time when we should be sending up our best and brightest to take them on, we have Condoleezza Rice negotiating for us. A woman who has done nothing, made not one deal in eight years. She goes to countries, shakes hands with lots of people and comes home with nothing. It's incredible. We need our best people to deal with countries like China, Russia and India as they get bigger and better. Instead we send average people.'

'Talking of average people, how much damage has George Bush done to America's reputation?'

'I think he has set back this country 50 years. We were a great country before he became president. A respected country. Whether you like Clinton or don't like Clinton, we had no deficit for the first time in many years, and were doing well economically. And then Bush came in, and wrecked it. After 9/11, America had the chance to be the most popular country in the world, and instead, in a matter of weeks, that man destroyed it. We are no longer respected like we used to be, no longer the place where people want to invest to the extent that they did before. We have been seriously hurt by Bush and his cronies. I think he will go down as the worst president in the history of the country. A disaster. Obviously we can make things up again, and recapture the glory. But right now, there is no glory for this country.'

It was astonishing to hear such a capitalist, republican businessman talk in this way. And indicates just how angry Americans are getting about the state of their country.

'How much of the damage is down to the Iraq war?'

'A lot. It's inconceivable what Bush has done. He invaded a country that had nothing to do with 9/11, absolutely zero. He purposely lied, and lied badly, and his lies got us into a war. But he wasn't impeached. Clinton was impeached for something that wasn't one millionth as important. Bush doesn't have the intellect to be president. When he said he reads 56 books a year...I say, give me a break. Of course he doesn't. And then he said he never watches television, which I don't believe either. Everyone does. Nothing he says is the truth.'

'Is America ready to vote for a black president?'

'Nobody knows. That is what makes it so fascinating. I like blacks and they like me. But in numerous other elections where a black candidate has been leading substantially, they either didn't win or it is a much closer "squeaker" than anyone predicted. Race is a huge factor.'

Trump almost went bust in the early nineties, so I was intrigued to see what his take is on the current credit crisis.

'Look, the last time this happened, I owed billions and billions of dollars, and nearly went under. Many of my friends went under. It was a very tough time. But I reacted positively. I went forward quite bravely I'd say given that so many people were going out of business. My theme was "survive till '95" and that turned out to be about right, because those who survived until then were OK.'

'What did you learn from that time?'

'A lot. Number one, I could handle pressure. A lot of my friends couldn't and just took the gas. I knew tough guys, or people who I thought were tough but who weren't with retrospect, who crawled into a corner, put their thumbs in their mouths and cried, "Mummy, I want to go home." I didn't lose sleep, I never ever gave up and I fought hard to survive. The biggest thing I learned is that economic cycles don't last for ever, they go up and they go down. And whatever you try and do to keep a cycle going, they end. Period. If you study the financial charts from 1900 to now, it's almost a perfect roller-coaster graph, it's amazing.'

'I studied your book *Think Big and Kick Ass* very carefully before doing the *Celebrity Apprentice*...'

'Ah...did you...that's probably why you won.'

'Yes, probably! But you have often renamed it in interviews as *Think Big, Be Paranoid.*'

'Yes, that's right. Paranoia means to me, as the boxers would say, "keep your left up". Never let your guard down. A lot of people rely on people, trust people, who betray them and take advantage of them.'

'How do you avoid that happening to you?'

'By hiring good people, and then watching them.'

'Do you actually fully trust anybody who works for you?'

'Very few, I don't want to trust people. Look, we are worse than the lions in the jungle. Worse than any predator. Lions hunt for food, to live. We hunt for sport. Our hunting involves doing lots of bad things to other people, whether it's stealing their money or whatever. People are bad, they really are! They're evil in many cases! So you have to keep your left up. People have to respect you. If they don't respect you then even if they are fairly honest they will start to steal from you. That's the way it is. Pretty sad, but true.'

'You've never touched alcohol?''

'No. Never. I had a brother who died of alcoholism. He was called Fred, and he was a very handsome guy, had the best personality. But he got into drinking at college and became an alcoholic, and I watched him disintegrate with alcohol. And he did something to me. He was 11 years older, and he told me never to drink or smoke. Drugs weren't really in vogue then or he would have added "don't take drugs either". He'd smoke three packs of cigarettes a day. And he hated smoking and drinking, but he couldn't stop it. He knew he had a problem, and didn't want me having it. I've never had a single glass of alcohol because I have genuinely never wanted to, and I'm proud of that. Alcohol is a terrible thing. I was with a very respected banker the other day, and we had to carry him out of the dinner because he was so drunk. And you lose respect for people when that happens. He is a smart, tough guy but he is unable to stop drinking. I've just seen too many people like that, men and women. And none of them can stop, it's unbelievable to watch. The reason they can stop drugs easier than alcohol is that drugs are a no-no. You can't go out to bars and openly shoot heroin into your arm. But you can drink anywhere. Society encourages it.'

'Are you a woman-holic?'

(Laughs.) 'Well, I love women, that's for sure. But I have a great wife, Melania, who is a spectacular mother. And we have a great relationship. But I do love women, definitely. I respect them, I think they're magnificent. And I don't just mean their physical beauty.'

'Are you a good husband?'

'I think I'm a great father'.

'That wasn't the question.'

(Laughs.) 'I answered a much easier question! I think I'm a good husband now. It's not easy for someone competing all the time with my business.'

'What have you loved more – your business or your wives?'

'I remember seeing John Paul Getty being interviewed on TV years ago, when I was very young. And they asked him a version of that question. They asked him if he had his time again whether he would rather be John Paul Getty the great financial genius, or would he rather have a great marriage. And he said he'd rather be John Paul Getty because many people have great marriages, but there is only one John Paul Getty.'

'Do you agree with that?'

'I do agree with that, but maybe you can have both.'

'What has brought you more happiness, women or money?'

'I know a lot of rich people who can't get a date. It's a funny thing. I read an article not so long ago that said women aren't just attracted to money, there has to be an attraction to the man as well. And I think that's true. I know rich, smart, cunning guys who just can't get a woman to go out with them.'

'Why?'

'Because they're missing something. I'll tell you a great story. A very, very rich friend of mine calls me recently because he knows I know a lot of great-looking women because I own Miss Universe and run a hot model agency. And they know I have a very good understanding with women. So he says he wants to go out with the particular woman, who I know very well. And this guy's got his G5, his beautiful houses, his cars – he's got everything money can buy. So I call this woman, and she's a top model, and she has no interest in going out with him at all. So I said, "Look, do me a favour, this guy's break-ing my ass, is it such a big favour to ask you to go out with him once?" And she just didn't want to. Then I said, "Look, he has a G5," and so on. And she still has no interest. But eventually she agrees to go on one date. And they go out, and she calls me afterwards and says, "Do me a favour now, never make me do that again. Just don't waste my time with guys like this." This is a guy who eats financial geniuses for a living, he beats up guys with his head. And he's got so much money he doesn't know what to do with it. But in front of a beautiful woman he gets lockjaw. Anyway, he calls me the next day and says, "Donald, that was the greatest woman I ever had dinner with. Would you do me a favour, and call her and ask if she will go out with me again?" Now think about that for a second. I can understand why I have to do it for the first date, but if I have to do it for the second one, too, then there's something wrong, right? And I know a lot of very rich guys who can't go out with a girl twice because they're so boring.'

'If I said to you now that you can have a cheque for ten billion dollars, but the proviso is you can't have sex for five years, would you take it?'

'No, I wouldn't. Because ten million dollars isn't a lot of money to me.'

'Ten *billion*.'

'Oh, ten *billion*. I might think about taking that!'

'And you could go five years without sex?'

'For ten billion dollars, sure. You can do a lot of things with ten billion dollars. You double up my net worth just by not having sex, sure. That's pretty good. I could do that.'

'So you're worth ten billion dollars already?'

'I think I'm worth around that neighbourhood, yeah.'

'That makes you one of the richest men in the world.'

'I live nicely, definitely.' (Smiles.)

'They say that every powerful man is good in bed. That true?'

'I think there is a certain truth to that, yes.' (Chuckles.) 'Now, some powerful men are gay, and I'm sure they're good in bed with their gay lover. But I think there is a truth to it. Put it this way, I've never had any complaints.'

'What is the secret to being good in bed?'

'I think there are a lot of secrets. A lot of it is down to The Look. Don King, the boxing promoter, is a great friend of mine, and he is a believer in The Look. He doesn't mean you have to look like Cary Grant, he means you have to have a certain way about you, a stature. I see some successful guys who just don't have The Look. And they are never going to go out with great women. The Look is very important. I don't really like to talk about it because it sounds very conceited…but it matters.'

'You're the perfect person to ask this question: can money buy happiness or not?'

'I couldn't live without money, not because I need the money so much because I don't need to live in lots of great places. No, I couldn't live without it because it's a game. I wouldn't be the same person without money.'

'Do you live for the money itself, or for the deal?'

'Both. Money is the scorecard. If I didn't have money then it would mean that I am not very good at what I do. Does that make sense?'

'Totally. You're motivated by success.'

'I am, I like success. And I like being successful. I am very competitive. I like winning when I study, when I play sport, when I'm in business. I like to win.'

'So what would your tombstone say?'

'I put a lot of people into work, I have done a lot of really good jobs and I really believe that in terms of the word 'quality' there is nobody that tops me.'

'And personally?'

'Good father, sometimes good husband' (laughs), 'a loyal friend. I'm a loyal guy, and I'll give you an example. Choosing you as my *Celebrity Apprentice* was a tough thing for me. Because you're a smart, tough guy, but you're abrasive, too, and everyone loved Trace Adkins, and the easiest and most popular thing to do would have been to let him win. I had so many people telling me to do that. But I did what was right, you deserved to win. And you had some pretty high-powered friends telling me I should choose you, too! I was surprised by that. The politically correct thing to do was choose Trace, but I did the right thing because I chose a winner. And a funny thing happened: from the day after the finale, everyone started saying, "Hey, you did the right thing choosing Piers."'

'But that's because America loves winners, period. And you, more than possibly anyone else in the country, personify the word "winner".'

'You've gotta win. That's what it's all about. You know, Muhammad Ali used to talk and talk, but he won. If you talk and talk but you lose, the act doesn't play. I gotta go.'

As he leapt from his seat, Trump invited me to join him later this evening at a £3 million party to launch some vast new hotel he's opening in Dubai.

It was a typically over-the-top lavish Trump affair: 600 VIP guests including Orlando Bloom, Hilary Swank and P. Diddy, entertained on a sprawling Bel Air estate. And when I say 'entertained', there were stilt-walkers, iced bowls of caviar, an Apple iPod Touch for everyone as they left and, most impressively of all, The Donald had arranged for Christina Aguilera to perform a surprise gig in the back garden.

As we listened to her belting out 'Beautiful', I asked one guest, a friend of The Ferret's called Brian, what he thought of Trump.

'He's a true American,' he replied, without hesitation.

'What do you mean by that?'

'I mean that he's a winner, a success story. He works hard, plays hard and believes in his country.'

'Isn't he too brash and arrogant?'

'Maybe, but what's wrong with that? It's that kind of attitude that made America the greatest country on the planet. Trump epitomises the "anything's possible" thinking that underpins the United States. Schwarzenegger has it, too. These guys go for it, they speculate to accumulate, they talk the talk and walk the walk. And they love their families, the military and America.

'And people respect them for that, hugely. It's a shame they're not actually running the country, because we wouldn't be in the mess we're in now.'

I came away from my day with Trump thinking the same.

What America needs is leadership with brains. Smart, confident guys who can instil a new sense of pride to the country, rebuild it economically and restore its reputation for fairness.

Trump, from what I saw during the making of *Celebrity Apprentice*, always had a keen sense of fair play. He didn't like bullying, and he treated everyone with respect until they disrespected them. And his own extraordinary self-confidence is just contagious.

Towards the end of tonight, Trump swaggered by and slapped me on the shoulder.

'Isn't this terrific?'

'Yes, Mr Trump.'

'I mean, this is the greatest party ever, right?'

'Yes, Mr Trump.'

And in that split second, I believed it to be true.

America needs a leader who can do that, who can look them in the eye, slap them on the shoulder, and say: 'We're the greatest country in the world, right?'

And the whole country feels compelled to shout back: 'Yes, Mr President.'

SUNDAY, 24 AUGUST 2008

Pounding away in the Beverly Wilshire gym this afternoon, I noticed a small, wiry old man creep in.

He was bespectacled and wearing a brown Oasis-style hat, white T-shirt, green shorts, multi-coloured Jon Snow socks and the latest hi-tech Nike trainers.

But there was something vaguely familiar about him, albeit through my sweat-encrusted, slightly glazed eyes, 20 feet away.

I continued running, as he clambered aboard a power-walking machine and began a slow but determined session that lasted more than 45 minutes, muttering to himself quite regularly.

As time wore on, he began to slump, clinging on to the handles either side for dear life. At one point I even thought he'd fallen asleep, despite the music blaring through his iPhone earplugs.

It was a curiously comical scene, and a familiar one in Hollywood where even 95-year-olds feel compelled to risk life and limb in constant strenuous training activity to keep 'The Look'.

We both finished around the same time, and limped like limbless tortoises towards the exit door, both broken men.

I opened it for him, and he looked up plaintively, and wheezed breathlessly: 'Thank you.'

And it was then that I realised I'd just shared a uniquely LA moment with one of my all-time movie heroes, Woody Allen.

We trudged back through the ranks of holidaymakers sunbathing by the pool, none of whom showing the slightest recognition or interest in this global legend amid their ranks. (And they didn't spot Woody, either…)

I got back to my room, checked him out on Google and discovered he's 72 years old.

And, to my amazement, the great man followed exactly the same gruelling 4 p.m. routine every day this week, without ever once cracking a smile.

It was all rather disheartening. Woody, of all people, should resist this self-improvement nonsense.

MONDAY, 25 AUGUST 2008

Barack Obama has snubbed Hillary Clinton, and chosen Senator Joe Biden as his vice-presidential running mate. The reason, when you read Biden's biography, is obvious – he's steeped in foreign policy history, the one area where Obama is deemed to be most inexperienced. Biden's also white, old, grey, reassuringly serious and boring, and, amusingly, prone to acute verbal diarrhoea with journalists. This might well prove to be Obama's most critical decision. He knows, as everyone knows, that America remains at its heart a very conservative, pretty racist country. And to make himself electable he needs people around him who tick all the boxes that his black, youthful skin most definitely won't in places like Houston and Kansas. Biden seems a smart move. The TV networks here are in complete election overdrive, clearing the decks for any tiny new development. It makes it all seem like the most important thing in the world, which in many ways it is. And come election day there can literally be nothing left that the American public haven't been told about the two candidates. It also means that whoever wins has built up a huge, and pretty deep, reservoir of fascination, support and warmth. In direct contrast to our own frantic six-week campaigns in Britain, where we're often left asking: 'Who IS this guy?'

Late tonight, Boris Johnson formally received the Olympic flag from the Chinese in Beijing.

'I say this respectfully to our Chinese hosts who have excelled so excellently at ping-pong,' he chortled, 'but ping-pong was invented on the dining tables of England in the nineteenth century, and it was called wiff-waff. And there you have the difference between us and the rest of the world. The French looked at a dining table and saw an opportunity to have dinner, we looked at it and saw an opportunity to play wiff-waff. That's why London is the sporting capital of the world, and that's why I say to the Chinese and to the world, ping-pong is coming home!'

I laughed watching him, as did the audience, and his fellow star hosts David Beckham and Gordon Brown.

And for the first time, I began to feel rather pleased that Boris is our mayor. Because in a world of war, terror and financial disaster, it's actually quite nice to have a laugh every now and again.

The Democratic Convention kicked off as well tonight, and there were two extraordinary moments on stage.

The first involved Teddy Kennedy, who was supposed to be too ill to attend but who flew in at the last minute, staggered to the podium and delivered a spellbinding tour de force oration in support of Obama.

The Kennedys have always been the nearest thing to America's Royal Family, and Teddy is the last survivor of the three great brothers.

Now 76, and devastated by a recent brain tumour, he brought the crowd to a rousing ovation by thumping the lectern and declaring: 'Nothing, NOTHING, is gonna keep me away from this special gathering tonight.' And then again by comparing Obama to JFK, a link that will resonate strongly with every American.

'We are told that Barack believes too much in an America of high principle and bold endeavour,' he roared, 'but when John F. Kennedy thought of going to the moon, he didn't say, "It's too far to get there – we shouldn't even try." Our people answered his call and rose to the challenge, and today an American flag still marks the surface of the moon.'

It was a thrilling, and extraordinarily emotional, affirmation of Obama's 'Yes, we can' mantra.

And it followed a similarly powerful contribution from JFK's daughter, Caroline, who said: 'They share a commitment to the timeless American ideals of justice and fairness, service and sacrifice, faith and family. Leaders like them come along rarely. But once or twice in a lifetime they come along just when we need them most.'

After the Kennedys came Michelle Obama. It was the first chance I've had to see and hear her in action. She has been a controversial figure since claiming recently that Barack's rise to be the Democratic nominee was the 'first time I've been proud of my country in my adult life'. Everyone knew what she meant, of course, but it sounded all wrong to many voters.

She was greeted by the soundtrack to 'Isn't She Lovely?' by Stevie Wonder.

I laughed out loud, watching it on TV. Can you even begin to imagine the gales of hilarity that would have greeted Cherie Blair if she'd come out at a Labour Conference to 'You're Beautiful' by James Blunt?

But Americans love all this gushing nonsense.

Michelle's speech was polished, poised, immaculate, and yet...I didn't massively warm to her.

What I saw was a smart, overtly ambitious woman with her determined, beady eyes on the biggest prize in world politics, hitting every emotional button she could to help her husband attain it. Even down to dragging on their sweet little daughters at the end to talk to Daddy on the video screen.

It was calculating, it was manipulative and it was, ironically, rather emotionless.

She got a huge reception, naturally, and everyone lavished praise on her afterwards.

But I felt slightly disconcerted by her, and can understand why some think she's a negative rather than a positive. What she lacks is Barack's natural charm.

TUESDAY, 26 AUGUST 2008

The live *America's Got Talent* semi-shows started today, and The Hoff was on surreal form even by his standards.

After I criticised one absurd Britney Spears impersonator ('I don't think grown men called Derek should be dressing up as schoolgirls'), he leapt to his feet, shrieked 'I'm confused about my sexuality', then bared his rear to me – which revealed the words 'Back' and 'Hoff' on each cheek of his jeans.

Words, temporarily, failed me.

Later, the Californian warm-up man – Ian Royce had flown home to do *X Factor* – rallied the audience by talking about the Olympics and how brilliantly America had done.

'Britain had its best Olympics for 100 years,' I pointed out.

'Who cares, we still beat you!' he retorted, to loud cheers.

And the truth is that they don't care how Britain did here. The TV coverage has been almost exclusively about American successes – led by everybody's hero Michael Phelps.

WEDNESDAY, 27 AUGUST 2008

Every day, I call the boys and ask them – to their increasing boredom – the same opening question: 'Hi guys, what's the news?'

Today, Stanley sent me an email before I called them saying: 'Dad, look at this before we talk later, love Stan.'

I clicked on the Internet link...and was directed to the BBC News website. The cheeky monkey.

THURSDAY, 28 AUGUST 2008

Obama made his big conference speech tonight, and it was undeniably powerful and eloquent. But then, all his speeches are. He's a great speaker. But I didn't think this was one of his best.

The 80,000-strong stadium still rocked with cheers throughout, though.

He spent much of the speech linking McCain to Bush, which has to be the right tactic, pointing out that despite his reputation as an 'independent maverick', McCain has actually voted with Bush 90 per cent of the time he's been president.

His strongest remark, I thought, came when he said: 'America, we are better than these last eight years, we are a better country than this. I will restore our moral standing, so that America is once again that last best hope for all who are called to the cause of freedom.'

That, surely, is the reality of what Obama offers: hope.

America is fast waking up to the reality that the party's over as far as their nation being the only global super-power. Russia, China and India are all emerging as genuine rivals. And there will be others, too.

America, as Obama realises, needs to reassert itself as the country that people turn to for help, not the place everyone hates because it is a bully.

Tomorrow, McCain announces his running mate and builds up the anticipation for his own Republican convention next week. The clever money is on another heavy-hitting big name with bags of political clout and history to re-emphasise the one major difference between the two candidates – experience. Someone like Mitt Romney.

It's McCain's best card, and he knows it. If he can make America really doubt that Obama's ready to lead, he can win.

The Lipstick Bulldog in all her idiotic glory. Sarah Palin wowed America for about three weeks, but cost McCain any chance of winning the election in the process.

11

'I just want to say this. I want to say it gently but I want to say it firmly: there is a tendency for the world to say to America "the big problems of the world are yours, you go and sort them out", and then to worry when America wants to sort them out.' TONY BLAIR

FRIDAY, 29 AUGUST 2008

What the fuck??????

McCain has picked a virtual unknown 44-year-old woman called Sarah Palin as his running mate.

She's the Governor of Alaska, got her first passport in 2007, thinks rape victims cannot be allowed abortions, hates gays, loves capital punishment and guns, and said publicly last month that her home state of Alaska should opt for her suggestion for a new oil pipeline over a rival's because 'God wants it'.

She's also three years YOUNGER than Obama.

It has to be one of the most astonishing decisions in American presidential race history, and seems totally inexplicable to me.

Why, when your best asset is your experience, do you make your No. 2 someone with absolutely no experience at all? Particularly when you're 72, have had serious health problems and most Americans fear you may not make it through a full presidential term anyway?

It's a suicide note, surely?

I went to the gym, where CNN was blaring out the news to stunned Americans as they worked out.

One middle-aged man walked to the screen, shook his head and said simply: 'That's it. All over. What a stupid man.'

'Why do you say that?' I asked.

'Because she's a woman, she's dumb and she has no experience. The game's over.'

'Are you a Republican?'

'Yep, but that call just lost us the election.'

And off he went, muttering in fury to himself.

They've started showing clips from Palin's old speeches, and she sounds like a virtual parody of the dumb red-neck American.

There must be method to McCain's madness – but I can't for the life of me see what it is.

I rang The Ferret for his verdict.

'It's the Hail Mary play,' he said.

'Which is?'

'You've run out of any other ideas, it's near the end of the game, you've slipped behind in the polls, so you say a Hail Mary prayer and do something crazy.'

SATURDAY, 30 AUGUST 2008

They say you can always tell when your number's up in Hollywood when the pool attendants can't find you a sun-bed.

So I'd start selling shares in Jerry Springer plc.

We were dining together tonight, when I casually asked if he'd caught any rays during the baking hot afternoon.

'Don't go there!' he exclaimed, bitterness etched in his globally renowned face.

'Why?'

'Because I went down to the pool with my towel, my books, my sunglasses and asked for a bed. And this young guy looks at me and says, "I'm really sorry, Mr Springer, but we don't have any free at the moment." So I had to turn round and walk back to my bedroom, feeling crushed.'

'What time was that?' I asked, loving every second of this humiliating incident.

'Around 3 p.m.,' replied Jerry, mournfully.

'How strange,' I chortled, 'because I went down around 3.05 p.m. and they found me a bed straightaway.'

'You…you…' Jerry is too nice to swear, so didn't finish the sentence.

'Rest assured, though, I won't tell a soul…'

'Piers, you'll tell *everybody*,' he grimaced. 'I'm finished in this town.'

SUNDAY, 31 AUGUST 2008

Sarah Palin is everywhere. Every front page, every TV show, every Internet site.

By 6 p.m. this evening, she had more hits on Google (16 million) than Nelson Mandela – my favourite yardstick for assessing global fame.

And, to my amazement, she's giving McCain a real bounce in the polls.

Her description of herself as 'an average hockey mom from Alaska' seems to have struck a chord with women. Many of whom were perhaps disappointed by the failure of Hillary Clinton to win the Democratic nomination.

And more and more colourful and media-friendly details are emerging about her life to titillate the airwaves.

One of her children has Down's syndrome (hence her views on abortion), and another is about to head off to serve in Iraq. She was nicknamed 'Sarah Barracuda' at school for her aggressive basketball playing style, wears conservative black power suits, her hair raised in an uptail, eats moose meat and has shot and hunted all her life.

I find her utterly terrifying, the worst kind of dim, right-wing nutcase imaginable.

But she's getting all the attention, and middle America is enthralled by this brand new face on the election scene.

McCain may not be so stupid after all. He's found his own rock star.

Tonight, I watched the news, and saw that a big new Hurricane, called Gustav, is sweeping through the country.

Ever since the Katrina disaster in 2005, these hurricanes – which are quite regular in America – have taken on new significance.

Katrina killed over 1,800 people, most of them in New Orleans – where the great unspoken divide of America's wealth culture was cruelly exposed.

As the rich, white politicians sat in Washington wondering what to do, hundreds of poor black people died in the eye of a storm that should never have killed them, if security measures had been taken more seriously.

Caroline, who is making fantastic progress from her cancer, rang for a chat and revealed that she had covered the story for the *Mail*.

'Katrina showed for the first time how a major US city could break down, quite literally, overnight. I'd seen poverty in America before, but it's never been obvious like it is in somewhere like India or Africa. Katrina was the first time middle-class America came face to face with its dirty little secret – that there was a huge stratum of people below the poverty line. It was the most awful job I've had to do – the Superdrome, where they took all the dead bodies, was unbelievable – it just had this horrific stench of death, a sickly sweet smell of rotting bodies, faeces and urine that was impossible to scrub out of your mouth, hair, or clothes. I interviewed several families where four successive generations had never worked. And when I went back there to check out the relocation centres they set up in places like Houston, I saw the victims who survived spending their welfare cheques on flat-screen TVs and strippers.

'The whole Katrina episode was a massive shock to the American system. Like 9/11, they just never thought this kind of thing could happen here. And the truth that it exposed, about the terrible conditions many Americans were living in, really stunned them.'

MONDAY, 1 SEPTEMBER 2008

Jerry Springer and I were guests on LA's top breakfast TV show this morning.

'Don't even think about it,' he warned, as we sat in the green room.

Ten minutes later, we were live on air.

'So how have you guys been?' asked one of the hosts.

'Great,' I replied. 'Ask Jerry how his sunbathing's going…'

Jerry had the last laugh, though, when we left the studio and found our two limos waiting for us (even though we were being picked up and dropped off at exactly the same place, at exactly the same time, the Hollywood system dictates that no two stars can *ever* use the same car).

Mine was a perfectly nice Mercedes S500.

Jerry's super-stretch version was so big it could barely get out of the parking lot.

'I'm so sorry, Piers,' he chuckled, catching my envious eye. 'But that's showbiz, I guess.'

And then we departed, the only common denominator being that both cars had (genuinely) the words 'DIVA LIMOS' printed in big letters on the number plates.

Stayed in tonight, and watched the TV news shows going overboard, quite literally, with Hurricane Gustav.

Geraldo Rivera, the 'most fearless man on TV', actually reported live for Fox from the ocean as Gustav gathered pace in Louisiana.

It was hilarious to watch.

As the waves got bigger, and the wind stronger, so Geraldo waded deeper.

Until eventually he started getting knocked over, repeatedly.

'Every time you think it's going to be OK, Gustav comes again and bites you,' he shouted, as he was thrown to the ground for the fifth time.

A viewer rang in, concerned: 'Does Geraldo have a Plan B?'

To which the obvious answer was 'Yes – get out of the water you silly man.'

But Geraldo has built his name on this kind of heroic nonsense, so he stayed and fought the Hurricane, for what purpose only he knows.

As the night wore on, news broke that 29 people had been killed in a Los Angeles train crash. Yet Fox stayed predominantly with Geraldo and his one-man battle with Gustav.

Incredible, and yet perhaps not when you think about it. Most Americans genuinely care more about the weather than a train crash.

TUESDAY, 2 SEPTEMBER 2008

Obama's speech was watched by a record 38.4 million Americans, a bigger audience than the Beijing Olympics opening ceremony, this year's *American Idol* final and the Oscars.

To put this into political perspective, it was 57 per cent higher than the number who watched John Kerry's equivalent Democratic nominee acceptance speech in 2004, and that at the time was the highest convention speech rating ever.

Modern politics is as much about image as substance, and Obama is drawing the masses like nobody before him.

Late in the day, Sarah Palin reveals that her 17-year-old unmarried daughter Bristol is pregnant. A fact that would depth-charge most right-wing politicians' careers. But she's come out fighting, talking of facing up to a typical family problem and people seem to be supporting rather than berating her. Extraordinary.

McCain received more good news when Hurricane Gustav, which is still ravaging the country, prevented George Bush from speaking in person at the Convention.

You could almost hear the sigh of relief booming all over Minnesota. Bush's public support would be like an injection of cyanide to McCain – potentially lethal. His chances of success depend a lot on his ability to distance himself from Dubya as much as he can.

WEDNESDAY, 3 SEPTEMBER 2008

It's never a question of 'if' Sharon Osbourne is going to hit me during a live *America's Got Talent* show, only 'when' and 'how hard'.

Today, she started simmering like a lobster being boiled alive in a pot as I verbally coated some early acts, before finally exploding over a group called 'The Dancing Dads'.

These clowns are a bunch of 20 or so ageing fathers who say they're in the show for one reason – to please their daughters.

And not, of course, for the chance to win $1 million.

'Do you want me to judge you as dads or dancers?' I asked, when they'd finished their latest train wreck routine.

'As dancers!' they responded defiantly.

'OK then, you asked for it. I think if Fred Astaire had seen that performance, he'd have turned in his grave.'

Cue the usual cacophony of booing, then Sharon erupted.

'You WHAT?' she screamed. 'How DARE you?'

Then she tore up her notes, and flung the pieces over me as the crowd cheered her on.

As I cowered in terror, she stood up and began belting me round the head. At which point, my wheeled chair began to head backwards fast towards the edge of the judges' podium, and possible oblivion.

'Get off me, you madwoman!' I yelped pathetically.

'No!' she barked back, giving me one last smack across the shoulder. All good TV.

Talking of dangerous unpredictable creatures, I got back to my room tonight and watched Sarah Palin address the Republican convention.

'What's the difference between a hockey mum and a pitbull?' she drawled. 'Lipstick.'

But after watching her sneering, nasty, right-of-Genghis-Khan rhetoric for an hour, I don't think either description even comes close.

This woman is a walking, talking time bomb of stupidity, arrogance and the worst kind of bigoted, 'conservative' extremism. And if McCain gets elected and suffers another health collapse, she could actually be running the free world.

As the shock jock DJ, Russ Limbaugh, put it today: 'Babies, guns and Jesus. Hot damn!'

THURSDAY, 4 SEPTEMBER 2008

Another day, another pounding session in my hotel gym with Woody Allen.

I'm not saying the old boy's getting competitive with me, but halfway through our separate workouts today he suddenly ripped his T-shirt off, threw it on the floor and continued dementedly power-walking – topless.

Now, no disrespect to one of the greatest living film-makers, but there are some world famous chunks of human flesh that I still want to see before I die (Scarlett – you know where to find me) and 72-year-old Woody's scraggly, size one-below-zero, gleaming white torso is not one of them.

Quite put me off my cholesterol-free egg white frittata.

Even stranger, American chat-show legend Larry King came in later, and started running very slowly on the treadmill in a pair of *jeans*.

I think they should rename this place Hollyweird.

This evening, the McCains spoke to the Republican convention.

First up was Cindy, who couldn't be more different from Michelle Obama. White, surgically enhanced, peroxide-haired, rich and privileged.

But she, too, did a nice line in shockingly fawning, and rankly insincere, rhetoric – even dragging Mother Teresa into it at one stage.

As for her husband John, well, of course, he is the greatest man on God's earth.

'I know John,' she sighed, 'you can trust his hand at the wheel. A loyal, loving and true husband.'

Not something his first wife Carol would have said, of course, given the numerous affairs trusty old John allegedly conducted during their marriage.

Cindy then banged on about his war record again, setting us up for McCain himself to be introduced.

And just in case we'd forgotten, a lengthy nauseating video was played on giant screens showing yet more footage of him being stretchered out of Vietnam.

Not content with that, a large chunk of his speech was then devoted to his account of his own courage in that conflict.

It was all said with apparent humility, but, of course, what he was really telling America was: 'I'M A WAR HERO.' And each time he pressed that button, he got met with resounding cheers of 'USA, USA, USA.'

If a British candidate tried this kind of stuff, he'd soon get told to shut up.

Boasting, repeatedly, about one's own war heroism is just not the done thing in Blighty. Particularly when his main achievement seems to have been getting captured. But over here, nobody would dare cast any aspersions over such a shameless piece of manipulation.

McCain is a hero, and that's the end of it.

What this speech illustrated, though, was the extraordinary contrast between the two candidates.

White vs black, age vs youth, warmonger vs peacemaker.

America faces a real choice this time. And the positive aspect of this choice is that both candidates represent a major improvement on Bush. That much is unquestionable.

SATURDAY, 6 SEPTEMBER 2008

Jerry came up to me by the pool, now virtually empty because the holiday season has ended.

'They let you in then...' I laughed.

'Yes! And more good news, I've become a grandfather,' said Jerry, with a huge beaming grin of pride.

'And be honest, how does that word make you feel?' I asked.

'Well, I'm thrilled to have a grandchild, obviously, but clearly this has made me even more finished in this town!'

Meanwhile, Heather Mills' former PR adviser Michele Elyzabeth has branded her ex-client a 'lying, gold-digging witch'. Which is probably the nicest thing anyone's said about her in years.

SUNDAY, 7 SEPTEMBER 2008

I'm making an ITV documentary on Hollywood, and decided to play a little game with the paparazzi – who now infest every street corner of Los Angeles like a shoal of ravenous piranhas.

I enlisted Sharon and Ozzy Osbourne to have lunch with me at the Ivy. 'Let's just cause mayhem,' I ordered.

'Marvellous!' giggled Sharon, who is nearly as shy and retiring as I am.

I drove us all there in Ozzy's spanking new Bentley, as he regaled me with hilarious stories about celebrities behaving like self-obsessed cretins – 'That bloke off *Miami Vice*, Donny whatever he is [Johnson], used to give fans who came up to him a card saying they should contact his agent for an autograph. The fucking twat.'

Ozzy had me laughing so hard I nearly crashed us into a Beverly Hills roadsign. (That would have been quite a cool way to die, if it were not for the fact that the headlines would have said 'OSBOURNES DIE IN CAR SMASH' with a tiny note on an inside page adding: 'National joy as mean judge Morgan also meets his maker'.)

We were mobbed by more than 40 photographers as we arrived, and duly posed and preened for all we were worth – as my film crew filmed everything from a few yards away.

Then my other guests turned up – Heidi and Spencer from the smash-hit MTV reality show *The Hills*. They are not the brightest spanners in the tool-box, but they're tabloid gold dust at the moment, the Beckhams of Beverly Hills, and created another huge onslaught of flashing cameras as they headed to our table.

And finally Mel B shimmied in wearing a stunning silver dress, and came and sat next to me.

The paps by this time were almost expiring from excitement, and complete bemusement. I could see them all thinking 'what the hell are this lot doing having lunch together?' No other reason than to get you all over-excited, chaps.

A sentiment I shared when I casually mentioned to young Heidi that she had nearly as many hits on Google as Nelson Mandela.

'Nel...Nelson who?'

Her doe-like eyes stared at me blankly.

'You know who he is,' said a desperate Spencer.

'No, I don't,' she replied, firmly. 'Is he an actor?'

MONDAY, 8 SEPTEMBER 2008

Met former It girl, Lady Victoria Hervey, for tea this afternoon.

'Do you see much of Robbie Williams?' I asked.

'Not at the moment,' she replied. 'He's at a UFO convention with some friends of mine.'

I nearly spat out my Earl Grey.

'UFOs are the new religion here,' she explained, calmly. 'It's like Kabbalah, only for people interested in flying saucers.'

Later she revealed that she and Rachel Hunter take their pet hounds to see a local dog psychic.

'He talks to our dogs and tells us what they are thinking,' she said.

'I see, and what does he charge you for that?'

'Oh, about $200.'

Hollywood does very strange things to people.

TUESDAY, 9 SEPTEMBER 2008

I was having drinks with The Ferret at the Four Seasons Hotel tonight when he suddenly spied one of the stars of *Entourage*.

'We call him the Dalmatian,' he said.

'Why?'

'Because he's pretty to look at, but stupid enough to eat his own shit.'

His BlackBerry buzzed again, as it always does.

'How many emails do you get a day?'

'I counted them recently – over 1,000.'

'God almighty! How do you possibly deal with them all?'

'I prioritise.'

'Which is why you always reply to me immediately?'

'At the moment, yes…'

We talked about how Obama has used modern technology to brilliant effect in this election.

'Communication is the key thing now,' he said. 'Since 9/11, every American wants to stay in touch with what's going on. I met some soldiers recently and when I asked them what their most important possession was, they all replied their cell phone. They wanted to stay in contact at all times with their friends and family.'

WEDNESDAY, 10 SEPTEMBER 2008

I have been in Los Angeles for nearly a month, and just realised this morning that I haven't walked.

At all.

Anywhere.

I have, literally, not taken more than a handful of steps since I landed. Car to studio, car to hotel, car to restaurant, car to cinema, car to shops, car to beach.

The furthest distance I have walked is the 100 yards to the local paper shop and back, which I do every three days or so.

Otherwise, I have become a typical LA sloth.

The reason is simple – the roads are huge, the traffic lights slow, jay-walking is strictly forbidden, and so it can take 15 minutes just to walk a couple of blocks. Whereas parking is cheap, and valet parking plentiful.

It's just a lot easier to take the car.

Spoke to Caroline about this tonight, and she laughed:

'I valet park everywhere – at the bank, the grocery store, the shops, of course, at every restaurant. I even valet park at the frozen yogurt store, the airport, the gynae and the bank.

'Actually, I can't think of anywhere I don't valet park. It's the greatest invention ever. It just makes life so much more pleasant for everyone involved. I don't have to drive around in circles getting stressed looking for a space, the valet guys make a living (many valet services also offer a car wash) and everyone keeps their blood pressure nice and low. I don't know how you drive in England. I tried it once and nearly had a nervous breakdown.'

THURSDAY, 11 SEPTEMBER 2008

Sarah Palin gave her first sit-down TV interview to ABC's Charlie Gibson today, and the following exchange took place:

CG: Do you agree with the Bush Doctrine?
SP: (shifting in her seat uneasily) In what respect, Charlie?
CG: Well, what do you interpret it to be?
SP: His world view?
CG: The Bush Doctrine that preceded the Iraq War in 2002.

Looking like the proverbial rabbit in headlights, Palin rambles off about Bush's foreign policy in general, until Gibson stops her and says: 'The Bush Doctrine is we have the right to self-defence, pre-emptive strike against any country we think is going to attack us.' At which point the penny finally drops and she answers the original question.

This was more than car-crash TV, it was a multiple freeway pile-up of epic proportions. The woman who might in six weeks be 'a heartbeat from the presidency' has absolutely no idea what the infamous 'Bush Doctrine' actually is.

By complete contrast, General David Petraeus, who has been promoted to run US Central Command, said today that he will 'never claim victory in Iraq'.

'This is not the sort of struggle where you take a hill, plant the flag, and go home to a victory parade, it's not a war with a simple slogan,' he said. 'The situation is hard but hopeful. The progress is a bit more durable but there are still many storm clouds on the horizon which could develop into real problems.'

There is no doubt that the troop surge has been a success, and that the carnage has been stemmed.

Countrywide, daily attacks in Iraq have fallen from 180 this time last year to around 25, and there has been a drop of 80 per cent in civilian deaths. Street markets, even swimming pools, have reopened. And the economy is very slowly picking up.

Crucially for the future, the extra troops ordered in the surge have now been withdrawn, but the gains have held up.

But rather than gloat about it, Petraeus hits just the right tone – measured, cautious, thoughtful. And by maintaining this manner for the last 18 months, Petraeus has gone a long way to transforming the way the world views the American military machine, from warmongers to genuinely committed peacemakers and nation-builders. A remarkable achievement.

SATURDAY, 13 SEPTEMBER 2008
Purely for the purposes of investigative reporting for my ITV show, I interviewed Hollywood's top plastic surgeon Garth Fisher today.

He's done everyone from Pamela Anderson to Jordan, and specialises in face lifts and boob jobs.

'What were the biggest breasts you've ever created?' I asked.

'1400cc of silicone each,' he replied. 'Took her to a size "I".'

'Did it work?'

'Well, there were some gravitational issues to deal with,' he admitted, with a wry chuckle. 'I don't do them that big any more, or we'd have women falling flat on their faces all over town.'

I was keen to see what he might do with my own face.

'Let's see what we've got here,' he said, throwing my head into a large computerised scanning machine, and tapping some buttons.

Two minutes later, a detailed printout of my skin readings arrived.

Garth was momentarily silenced.

'Very disappointing,' he said.

'Really?'

'Yes, you're an 82 percentile.'

'What?

'That means you've got better skin than 82 per cent of men your age in Los Angeles.'

'That sounds good?'

'Good? It's brilliant. But it means I can't do anything with you, unfortunately.'

SUNDAY, 14 SEPTEMBER 2008

Spent the morning with Vinnie Jones and his new Hollywood Allstars football team.

'I'll get found out one day,' he laughed, as we enjoyed a big fry-up at his local café. 'But until then, I'm going to love every minute of it, my son!'

Vinnie's team is a hilarious mixture of former pros, ex-pat Brits, and Americans high on enthusiasm but low on technical expertise.

His star striker is Danny, a former Southampton player who is now a full-time porn star.

'He's not very good when he's had a long day at the office,' observed Vinnie.

By the side of the pitch was Danny's wife, adult entertainment legend Eva Angelina.

'We fell in love during a scene together,' she sighed. 'Danny was everything I've been looking for. And I mean *everything*!'

At the end of a ferocious training session, Vinnie shouted, 'Get him!' and his entire squad threw themselves on top of me, then threw me into the air ten times and engulfed me with water.

You can take the boy out of the Crazy Gang...

MONDAY, 15 SEPTEMBER 2008

The global economy has been deteriorating for months, and today it finally went into spectacular meltdown. Lehman Brothers, one of the biggest banks in the world, has collapsed. And another, Merrill Lynch, is under threat.

More immediately worrying for me is that AIG, the giant American insurance firm, is also in big trouble, and I have £175,000 saved in one of their premium bonds at the moment.

I rang my bank Coutts to try and get my money out, but was told that it wasn't possible, and that it may not be possible if AIG goes under. Only 10 per cent of my investment, which Coutts encouraged me to take out in the first place, is 'protected'.

I was stunned, and appalled.

If this is happening to me, then it's happening to everyone who has any money to invest. Banks, once the safest port in any storm, have just become the least secure.

Stock markets dived everywhere in this tumultuous day, and it will change the political, as well as the financial, landscape for years.

The credit crunch is all being blamed on American banks betting huge sums on those 'sub-prime' mortgages. And since this has all happened on the Republican administration's watch, it could have a devastating effect on McCain's chances of winning the election.

That careworn phrase about all elections coming down to 'the economy, stupid' has never seemed more appropriate.

I picked up the *LA Times* tonight and saw that *Little Britain* stars David Walliams and Matt Lucas have taken their show to America, which surprises me because but I just can't see their extreme, crude, lewd, lavatorial humour working here. Americans are strangely prudish, and easily offended by the kind of schoolboy filth that makes Brits fall about laughing.

Walliams tells the paper that British humour is 'much more cynical'.

'We have more losers, too,' says Lucas.

'Yes,' agrees Walliams, 'we have Mr Bean, we're the little men, we're nebbishes, we're the little man against the world, the underdog. America has The Fonz.'

But that's not really true any more.

The Brits who are successful over here these days are no longer the bumbling fools of Monty Python, Benny Hill and Bean.

They're the cool dudes like Hugh Laurie, tough guys like Daniel Craig, or the 'frank and honest' brigade like Simon Cowell and Gordon Ramsay.

And that's why I think *Little Britain USA* won't really work – it's celebrating a form of British eccentricity and failure that no longer resonates in America.

TUESDAY, 16 SEPTEMBER 2008

The Beverly Wilshire was in turmoil all day today, with security guards and police marksmen everywhere.

'What's going on?' I asked.

'Obama,' came the reply.

I felt a rush of excitement. I'd never seen him in the flesh, and was fascinated to discover what he actually looks like. McCain had been such a disappointment when I'd seen him in Dallas – small, old, tired and creased.

At 6 p.m., a cavalcade of cars swept into the valet parking area of the hotel and out stepped Obama.

He looked magnificent – tall, lithe, straight-backed.

Hundreds of people waiting to go into the event broke into wild cheering and applause.

He turned, waved and flashed that gigantic smile, and they went even crazier.

I haven't seen anything quite like it since I saw the Rolling Stones emerge from their Philadelphia hotel at the start of their *Steel Wheels* tour, to be met by a howling mob of devotees.

Obama strode inside with confidence and grace.

After he disappeared from view, the excitement lingered on in the crowd for some time.

This guy is political Viagra.

WEDNESDAY, 17 SEPTEMBER 2008

'Fancy dinner tonight?' read the email from Robert Earl, the billionaire tycoon behind the Planet Hollywood phenomenon.

At 9 p.m., I arrived at Koi, one of LA's hippest restaurants, and found Robert holding court out in the back terrace.

'An old friend is waiting for you,' he chuckled.

I turned to see Sylvester Stallone sitting at the head of the table.

'Sly!' I cried.

'Yo, Piers, how ya doing?' he drawled, standing up and bear-hugging me.

Stallone is perhaps my favourite celebrity in the world – I worshipped the Rocky movies as I grew up, and I've interviewed the great man everywhere from Aspen to Cannes.

I sat next to him, with Jim Belushi to my left.

'I took my kids to see *Rocky 6*,' I told Sly immediately. 'It was like a father-son pilgrimage. They loved it.'

Sly nodded. 'You know, I was so glad I did that movie. It brought me closure on *Rocky*. The fifth film was so bad, it always nagged me that I didn't make another one.'

'Will you make any more?'

'No, that's it. They want me to do him fighting some UFC champion, but why would I do that? Rocky is retired, it's over now.'

He still looks in incredible shape.

'How often do you work out?'

'I do three days on, three days off. And I push myself pretty hard…'

He flexed his absurdly large biceps and laughed. 'Well, my personal trainer pushes me hard!'

'Do you ever see Arnie these days?'

'Oh yeah, all the time. Actually, we meet for lunch every Saturday at the Café Roma in Beverly Hills. Arnold is a creature of habit so it's always the same time, same restaurant. I love seeing him, but it gets pretty competitive. If I turn up wearing a big new watch, then the next week he'll come with an even bigger more expensive one. If I wear some cool new boots, he'll turn up the next week in huge new cowboys! We're always trying to outdo each other, even now.'

'Do you think he'll ever make another movie?'

'No, I don't think so. He loves the politics. Arnold's had an amazing life, how many people have reached the top in three completely different careers – one physical, one visual, one intellectual? He's incredible.'

'Would you beat him in a fight?'

'Oh yeah, of course. Arnold's never been a street fighter… I know how to fight, you know what I mean?'

He fixed me with that Rocky Balboa stare.

I grinned, slightly nervously. 'I know exactly what you mean, Sly…would you have beaten Steven Seagal too?'

Sly nearly spat out his sushi.

'The last time I saw Seagal, I pushed him up against a wall and told him what I'd do to him if he went around badmouthing me any more. He's just a phony.'

Nelly, the rapper, arrived with his girlfriend Ashanti. This evening was getting more surreal by the minute.

'Who do you want to win the presidential election?' I asked Sly.

'McCain has to win,' he retorted angrily. 'I've never seen anyone as young and inexperienced as Obama even try to get to the White House. It's ridiculous. McCain is the real deal, he was a hero in Vietnam, he's fought for and served his country. What's Obama ever done?'

At 11 p.m., Sly got up to leave.

'I gotta go or my wife's gonna have my ass,' laughed the finest swordsman in Hollywood history.

'You've changed!' I said.

'I had to…when your back catalogue includes Brigitte Nielsen and Janice Dickinson, you have to keep a good woman when you get one!'

And with that, we exchanged another bear hug, one that nearly broke my shoulder.

'It was so good to see you again,' I whimpered.

'You too, man,' he replied. 'I like watching you on that *Talent* thing, you're quick with those buzzers…'

I nearly expired from joy.

THURSDAY, 18 SEPTEMBER 2008

I received an invitation today to attend a pre-Emmy 'gifting suite'.

'What are these all about?' I asked The Ferret.

'They're about grasping celebrities going to hotel suites to pick up a load of free presents in the run-up to the Emmy awards just because they're famous,' he scoffed.

'Seriously? You just turn up and help yourself to a load of expensive clobber, when you're not even an Emmy nominee?'

'Yep. Of course, no real star would be seen dead in one…'

An hour later, I arrived with Caroline at the venue, where I was greeted with huge excitement by a heavily sweating man with Cowell-esque teeth, and a loudhailer.

'Oh, this is AWESOME! From *America's Got Talent*, it's Pierce Morgan!' he exclaimed, getting my name wrong, as most Americans usually do.

But no matter, there was 'work' to be done.

A smiling woman appeared at my side clutching two vast holdalls.

'These are your bags,' she squealed. 'And we're gonna fill 'em all up for you!'

And for the next hour, that's exactly what we did, moving from stall to stall helping ourselves to designer clothes, jewellery, video games, dental care kits (the yanks just love their teeth…), huge whisky bottles, sunglasses, iPods, hats, cigars and even cuddly toys.

It was like the old conveyor belt on *The Generation Game*, only I didn't have to remember anything. They just piled it on, and my only requirement was to pose for a photo with each stall owner.

By the end, my poor aide was struggling to maintain her balance under my now mountainous bags.

'Who else has been in today?' I asked.

'Oh, lots of big stars like…erm…Bobby Brown!' she gasped.

At which I began to feel slightly uncomfortable.

'Anyone else?'

'Well, let me see now…'

As she gave it some thought, I spied Cuba Gooding Jnr leaving with his swagbag, and Paula Abdul heading in.

And I relaxed.

Later, watching TV back in my hotel, I caught Oprah Winfrey marauding around another gifting suite. And she's worth $4 billion.

America's the land of the free all right – the utterly shameless free-bie.

FRIDAY, 19 SEPTEMBER 2008

I flew to New York today to take part in a Dunhill-sponsored London vs NYC debate.

The flight took nearly six hours, which reminded me again of what an absolutely vast country America is. It takes a quarter of that time to fly from John O'Groats to Land's End.

And as you look down during the flight from the West to East coasts, all you can often see is large swathes of nothingness.

Prairies, mountains, lakes, desert. America has it all, and it's almost mind-bogglingly massive.

The 52 states that make up this extraordinary place are all basically countries in their own right. They have their own laws, their own moral codes, their own particular issues.

Yet despite the big social and cultural differences between many of them, America remains at its heart one entity.

Take one of them on, and you take them all on.

For pure patriotism, there is nowhere like it anywhere else in the world.

They were born with the stars and stripes imbedded in their psyche.

My debating opponent was Donny Deutsch, the American equivalent of Sir Philip Green.

The categories included black cabs vs yellow cabs, football vs 'football', and the relative merits of our current Queen vs President George W. Bush.

We both hurled insults at each other for two minutes on each topic, then the audience voted with little flags – American or British. Given that 90 per cent of them were Americans, I didn't hold out much hope of winning, but it was close. In fact it went down to a tiebreaking seventh subject – the Queen vs Dubya.

And when I tell you that I lost, you'll perhaps understand just how far that patriotism goes, and how blind it can be.

But it was more a vote for the presidency than for the current incumbent.

All Donny had to do was say, 'Wait a minute, are you going to let a Brit insult our president in our own country???' And suddenly all the Union Jacks got dumped.

Afterwards, Donny and I had a chat about the financial crisis.

'America is in big trouble,' he said. 'We don't produce anything, and our banks are fucked.'

When even guys like him are talking like this, you know that this country's problems run very, very deep.

I am detecting a real sense of vulnerability among Americans at the moment, of the kind we saw in the immediate aftermath of 9/11. I remember flying to New York three weeks after that atrocity, and it was like a ghost town, as everyone tried to come to terms with the enormity of what had happened. New York today seems pretty much the same. Cowed by the financial crisis, humbled by the speed and scale of the economic meltdown. Gone is that inherent cockiness that drove Wall Street to ever-greedier heights. I walked around the streets tonight and saw a lot of furrowed brows and tight-lipped faces. People here are worried, and nervous. Just as with 9/11, they don't understand what's happening, or why it's happening. And they are very uneasy about what it means for their future. Americans like to feel secure, perhaps more than any other nation in the world. They don't like disorder, or chaos. They like order, and routine. They want to get up in the morning knowing what the weather will be like, knowing what coffee they're going to have and knowing they are not going to get blown up by a terrorist or go lose all their money. Right now, that security has gone, and Americans are feeling exposed.

And I feel sorry for them. It can't be easy being an American citizen in this fast-changing modern world. Since the Second World War, they have stridden like the proverbial Colossus around the globe, feared and respected by all. Their hugely superior economic and military power has made them an unassailable force. But for how much longer? The Chinese, Russians and Indians are coming, and coming fast. What is encouraging, though, is that the Americans seem to finally realise that they have to adapt. The swaggering arrogance has been replaced by a caution and curiosity. Perhaps the best thing about America is its willingness to adapt, to move with the times. It has always led the way in this – just look at innovations like the Internet. Google, Yahoo, Microsoft and Apple are all American companies. What Barack Obama has tapped in to so brilliantly is the need for 'change'. The American people want it, need it and will vote for it. All he has to then do is deliver it.

SATURDAY, 20 SEPTEMBER 2008

Celia flew out to join me today, and decided to celebrate this fact by wearing the hottest pair of black PVC trousers imaginable to dinner at Nobu restaurant.

As we arrived, I could see every pair of male eyes transfixed by this shimmering six-foot vision of blonde, biker-chick beauty.

Everything went swimmingly until we got up to leave, or rather I got up and Celia stayed resolutely seated.

'Come on,' I barked, 'let's move.'

'I can't,' she whispered.

'Why not?'

'I'm stuck.'

'What do you mean, stuck?'

'I mean, Piers, that I'm stuck to the chair.'

At which point she slowly tried to raise herself up again, and I could see the PVC stretching, but not releasing itself from the leather banquette.

'How hilarious,' I observed, unhelpfully.

'Get me out of here, you goon,' she snarled.

I knelt down and began to gently prise the trousers away from their captor. It must have looked extremely odd to the other diners, but there was no time for decorum. Eventually, Celia sprang free and was nearly propelled right across the stairwell, catapult-style.

The same eyes that had greeted her with such lustful admiration were transfixed again, with horror.

'Don't,' she snapped, 'even think about making any jokes.'

SUNDAY, 21 SEPTEMBER 2008

Sarah Palin has sparked an astonishingly fevered debate among Americans, and what's clear it that she polarises this country's supposedly non-existent class system in the most glaring way that any politician has done here for decades.

On the one side, you have this view:

'Do we really want a "hockey mom" as leader of the free world?' wrote one *LA Times* reader today. 'Do we want someone who believes that decisiveness without prior thought is a good thing? I think we've had enough of that in the last eight years. I want an elitist in office, someone who is smarter than average.'

But on the other side, you have the Pro-Palin lobby who say that if you sneer at her, then you sneer at the real heartland of America.

Ralph Peters, a top columnist on the *New York Post*, put it this way: 'The sneering elites and mediacrats just don't get it. They think she's just a country bumpkin chumpette from a hick state with low latte availability. She's not one of them, and never will be with her busy mom beehive 'do and hick accent. Bet she hasn't even read Ian McEwan's latest novel and can't explain Frank Gehry's vision for a new architecture... But when these people insult Palin, they are smearing every American who actually works for a living, who doesn't expect a handout, who doesn't have a full-time accountant, who believes in the Pledge of Allegiance, and who thinks a church is more than just a tedious stop on daughter Emily's 100k wedding day. Sarah Palin sounds more like most of us than any Harvard man ever will. And she energises us because she *is* us. We sat beside her at school, we've hung out with her, and now she lives next door with her kids. And for the first time since Reagan we see a chance that one of us might have a voice in governing our country.'

And he may be absolutely right. Because let's face it, the same people who voted George Bush back for a second term of office are the ones who look at Sarah Palin and think she'd make a great vice-president.

Tonight, Celia and I had dinner at an Italian restaurant in Soho, and were led to our table by two handsome young male waiters, who jabbered excitedly to each other in their native tongue as they did so – blissfully unaware that Celia speaks fluent Italian.

She started laughing as we sat down.

'What's so funny?'

'They were. One of them said to the other, "Where shall we put them?" and the other one replied, "I don't know about him – she's going in my bedroom."'

MONDAY, 22 SEPTEMBER 2008

America won the Ryder Cup golf last night, and everyone went bonkers – the chant of 'USA, USA, USA' filling the airwaves.

It may be annoying to some, but I like their patriotic fervour.

What's so wrong with being ferociously proud of your country?

TUESDAY, 23 SEPTEMBER 2008

Back to LA. I walked into the gym this afternoon, and found a grimacing Jason Orange from Take That bunched into an extraordinarily tight, crab-like, yoga position.

'Need some help, mate?' I joked. 'You look stuck.'

'I'm fine, thanks,' he grimaced.

Half an hour later, he reappeared as I was trying (with excruciating difficulty) to repeatedly, and pointlessly, lift two 60-pound dumbbells high above my head.

'Need some help, mate?' he chuckled. 'I could hear you grunting and groaning in the room next door…'

The whole band are here for two weeks finishing their new album.

This afternoon, I popped down to my local Duane Reade Beverly Hills supermarket to get some sleeping tablets. My almost perpetual jetlag remains a constant aggressor.

The choice was ridiculous – row upon row of tablets, all with different names like 'Sleepeaze' or 'NiteNite'. I examined a few of the bottles, and then started to laugh, because all of them contained exactly the same ingredients. The whole thing was just one massive con trick on the American consumer, designed to make them think there was a huge array of varying degrees of sleep-inducing pills for them to inspect. When, in fact, there was one – but hey, if you want to spend an extra dollar on a fancy name, who's gonna stop you?

Celia and I stayed in tonight and decided to watch TV, something we hardly ever do because there is usually so little good stuff to watch.

American television is a weird thing. They've produced some of the greatest shows ever – *The West Wing*, *The Sopranos*, *The Simpsons*.

But in between, they churn out more horrific dross than you could possibly imagine in your worst viewing nightmares.

The sheer mind-numbing cretinousness of some of it almost defies belief.

You end up insanely, incessantly, channel-hopping like some OCD wacko, desperately trying to find something, anything, to test your brain.

And the only thing that does in the end is their political coverage, which is rough, tough, vigorous and often highly stimulating. And in many ways, America's saving TV grace.

A night spent listening to Bill 'right of Genghis Khan' O'Reilly and Bill 'left of George Galloway' Maher gives you an intense, opinionated, emphatic overview of where the day's political issues have moved.

America may well, because of its size, have more stupid people than Britain. But it also has more people actively engaged in the political process.

WEDNESDAY, 24 SEPTEMBER 2008

George Bush addressed the American people tonight, and practically begged for their support in getting through what he said could be a period where retirement savings, jobs, homes and businesses could all be lost in a 'long and painful recession'.

It was pathetic to watch. This is the man, after all, who allowed the sub-prime fiasco to take a grip of his country, and who dragged America into senseless war in Iraq.

He looked grey, timid and pitiful.

For weeks he has been insisting 'everything will be fine'. But now he has been forced, just as he was with Iraq, to admit it won't be for a long, long time.

This was not the face of a confident leader, in charge of a confident, successful country. It was the face of a man who has shot his bolt, who's washed up and history before his tenure is even over.

Bush and his administration have dragged America into the gutter of economic and military humiliation, and the new president, whoever it is, will have to try and drag it back out again.

Like all bullies, Bush has got his come-uppance, and his people deserve so much better than what he gave them.

But I wouldn't underestimate America's ability to bounce back from this shocking Armageddon. It has in the past, after the Great Depression, Pearl Harbor and 9/11.

If what we've seen under General Petraeus in Iraq is anything to go by, then America still has the power to change, and to change quickly and for the better.

And I hope it does, because a successful America, with a new-found humility about itself, and respect for others, would be of huge benefit to the world.

What is definitely not a great thing for the world is Sarah Palin, who has given another TV interview, this time to CBS anchorwoman Katie Couric, and, again, it almost defied belief in parts for sheer ignorance.

As Palin tried to paint an entirely false picture of John McCain having pushed for regulation in the financial markets, rather than the reality of his constant demands to relax them, Couric asked if she could offer any actual examples of him 'pushing'.

Palin avoided the question, so Couric asked her again.

At which point, Palin actually smirked and said: 'I'll try to find you some, and I'll bring 'em to ya!'

It was toe-curling.

Palin is single-handedly destroying McCain's election chances. He gambled on her because she was a woman, and he thought he'd pick up the female vote disappointed by Hillary Clinton's departure from the race.

But this outrageous piece of tokenism is now coming back to haunt him with every word she utters in public. And his one great argument against Obama, that he lacks experience, looks less convincing every day given Palin's obvious shocking lack of experience herself.

FRIDAY, 26 SEPTEMBER 2008

The first of the three presidential debates was held tonight, and was a fairly tame affair that most pundits declared a draw. Both Obama and McCain seemed nervous, and determined not to make a mistake. What struck me most was that McCain seemed more volatile and defensive than Obama. The older man displaying less self-control and calmness under fire. This can't play well for him when he's put such a premium on having more experience than his rival. You can have all the experience you like, but if you've got a short, testy fuse, then that makes you dangerous. McCain didn't even look at Obama during the debate, which just looked petty. And that frequent lopsided smirk of his grates.

It was, though, gratifying to see two men running for president who could intelligently articulate their views, and form clear, cogent arguments.

SATURDAY, 27 SEPTEMBER 2008
Paul Newman died today, and what a life he had.

A modest man with an extraordinary talent who rose to the top of the acting profession, then used his celebrity power to raise hundreds of millions of dollars for kids' charities by selling his own home-made salad sauces.

He also managed to stay married to the same woman, the actress Joanne Woodward, for 50 years.

And watching the tributes pouring in today, there's no doubt that this last achievement is considered by many Americans to be at least as commendable as anything he did in movies.

'I loved Paul Newman because he loved his family,' said one woman caller to Larry King's show tonight.

When asked why his marriage had lasted so long, Newman replied recently: 'In this family, we don't throw things away. If they're broken, we fix them.'

And that, in many ways, is an attitude that pervades the average American's attitude to life and to the rest of the world.

If their teeth are bad, they fix them.

If there's a problem in the world, they want to fix it.

They see themselves as a global Bob The Builder, a positive force for good.

And that's why the current hatred towards their country has left Americans so baffled, and upset.

America wants, and needs, to be loved.

SUNDAY, 28 SEPTEMBER 2008
Jonathan Ross has actually gone ahead with his lawsuit against me, and I have been compelled to write an apology in my *Mail* column, saying:

'Jonathan Ross and I have had a little bit of a tiff recently.

'He called me a fat waste of space, so I called him an equally fat, talentless, overrated has-been.

'All a bit like Colin Firth and Hugh Grant handbag-fighting in the fountain in *Bridget Jones 2*.

'And it got worse.

'During my revenge attack, I said Jonathan secretly had a junior member of staff write large chunks of his *Mirror* film reviews for him when I was the editor.

'"Not true," he responded by email. "However, am happy for you to place a small apology in next column – feel free to serve it up dressed heavily with bile and sarcasm, and to call me a fat, talentless, whinging, thin-skinned fuckwit while you're at it but it needs to be clear that you were 'mistaken'. If not then my lawyers will start earning…"

'So, deep regretful gulp, here goes: "I'm sorry for saying that Jonathan Ross secretly got a junior member of *Mirror* staff to write large chunks of his reviews for him. I was mistaken. I also accept his invitation to call him a fat, talentless, whinging, thin-skinned, fuckwit." And I'd like to brand myself a fat, talentless, whinging, thin-skinned fuckwit, too. Just to balance things out.'

As apologies go, it's quite a good one. In fact most people might assume by the language deployed that this might be some sort of piss-take.

But the mere fact I've had to do it at all really, really rankles with me.

Ross sues everyone at the drop of a hat these days. He boasted to me that he'd won money off the *Mail* twice in the last two years alone, whilst letting off a diatribe of abuse about the paper at the same time.

It's the kind of bragging, swaggering, bully-boy nonsense I'd expect from a city trader at closing time. Not a guy I once paid £100,000 a year to write about movies, and who, before his jibes, I had never been anything but respectful towards in public and in private.

Ross has, I am sad to see, disappeared up his increasingly big, fat, overpaid arse.

Celia and I went down to a big street festival near Venice Beach today, which turned out to be a fascinating snapshot of modern-day America. Stall after stall sold Obama T-shirts, posters, books and photos. And then I arrived at one that contained the following words in large lettering: 'NO ONE EVER RAPED ANNIE OAKLEY.' I laughed, and read on. 'Help us defend a woman's right to defend herself,' said the next sentence. Very laudable, I thought, but who were these shining knights in white armour? 'I'M A BITTER GUN OWNER, AND I VOTE!' screamed another banner head-line. Ah yes, it was of course the National Rifle Association. And they're gunning, quite literally, for Obama, claiming he would ban handguns, hunt-ing ammunition and the use of a gun for defence in one's home. In fact, he's threatening nothing of the sort. Obama knows that such a policy would make him unelectable. What he has said is that he would seek to strengthen exist-ing gun laws to keep them away from children and criminals. All eminently mature and sensible. But these NRA guys don't really do 'mature and sensi-ble' as I discovered when I started talking to them.

'Obama would make all our children and women unsafe,' insisted one huge pock-marked man in a Stetson that Jock Ewing would have been proud of, and giant glinting spurs on his boots.

'No, he wouldn't,' I replied. 'His proposals would actually make them safer. What's dangerous is having so many guns lying around for people who shouldn't be anywhere near them to use.'

He peered at me like I'd just suggested paedophiles should be allowed to teach at primary schools.

'Don't get into what you know nothing about, boy,' he snarled, with genuine loathing and menace in his voice. 'Obama don't understand, and you don't understand.'

I do understand, actually. But I could see that further argument was futile. What was extraordinary was that he was able to hold these views, and articu-late them with extreme vehemence, in a street festival where I'd say 90 per cent of the people were liberal and pro-Obama. But then America can, despite its latent, widespread bigotry, be surprisingly tolerant of opposing views too.

As if to prove the point, a few stalls down I found an Islamic stall giving away free copies of the Koran. It was staffed by Muslims dressed in full Islamic regalia. Yet I watched for more than 15 minutes, and they never received a single word of dissent from anyone passing by, not even the redneck gun-freaks next door.

Every stall took credit cards, cash-point machines were freely available every block or so and the staff were almost always unfailingly polite and cour-teous. Americans really do show more respect for each other than British people. It's instinctive, and it's genuine. Their first thought on seeing a stranger is 'I wonder who this nice person is?' rather than our more cynical 'I wonder if he'll stab me?' thought process. Where we lambast Americans for the lack of sarcasm or irony in their humour, we forget that they also lack the cynicism that comes with highly developed senses of sarcasm and irony. Americans are an extraordinarily positive bunch. Their collective glass is usually brimming over, never mind half full. When an American says 'have a nice day' they actually mean it. And if you react towards it with jokey negativity, saying something like 'I will if I don't get run over by a bus', they will take you literally. 'That won't happen here,' they will reply in all seriousness, 'the bus drivers are very good.'

One odd contradiction to all this innocent politeness is on the roads. Americans are appalling, ruthless and utterly selfish drivers. Get on the freeway, even in a civilised oasis like LA, and see how many people let you pull into a different lane. They'll accelerate rather than do that, or deliberately block your way, and gesticulate angrily or toot their horn if you dare to cut them up if you're in danger of missing a turning off. I consider myself a pretty good, if rapid, driver. But going on the busy LA freeways in rush hour (the 405 or 10 in particular) is like entering *Wacky Races*.

TUESDAY, 30 SEPTEMBER 2008
I stumbled across a hilarious glossy magazine in my local Hollywood store this morning.

Entitled *Celebrity Staff*, it contains pages of splendid advice for servants to the stars.

'The unprofessionalism of some celebrity assistants shocks me,' wrote one reader called Michelle D this month. 'If you do not stay grounded and remember that all the glitz and glamour around you is only compliments of your employer, you can get carried away. Don't forget your place!'

I immediately faxed this to my PA, Tracey (well, you can't be too careful, can you?) 'Relax, Piers,' she replied, 'you're not even the most famous person I work with…' Which is tragically true, as the other person she's currently looking after is *Britain's Got Talent* winner George Sampson.

A second piece of valuable advice in the magazine came from an assistant whose famous movie star husband-and-wife employers used to row incessantly in front of her, and tried to get her to snitch on each other's whereabouts.

'The bottom line,' she wrote, 'is that love may come and go in your boss's life (especially in Hollywood) but keeping your distance when it turns ugly is not just the smart thing to do, it's the only thing to do.'

'Just remember that when you hear Scarlett and me having an argument,' I ordered Tracey. At which point she sighed, wearily, and pointed out a reference later in the article to 'celebrity staff salaries'.

Apparently top nannies to the stars can get up to $150,000 p.a., PAs $200,000 p.a., hairdressers $300,000 p.a., and, in what sounds like the best job of all, a golf instructor called Derrick Allen charges VIP clients including Morgan Freeman and Bill Clinton $350 an hour just to whack a few balls around.

'I think it's time we renegotiated, don't you?' Tracey suggested.

WEDNESDAY, 1 OCTOBER 2008

America's Got Talent had its third series finale tonight, and was won by a large, unassuming salesman who sings opera. Sound familiar? Neal E. Boyd, who flogs insurance by day and sings like Pavarotti by night, could be Paul Potts' long-lost brother. Leona Lewis was the show's star guest, and I went up to see her in her dressing room – only to be blocked entry by the largest entourage I've seen since word got out that Jude Law was sleeping with his staff.

But I needn't have worried about fame going to her head. Leona herself, who sounded spine-tinglingly good during her live performance, was just the same sweet, unaffected young lady we all remember from *X Factor*.

'You having fun?' I asked, when I finally got through.

'I'm loving it!' she smiled. And who can blame her?

Two years ago she was working as an office receptionist; now she's one of the world's biggest singing stars. I was assigned one line to say during the finale – which was then cut at the last second as we over-ran. Meaning I sat there for an hour doing precisely nothing. 'Should I be feeling bad about this?' I asked The Ferret afterwards. 'Bad? Are you crazy? Your rate per word just went through the roof!'

THURSDAY, 2 OCTOBER 2008

Had a farewell drinks party at the hotel tonight with a few friends, including Caroline. She is unrecognisable from the woman ravaged by cancer this time last year – glowing with health, superfit from four gym sessions a week with Alex and full of optimism for the future.

We discussed the economy.

'Looking back on it,' she said, 'I think the problem started after 9/11. The whole nation went collectively nuts. Normally sane friends of mine started buying bigger and better SUVs, getting bigger mortgages and second homes and more weekend toys like boats and horses. They were so stunned by what happened in their own back yard that they honestly believed the end of the world was nigh, so they might as well do the good old American thing of spending themselves into oblivion before Armageddon came. That's why the country's economy is in such a mess now, I'm sure of it.'

She's probably right. I remember hearing the new New York mayor Rudi Giuliani speak after 9/11, and urging everyone to 'get back out there spending'. As if, somehow, that alone would restore America's power.

We also discussed the significance of this election.

'I would vote for McCain because I'm a conservative at heart,' said Caroline, 'but the thing about Obama that is so powerful is that he offers genuine hope. This is a country that's been ravaged in the last decade by acts of terrorism, acts of God and acts of greed, and it is desperate for an answer to it all. I don't think Obama's got all the answers, but he has the ability to make them think he has, and that's why they love him.

'And I really hope he can turn things around because I love this country.

'I came to America in 1992, and since then, I've managed to visit every one of the 52 states, and I feel like it's now my adopted home. When I came here I remember being quite British and cynical about something one day and my friend Cathy, a ballsy PR girl from Texas, shut me up by saying: "Hey, stop that negative talk. I'm an Ameri-CAN!" That was how it was when I first arrived. I loved the positive attitude. In England when I bought my first new car someone keyed the side of it the first week I had it. Here I bought a Porsche and a stranger came up to me on the second day and high-fived me in the street.'

That's so true. I was out driving an Aston Martin the other day, and a guy came up to me at some traffic lights, stared at it for a few seconds, then said: 'Nice wheels, man.' Whereas back home, he'd stare at it, then me, and mouth 'wanker' to himself. Americans don't do envy, it's another very endearing trait.

Caroline and I both agree that probably the best thing about living in America is that things work.

'Things like getting cable/telephones/removal men/painters/electricians/plumbers are a doddle,' she said. 'Call them, they come out the next day (or increasingly now, the same day). Compare that to Britain. I know when friends of mine there move home I can count the days until I get an apoplectic email about the incompetence of the British system. Americans simply wouldn't stand for that. This is a service country. You've got cash and they want it. They do a job and they get it. Simple, really...'

The dream is realised.

12

'I have a dream that my four little children will one day live in a nation where they will not be judged by the colour of their skin, but by the content of their character.' MARTIN LUTHER KING, JNR

SATURDAY, 4 OCTOBER 2008

I flew back to Britain today after six weeks of ceaseless 85-degree sunshine, and smarmy arse-licking in Tinsel Town, to be greeted by cold drizzle, appalling traffic up the M4, and a cheeky young scamp in Earl's Court shouting out 'Britain's Got WANKERS!' as I sped past in the Maserati, splashing his shellsuit as I did so.

God (and I really do mean this...), it's good to be home. There is something incredibly comforting about British weather at this of year, something that LA people would never be able to appreciate. Too much of anything good makes you lazy, and complacent. And sunshine is the most mind-fogging element of all. It might brighten your mood, but it also saps your energy. Rain, cold, snow, wind – they all conspire to sharpen the brain.

I bought the papers to discover that Peter Mandelson is back in the Cabinet. And to my surprise, I found myself nodding with approval. Brown needs some big beasts in his jungle to deflect all the crap from his own shoulders, and Mandelson is not only a very experienced politician, but he's also respected by the business community, which right now is crucial, obviously.

But even back here, the news media are just as obsessed with Sarah bloody Palin as the Americans.

I watched her on TV at a rally today, accusing Obama of 'palling around with terrorists', and winced. This was a truly pathetic attempt to smear him by association with a sixties' radical called Bill Ayers, who he barely knows. I watched Palin as she sneered away, curling up her face in faux horror as she played to the equally dumb gallery. It was embarrassing to watch, like seeing the deputy vice-president of your old school debating society trying, and failing, to belittle her opposite number with a vacuous, age-old rumour that everyone knows is nonsense. It's extraordinary that anyone is taking this imbecilic woman seriously, but they are. And the sole reason is that she is good TV. Sarah Palin's the Jade Goody of world politics – ignorant, bigoted, stupid, but undeniably charismatic, and great for ratings.

But when push comes to shove on 4 November, I think John McCain will look back on his decision to select her as his running mate and think, 'Doggone it, I wish I'd never gone and done that!'

MONDAY, 6 OCTOBER 2008

Sarah Palin made a speech in San Francisco yesterday in which she described Afghanistan as 'our neighbouring country'. And what's worse is that she clearly meant it. Can you imagine if a serious British politician suddenly described Iraq as 'our neighbouring country'? He or she would be a laughing stock. And these aren't inadvertent slips of the tongue, either. The woman only got her passport last year (less than 25 per cent of American citizens hold passports according to the latest survey), and clearly has no idea where anywhere is outside of Alaska. It's terrifying. As a reader in the *New York Times* put it today: 'She's like a hapless contestant on *American Idol* who doesn't realise that she just doesn't have what it takes. It's deluded and sad.'

An email arrived from Dame Helen Mirren, following my recent *GQ* interview with her in which she raised a few eyebrows with her 'I loved cocaine' confession, and controversial views on date rape.

'Well, didn't you get me into trouble!' she said. 'Or rather, didn't I get myself into trouble with your good help. Oh well... On we go...'

I love her.

WEDNESDAY, 8 OCTOBER 2008

Still hideously jet-lagged, I stayed up until 4 a.m. to watch the second presidential debate. It was like watching a young Muhammad Ali fighting Sonny Liston. Obama was young, direct, supremely confident, and none of McCain's blows got near to hurting him. McCain, by contrast, looked older than ever, slightly desperate, lost his temper several times, and at one stage even snapped at Obama – calling him 'that one', which was just plain offensive.

It was fascinating to observe their behavioural ticks as the debate went on.

McCain smirks, all the time. He can't stop himself, and it's exactly the same incredibly annoying mannerism that George Bush has. He also sneers, another Bushism. And he has an even more irritating habit of saying 'my friends' every five minutes, trying to smarmily ingratiate himself with the audience and the people watching at home.

But when it comes to actual substance, he just comes across as a tired old man with tired old ideas. He loves calling himself a 'maverick', but has precious little to back up the mantle. His rhetoric always falls back on war, his military record and his desire to kill people in the name of his country.

'We will take bin Laden out,' he shrieked. But when asked how he intended to do that, he retorted: 'I know how...but I'm not going to tele-graph it.' Which was a bit like saying, 'I know a cure for cancer, but I won't tell you what it is until you make me President.'

His biggest mistake tonight, though, came when he tried to accuse Obama of being too bombastic about foreign policy.

Obama smiled, almost pityingly, and said simply: 'John McCain is a man who joked about attacking Iran, singing "Bomb, Bomb, Bomb, Iran". And he said we should annihilate North Korea. That is not an example of speaking softly!'

Obama wasn't perfect. He is a bit too slick sometimes, which can come over as insincere. And he remains curiously unconvincing on Iraq given he has always rightly opposed it, probably because he knows a lot of Americans still feel a need to 'win' the war there, for national pride reasons.

But he was cool, calm, professional and impressive tonight. Very much in keeping with his campaign slogan: 'No drama, Obama'. And McCain looked more and more like the old right-wing hothead that everyone suspects he really is underneath all the false bonhomie.

In other presidential news, Brigitte Bardot has branded Sarah Palin a 'disgrace to women'.

In a letter to the French media, she raged: 'I knows dogs well, and I can assure you that no pitbull, no dog, nor any other animal is as dangerous as you. By denying the responsibility of man in global warming, by advocating gun rights, and making statements that are disconcertingly stupid, you are a disgrace to women and represent a terrible threat, a true environmental catastrophe.'

THURSDAY, 9 OCTOBER 2008

Spencer was playing football at school today, and I drove down to watch him. The thing I miss more than any other about working abroad is the boys' sports stuff. And I suspect it's the thing they miss most about me being away, too. Every son wants their dad to see them score a great goal, take a fantastic wicket, run over a brilliant try. And vice versa.

I was, to my surprise, one of only two parents who turned up today, on either side. It was easy to find Spencer, as he has taken to wearing bright yellow boots in honour of his footballing hero, the Argentinean genius Lionel Messi.

He saw me out of the corner of his eye, and gave an imperceptible flick of a hand, which, for him, is a greeting of extraordinary public affection.

After ten minutes, he picked up the ball 30 yards out, and started a mazy dribble that took him past four of the opposition players, jinxing left and right at increasing speed, before getting inside the penalty area and smacking it right-footed (his wrong foot) into the corner.

I was on the phone to someone at the time, and nearly combusted with excitement.

'Are you OK?' asked the caller.

'Yes, yes, sorry. My eldest son just did a Messi.'

'A what?'

'A…oh, no matter.'

I caught his eye again, as he was engulfed with delirious teammates, and received a double hand flick – denoting major, stratospheric, satisfaction.

And in that moment, I honestly wouldn't have wanted to be anywhere else in the world. Hollywood can provide many delights, but not that.

SUNDAY, 12 OCTOBER 2008

John McCain's rallies have grown increasingly unruly, with people shouting out abuse about Obama.

Today, in Minnesota, that abuse turned very nasty, with one supporter shouting out that Obama was 'an Arab', another calling him a 'terrorist', and even chants of 'kill him!' being picked up on microphones.

McCain, to his credit, denounced all this nonsense, saying: 'Senator Obama is a decent person, a decent family man, he's not an Arab, and he's not a person you have to be scared of as a president of the United States. I admire him, and I respect him.'

But his comments were roundly booed.

If McCain wants someone to blame, then he should look no further than The Idiot Palin, who has of course effectively been branding Obama a terrorist all week.

Whipping up all this Obama-hatred is totally self-defeating for the Republicans. It just makes more people feel more empathy towards him, not less.

MONDAY, 13 OCTOBER 2008

The British government has effectively nationalised three big banks – Royal Bank of Scotland, Lloyds and HBOS.

Gordon Brown has been pumping huge sums into our economy, and generally taking charge of the crisis like a Great White Shark devouring a shoal of fish.

And it's working. His poll ratings are moving up, David Cameron's moving down.

Some of the tributes flooding his way are almost embarrassing.

The new winner of the Nobel Prize for Economics, Paul Krugman, for instance, said today that Gordon has effectively saved the world!

He cooed: 'The Brown government has shown itself willing to think clearly about the financial crisis, and act quickly on its conclusions. And this combination of clarity and decisiveness hasn't been matched by any other Western government, least of all our own [the US]... At a special European summit meeting on Sunday, the major economies of continental Europe in effect declared themselves ready to follow Britain's lead, injecting hundreds of billions of dollars into banks while guaranteeing their debts... Luckily for the world economy, however, Gordon Brown and his officials are making sense. And they may have shown us the way through this crisis.'

What an extraordinary turnaround in Brown's fortunes. This time last year, he was accused of 'bottling' the election and very quickly became a dead political duck.

Now, he has finally found a major global issue to tackle, and is emerging better than any other world leader.

And it's the perfect issue for him – a grotesquely complicated financial crisis that needs serious, intellectual, thought.

Cameron, by contrast, is floundering and looks completely out of his depth.

WEDNESDAY, 15 OCTOBER 2008

Watched Stanley play in his inter-house school football tournament today.

'You'll have to go some to beat Spencer's goal,' I teased this morning.

During the second of his three matches, Stanley picked up the ball just inside his own half, moved swiftly forward, looked up and smacked it from a good 35 yards straight into the top corner of the goal.

Then turned to me, flashed the cheekiest of grins and performed a deep theatrical bow.

THURSDAY, 16 OCTOBER 2008

I taped the third, and last, presidential debate last night, and watched it with Celia at 6 a.m. this morning.

It wasn't massively revelatory, though I was struck once again by Obama's 'no drama' coolness, and his warm smile every time McCain insulted him.

And also by McCain's head, which resembles a large gnarled turtle. He's got no neck, a mashed-up jaw that juts alarmingly when he gets angry and a horrible tendency to do that sneering Bush-style smirk every three minutes.

He wants us all to think he's Mr Nice Guy, but he's not. He's just another warmongering old conservative who wants to kill all the baddies.

The unlikely star of the debate, though, turned out to be a tall, bald guy called Joe the Plumber, who Obama met in Ohio last weekend. He'd told Obama that he was about to buy a company that makes $250,000 a year, and was concerned that the Democrat nominee's tax plans would punish him.

Joe's name was mentioned 11 times during the debate, more than bin Laden, Iraq and the global economic meltdown.

I turned to Celia. 'Joe's going to wish he'd never spoken to Obama.'

'Why?'

'Because by the end of today, he'll probably have been exposed as a wife-beating, tax-dodging, drug-dealing sleazeball who is probably not even a licensed plumber.'

Such is the speed and aggression of the modern global media, people like Joe become instant superstars, and have their lives dissected so fast they barely have time to enjoy their 15 minutes of fame before it comes crashing down and flattens them.

Sure enough, by the ten o'clock news bulletins tonight, doubts were already being raised about the legality of Joe's plumber licence, and the taxes he is said to have avoided.

FRIDAY, 17 OCTOBER 2008

Today, it was time for Bertie's inter-house football tournament.

'No pressure, mate,' I reassured him, 'but your two older brothers have both scored wonder-goals in the last week.'

Bertie's team were 5–0 up in the first match after just six minutes, and he'd scored a blistering hat-trick, never once even cracking a smile.

Tonight, Spencer rang to say that his teachers have all been asked to come up with likely career paths for him.

'And?' I asked, intrigued.

'And,' he chuckled, 'one of them thinks I would make a good *journalist*.' The last word was delivered with serious derision!

SATURDAY, 18 OCTOBER 2008

Madonna and Guy Ritchie are to divorce, as I confidently predicted back in June.

'Thanks, Godzilla,' I thought as I went to collect my winnings from the bookies...

SUNDAY, 19 OCTOBER 2008

Colin Powell has come out in support of Obama, in what is a shattering blow to McCain.

Powell is still seen by most Americans as just about the one acceptable face of the eight-year Bush regime.

And his endorsement is memorable both for its eloquence and the damning nature of its verdict on McCain.

'An Obama victory,' he said, 'would not just electrify our country, but would electrify the world.'

As for McCain, he observed: 'You get the sense that he didn't have a complete grasp of the economic problems that we had.'

And then added: 'I'm also troubled by what members of the Republican party say...such things as, "Well, you know that Mr Obama is a Muslim."

'Well, the correct answer is, "He's not a Muslim, he's a Christian, he's always been a Christian." But the really right answer is, "What if he is? Is there something wrong with being a Muslim in this country?" The answer is "No", that's not America.'

And he's right, it's not. The America I have experienced for the last three years is a country that increasingly encompasses tolerance and fairness to ethnic and religious minorities.

Which is precisely why it is on the verge of electing its first-ever black president.

McCain, by picking an idiotic bigot like Sarah Palin as his running mate, and allowing her to openly ferment the whole ludicrous 'Obama pals around with terrorists' rhetoric, has discovered to his cost that the American people have changed, and started to recoil from that kinda talk.

MONDAY, 20 OCTOBER 2008

'Come and see me in my new office,' commanded Simon Cowell.

But the word 'office' barely does justice to the vast, sprawling Sony/BMG emporium that I found myself in this afternoon.

After yomping for what seemed like several days, up and down various floors, and through endless sweeping long corridors, I finally arrived at Simon's mammoth, L-shaped lair.

After his unfortunate failure to remember two *X Factor* contestants' names in successive weeks, I decided to take no chances, and hastily attached a large badge to my suit lapel saying 'PIERS'.

Simon sniggered when he saw it, but only in that way I suspect Idi Amin used to snigger before inserting the head of a political opponent into a vat of boiling oil.

Having had my little joke, it was time to cheer him up (the trouble with being a demented perfectionist like him is that you don't recognise real perfection when you see it, as I felt like pointing out when he was explaining my numerous televisual deficiencies...)

'*Glamour* magazine have done a "Who would you rather?" vote between me and you in their next issue,' I said.

He looked bemused. 'Who would you rather what?'

'Well, put it this way, I don't think they're talking about who they'd rather have a cup of tea with...'

Simon dropped the papers he was holding, and sat bolt upright.

'*And*?'

'And you won – 65 per cent to 35 per cent.'

I waited for the inevitable smug smirk, but it never came.

'What? You mean to tell me that 35 per cent of *Glamour* readers would actually rather sleep with you than me? I'm astonished you got that many votes. In fact, I'm appalled.'

At the end of our meeting, Simon stood up, said goodbye, then suddenly vanished through a secret doorway in the wall that I didn't know existed.

It was all a bit sinister, like something out of a John Grisham thriller.

After my audience with the country's most powerful man, I caught a cab down to Downing Street for a private cup of tea with Gordon Brown.

I hadn't seen him since early summer, when he was dead and buried in the polls, and taking it all quite badly. Then, he'd looked gaunt, pale, hunted and dejected.

Today, I was greeted by a completely different person.

'How are you, Piers!' he boomed, swaggering into his prime ministerial reception room like Guy the Gorilla used to move when it was morning banana feed at London Zoo.

'Not as well as you by the look of things,' I replied. 'I'm still jetlagged.'

Gordon beamed a huge grin.

'I'm very well. Though I've put on a bit of weight since we last met. I haven't had time to do any workouts.'

'Not surprised, and anyway, you shouldn't be pumping iron at your age.'

'I don't do weights. I got quite fit on our holiday in Suffolk, I was doing that thing called P...oh, what's it called...Pillow...'

'Pilates?' I suggested.

'That's it. Pilates. I had a personal trainer.'

'Yes, I know, I read about her in the papers.'

The lady concerned, Miss Millie Dobie, was alleged to have taken part in three-in-a-bed sex sessions with another woman and an unnamed Hollywood star.

'I felt very sorry for her, poor girl. She was a very good trainer.'

'I bet she was.'

We discussed his astonishing political comeback.

'This crisis has been perfect for you,' I said. 'Because absolutely nobody else knows what the hell is going on.'

He frowned.

'It's very serious, but I am determined to do everything I can to help get people through it. The British public are remarkably resilient.'

'Cameron's been exposed for what he is,' I said.

'And what's that?'

'A rich, posh lightweight. The reason he's been so quiet on all this economic stuff is because he can't get his head round it. And the public aren't stupid, they can tell he's out of his depth. Anyone can be prime minister in the good times. It's when the bad stuff happens that you need leadership. You should stop him mid-sentence during the next PMQs, and just say: "With the greatest of respect, you don't understand a bloody word of this, do you, you Tory halfwit?"'

Gordon chuckled. 'I'll bear that in mind, Piers, thank you. What did you think of Mandelson returning?'

'I thought it was genius. He'll take all the media heat off you, he's respected by the business world, and for all his faults he's got a brilliant, strategic political brain.'

There was a sudden burst of noise, and into the room raced John and Fraser, Gordon's two sons.

He embraced them both warmly.

'Say hello to Piers,' he said.

Fraser, two, stared at me for a couple of seconds, then shouted: 'I don't like you!'

Gordon burst out laughing.

'Fraser! Be nice to Piers, please.'

'Relax, Prime Minister. His judgement appears to be very sound.'

They'd recently returned from a trip to Disneyland.

'What did you like best?' I asked Fraser, desperately trying to secure his approval.

'I liked shooting baddies,' he replied, with a huge cheeky grin.

'I see, well that should come in handy next time your daddy takes you to work with him.'

Sarah arrived, looking very svelte.

'Ah, First Lady, I was just telling Gordon how it's just as well he's finally pulled something out of the bag, because it was getting lonely being a Brown supporter...'

Sarah smiled. 'People just needed to be patient. My husband knows what he's doing.'

He certainly did when he married Sarah, she's fast becoming his greatest electoral asset.

I left after an hour and a half, rather stunned by the transformation in our prime minister. He's pumped up, got his confidence back and knows this global financial crisis has given him a chance to show everyone what he can really do.

Just when I thought my day couldn't get any more surreal, I rang Celia.

'Can't talk now,' she said, 'I'm lying in bed with Paris Hilton.'

TUESDAY, 21 OCTOBER 2008

Peter Mandelson and George Osborne have both been embroiled in an amusing scandal involving their dealings with some Russian oligarch on a summer yacht in Corfu.

Nobody seems too sure precisely what went on, but it would appear that Osborne started the mud-slinging, and Mandelson has finished it in spectacularly effective style. If you dance with the devil…

I flew to New York today to play a cameo role in the new series of *Celebrity Apprentice*. The show's Australian producer Eden Gaha sold it to me as 'Jaws goes back into the ocean', and when I asked for clarification, laughed: 'Just do what you do best, Piers – be obnoxious, arrogant and vile.'

I asked the driver who took me to the set today what he thought of the election battle.

'Obama's got New York,' he said. 'But it's what happens outside of the big cities that will decide who wins, and I don't think any of us really knows whether this country is really ready to elect a black president yet, and we won't until people go into those polling stations and vote.'

'What do you make of Sarah Palin?'

'Well, I'd quite like to marry her…but I sure as hell wouldn't want her running the country!'

Despite his thick New York accent, it turned out the driver was Swedish.

'You know, Bush has done so much damage to America's reputation that when I go home, I never speak English because they would think I'm an American, and they would hate me for that.'

Ivanka Trump, who had joined us by now, offered an extraordinary view on the message an Obama election would send to the wider world.

'Europeans all love Obama, and the whole idea of America electing its first black president. But I've spent time with the Russians, Arabs and Chinese recently,' she said, 'and a lot of them find it laughable that America would even consider electing a woman as president, as we did when Hillary was doing well, and now an African-American man. They see it as weakness, and something that makes America a laughing stock.'

As for the credit crunch, Ivanka was equally revealing: 'A lot of the big players learned nothing from previous crashes, and just let greed rule their heads. I'm just glad it blew up when it did, because if it had gone on much longer then the whole global financial system might have collapsed.'

WEDNESDAY, 22 OCTOBER 2008

Not a great day for John McCain. It began with a *Washington Post* revelation that al-Qaeda supporters are clamouring for him to win the election, because he would 'continue the failing march of his predecessor Bush'. In sinister undertones, the website spouting these thoughts suggested that a big terrorist strike in the next fortnight would 'push the Americans into voting for McCain so he takes revenge against al Qaeda'.

The worst thing about this theory is that it's plainly correct. Just about the only thing that could suddenly swing the presidency to McCain now judging by the latest polls is a cataclysmic attack on America by Islamic fundamentalists. I can see the TV ads now – 'Who would you rather trust to deal with these evil ragheads? The bravest Vietnam vet in history? Or the black guy with *Hussein* as his middle name?'

The second blow to McCain came in the unlikely form of actor Daniel Craig, who, when asked which candidate would make the better James Bond, replied: 'Obama, because – if he's true to his word – he'd be willing to quite literally look his enemy in the eye and go toe-to-toe with them. McCain would be a better M, there is a kind of Judi Dench quality to him...'

But perhaps the worst moment of a truly bad day at the office erupted later when it was disclosed that the Republican Party has spent $150,000 on clothes since Sarah Palin was appointed VP nominee.

This astonishing sum included $75,000 in one designer dress spree at the Neiman Marcus department store. And is, of course, slightly at odds with her 'I'm just your good ole average hockey mom' positioning.

To put it into perspective, the average American spends $1,874 a year on clothes. And $150,000 would pay for a fairly nice little house in a lot of the Southern states that Ms Palin was supposed to be representing.

I've got a feeling that this story, more than any other that's emerged so far about Palin, could be the most devastating.

McCain responded to this hiccup as he always does, by trying to switch the agenda back to what a bloody war hero he was.

'Joe Biden referred to the Cuban missile crisis,' he told a rally this afternoon. 'Well, I was there, as a combat pilot, ready to go into battle!'

This was 46 years ago, for God's sake, he didn't actually do anything and the anecdote merely serves to remind us all what an ancient old crock McCain really is.

THURSDAY, 23 OCTOBER 2008

Picture the scene.

It's 9.45 p.m., and I've just arrived in the luxurious British Airways Concorde lounge at New York's JFK airport, exhausted after two days' intensive filming on a TV project I'm not allowed to talk about yet.

I sit down for dinner in the small restaurant with one of my closest friends, Martin Cruddace, who happened to be in town at the same time and we ordered our meal. The lounge is virtually empty, save for a few businessmen in suits dotted around.

Then Martin suddenly leans forward with a huge grin on his face, and gasps: 'Oh my God, it's Tony bloody Blair!'

I turned slowly to where he was looking, and there, sat just five yards away, was the former prime minister, accompanied by two assistants.

A little greyer than I remembered, but looking pretty fit.

As we chuckled to ourselves about this bizarre coincidence, I noticed another familiar figure tottering into the lounge.

Heather Mills.

Or rather, the female British Airways special services assistant was tottering under the weight of Heather's five-year-old daughter Beatrice – while Heather marched on grandly ahead.

Then she glanced over and caught my eye. Ooooh, if looks could kill she'd have decimated the entire Parachute Regiment with that icy, beady stare.

Five minutes later, the special services lady went over to Blair's table, and said loudly: 'Excuse me, sir, but Heather would like to send her regards.'

Blair looked completely bemused, but thanked the lady anyway, and went back to his food.

Ten minutes on, Ms Mills strode back past Blair to the ladies' room, wiggling her backside for all she was worth in a desperate, and fruitless, attempt to attract his attention.

On her return journey, she tried even harder, but still to no avail.

But our Heather's nothing if not a fighter, and after ten more minutes elapsed, she was back again, performing another fly-by right past Blair on her way to the bar.

Still, he completely ignored her.

I caught the eye of Blair's bodyguard, sitting at a nearby table.

'You couldn't make this up, could you?' I said. And he laughed.

Heather pulled out all the stops on her second return leg, slithering within inches of Blair's seat.

But nothing, not even a raised ex-prime ministerial eyebrow.

This was one of the great blankings of our time, and I was loving it.

When boarding started, Blair and his entourage went first. Then Heather came by, this time visibly struggling to carry her own child, and making very sure I noticed her heroism. Though it wasn't quite as heroic as the poor bloke with her, who was left ten yards behind to push the buggy.

I got on the plane, assuming we'd all be crammed into the tiny first-class cabin together, in what would be a recipe for the biggest uproar since Naomi Campbell found her bags had gone missing.

But there was no sign of Heather.

Blair, though, was at the next seat to me. Well, actually, I was in 1K and he was in 2A. So, technically, I'd got a better one.

We turned to each other, there was a slightly uncomfortable silence, then Blair stuck out his hand and said: 'Piers, of all the places...how are you?'

'I'm very well, thanks, Tony. That was funny with Heather.'

'Who?'

'Heather Mills, Paul McCartney's ex, she kept trying to get your attention in the lounge.'

He frowned.

'Was she the blonde or redhead?'

'She was the fake blonde with one leg...'

He smiled in that frozen way he used to smile when a journalist asked him something unspeakable in a press conference.

'...and she wants to kill me even more than you do.'

'I don't want to kill you, Piers.'

'What are you doing in New York?'

'I've been doing a speech at Yale...'

Ah yes, he is now, amusingly, a highly paid professor in 'faith and globalisation' at the famous American college.

'...I travel all the time at the moment, I'm hardly ever in Britain.'

'Don't you get jetlag?'

'No, never have. I'm lucky. What do you think of the George Osborne story?'

'I think he's in big trouble. They've all been exposed as lightweights on this financial stuff, while Gordon's like a pig in a sty with it.'

'I know, it's amazing, isn't it? Everything's changed.'

'Indeed...even Peter's back.'

That frozen, suspicious smile again. 'Yessss.'

'Actually, I thought that was a smart move, lets all the papers lay into Mandelson instead of Gordon. Just what the doctor ordered! And talking of which, I had a doctor treat me in LA three weeks ago who says he treated you there the week before...'

Blair nodded.

'Yes, I had a nasty bug. He was very good.'

'He told me you sent him a very nice letter afterwards and that you were "very impressive". I said you were always good with the letters, it was just the wars that weren't your strong point...'

Blair laughed, and not even in a frozen way. He was relaxed in my presence now, just how he used to be before we all fell out.

'Are you enjoying your new life?'

'Yes, it's very different, obviously, but I am,' he replied. 'How about you?'

'Well, judging piano-playing pigs with David Hasselhoff is a bit different to my old job, too.'

After 20 minutes or so, we prepared for take off.

I asked a steward where Heather was.

'She's in business class, sir.'

'Thank God for that, she wants to kill me...'

'We know, sir, that's why she's back there.'

I then noticed there were still three empty seats in first class. But Blair's bodyguard reappeared with an even bigger grin than before – he'd been upgraded.

Martin texted me: 'I'm sitting next to Heather. She's not happy...'

Half an hour after take-off, Blair was fast asleep, and I pondered on the absurdity of finding myself effectively going to bed two feet from the man who had played such a large part in my life as an editor for more than a decade.

When we landed, he shook my hand again.

'It's good to see you again, Piers.'

'Likewise, Tony.'

And it had been, curiously.

I followed him off the plane and headed with him through what I thought was the exit door to customs.

A firm hand stopped me in my tracks.

'Sorry Mr Morgan,' said a burly security man, 'that is the VIP exit. Maybe next month...'

SUNDAY, 26 OCTOBER 2008

An extraordinary story has appeared on the front page of the *Mail on Sunday* this morning involving Jonathan Ross and Russell Brand.

Apparently they recorded Brand's Radio 1 show together a couple of weeks ago, and during it they called former *Fawlty Towers* star Andrew 'Manuel' Sachs, and made a series of obscene remarks to him.

At first I thought this was obviously just a silly joke that had been exaggerated, but then I read the transcript and realised it was actually a very nasty piece of gratuitous bullying masquerading as comedy.

At one stage Ross shouts 'He fucked your granddaughter!' down the phone to Sachs in a series of six messages they left on his answering machine.

'I had sex with your granddaughter,' adds Brand, 'though it was consensual...it was consensual lovely sex. It was full of respect. I sent her a text, I've asked her to marry me, Andrew Sachs...I wore a condom!'

Later in the programme, Brand even joked about the idea that Sachs might consider suicide as a result of their comments. Imagining a news bulletin, he said: 'The main news again. Manuel Andrew Sachs hung himself today...'

What is beyond belief is that this was all pre-recorded and *then* released on air!

The more times I read this transcript, the more appalling it seems. With the *Mail on Sunday* splashing on it, I think Brand and Ross are in big, big trouble.

MONDAY, 27 OCTOBER 2008

The Ross/Brand scandal is exploding, with thousands of people complaining to the BBC, MPs queueing up to lambast them, and Andrew Sachs and his family demanding apologies. Quite right, too. And how tragic if this bizarre incident should now pop Mr Ross's massively overblown balloon of an ego, and his obscene £18 million BBC contract. I've been getting endless texts and emails from people of the 'You must be LOVING this!' variety. And they're right. I'm afraid I am.

What I'm not loving so much is the announcement that Harry Redknapp is to be the new Spurs manager.

He's my favourite character in football, and now I have to hate him.

TUESDAY, 28 OCTOBER 2008

The *Daily Mail* rang.

'Would you like to write a piece about Jonathan Ross…'

They had barely finished the sentence before I gleefully shrieked, 'OH YES!!!' and sat down to pen 1200 gleeful words of vitriol demanding he get fired.

Oh, I know one should 'rise above these things', be 'better than that', let 'others do the talking'.

But I've never been like that, and never will.

He started this.

WEDNESDAY, 29 OCTOBER 2008

Out in Dubai for a week to film an ITV documentary about the place, my phone rang.

'Piers, it's Katherine Jenkins. I need to tell you something that's been bothering me, and I want you to publish it.'

Blimey, what the hell was this all about?

'When I said I'd never taken any drugs…'

Oh. My. God.

My mind raced back to the relevant part of our interview two months ago.

Q: Have you ever taken any drugs?
A: (Shakes head.)
Q: Whoa…was that a hesitation there?

A: No! I've never taken drugs.

I laughed.

'Did you tell me a little fib, Katherine?'

'Yes,' she said, sheepishly. 'It's not something I ever wanted to talk about publicly,' she admitted, 'because taking drugs is the biggest regret of my life. But I've always tried to be honest about my life, and I've had sleepless nights since that interview appeared because I knew I'd lied to you.'

Her voice sounded trembly.

'Are you OK?' I asked.

'Yes. But I'm very, very nervous about admitting what I did, and I know some people may be shocked.'

'When did you first try drugs?'

'I was offered cocaine by someone at a friend's house in London, and having said no so many times before, curiosity just got the better of me, and I said yes.'

'Did you enjoy it?'

'It wasn't what I thought it would be like,' she said. 'I thought it would have some massive, dramatic effect on me, but it didn't. It made me feel powerful, though, and I felt like I had so much energy. I became really talkative, too – even more than usual if you can believe that!'

Katherine laughed, a little nervously, at her attempt to bring a bit of levity to the conversation. I could tell she was hating every second of having to do this, but at the same time knowing in her heart that it was better in the long run to come clean now.

'I took cocaine a handful of times more after that, maybe five or six. It was usually in private at friends' houses, though I did once take it in the loo of a club.'

'How much did you take?'

'I'd take up to three lines a night, a bit of a lightweight compared to some of them. The truth about drugs like cocaine is that after a while you see what it does to people around you and it's not pretty, is it?'

'Why did you do it?'

'I was young, and silly, and never really thought about the consequences,' she admitted. 'I didn't know I'd ever become famous, and I was at an age where you just don't care about the future much, do you? I just liked going out with friends, getting drunk on too many Malibus and cokes, and then someone would usually produce some drugs and occasionally I'd take some. I was just hanging around with a bad crowd. Coming from where I come from, it tends to take me a while to see the bad in people. I was very trusting, and keen to please.'

'How would you feel afterwards?'

'After taking cocaine, absolutely terrible. It was like the worst hangover in the world times ten, times a hundred. And I'd not be in a good mental place afterwards either. I'd feel depressed and paranoid, it was awful. And I was shocked that something could affect me in such a massive way like that. I'd feel horrible for at least a day, sometimes longer.'

'Did you try any other drugs?'

'I also tried ecstasy and MDMA. That had a totally different effect, a really massive one. I took half a pill the first time, and it made me feel excited, passionate, in love with everyone and everything, and really happy, very, very happy. I took ecstasy pills after that four or five times, and MDMA too. But that made me feel worse than cocaine. I didn't want to live the next day, it made me feel so depressed. It was horrible, just horrible.'

On other nights, she tried cannabis.

'I never smoked it, I just used to eat these cakes with cannabis in them. I did that seven or eight times. I can't remember the exact number. It seems so long ago now. It just made me feel relaxed and sleepy. And slightly out of control again.'

'What made you stop?'

'When I got offered my first big record deal. I knew in that moment that I had to stop taking drugs. I'd been given this amazing opportunity and I just couldn't let myself mess it all up for the sake of cocaine or ecstasy.'

'Did you tell your family?'

'Only my mother. We have a great relationship, and I wanted to be honest with her. I went back home to Wales, sat her down and told her about the drugs. And she was shocked and asked me why I'd done it, and wanted to make sure I wasn't still taking them, and I said I wasn't, and wished I never had, and would never, ever take them again. And then she just gave me a disapproving look that said it all – it was like, 'KATHERINE!' I feel so ashamed. Drugs are dangerous and destroy lives. Look at Amy Winehouse. She's an amazing talent but she is in such a bad way, it's such a shame. I could have ended up like her. It's possible. I don't think I'd ever have got that bad, but who knows with drugs? They're frightening. And that's why I feel so lucky to have stopped when I did.'

'I don't think we've had a cocaine, ecstasy and cannabis scandal rocking the classical music world before, how do you think they will react?'

Katherine gasped with a mixture of unsuppressed horror, and just the merest hint of hilarity.

'Oh, goodness me… I don't want to cause a stir, I just want to be honest.'

We finished the interview. 'How bad will it be for me next week?' she asked.

'Well, put it this way,' I replied, 'probably not half as bad as Jonathan Ross or John McCain's week is going to be.'

And Katherine laughed again, in that delightfully natural way that has, together with her regular trips to perform for British troops abroad, made her the modern-day Vera Lynn.

She never cried during the interview, never shirked a question and never asked for any sympathy.

She just said what she wanted to say, and that was that.

It's hard not to admire the courage it took to talk in such a frank and self-condemnatory way.

Later, I dug out the tape of our *GQ* interview and chuckled at the following exchange:

Q: Is there a devil hiding inside you, Saint Katherine?
A: That's for me to know, and you to find out, Piers…

THURSDAY, 30 OCTOBER 2008

Jonathan Ross has been taken off air by the BBC, without pay for three months, which amounts to an expensive slap on the wrist.

Brand has resigned, as has Lesley Douglas, the hugely popular Controller of Radio 2.

The feeling at the BBC is mutinous, with many people I've talked to there feeling Ross has got away with not being fired simply because of who he is.

Either way, this story isn't over yet.

Ross has got to come back to work in January – with a clean act, and in a building where he's not exactly Mr Popular.

One thing's for sure, I don't think he'll be using his 'expensive lawyers' to sue newspapers left, right and centre any more.

Not now that he's been exposed as a nasty, arrogant, intrusive, rude, insensitive bully.

FRIDAY, 31 OCTOBER 2008

Sarah Palin has now had 60 million hits on Google.

Yet six weeks ago, nobody outside of Alaska had ever heard of her.

Isn't this the most stunning evidence yet of the speed and breadth of the modern Internet-fuelled media?

SATURDAY, 1 NOVEMBER 2008

Arnold Schwarzenegger has hit the campaign stump with McCain, and hilariously laid into Obama for having 'skinny legs'.

'I'm going to make him do some squats,' he told a huge, cheering crowd in Ohio. 'And then we're going to make him do some biceps curls to beef up those scrawny little arms. But if he could only do something about putting some meat on his ideas. Senator McCain on the other hand is built like a rock. His character and his views are solid.'

I could have predicted what was coming next...

'John McCain's character has been tested as no other presidential candidate in the history of this nation,' Schwarzenegger said. 'He has spent five and a half years as a prisoner of war. He has been tested under torture, under temptation, under deprivation, under isolation.

'He has proven what kind of a man he is. John McCain has served his country longer in a POW camp than his opponent has served in the United States Senate.

'I only play an action hero in the movies but John McCain is a real action hero. And when John McCain is elected you will see all kind of action.

'When Americans go into that voting booth on Tuesday I hope they will think about this: if you were in a POW cell, who would you want in that cell with you? Do you want a man of eloquence or a man of proven courage?'

So there we have it – the Terminator says they all have to vote for McCain because he got caught in a war America lost 40 years ago.

How ridiculous!

Obama, meanwhile, is spending a small fortune on extensive last-minute

TV commercials, highlighting the extraordinary financial advantage he has enjoyed throughout this campaign.

The unique Internet fundraising system he set up through groups like Facebook and MySpace has allowed millions of ordinary Americans to donate a few dollars online. More than three million have so far donated a total of $650 million – more than both presidential contenders in 2004 combined. Obama has thus entered this final stage of the race with four times as much cash as McCain to lavish on TV advertising.

Crucially, these online donors were predominantly younger people, too, who bought themselves a vested interest in Obama and would therefore be more inclined to vote.

I spoke to The Ferret on the phone tonight.

'Obama's going to walk it,' he said.

'Why are you so sure?'

'Hey, no drama Obama. That was their strategy, and it's worked. There has been no drama, and McCain's chances have collapsed with the economy.'

'Has America changed a lot in the last two years?'

'Oh my God! It's been a revolution. If you had said then that we'd still be at war in two countries, that our economy would be in the toilet, that we'd be about to elect a young African-American president with the middle name of "Hussein", that all the top television shows would be reality, not scripted stuff, and that the Phillies would win the world series – nobody would have believed you! It's been unbelievable, and what's even more extraordinary is that it's been achieved by acclamation. People really want this.

'I told you last year that what America needed was a good press agent – and we found one in Barack Obama.

'If he wins on Tuesday then he is proof that America is still the place where anything can happen if you believe in it hard enough. You're a young black American who wants to be president? You can. You want to go on a reality TV show and become a movie star? You can. You've got no money but want to go to college and then run a big company? You can. Obama has given America its pride back, and offers real hope for the future.'

SUNDAY, 2 NOVEMBER 2008

Sarah Palin has been tricked into talking to a Canadian prankster on the phone who convinced her he was French president Nicolas Sarkozy.

Marc-Antoine Audette, who has conned numerous public figures like this, told Palin he wanted to go moose-hunting with her.

'I just love killing those animals! Taking away life, that is so fun!'

And Palin laughs.

He then says: 'You know we have a lot in common also because from my house I can see Belgium.'

And she laughs again.

Audette, who clearly can't believe his luck, tells Palin, as Sarkozy, that Carla Bruni is 'hot in bed', and then informs her that Bruni has written a song for her about Joe The Plumber called '*Du rouge levres sur une cochonne*'. Which actually means 'lipstick on a pig'. He then says that France has its own Joe – 'he's called Marcel, the guy with bread under his armpit!'

Another Palin snigger.

Audette ends by telling her that he 'loved the documentary' about her – referring to the porn movie made by *Hustler* king Larry Flynt featuring a Palin lookalike. 'Oh, good,' she replies, 'thank you.'

The whole thing is humiliating, obviously, but I doubt it will do much damage to Palin.

She just comes over as 'stoopid', which almost everyone now accepts she is.

And on the subject of 'stoopid' people, what the hell has happened to George W. Bush? He has literally vanished. I haven't seen or heard from him in a month.

This has to be the most ignominious exit ever by an American president, particularly one who served two terms.

But then, his approval ratings have slipped below 30 per cent, so you can't blame McCain for wanting Bush nowhere near his campaign.

Not everyone is happy with Dubya's isolation, though.

A writer in today's *Wall Street Journal*, which has recently been bought by Rupert Murdoch, raged: 'The treatment President Bush has received from this country is nothing less than a disgrace, proving to the world what little character and resolve we have. The president never lost faith in America or her people, and has tried his hardest to continue leading our nation during a very difficult time. Our failure to stand by him is a shameful display of arrogance and weakness that just shows the world how disloyal we can be.'

Which I think can safely be translated to 'Mr Murdoch backed this chump on Iraq, and we need to somehow make this look better than it is...'

Tonight, Lewis Hamilton became World Motor-racing Champion, the youngest to ever achieve that title.

Who would have predicted 20 years ago that the world's best golfer and driver would be black, and that we'd be on the verge of a black president, too?

The collapse of racial barriers has been one of the most notable, and beneficial, aspects of globalisation.

MONDAY, 3 NOVEMBER 2008

If Obama was white, he'd be heading for a guaranteed landslide by now.

But he's not, his skin is black. And I still don't know what the hell those ultra-conservative, Bible-bashing, 'race-concerned' folks who voted Bush back in for a second term are going to actually do when they enter those polling booths tomorrow.

But one thing IS certain. This is the most important presidential vote in America since the Second World War.

The race has been electrifying, and I've been totally gripped by it. Perhaps because I'm spending so much time out there now. Or perhaps because I feel such a vested interest in what happens after spending the latter years of my newspaper editing career lambasting George Bush, and feeling a mixture of incredulity and fury that Americans voted him back to power soon after I was fired from the *Daily Mirror*.

It's hard to exaggerate the terrible damage that Bush has done to America's reputation in the last eight years.

As Donald Trump told me: 'He's put this country back 50 years.'

Bush, with his blinkered, hideously right-wing, old-fashioned attitudes, has made America the most hated nation in the world.

Which is just shockingly unfair to the people who live there.

Most Americans from my experience, are, in the main, thoroughly decent people. They're polite, civilised, big-hearted and generous to a fault.

Americans have an astonishingly intense patriotic fervour, much more evident than the modern-day British.

English soccer fans, for example, will boo their national team all day long. Americans would never dream of doing that.

Americans talk up their country, even when times are tough. Brits like nothing more than trashing their homeland.

The Yanks have, and I say this with regret more than anything else, more basic respect for each other than we do.

And they're a really positive, glass-half-full bunch, devoid of the ludicrous envy that we Brits are so susceptible to. They're warm, friendly, accommodating and welcoming.

They're also great with anything to do with service – whether it's meals or catheters. They're creative, very hard-working, loyal, dependable and energetic.

And they don't have the ridiculous class system that creates such silly social barriers in Britain.

Americans are not perfect, of course they're not.

They're prone to arrogance, and loud noise. You wouldn't want to be trapped with a group of young male Americans on a Maldives island for very long.

They're oddly insular – just 1 in 4 of them have passports. And this makes them blissfully, or should I say woefully, ignorant of almost anything that happens outside of America.

They're lemming-like in their tastes and habits. Hence the omnipresence of chains like Starbucks and McDonalds on every street.

Their religious zealotry – 80 per cent go to church – can be overbearing and irritatingly moralistic.

Their aversion to sarcasm is just a shame, because they'd be rather good at it if they tried.

And their obsession with self-improvement, plastic surgery and white teeth is fake and self-defeating, because they all end up looking the same.

But Americans have a loyalty and unity about themselves that is admirable.

Which is why this election matters so much. Because Americans take their lead from their president. The occupant of the White House is their spiritual, emotional and psychological mentor. They revere the office of the presidency, and the words that emanate from it.

The president *is* America. He, or she, represents the hopes and fears of 300 million people.

And I just can't bear the thought of it being John McCain.

He's not a bad man, not in the way that Bush became.

But nor is he a force for good.

McCain is old in age, and in his ways.

He thinks America's strength is its military. His views are black and white, 'with me or against me'.

Obama is youthful without being young, smart without being a smart-aleck, articulate without being hectoring, calm not excitable, proud but not stubborn; he loves his family, he's travelled the world and he voted against the Iraq war when to do so was virtual heresy in America. He inspires. When Obama cried, 'Yes, we can!' I felt like shouting it back at him through the TV screen, and I'm not even American. He's a man of hope, not despair. An extraordinary fusion of John F. Kennedy and Martin Luther King, with a dash of Clinton and Mandela.

I'm not blinkered; I know Obama's not going to rescue America overnight. If he wins, he will face huge problems, some of them perhaps insur-mountable. We're in the grip of the world's worst-ever financial recession. There are wars in Afghanistan and Iraq raging more violently than ever. And America's status as both the globe's respected policeman, and banker, lies in tatters.

Obama is untried, and untested. Nobody ever truly knows what a leader will be like until that person has the chance to lead, and to prove themselves under pressure.

I remember newspaper executives working under me who I thought would be brilliant editors, but who, when they got the top job, turned out to be weak, indecisive failures.

So if, as I so sincerely hope, he gets that chance, he will need our patience, support and understanding – even as more banks collapse, and more bombs explode.

But if Barack Obama is made president, then at least the world will have a man at the helm of the No. 1 superpower who understands the preference of peace to war, of talking to fighting, of unity to disharmony, and who can string a sentence together.

He has also fought a magnificently competent and inspired 'no drama' campaign – the Internet fund-raising, the radical health care plan, the wooing of the Hispanic and Latino vote, and securing the support of pivotal figures like Oprah, Warren Buffett and Colin Powell.

His book was called *Audacity of Hope*, and that's where we are with Obama. He offers up hope, all we need is the collective audacity to follow him.

Fortune, they say, favours the brave.

And I, for one, am prepared to take a big bold step into the unknown with Barack Hussein Obama. Because he's the right man, in the right place, at the right time.

And because, let's be brutally honest here, the world needs him now.

Come on, America, you can do this.

Yes. You. Can.

WEDNESDAY, 5 NOVEMBER 2008

Obama won.

God Bless America!

R.I.P. DUBYA

'This is your farewell kiss, you dog!'
MUNTADAR AL-ZEIDI, REPORTER WITH AL-BAGHDADIA TELEVISION

'I don't what his beef is, but whatever it is, I'm sure someone will hear it.'
GEORGE W. BUSH, PRESIDENT OF THE UNITED STATES OF AMERICA, 2000-2008